T. W. Allies

The Formation Of Christendom Vol. 4

As Seen in Church and State

T. W. Allies

The Formation Of Christendom Vol. 4
As Seen in Church and State

ISBN/EAN: 9783742835765

Manufactured in Europe, USA, Canada, Australia, Japa

Cover: Foto ©Lupo / pixelio.de

Manufactured and distributed by brebook publishing software (www.brebook.com)

T. W. Allies

The Formation Of Christendom Vol. 4

CHURCH AND STATE

AS SEEN IN

THE FORMATION OF CHRISTENDOM.

BY

T. W. ALLIES, M.A.

AUTHOR OF

"PER CRUCEM AD LUCEM, THE RESULT OF A LIFE,"
"A LIFE'S DECISION," "JOURNAL IN FRANCE AND LETTERS FROM ITALY,"
"THE FORMATION OF CHRISTENDOM," ETC.

LONDON: BURNS AND OATES.
1882.

TABLE OF CONTENTS.

PROLOGUE.

	PAGE
THE KINGDOM AS PROPHESIED AND AS FULFILLED,	xix

CHAPTER I.

RELATION BETWEEN THE CIVIL AND THE SPIRITUAL POWERS FROM ADAM TO CHRIST.

1. *The Divine and the Human Society, founded in Adam, refounded in Noah.*

The origin of man, of woman, of marriage, and of the human family,	1
Archetypal character of the fact that man is created a Race,	3
Sole creation of Adam in the maturity of thought and speech and the perfection of knowledge, as shown in the naming of creatures,	4
Subsequent building of woman from man,	5
The divine Image and Likeness in the individual man,	5
A further Image of the ever-blessed Trinity in the Race,	6
Indication of the Headship and the Passion of Christ in the original creation,	8
Beauty and splendour of the divine plan,	9
The part in the divine plan which belongs to man's free-will,	10
The divine treatment of man as a Race not broken by the Fall,	11
Adam after the Fall the head of the civil and the religious order,	12
Bearing of man's condition before the Fall upon his subsequent state,	13
Adam receives in a great promise a disclosure of the future,	14
He becomes the Teacher and likewise the Priest of his Race,	15
The rite of sacrifice,	15

	PAGE
Triple dignity of Adam in this first society,	16
Man breaks up this society by the misuse of his free-will,	17
Resumption of the unity of the Race and its reparation in Noah,	18
Condition of man, individual and collective, at this new beginning of the race; marriage and sacrifice,	19
Express establishment of civil government by divine authority,	20
Union of religion with civil government from the beginning,	21
Parallel between Adam and Noah,	22

2. *The Divine and Human Society in the Dispersion.*

Unity of human language withdrawn on account of a great sin,	24
Coeval with which the various nations spring forth out of the one original society,	26
Injury to human society by the degradation of the conception of God,	28
Loss of belief in the divine unity followed by loss of the sense of man's brotherhood,	29
Proof of this brotherhood recovered by science in the case of the Aryan family of nations,	31
The one universal society becomes many nations at enmity with each other,	32
Their state after a long lapse of time, when their several histories begin,	33
Original goods of the race still remaining—	
1. Marriage,	35
2. Religion as centered in the rite of sacrifice,	37
3. Civil government,	38
4. Alliance between government and religion,	41
Cumulative testimony of the four in their contrast with slavery to the unity of man's Race, as its origin is recorded by Moses,	43
Summary of the course of mankind from the Dispersion to Christ,	44

3. *Further Testimony of Law, Government, and Priesthood in the Dispersion.*

The fiction of universal savagery, or different races, or simial descent,	45
The author of "Ancient Law" upon original society,	46
Proof from comparative jurisprudence of the patriarchal theory,	47
Law and government in their commencement,	48
Family the ancient unit of society,	49

CONTENTS.

	PAGE
Universal belief or assumption of blood-relationship,	50
The Roman Patria Potestas a relic of the original rule,	52
Family everything, the individual unknown,	52
Original union of religion with government,	53
Origin of law and property,	54
Summary of the foregoing witness,	55
The Two Powers from the beginning,	56
Degradation of worship and degradation of society in Gentilism,	57
Deification of the State,	58
Which, however, remains a lawful power,	59
The distinction between sacerdotal and civil power in the Roman republic,	60
The power of the Pontifex Maximus united to that of the Principate,	62
The College of Pontifices reversing a tribunitial law,	63
The distinction between Sacerdotal and Civil Power running through all ancient nations,	64
Witness of the heathen priesthood to the unity of man's Race,	65
The providence of Abraham's call,	66
Relation of the Two Powers in the Mosaic law,	67
The actual result of the coming of Christ,	68

CHAPTER II.

RELATION BETWEEN THE SPIRITUAL AND THE CIVIL POWERS AFTER CHRIST.

1. *The Spiritual Power in its Source and Nature.*

The Spiritual Power not only allied but subordinate to the Civil throughout the Gentile world at the death of Christ,	70
1. Its independence in Israel alone, as acknowledged by the people, a result of the creation of the Aaronic priesthood,	72
Special offices of the High Priest,	73
2. The part of the High Priest through the whole history from Moses to Christ,	75
3. The actual jurisdiction of the High Priest under the Roman Empire,	77

4. The High-priesthood and the system of worship over which it presided viewed as a prophecy and preparation for Christ, ... 80
Bearing of the High-priesthood to Christ at His coming, . . 82
The undisputed circumstances of Christ's death, . . . 83
Extreme antecedent improbability of what followed, . . . 84
Its dependence upon a supernatural and miraculous fact, . . 85
As the Race springs from Adam in Paradise, so the Spiritual Power from Christ at His Resurrection, ... 86
The inward cohesion of Priesthood, Teaching, and Jurisdiction, . 87
The two forces of the Primacy and the Hierarchy from the beginning, 90
The unity and triplicity of power in the regimen of the Church an image of the Divine Unity and Trinity, ... 92

2. *The Spiritual Power a Complete Society.*

The supernatural society exists for a supernatural end, . . . 93
To which the present life is subordinated, ... 94
And which is beyond the provision of temporal government, . . 95
Analogy between the Two Powers, ... 96
Complete philosophical basis on which the Spiritual Power rests, . 98
How the inward life which it imparts is united with the Person of Christ, ... 99
From whom, in worship, belief, and conduct, the Christian people derives, ... 101
The King and the Kingdom not of this world but in it, fulfilled in thirteen particulars, ... 103
  1. A kingdom ruling all the relations of man Godward, . 103
  2. Having an end outside this life, ... 103
  3. Deriving all authority from Christ as Apostle and High Priest, ... 103
  4. Producing its people from its King, ... 103
  5. Imparting grace from the King in its sacraments, . . 104
  6. Transmitting the King's truth by the order of its regimen, 104
  7. Having a complete analogy with civil government, . . 104
  8. Fulfilling man's need of supernatural society, . . . 105
  9. Generating an universal law for all relations of public and private life, ... 105
  10. Possessing independence of the Temporal Power, . . 106
  11. Not limited in space, ... 106
  12. Not limited in time, ... 107
  13. A kingdom of charity through union with its King, . . 107

3. *Relation of the Two Powers to each other.*

	PAGE
Principles which ruled the relation between the Two Powers before Christ,	108
A new basis given to the Spiritual Power by Christ, from which every relation to the Temporal Power springs,	110
1. All Christians subject to the Spiritual Power,	112
2. And likewise to the Temporal Power as God's Vicegerent,	112
3. The relation between the Two Powers intended by God is amity,	114
4. A separate action of the Two Powers, without regard to each other, not intended,	115
5. Persecution of the Spiritual by the Temporal not intended,	119
6. Contrast between human kingdoms and the divine kingdom,	120
The *end* the ground of the subordination of the one to the other,	122
Doctrine of St. Thomas to that effect,	123
The indirect power over temporal things,	124
Sum of the foregoing chapter ; Orders of Nature and Grace,	125
Co-operation of the Two Powers as stated by St. Gregory VII.,	126
The image of marriage, as describing the ideal relation and the various deflections from it,	128

CHAPTER III.

TRANSMISSION OF SPIRITUAL AUTHORITY FROM THE PERSON OF OUR LORD TO PETER AND THE APOSTLES, AS SET FORTH IN THE NEW TESTAMENT.

The Church a kingdom subsisting from age to age by its own force, but its original records to be considered,	131
Institution of the Priesthood ; St. Paul's and St. Luke's testimony,	132
St. Matthew, St. Mark, and St. John,	133
Transmission of Spiritual Power as recorded by St. Matthew,	136
The same according to St. Mark,	138
The same according to St. Luke in his Gospel,	139
And in the Acts,	139
His record of a peculiar promise made to Peter,	141
Conversation which forms his main addition to the narrative,	141
Contrast between Gentile and Christian rule,	143

CONTENTS.

	PAGE
The kingdom disposed to the Apostles,	144
The confirmation of the brethren,	145
The time of the confirming marked out,	146
St. Luke distinguishes Peter as markedly as St. Matthew and St. John,	148
Testimony of St. John as to the promises made to the Apostles,	149
And as to the universal pastorship bestowed on St. Peter,	152
Two classes of passages,	153
Comparison of the two,	154
And of the testimony of the four Evangelists,	156
Caution that what is recorded is not all that passed,	157
Perfect instruction of the Apostles in the forty days,	158
The powers comprising the Apostolate,	159
The powers bestowed on Peter,	160
Testimony of St. Paul; conception of the Church as the Body of Christ,	161
Of the one ministry by which the Body is compacted together,	162
Of mission from this Body as necessary to every herald of the gospel,	164
Of the grace given by ordination,	165
How the unity set forth by St. Paul bears witness to the Primacy of St. Peter,	166
Of the inseparable bond of unity, truth, and government in St. Paul's mind,	167
Six names by which he designates the principle of his own authority,	168
The great vision of our Lord and His Church in the Apocalypse in accordance with St. Paul and the Evangelists,	171
Four qualities of Spiritual Power in this Scriptural testimony,	175
1. The coming from above,	175
2. Its completeness,	176
3. Its unity,	179
4. Its independence,	181
How the idea of perpetuity pervades all these qualities,	182

CHAPTER IV.

TRANSMISSION OF SPIRITUAL AUTHORITY, AS WITNESSED IN THE HISTORY OF THE CHURCH FROM A.D. 29 TO A.D. 325.

	PAGE
The letter of St. Clement of Rome,	184
Description of this letter by St. Irenæus,	185
St. Clement urges the Roman military discipline as an example for Christian obedience,	186
Minute regulations given by Christ as to religious ordinances,	187
The descent of all spiritual order from above,	188
Example of Moses in establishing the Jewish Pontificate,	189
How the Apostles appointed everywhere Bishops with a rule of succession,	190
St. Clement fills up details omitted in the Gospel record,	190
How he attests the continuation of the Mosaic hierarchy of high priest, priest, and levite in the Christian Church,	191
How he says that Christian ordinances are to be observed more accurately than Mosaic,	193
How the Apostles carried out the descent of power from above,	194
Why St. Clement instances the origin of the Jewish hierarchy,	195
How St. Clement exercises the Primacy,	197
St. Ignatius of Antioch supplements St. Clement of Rome,	200
His statement as to Bishops throughout the world, combined with his statement as to the authority of the local Bishop,	201
The complete testimony of St. Clement and St. Ignatius,	203
The historian Eusebius notes three periods in the first ninety years,	205
Sum of his testimony as to the great Sees and the Episcopate,	206
How Tertullian describes the first propagation of the Church,	211
And how Irenæus,	213
Concordance with the Gospels of these statements of St. Clement, St. Ignatius, Eusebius, St. Irenæus, and Tertullian,	215
Bishops in every city and town of the Empire before the peace of the Church,	216
St. Peter, St. Paul, and the Apostles appointed everywhere local Bishops,	217
The Bishop universally said to wield a government,	218
Bishops sent out from Rome to convert the nations,	219
Episcopal government universal,	220

CONTENTS.

		PAGE
But the One Episcopate much more than this,		222
St. Cyprian's One Episcopate illustrated by St. Leo the Great,		223
What the One Episcopate adds to the universal establishment of Bishops,		224
The special character of the miracle which St. Chrysostom and St. Augustine proclaimed		227
St. Augustine's criterion in the fourth century applied to the nineteenth,		229
St. Chrysostom's epitome of the Church's course preceding his time,		230
Christ's special miracle is that He founds the race of Christians,		231
Contrast of the race with that out of which it was formed,		232
The incessant conflict amid which it was done,		233
A reflection upon this picture of the Church,		236

CHAPTER V.

The One Episcopate Resting upon the One Sacrifice.

St. Clement's assertion of the care with which our Lord instituted the government of His Church,		238
Christ's High-priesthood consisting in two acts,		239
1. The assumption of a created nature,		240
2. The offering that nature in sacrifice,		241
His union of these two acts in instituting the Priesthood of His Church,		242
The institution of bloody sacrifice in the world before Christ,		243
Lasaulx's statement how it enters into all the acts of human life,		245
What the ceremonial of Gentile sacrifice was,		250
Union and correspondence of prayer and sacrifice,		253
The sense of guilt in bloody sacrifice,		254
Bloody sacrifice a positive divine enactment,		254
Statement of St. Augustine to this effect,		255
St. Thomas on sacrifice as offered to God alone,		256
Bloody sacrifice the most characteristic fact of the pre-Christian world,		257
The practice of human sacrifices running through the history of ancient nations,		259

	PAGE
Conclusion as to the divine appointment of sacrifice,	261
The Christian Sacrifice the counterpart of the original institution,	263
And the compendium of the whole dispensation,	265
Containing in itself all the original force of sacrifice,	267
But besides it is guardian of the Divine Unity,	268
And of the Divine Trinity,	268
And of the Incarnation,	269
And of the Redemption,	270
And of the adoption to Sonship,	271
It contains also the fountain of spiritual life,	272
And the source of sanctification,	273
And the medicine of immortality,	274
The presence of Christ's physical body, St. Chrysostom,	275
The unity of the Christian people its result, St. Augustine,	276
How our Lord impressed His High-priesthood on the world,	276
Jurisdiction necessary to constitute a kingdom,	278
Jurisdiction in the diocese and in the whole Church,	279
The fulfilment of the parable, "I am the true vine,"	280
The Eucharistic Sacrifice the centre of life in the Church during eighteen hundred years,	283

CHAPTER VI.

INDEPENDENCE OF THE ANTE-NICENE CHURCH SHOWN IN HER ORGANIC GROWTH.

The Church's triple independence in government, teaching, and worship as actually carried out,	287
Occasion of the Nicene Council's convocation,	289
The Emperor thereby recognised the Church as a divine kingdom,	290
This kingdom, as it appeared in A.D. 29 and in A.D. 325,	291
The Emperor also acknowledged the solidarity of the Episcopate,	292
The Christian Council and the Roman Senate,	293
Force of the Council as to the relation between Church and State,	294
A. Independence of the Church's government shown in five points,	295
1. The ordered gradation of the hierarchy in mother and daughter churches,	296
Recognised as original in the 6th canon of the Council,	297

This principle carried through the whole structure of the Church,	298
Symbolised in the building of the great medieval cathedrals,	301
2. Development of Provincial Councils,	302
3. Action of the Church in hearing and deciding causes,	303
Her proper jurisdiction in the exterior and interior forum,	304
The episcopal magistracy exercised in a fourfold gradation,	306
4. Election of Bishops and the inferior ministers,	307
St. Cyprian's testimony,	308
Outcome of the three centuries in this respect,	309
The principle upon which all this practice was built,	310
5. Administration of temporal goods,	311
Three states as to these goods in the early Church,	312
Acquisition and usage of temporal goods,	313
Temporal goods in A.D. 29 and in A.D. 325,	315
B. Independence of the Church's teaching,	316
The first teaching purely oral, based upon authority,	317
Three classes of truths forming the divine and the apostolical tradition,	319
Importance in this period of exclusively oral teaching in exhibiting the Church's office of teacher,	320
Seen in the rite of baptism,	321
In the Eucharistic Liturgy,	322
Picture of the Eucharistic Sacrifice by an Apostle,	324
Further exhibition in the rite of Ordination,	328
Fulness of the Magisterium expressed in these rites,	329
The Church's teaching office neither changed nor diminished by the writings of the New Testament,	331
Shown by the nature of the office in itself,	331
By the circumstances under which these writings came,	331
By their internal arrangement,	332
By their own positive testimony,	335
The living personal authority an unchangeable principle,	335
Things in the Church which preceded the publication of the New Testament,	336
The written record of our Lord's words and acts,	337
The various parts of ecclesiastical tradition,	338

CHAPTER VII.

INDEPENDENCE OF THE ANTE-NICENE CHURCH SHOWN IN HER MODE OF POSITIVE TEACHING AND IN HER MODE OF RESISTING ERROR.

	PAGE
Germ of the Church in the missionary circuits of our Lord,	340
The mission carried on by the Apostles,	341
Its two parts: work of positive teaching and defence against error,	343
As to the first—	
1. The system of catechesis,	344
2. The employment of a Creed,	347
3. The dispensing of Sacraments,	349
4. The system of Penance,	351
5. The Scriptures carried in the Church's hand,	352
This mode of promulgation continued during fifteen centuries,	355
Substitution of a private interpretation of Scripture by the individual attempted in the sixteenth century,	356
Summary of the mode in which the Church promulgated the faith,	358
As to the second, the Church's defence against error lay in the principle of her own authority,	360
The first conflict with unbelieving Judaism,	362
Three incidents of it—	
The proclaiming Jesus to be the Christ,	362
The receiving the Gentiles without Circumcision,	363
The protection of being Jews enjoyed by the first preachers of Christ,	364
Gradual severance of the Christian Church from the Synagogue,	369
Circumstances and peculiar difficulties of the Ante-Nicene Church,	371
The first condition of Christians one of simple faith,	376
The two opposed principles of orthodoxy and heresy,	378
Contest between them indicated in the Apostolic writings,	380
Character of the first writings after the Apostles,	381
Christian learning in the second century; conversions of heathens who became Christian apologists,	382
Extension of education given in great catechetical schools,	385
The defence against error lodged in the Magisterium,	387
The Magisterium lies in the Church's divine government and concrete life,	388
Athanasius as the expounder of it; his fundamental idea,	389

xvi CONTENTS.

	PAGE
His statement as to the authority of Scripture,	391
As to the Rule of Faith,	392
As to private judgment,	393
His tests of heresy,	393
Definitions,	394
How the Magisterium embraces Scripture and Tradition, and employs them as a joint rule,	395
Testimony of the Council of Arles to the above principles,	397
And Constantine's public recognition that the Magisterium of Christ is lodged in the Bishops,	398

CHAPTER VIII.

THE CHURCH'S BATTLE FOR INDEPENDENCE OVER AGAINST THE ROMAN EMPIRE.

Alliance of the Two Powers in the Roman Empire at the Advent of Christ,	400
The Emperor official guardian of all religions,	401
The Christian religion a singular exception,	403
Its cause the position of Christians towards heathendom,	404
Contradiction in belief, worship, and government,	405
The Christian people as the outcome of these three constituents,	411
The course of the Roman Empire and the Christian Church in three hundred years,	414
The ten persecutions from Nero to Diocletian,	417
The Martyrs champions of a great army,	421
St. Paul's account of this army's creation,	422
The wonder of this creation,	424
Supernatural character of the conversion wrought in these times,	426
Accounted for only by the internal action of the Holy Ghost,	427
Power of the κήρυγμα insisted on by Clement of Alexandria,	429
Contrasted by him with the impotence of philosophy,	430
Sufferings which followed on conversion according to Tertullian,	431
Martyrs enduring for God what heroes endured for goods of nature,	432
Origen insists on the divine power shown in converting sinners,	434
On miracles of conversion as greater than bodily miracles,	435
The spread of the Church and the conversion of sinners viewed together,	436

	PAGE
Miracles only could account for the spread of the Church,	437
Statement of Irenæus as to miraculous powers exercised in his time,	438
Athanasius on the cessation of idolatry, oracles, and magic,	440
And on the greatness of the conversion wrought by Christ,	442
The necessity of miracles in proof of our Lord's mission,	444
The connection between miracles and martyrdom,	445
Parallel between them as to their principle, witness, power, and perpetuity,	449
How the liberty of the Church was gained against the empire,	455
How the Martyrs constructed a basis for civil liberty,	456
The five conflicts of the Church with Judaism, Heresy, Idolatry, Philosophy, and the Roman State,	459

PROLOGUE.

THE KINGDOM AS PROPHESIED AND AS FULFILLED.

This volume, though entire in itself, is also the continuation of a former work, the "Formation of Christendom," already written and published by me in three volumes. It is, in fact, the further unfolding of the subject under a particular aspect. In truth, the relation between Church and State leads perhaps more directly than any other to the heart of Christendom; for Christendom, both in word and idea, means not only one and the same Church subsisting in all civil governments, but also a community of Christian governments, having a common belief and common principles of action, grounded upon the Incarnation of the Son of God, and the Redemption wrought thereby. For this reason, the Formation of Christendom can hardly be described, unless the relation which ought by the institution of God to subsist between the two great Powers, the Spiritual and Civil, appointed to rule human society, is first clearly established.

In this volume, therefore, I treat first of the relation of these two Powers before the coming of Christ. Secondly, of their relation as it was affected by that coming, in order to show what position the Church of

Christ originally took up in regard to the Civil Power, and what the behaviour of the Civil Power towards the Church was. And, thirdly, the question of principles being thus laid down, the remainder of the volume is occupied with the historical exhibition of the subject during the first three centuries; that is, from the Day of Pentecost to the Nicene Council. The supreme importance of that period will appear to all who reflect that the Church from the beginning, and in the first centuries of her existence, must be the same in principles with the Church of the nineteenth and every succeeding century. And this volume is, in fact, a prelude to the treatment of the same subject in the last three centuries, down to the Ecumenical Council of the Vatican.

The subject which I am treating is, then, strictly historical, being the action of a King in the establishment of a kingdom; the action of a Lawgiver in the legislation which He gave to that kingdom; the action of a Priest in founding a hierarchy, whereby that kingdom consists; but, moreover, which is something much more—the action of One who is Priest, Lawgiver, and King at once and always, and therefore whose work is at once one and triple, and indivisible in its unity and triplicity, and issuing in the forming of a people which is simply the creation of its King.

1.—*The Kingdom as Prophesied.*

As an introduction to it, let me refer to the distinct and explicit prediction of such an event at a point of time six centuries before it took effect, as well as now distant from us almost 2500 years, under circumstances upon which it is most instructive to look back. For not only did the secular and the religious histories of mankind then meet together, as they had met before, but they began to stand in a certain relation to each other, which continues from that time to this. The intersection of two societies which work themselves out in the one human history became permanent. At that moment a revelation was given, which is perhaps the most definite detailed and absolute prophecy concerning the whole compass of human society, as viewed in its relation to God, which is to be found in the Old Testament. And the occasion upon which it was given makes it even more significant, for it was like a burst of sunlight suddenly scattering the darkness of a storm and bathing the whole landscape in radiance.

That darkness indeed was terrible, for the ancient people chosen by God to support His name among apostate nations no longer lived apart from those nations in their own land which God had provided for them, with an independence based upon the law especially given to them, but lay prostrate under the feet of a heathen invader, who had placed a vassal upon the diminished throne of Solomon, and the royal line of David seemed on the eve of expiring in a degenerate descendant. For the continued infidelities of four hundred years had worn out even the divine patience. In vain had the ten tribes of schismatic Israel been carried into captivity by Assyria. It needed that the remaining kingdom of Judah should be broken up and its chiefs deported to Babylon, whose monarch was now the heir of Assur's great empire, the king of kings, the sceptred head of heathendom. Moreover, in a few years he was to punish the vassal, rebellious to himself, but yet more faithless to the God of Israel, whom he had placed on David's seat, and to burn that glorious Temple which the wisest of kings had erected to the majesty of the one true God. And with that fall of Zedekiah the line of David would cease for ever to sit upon a temporal throne.

A darker moment in the history of the chosen people could not be found, nor a more hopeless prospect, to all seeming, for the carrying out the promises made to Abraham and his seed. What was a divine judgment on the breakers of a special covenant with the one true God appeared to be the triumph of a heathendom which had set up many false gods. Yet it was the moment chosen to send to that very king, who was the executor of the divine chastisements upon a faithless people, a revelation which contained the future lot not only of the people which he had humbled, but of the heathendom of which he was the crown. As he lay upon his bed, Nabuchodonosor had a dream, "and his spirit was terrified, and the dream went out of his mind." He strove in vain to recover it, either by the efforts of his own memory or by the skill of the wise men and soothsayers of Babylon. But among the captives in the imperial city was a youth of David's lineage, nourished at the king's court, and a member of his household. And when Daniel heard the decree of the great king ordering the death of the wise men who failed to interpret a dream which the king could not disclose to them, Daniel turned himself and his three fellow-captives and companions to prayer and supplication, "to the end that they should ask mercy at the face of the God of heaven concerning this secret. Then was the mystery revealed to Daniel by a vision in the night: and Daniel blessed the God of heaven, and speaking he said : Blessed be the name of the Lord from eternity and for evermore : for wisdom and fortitude are His. And He changeth times and ages : taketh away kingdoms and establisheth them, giveth wisdom to the wise, and knowledge to them that have understanding : He revealeth deep and hidden things, and knoweth what is in darkness, and light is with Him. To Thee, O God of our fathers, I give thanks, and I praise Thee; because Thou hast given me wisdom and strength : and now Thou hast shown me what we desired of Thee, for Thou hast made known to us the king's discourse. After this Daniel went in to Arioch, to whom the king had given orders to destroy the wise men of Babylon, and he spoke thus to him : Destroy not the wise men of Babylon: bring me in before the king, and I will tell the solution to the king. Then Arioch in haste brought in Daniel to the king, and said to him : I have found a man of the children of the captivity of Judah that will resolve the question to the king. The king answered and said to Daniel, whose name was Baltassar : Thinkest thou indeed that thou canst tell me the dream that I saw, and the interpretation thereof? And Daniel made answer before the king and said: The secret that the king desireth to know, none of the wise men, or the philosophers, or the diviners, or the soothsayers can declare to the king. But there is a God in heaven that revealeth mysteries, who hath shown to thee, O king Nabuchodonosor, what is to come to pass in the latter times. Thy dream, and the visions of thy head upon thy bed, are these: Thou, O king, didst begin to think in thy bed what should come to pass hereafter: and He that revealeth mysteries showed thee what shall come to pass. To me also this secret is revealed, not by any wisdom that I have more than all men alive, but that the interpretation might be made manifest to the king, and thou mightest know the thoughts of thy mind. Thou, O king, sawest, and behold there was as it were a great statue: this statue, which was great and high, tall of stature, stood before thee, and the look thereof was terrible. The head of this statue was of fine gold, but the breast and the arms of silver, and the belly and the thighs of brass: and the legs of iron, the feet part of iron and part of clay. Thus thou sawest, until a stone was cut out of a mountain without hands, and it struck the statue upon the feet thereof that were of iron and of clay, and broke them in pieces. Then was the iron, the clay, the brass, the silver, and the gold broken to pieces together, and became like the chaff of a summer's threshing-floor, and they were carried away by the wind, and there was no place found for them: but the stone that

struck the statue became a great mountain, and filled
the whole earth. This is the dream: we will also tell
the interpretation thereof before thee, O king. Thou
art a king of kings: and the God of heaven hath given
thee a kingdom, and strength, and power, and glory:
and all places wherein the children of men and the
beasts of the field do dwell: he hath also given the
birds of the air into thy hand, and hath put all things
under thy power: thou therefore art the head of gold.
And after thee shall rise up another kingdom, inferior
to thee, of silver: and another third kingdom of brass,
which shall rule over all the world. And the fourth
kingdom shall be as iron. As iron breaketh into pieces
and subdueth all things, so shall that break and destroy
all these. And whereas thou sawest the feet and the
toes part of potter's clay, and part of iron: the kingdom
shall be divided, but yet it shall take its origin from
the iron, according as thou sawest the iron mixed with
the miry clay. And as the toes of the feet were part
of iron and part of clay, the kingdom shall be partly
strong and partly broken. And whereas thou sawest
the iron mixed with miry clay, they shall be mingled
indeed together with the seed of man, but they shall
not stick fast one to another, as iron cannot be mixed
with clay. But in the days of those kingdoms the God
of heaven will set up a kingdom that shall never be
destroyed, and His kingdom shall not be delivered up to
another people, and it shall break in pieces and shall consume all these kingdoms, and itself shall stand for ever.
According as thou sawest that the stone was cut out of

the mountain without hands, and broke in pieces the clay, and the iron, and the brass, and the silver, and the gold, the great God hath shown the king what shall come to pass hereafter, and the dream is true, and the interpretation thereof is faithful."

No one can study the vision and its interpretation without seeing that the fabric of a great temporal empire, whose ruler is called a king of kings, and whose seat is the city wherein Nimrod, "the great hunter before the Lord," set up the first kingdom, to stand for ever at the head of human history a kingdom symbolical not of justice but of force, is therein contrasted with the fabric of a kingdom which the God of heaven should set up. And it is specially noted that He should set up this kingdom in the times of the empires denoted by the statue. And of the kingdom so to be set up four things are predicated in, as it were, an ascending scale. First, there is its divine institution: "the God of heaven shall set up a kingdom," and that in a manner wholly unexampled, which is expressed by "a stone cut out of a mountain without hands." Secondly, "the kingdom shall never be destroyed." Thirdly, and further, "it shall not be delivered up to another people;" a process which, according to the interpretation of the vision, was to take place three times in the empires represented by the statue. Fourthly, "that it should break in pieces and consume all these kingdoms, while itself should last for ever."

Moreover, as the earthly kingdom was really a kingdom, so the force of the similitude running through the whole, and heightened by the effect of contrast, declares that the heavenly should be a kingdom. As the seat of the earthly kingdom was this world, so evidently the seat of the heavenly is this same world. As the earthly kingdom should be destroyed, so the heavenly should be exempt from destruction. As the earthly kingdom was to pass from one people to another, so the heavenly kingdom should not pass from one people to another. But then comes a culmination which no one could anticipate. For not only is there an antagonism between the earthly and the heavenly kingdom, but by force of it, and in consequence of it, the heavenly should consume and break in pieces the earthly. Whereby the hearer is given to understand that the earthly kingdom, terrible and grand and all-powerful as it seemed to be, was created for the sake of the heavenly, which in due time should be set up in it, but not of it nor from it.

It is no less implied through the whole tenor of the vision that the authority which constitutes the essence of a kingdom—that is, supreme and independent authority, which is expressed in legislation and administered in government—subsists as much in the heavenly as in the earthly kingdom, with this marked distinction, that it is transitory in the one case and permanent in the other.

And, finally, the power by which all this should be done was something beyond human power, and without parallel, very strange and astonishing, "a stone cut out of a mountain without hands," which should not only strike the statue upon its feet, but itself grow, "until it became a great mountain, and filled the whole earth."

Thus the filling of the whole earth with the stone which struck the statue and then became a great mountain terminates the vision. But it is no less its scope and object. The statue exists before that the stone may come after. The statue and the stone, as thus exhibited, indicate the respective value in the divine counsels of the powers which they represent; that is, the subordination of the human kingdom to the divine, both in the order of causality and in duration, is distinctly laid down. And the end of both accords with this. The great statue, when struck by the stone, became like the chaff of a summer's threshing-floor; but the stone which struck it filled the whole earth. And the vision leaves it in possession.

The vision also reaches from end to end. It begins with the first empire, which is human, and runs back by the place in which it is seated to the commencement of actual things; and it ends with the last, which is divine, and which shall consume all the other kingdoms recorded, and itself last for ever. Thus the vision grasps the whole organism of society in the human race, as it lies unrolled before the providence of God.

2.—*The Kingdom as Fulfilled.*

Such was the prophecy. Now let us pass over a thousand years, and take the first fulfilment of the vision as it presented itself to an ancient saint at the beginning of the fifth century. We will only note that in the interval Nabuchodonosor and Cyrus and Alexander and Cæsar had set up the four world-empires.

They were four indeed, for they passed three times from one people to another—from Chaldean to Persian, from Persian to Grecian, from Grecian to Roman, as the variety of metals in the statue was interpreted to mean. Yet were they also one—a unity which, as that of a single person, the great statue so faithfully represented. For they were one with each other in the character and unbroken tradition of the same civilisation, and in the principle of their authority, which was conquest. They were filled with the same spirit of heathen domination, which was in truth the voice and the power of a false worship, as with the spirit of one man who rose in Babylon to set in Rome.[1] Two Apostles, special friends and constant fellow-workers, had marked this identity by giving the mystical name of Babylon to heathen Rome—St. Peter[2] in the epistle which he dates from Babylon, St. John in his vision of the woman drunk with the blood of saints and martyrs, and seated upon the seven hills, whom he himself interprets to be "the great city which had kingdom over the kings of the earth." These empires had run their appointed course, and the last and greatest of them, which was likewise the heir and successor of the three preceding in power and thought, as well as in the body of their territories and the soul which ruled therein, was ending in disgrace and dissolution. For at length the tribes of the North

---

[1] "Dentro dal monte sta dritto un gran veglio,
  Che tiene volte le spalle inver Damiata,
  E Roma guarda sì, come suo speglio."
      —DANTE, *Inferno*, 14, 101.

[2] 1 Pet. v. 13; Apocal. xvii. 18, xviii. 2, 20.

had broken through the long-guarded frontiers of Roman power. Alaric with his Goths had taken Rome, and a deep cry of distress arose through all the vast provinces of her empire. Every city in that wide domain trembled with the sense of insecurity for the present and fear for the future which the fall of Rome inspired. Just at this moment the great Western Father, whose voice sounded like the voice of the Church herself, wrote thus to a heathen inquirer:—

"Faith opens the door to intelligence, while unbelief closes it. Where is the man who would not be moved to belief, simply by so vast an order of events proceeding from the beginning; by the mere connection of various ages, which accredits the present by the past, while it confirms antiquity by what is recent? Out of the Chaldean nation a single man is chosen, remarkable for a most constant piety. Divine promises are disclosed to this man, which are to find their completion after a vast series of ages in the last times, and it is predicted that all nations are to receive a benediction in his seed. This man being a worshipper of the one true God, the Creator of the universe, begets in his old age a son, of a wife whom barrenness and age had long deprived of all hope of offspring. From him is propagated a most numerous people, which multiplies in Egypt, whither a divine disposition of things, redoubling its promises and effects, had carried that family from eastern parts. From their servitude in Egypt a strong people is led forth by terrible signs and miracles; impious nations are driven out before it; it is brought into the promised land, settled therein, and exalted into a kingdom. Then it falls more and more into sin; it perpetually offends the true God, who had conferred upon it so many favours, by violating His worship; it is scourged with various misfortunes; it is visited with consolations, and so carried on to the incarnation and manifestation of Christ. All the promises made to this nation, all its prophecies, its priesthoods, its sacrifices, its temple, in a word, all its sacred rites, had for their special object this Christ, the Word of God, the Son of God—God that was to come in the flesh, that was to die, to rise again, to ascend to heaven, that by the exceeding power of His name was to obtain in all nations a population dedicated to Himself; and in Him remission of sins and eternal salvation unto such as believed.

"Christ came. In His birth, His life, His words, His deeds, His sufferings, His death, His resurrection, His ascension,—all the predictions of the prophets are fulfilled. He sends forth the Holy Spirit; He fills the faithful who are assembled in one house, and who by their prayers and desires are expecting this very promise. They are filled with the Holy Spirit; they speak suddenly with the tongues of all nations; they confidently refute errors; they proclaim a most salutary truth; they exhort to penitence for the faults of past life; they promise pardon from the divine grace. Their proclamation of piety and true religion is followed by suitable signs and miracles. A savage unbelief is stirred up against them. They endure what had been foretold;

hope in what had been promised; teach what had been commanded them. Few in number, they are scattered through the world. They convert populations with marvellous facility. In the midst of enemies they grow. They are multiplied by persecutions. In the straits of affliction they are spread abroad over vast regions. At first they are uninstructed, of very low condition, very few in number. Their ignorance passes into the brightest intelligence; their low ranks produce the most cultivated eloquence; their fewness becomes a multitude; they subjugate to Christ minds the most acute, learned, and accomplished, and convert them into preachers of piety and salvation. In the alternating intervals of adversity and prosperity, they exercise a watchful patience and temperance. As the world verges in a perpetual decline, and by exhaustion expresses the coming of its last age, since this also is what prophecy led them to expect, they with greater confidence await the eternal happiness of the heavenly city. And amid all this the unbelief of impious nations rages against the Church of Christ, which works out victory by patience, and by preserving unshaken faith against the cruelty of opponents. When the sacrifice unveiled by the truth, which had so long been covered under mystical promises, had at length succeeded, those sacrifices which prefigured this one were removed by the destruction of the Temple itself. This very Jewish people, rejected for its unbelief, was cast out of its own seat, and scattered everywhere throughout the world, to carry with it the sacred writings; so that the testimony of prophecy, by which Christ and the Church were foretold, may not be thought a fiction of ours for the occasion, but be produced by our very adversaries— a testimony in which it is also foretold that they should not believe. The temples and images of demons, and the sacrilegious rites of that worship, are gradually overthrown, as prophecy foretold. Heresies against the name of Christ, which yet veil themselves under that name, swarm, as was foretold, in order to call out the force of teaching in our holy religion. In all these things, as we read their prediction, so we discern their fulfilment, and from so vast a portion which is fulfilled we rest assured of what is still to come. Is there a single mind which yearns after eternity and feels the shortness of the present life, that can resist the light and the force of this divine authority?"[1]

St. Augustine wrote thus to his friend Volusian, the uncle of St. Melania, a Roman nobleman of high reputation, who was then, as he continued for many years

[1] St. Aug. Epist. 137, ad Volusianum, § 15–16. A.D. 412. It is remarkable that Volusian, who held the highest offices in the Roman Empire, and among the rest was Prefect of the City, was not converted either by the genius or the saintliness of Augustine. But more than twenty years after this letter, about A.D. 435, he was sent on an embassy from the Emperor of the West to the Emperor of the East at Constantinople. His niece, St. Melania the younger, left the seclusion of her monastery at Jerusalem, and travelled all the intervening distance to see him. When he met in the garb of humility and poverty the niece whom he remembered at Rome in all the splendour of youth, rank, and beauty at the head of the Roman nobility, he was so impressed by the force of Christian charity which had wrought such a change, that he was converted and baptized by the Patriarch Proclus, and died shortly afterwards. God did by the sight of the nun what He had not done by the learning of the theologian and the philosopher.

to be, a heathen. But we must also take note that he wrote at a point of time scarcely less remarkable than that of the vision interpreted by Daniel. The old world with its sequence of world-empires was passing away. And so soon as it passed another travail of extraordinary severity was preparing for the Church, such a travail as even the eagle eye of the Bishop of Hippo could not discern as he stood before the beginning of its accomplishment. When he wrote there was a Catholic Church, the fulfilment of a long train of prophecies in that "connection of ages" which he has so wonderfully drawn out, but there was not yet a Christendom. Nor could he the least foresee what was to take place before that Christendom could be formed. Only, as he spoke, the iron of Roman discipline—the inflexible Romulean mind—which had held together the miry clay of so many various and divergent nationalities, European, Asiatic, African, so that "the kingdom took its origin from the iron," was losing its tenacity. That vast structure of Roman power, the breaking up of which had been feared in the wars and insurrections arising upon the death of Nero, and extinction of the family of Augustus, was in truth dissolving.[1] The western and eastern limbs of the statue were parting away from each

---

[1] The words which Cerialis addressed to the Gauls, as recorded by Tacitus, Hist. 4, 74, apply in all their force to the times when the transmigration of the northern tribes took effect, four hundred years after they were written. "Octingentorum annorum fortuna disciplinaque compages hæc coaluit, quæ convelli sine exitio convellentium non potest." And every city of the Roman empire could testify to the truth of what he added: "Sed vobis maximum discrimen penes quos aurum et opes, præcipuæ bellorum causæ."

other, and the toes were crumbling. But though Augustine heard the sound of the advancing tide, he saw not yet the full flood of the deluge from the north; and still less could he foresee the counter desolation from the south; Teuton flood and Arab desolation which in their joint effect would blast utterly the Roman Peace, and break the iron, the clay, the brass, the silver, and the gold in pieces together, until they became like the chaff of the summer's threshing-floor.

As little could he anticipate another sight, the further fulfilment of the vision, when the provinces, those crumbling toes of the statue, which lay before him in an impending dissolution, were to be formed into great independent kingdoms, having for the common foundation of their power "the Word was made flesh and dwelt among us." Then in that "connection of ages" which should be drawn out after the time of Augustine in even greater distinctness than before him, and with greater claim upon the believing mind, which "yearns after eternity," a grander fulfilment of the vision would be disclosed. The royalties set up by barbarian chiefs of tribes among incoherent populations of victors and vanquished were to educate mature nations with individual character in the one Christian faith, and shine as distinct stars set in the crown of the Successor to Peter's pastorship. For as the Word made flesh created Christian monarchies and Christian nations in their several being, so the charge of the Word to a disciple by the lake of Gennesareth, "Feed My Sheep," created the great unity of Christendom which bound them together. In Constantine one empire had acknowledged the reign of Christ, and bent the neck of heathen domination to raise the cross upon a heathen crown. But then a group of nations should base the fabric of their laws, and the whole civilisation which redeemed them from barbarism, upon the truth that God assumed flesh for man's sake, and should acknowledge in Peter's Successor the Vicar of that God, who by and in that pastoral rule of Peter made them members of one Body, and in so making them "took the Gentiles for His inheritance, and the utmost parts of the earth for His possession."

This was a second and further fulfilment of the vision, which as yet Augustine saw not, nor even anticipated; but after thus writing he set himself in the last years of his life to a great task, even that of comparing together from their origin to their end the course of the two societies, not national, but world-wide, which run out through human history, intermingled together, and claiming possession of the same man. First, the natural society of the human race played upon by all the passions and infirmities which are the effect of man's original Fall; and secondly, that other society chosen by God from the beginning in view of His Son's Incarnation, for the purpose of repairing and counterworking that Fall. It was the capture of Rome by Alaric, and the deep despondency which thence arose in the minds of many, both Christian and heathen, that moved him originally to this design, of which the first tracing is seen in the letter to Volusian just quoted. He sought to meet conclusions unfavourable to the Christian faith, which were drawn by weak, or narrow, or unbelieving minds from the fall of the imperial city. His plan accordingly led him to take a complete view of all human history; and the result has been that one of the last representatives of the old world, and certainly the greatest of all as thinker, philosopher, and theologian, the most universal genius of the patristic ages, whether among Greeks or Latins, has left us a Philosophy of History, the first in time, and as yet unequalled in ability; for it supplies a key to the acts of man and the providence of God in that masterly comparison between the City of God and the City of the devil in their origin, their course, and their end.

The leading thought of this great work gives me a final text bearing on the subject of this volume.

"Thus, then, two Cities have been created by two loves: the earthly, by that love of self which reaches even to the contempt of God ; the heavenly, by the love of God which reaches even to the contempt of self. The first has its boast in self; the second in its Lord. For the first seeks its glory from men; whereas to the second, God, the witness of conscience, is the greatest glory. The first in that glory which it has made for itself exalts its own head; the second says to its God, 'Thou art my glory and the lifter up of my head.' In the first the lust of domination sways both its rulers and the nations which it subjugates. In the second a mutual service of charity is exercised by rulers who consult the good of subjects, and by subjects who practise obedience to rulers. The first loves in its own potentates its own excellence; the second says to the God of its choice, 'I will love Thee, O Lord, my strength.' And thus in the first its own wise men, living after human fashion, pursue the goods of their body or their mind, or both at once, or they who might have known God, have not 'glorified Him as God nor given thanks, but became vain in their thoughts, and their foolish heart was darkened; professing themselves to be wise,' that is, extolling themselves in their own wisdom through the pride that mastered them, 'they became fools, and changed the glory of the incorruptible God into the likeness of the image of a corruptible man, and of birds, and of four-footed beasts, and of creeping things;' for they either led their peoples or followed them in the adoration of such-like images; and 'worshipped and served the creature rather than the Creator, who is blessed for ever.' But in the second there is no wisdom of man save piety, by which the true God is rightly worshipped, awaiting its reward in the society of saints, not men only, but angels, that God may be all in all."[1]

I put together these three facts of human history, the vision of the King of Babylon interpreted by Daniel six hundred years before Christ, the summary of its fulfilment down to his own age written by St. Augustine four hundred years after the coming of Christ, and his delineation, a few years later, of the Two Cities, as set forth by him in a work on which the Christian mind

[1] De Civ. Dei, xvi. 28.

has now been nurtured for fourteen hundred and fifty years. The simple juxtaposition of these shows how Babylon stretches to Rome, and Rome is heir of Babylon; and the heathen man thus formed illustrates "the Man who is born in Sion, the city of the great King."[1] It is true that the two great Powers of Civil and Spiritual government, the relation between which forms the subject of this volume, are not exactly represented as concerns that relation in the vision of Daniel; but only the heathen growth of the Civil Power, and the miraculous rise, permanent rule, and progressive growth of the Spiritual Power in the midst of it; yet the mighty promise is recorded that in presence of the Civil Power the Spiritual shall never pass away; rather that it shall last unchanged, while the other is shifting and transitory; and also the cognate truth, that the great and terrible Power represented by the Statue is, in the counsels of God, subordinate in its scope to the Power represented by the Stone.

It is true, again, that the vivid contrast of the Two Cities as drawn by St. Augustine does not represent the legitimate relation of the Two Powers to each other, but only the perversion of the one Power from its true end and object, and the perfect antagonism of the other to that perversion.

But the kingdom set up by the God of heaven in the vision interpreted by Daniel, and the connection of ages dwelt upon by St. Augustine, which leads up to the Person of Christ, and then starts afresh from Him, and

[1] Ps. lxxxvi. 5.

the Divine City delineated by St. Augustine, fit exactly into each other, and so they seem to me to form together an appropriate introduction to that most remarkable period of history with which the present volume is occupied, when the Stone cut out without hands struck the Statue, and became a great mountain, in preparation for that further growth when it would fill the whole earth.

The Statue presented in vision to the heathen king has indeed been swept away, but in every country a reduced likeness of it, "the look whereof is terrible," stands over against "the Man born in Sion." And the Two Cities everywhere run on in their predestined course until the end contemplated by Augustine takes effect. But as he did not discern the second fulfilment of the divine kingdom which followed upon the wandering of the nations, so neither can we discern the third and yet grander fulfilment when the divine kingdom shall become to the whole world what once it was in the Roman Empire. For, to repeat St. Augustine's words, "In all these things as we read their prediction, so we discern their fulfilment, and from so vast a portion which is fulfilled we rest assured of what is still to come." And "the stone that struck the statue became a great mountain, and filled the whole earth."

FEBRUARY 12, 1882.

CHURCH AND STATE

AS SEEN IN

THE FORMATION OF CHRISTENDOM.

———•———

CHAPTER I.

RELATION BETWEEN THE CIVIL AND SPIRITUAL POWERS
FROM ADAM TO CHRIST.

1.—*The Divine and Human Society founded in Adam,
refounded in Noah.*

IN one of the most ancient books of the world, which, in addition to its antiquity, all Christians venerate as containing the original tradition of man's creation, guaranteed in purity and accuracy by divine assistance given to the writer, we read the following words :—
" God made the beasts of the earth according to their kinds, and cattle, and everything that creepeth on the earth after its kind. And God saw that it was good. And he said : Let us make man to our image and likeness : and let him have dominion over the fishes of the sea, and the fowls of the air, and the beasts, and the whole earth, and every creeping creature that moveth upon the earth. And God created man to his own

A

image: to the image of God he created him: male and female he created them." And further: "The Lord God formed man of the slime of the earth; and breathed into his face the breath of life, and man became a living soul. . . . And the Lord God took man and put him into the paradise of pleasure, to dress it and to keep it. And he commanded him, saying, Of every tree of paradise thou shalt eat; but of the tree of knowledge of good and evil thou shalt not eat. For in what day soever thou shalt eat of it, thou shalt die the death. And the Lord God said, It is not good for man to be alone; let us make him a help like unto himself. And the Lord God having formed out of the ground all the beasts of the earth, and all the fowls of the air, brought them to Adam to see what he would call them: for whatsoever Adam called any living creature, the same is its name. And Adam called all the beasts by their names, and all the fowls of the air, and all the cattle of the field; but for Adam there was not found a helper like himself. Then the Lord God cast a deep sleep upon Adam: and when he was fast asleep he took one of his ribs and filled up flesh for it. And the Lord God built the rib which he took from Adam into a woman: and brought her to Adam. And Adam said, This is now bone of my bones, and flesh of my flesh: she shall be called Woman, because she was taken out of man. Wherefore a man shall leave father and mother, and shall cleave to his wife: and they shall be two in one flesh. And they were both naked, Adam and his wife, and were not ashamed."

Such is the account of the origin of man, of woman, of marriage, as the root of human society, and of that society itself, beginning in the absolute unity of one who was father and head of his race, created in full possession of reason and language, and exercising both by an intuitive knowledge of the qualities of living creatures as they are brought before him by his Maker. This account stands at the head of human history, and has been venerated as truth by more than a hundred generations of men since it was written down by Moses, not to speak of those many generations among whom it had been a living tradition before he had written it down. Human language scarcely possesses elsewhere such an assemblage of important truths in so few words. Perhaps the only parallel to it is contained in the fourteen verses which stand at the opening of St. John's Gospel, wherein are recorded the Godhead and Incarnation of the Divine Word. The first creation has its counterpart only in the second; and the restoration of man by the personal action of God alone surpasses, or, perhaps, more truly may be said to complete, the Idea of his original formation by the same personal action of the same Divine Word, who, great as He is in creating, is yet greater in redeeming, but is one in both, and in both carries out one Idea.

For the creation of man as one individual, who is likewise the head and bearer of a race, is the key to all the divine government of the world. The fact rules its destinies through all their evolution. The world, as it concerns the actions, the lot, and the reciprocal effect of men upon each other, would have been quite a different world if it had not sprung out of this unity. If, for instance, mankind had been a collection of human beings in all things like to what they now are, except in one point, that they were independent of each other and unconnected in their origin. This unity further makes the race capable of that divine restoration which from the beginning was intended, and with a view to which man was made a race : which in restoring man likewise unspeakably exalts him, for He who made Adam the father and head of the race, made him also " the figure of One that was to come."

Let us briefly enumerate the parts of the divine plan as disclosed to us in the narration just given.

In the council held by the Blessed Trinity it is said, " Let us make man to our image and likeness ; " not, Let us make men, but man : the singular number used of the whole work indicates that the creation to be made was not only an individual but a family. From the beginning the family is an essential part of the plan. This is no less indicated in the single creation of Adam first, not the simultaneous creation of the male and female, as in the case of all other creatures, but the creation by himself of the head alone, from whom first woman by herself, and then from the conjunction of the two his family is drawn. In Adam first, while as yet he is alone, the high gifts of reason, speech, and knowledge indicated in the twofold and also congenital possession of reason and language, are exhibited as residing as in a fountain-head, when all creatures of the earth and the air are brought before him by his Maker, and he with intuitive understanding of their several qualities and uses imposes on them the corresponding name. Thus Adam is created complete, a full-grown man, in whom the divine gift of thought finds expression in the equally divine gift of language, both exerted with unerring truth, for it is intimated that the names which he assigns to the creatures thus passed in review render accurately their several natures. It is not said that the Lord God intimated to Adam the names which he should give; but the knowledge by which he gave the names was part of his original endowment, like the gift of thought and language, which answer to each other and imply each other, and in a being composed of soul and body complete by their union and joint exercise the intellectual nature. "The Lord God brought all beasts and all fowls before Adam to see what he would call them; for whatsoever Adam called any living creature, the same is its name."

This presentation of the creatures before Adam, and their naming by him, is the token of the dominion promised to him "over the fishes of the sea, and the fowls of the air, and the beasts, and the whole earth," as the result of his being made to "the image and likeness" of the Triune God. Only when he has thus taken possession of his royalty is the creation of the family completed out of himself. For when "for Adam there was not found a helper like himself," the Lord God took not again of the slime of the earth to mould a woman and bring her to man, but "He cast a deep sleep upon Adam, and built the rib which He took from Adam into a woman, and brought her to Adam." And then He uttered the blessing which should fill the earth with the progeny of the woman who had been drawn from the man her head, saying, "Increase and multiply and fill the earth, and subdue it, and rule over the fishes of the sea, and the fowls of the air, and all living creatures that move upon the earth."

What, then, is the image and likeness of the Triune God? The image consists in the soul, with its two powers of the understanding and the will, proceeding out of it, indivisible from it, yet distinct. May we not infer that the likeness is the obedience of the soul, with its powers, to the eternal law? This law, viewed in the Triune God, the prototype of man's being, is the sanctity of the Divine Nature; but in man, thus created, the obedience to it was the gift of original justice superadded to his proper nature: the gift by which the soul, in the free exercise of the understanding and the will, was obedient to the law of God, its Creator.

This was an image and likeness which belonged to Adam in a double capacity, firstly, as an individual, secondly, as head of a family; for it was to descend to each individual of the family in virtue of natural procreation from Adam. The man created after the image and likeness of the Triune God was, according to the divine intention, to be repeated in every one of the race.

But what of the family or race which was to be evolved out of Adam alone? Not the individual only but the race also is in the divine plan. Is there a further image of the Triune God in the mode of the race's formation?

To give an answer to this question, we must first consider what is the prototype of that singular unity according to which the first parents of the race are not formed together out of the earth, male and female, like the inferior creatures. For in most marked distinction from all these man is formed by himself, and alone; receives the command to eat of all trees in the garden except the tree of the knowledge of good and evil, under penalty of death if he take of it; and then is shown exercising the grandeur of his knowledge and the fulness of his royalty in the naming of the subject creatures. But inasmuch as none of them could supply him with a companion, and as "it was not good for him to be alone," a council of the Triune God is held again, and a help like to himself is taken out of himself. Is there not here, with that infinite distance which separates the created from the Increate, a yet striking image of the Divine Filiation?

Again, from the conjunction of the two, from Adam the head, and from Eve when she has been drawn out of him, proceeds, in virtue of the blessing of God, the human family. Is there not here, again, at that distance which separates divine from human things, an image of the procession of the Third Divine Person, the Lord, and the Giver of life, from whom all life proceeds?

May we not then say with reverence, that from the

council of the Triune God, "Let us make man to our image and likeness," proceeds forth the individual man, an earthly counterpart in his memory, understanding, and will to the divine Creator, and likewise man, the family, a created image of the primal mystery, the ineffable joy of the Godhead, the ever blessed Trinity in Unity? And since the origin of creation itself is the free act of God, it ought not to surprise us that the chief work of His hands in the visible universe should reflect in the proportion of a creature the secret life of the Divine Nature, the Unity and Trinity of the Godhead.

But next to this primal mystery, which is the source of all creation, stands that unspeakable condescension, that act of sovereign goodness, by which God has chosen to assume a created nature into personal unity with Himself, and to crown the creation which He has made. As to this the first Adam, in all his headship, with the privileges included in it, the transmission to his family of original justice, and of that wonderful gift of adoption superadded to it, is "the figure of Him who was to come." But more also, St. Paul tells us, is indicated in the formation of Eve out of Adam during the sleep divinely cast upon him. This was the "great sacrament of Christ and of His Church" (Eph. v. 32), to which he pointed in reminding his hearers of the high institution of Christian marriage. And thus we learn that God, in the act of forming the natural race, supernaturally endowed, was pleased to foreshadow by the building of Eve, "the mother of all living," out of the first Adam, the building of another Eve, the second and truer mother of a divine race, out of the wounded heart of the Redeemer of the world asleep upon the cross. As then in Adam's headship we have the figure of the Headship of Christ, so in the issuing of Eve from him in his sleep we have the Passion of Christ and the issuing forth of His Bride from it, when His work of redemption was completed and His royalty proclaimed.

Thus the mysteries of the blessed Trinity, that is, of God the Creator, and of the Incarnation and Passion of Christ, that is, of God the Redeemer, lie folded up, as it were, in the Mosaic narrative of the mode in which Adam was created, and in the headship of the race conferred upon him.

Before we approach the sin of Adam and its consequences to human society, let us cast one glance back upon the beauty and splendour of the divine plan in the original creation as it is disclosed to us in the narrative of Moses. As the crown of the visible creation is placed a being who is at once an individual and the head of a family, representing in his personal nature the divine Unity and Trinity, and in the race of which he is to stand at the head the same divine Unity and Trinity in their aspect towards creation; representing the royalty of God in his dominion over the creatures, a dominion the condition of which is the obedience of his own compound nature to the law given to it by the Creator; representing again in the vast number to which his race shall extend the prolific energy of the

Lord of Hosts; representing also in that secret and altogether wonderful mystery, out of which the multiplication of his race springs, the yet untold secret of the divine mercy, in virtue of which his fathership is the prelude to a higher fathership, the first man is the pattern of the Second, and the royalty of his creation but a rehearsal at the beginning of the world of the reparation which is to crown its end.

The whole work of creation as above described depends in its result upon the exercise of man's free-will. His value, before God, lies simply in the way in which he exerts this great prerogative of his reasonable nature. Without it he would be reduced from one who chooses his course, and in that choice becomes good or evil, to the condition of a machine devoid of any moral being. To test this free-will man was given a commandment. We know that he failed under the trial; that he broke the commandment. His disobedience to his Creator was punished by the disobedience of his own compound nature to himself. That divine grace, which we term the state of original justice, and in virtue of which his soul, with its understanding and will, illuminated and fortified, was subject to God, and the body with all its appetites was subject to the soul, was withdrawn. He became subject to death, the certain death of the body, with all that train of diseases and pains which precede it; and the final separation of the soul from its Creator, unless by the way which God indicated to him he should be restored. Becoming a sinner, his refuge was penitence; henceforth his life was to be the life of a penitent; he had lost the grace which was bestowed royally on the innocent; he was left the grace which was to support and lead on the penitent. From the garden of pleasure he is expelled, to go forth into a world which produces thorns and thistles, unless he water it with the sweat of his brow. To all this I only allude, since my proper subject is to trace the first formation of human society as it came forth from the fall. But the primal state of man could not be passed over, because the state in which he grew up, and the state in which he now stands, cannot be understood nor estimated rightly without a due conception of that original condition.

With the loss of original justice Adam does not lose the headship of his race. All men that are to be born remain his children, and continue to be not a species of similar individuals, but a family, a race. All the dealings of God with them continue to be dealings with them as a race. Adam's fathership, had he not fallen, would have been to them the source of an inestimable good, would have secured to them the transmission of original justice, crowned as it further was by a wholly gratuitous gift, the gift of adoption to a divine sonship. But that fathership, in consequence of his sin, actually transmitted to them a nature penally deprived both of the original endowment and of the superadded adoption; and, as a fact, all the difficulties which occur to the mind in the divine government of the world spring out of this treatment by God of man as a family, a race. But likewise through this continuing fathership of Adam, the Fathership of Christ appears as the completion of an original plan, devised before the foundation of the world, and actually carried out at the appointed time. He was to be son of David and son of Abraham in order that He might be Son of man. This original plan of God is not frustrated but executed by the fall of Adam. The yet undisclosed secrets of human lot have their origin in Adam and their solution in Christ. We are allowed to see that they belong to one plan. No doubt the hidden things of God in this dispensation baffle our scrutiny: they remain for the trial of faith until faith passes into sight, but we are allowed to see the fact of a vast compensation; and over against the fathership which brought death and corruption and the interminable ills of human life, we see all the supernatural blessings of the new covenant, consisting in the triple dowry of adoption, betrothal, and consecration, come to man as a spiritual race descending from the Second Adam.

Thus, not only the primary but the actual state of man in society springs out of an absolute unity. We have here to note two great truths. Adam, as he was expelled from paradise to till the earth and subdue it, was the head of his race in two particulars: first, as to natural society, whence springs civil government; and secondly, as to the worship of God, and the promises included in that worship, whence springs priesthood and all the fabric of religion. The two unities, the social and the religious, had in him their common root; and man thus comes before us in history as a family in which the first father stands at the head of the civil and religious order in most intimate intercourse with God. The only description which we possess of that first period of human society from the Fall to the Deluge, suggests to us a state which seems absolutely walled round by God with securities, both as concerns human life in the intercourse between man and man, and as concerns the purity of their worship of God. As to the first, have we not said all which can be said when we say that they were a family? The king of the human race was the father of every one in it. Certainly if any king could ever command the love and respect of his subjects it must have been Adam in that royalty.

But let us very briefly consider the bearing of man's condition before the fall, as set forth to us in the sacred records which have been so far followed, upon his knowledge of divine and human things, and his moral state in his first society after the fall.

We have seen Adam in possession of a great dignity, created in the maturity of reason, exercising the full power of thought and speech as directed to truth by an inward gift, which conveys to him the knowledge of the creatures surrounding him; moreover, taught by God as to his present duties and future hopes. We have seen a wife bestowed upon him, who is, as it were, created for him and drawn from him, and a vast family promised to him. He is thus made father and head of his family and his race, and his Creator is his immediate Teacher. After his fall these privileges do not become to him as if they had never been. The memory of them all is complete in him, but a very large portion of their substance remains. Let us take three points, which are enough for our purpose. He receives, at the fall itself, firstly, a great promise of God; secondly, he becomes the Teacher and, thirdly, the Priest of his race. As to the promise, God declares to him that, as the result of the serpent seducing the woman to sin, He will create enmity between the serpent and the woman, the seed of the serpent and the seed of the woman; the seed of the woman should crush the serpent's head; the serpent should lie in wait for his heel. All human history is gathered up in that division of the race, between the seed of the woman, from which springs the City of God, and the seed of the serpent, from which springs the City of the Devil. That is a communication of fresh knowledge to Adam, knowledge of good and evil, a mixture of consolation and sorrow. That is a disclosure of the issue of things stretching to the very end of the world, which comes to sustain Adam in his penitence, to complete the knowledge which he previously had of God and of himself.

In this first great prophecy, which embraces all the religion, the hope, and the destiny of man, the consequences of which are not yet worked out, man is treated as a race. The punishment falls on him as a Father; the Woman through whom it comes, the Mother of his children, points to another Woman and Mother, through whom it is to be reversed, and the Deliverer is to come to him as a Descendant.

Adam, then, was cast out of paradise, but not without

hope, still less without knowledge, for he carried with him the knowledge which God had given to him, and the lesson of a great experience. Thus he became the great Teacher of his family. Through him from whom they received natural being and nurture, they received the knowledge of God, of their own end, of all which it behoved them to know for the purpose of their actual life. The great Father was likewise the great Penitent; and the first preacher of God's justice to men told them likewise of His mercy: a preacher powerful and unequalled in both his themes.

But, by the fall, Adam became likewise the Priest in his family. We learn from the narrative of Cain and Abel that the worship of God by sacrifice had been instituted, and it is not obscurely intimated that it was instituted even before he was cast out of paradise, since God Himself clothed Adam and Eve with skins of beasts, which, doubtless, were slain in sacrifice, since they were not used for food.[1]

The rite of bloody sacrifice, utterly unintelligible without the notion of sin, and inconceivable without a positive divine institution, so precise in its formularies about the statement of sin, and the need of expiation, is an everliving prophecy of the great sacrifice which God had intended "before the foundation of the world," and a token of the knowledge which He had communicated to

[1] St. Aug. cont. Faustum, 22, 17. Antiqua enim res est prænuntiativa immolatio sanguinis, futuram passionem Mediatoris ab initio generis humani testificans; hanc enim primus Abel obtulisse in sacris litteris invenitur.

Adam before he became a father. Unfallen man needed to make no sacrifice, but only the triple offering of adoration, thanksgiving, and prayer. These Adam would have given before he fell; after his fall he became a priest, and the bloody sacrifice to God of His own creatures, a mode of propitiating God which man could never have invented or imagined of himself, is a token of the ritual enjoined upon him, and of the faith which it symbolised and perpetuated.

Such, then, was the condition of the children of Adam, the first human society, in those "many days" which passed before Cain rose up against Abel: the state of a family living in full knowledge of their own creation, being, and end, in vast security, for who was there to hurt them? worshipping God the Creator by a rite which He had ordained in token of a great promise, at their head the Father, the Teacher, and the Priest, with the triple dignity which emanates from the divine sovereignty, and makes a perfect government.

The two powers which were to rule the world rested as yet undivided upon Adam after his fall.

It is evident that nothing could be further from a state of savagery or barbarism, from a state of defective knowledge of God and man, and his end, than such a condition as this, which suggests itself necessarily to any one who considers attentively the sacred narrative.

But as Adam in paradise was left to the exercise of his free-will, and fell out of the most guarded state of innocence by its misuse, so the first-born of Adam broke out of this secure condition of patriarchal life through the same misuse, and begun by fratricide the City of the Devil. We are told that God remonstrated with him when he fell under the influence of envy and jealousy, but in vain. He rose against his brother and slew him; he received in consequence the curse of God; "went out from his face, and dwelt a fugitive on the earth at the east side of Eden." There it is said that he built the first city, on which St. Augustine comments: "It is written of Cain that he built a city; but Abel, as a stranger and pilgrim, built none."

The fratricide of Cain leads to a split in the human family. The line of Cain seems to depart from Adam and live in independence of him. It becomes remarkable for its progress in mechanical arts, and for the first example of bigamy. The end of it is all we need here note. In process of time, "as men multiplied on the earth," two societies seem to divide the race of Adam— one entitled that of "the sons of God," the other that of "the daughters of men." But the ruin of the whole race is brought about by the blending of the better with the worse: the bad prevail, the two Cities become mixed together in inextricable confusion. God left to man throughout his free-will, but when the result of this was that "the wickedness of men was great upon the earth, and that all the thoughts of their heart was bent upon evil at all times," that is, when the City of the Devil had prevailed over the City of God in that patriarchal race which He had so wonderfully taught and guarded, He interfered to destroy those whose rebellion was hopeless of amendment, and to make out of one who had remained faithful to Him a new beginning of the race.

The race had been cut down to the root because in the midst of knowledge and grace it had deserted God; and Noah, as he stepped forth from the ark, began with a solemn act of reparation. He "built an altar to the Lord and offered holocausts upon it of all cattle and fowls that were clean." God accepted the sacrifice, inasmuch as it was in and through this act that He bestowed the earth upon Noah and his sons, and gave him everything that lived and moved on it for food. He consecrated afresh the life of man by ordaining that whoever took human life away, that is, by an act of violence, not of justice, should himself be punished with the loss of his own life; and He grounded this great ordinance upon the fact that man was made after the image of God. At the same time God repeated to Noah and his sons the primal blessing which had multiplied the race, and was to fill the earth with it, and made a covenant with him and with his seed for ever, a covenant to be afterwards developed, but never to be abrogated. It is to be noted that the sacred narrative dwells rather upon the sacrifice made by Noah immediately upon issuing from the ark than upon the original sacrifice offered by Adam. Of the first institution of sacrifice it makes only incidental mention, referring with great significance to those skins of beasts, of which God provided a covering for the nakedness of Adam and Eve. It is as if the rite of sacrifice, instituted as a prophecy of the future expiation of sin, might fitly supply from the skins of its victims a covering for that nakedness which sin alone had revealed and made shameful. The mention of this fact ensues immediately upon the record of the fall, before Adam is cast out of paradise. And again, by the mention of the sacrifice of Abel, and of its acceptance, it is shown that the rite already existed in the children of the first man. But now the sacrifice of Noah, and the covenant made in it, as being of so vast an import to every succeeding generation, is described at length as the starting-point of the whole renewed, that is, the actual race of man. In this sacrifice it is emphatically declared that "the Lord smelled a sweet savour," since it stood at the beginning of man's new life, coming after the waters of the deluge as the image and precursor of the Sacrifice on Calvary, which was to purify the earth, and which those waters typified.

As, then, we considered lately the position of man as to his knowledge of God and of himself in the "many days" which ensued after the fall before the death of Abel, so let us glance at his condition in these same respects at the starting-point of this new life of man. First of all, out of the wreck of the old world Noah had carried the two institutions, one of which makes the human family in its natural increase, while the other constitutes its spiritual life—marriage and sacrifice. In marriage we have the root of society; in sacrifice the root of religion. These had not perished, neither had they changed in character. They were the never-displaced foundation of the race, an heirloom of paradise never lost; marriage, as established in the primeval sanctity before man fell, sacrifice as superadded to man's original worship of adoration, thanksgiving, and prayer immediately upon his fall, in token of his future recovery. God, in selecting Noah to repair the race, made him, in so far like to Adam, the head of the two orders, King and Priest, and from that double headship the actual government of the world through all the lines of his posterity descends.

Thirdly, we find in Noah's family the divine authority of government expressly established; for in the protection thrown over human life the power to take it away in case of grievous crime is also given. Authority to take life away belongs of right to the giver of life alone. He here bestows the vicarious exercise of it upon that family which was likewise the first State, and the fountain-head of actual human society. "At the hand of every man, and of his brother, will I require the life of man: whosoever shall shed man's blood, his blood shall be shed, for man was made to the image of God. But increase you, and multiply, and go upon the earth, and fill it." We have then the charter here of human society;[1] the delegation to it of supreme power by the Head of all power, to be vicariously exercised

---

[1] Leo XIII., in the great Encyclical of June 29, 1881, says: "It is also of great importance that they by whose authority public affairs are administered may be able to command the obedience of citizens, so that their disobedience is a sin. But no man possesses in himself or of himself the right to constrain the free-will of others by the bonds of such a command as this. That power belongs solely to God, the Creator of all things and the Lawgiver; and those who exercise it must exercise it as communicated to them by God. 'There is one lawgiver and judge who is able to destroy and to deliver' (James iv. 12).'

henceforward over the whole race as it went out, conquered, and replenished the earth; the sacredness of man's life declared, in virtue of that divine image according to which he alone of all creatures upon the earth was made, yet power over that life for the punishment of crime committed to man himself in the government established by God. An absolute dominion over all beasts was given at the same time to man; first for himself, in virtue of his distinction from the beast, in virtue of the divine image resting upon him, a delegation of divine power was set up in the midst of him, the supreme exercise of which is the power of life and death. Civil government therefore was no less created by God than marriage, and sacrifice, with the religious offices belonging to it. Like them it was ratified afresh in the race at this its second starting-point.

But, fourthly, it was as Father and Head of the race that the first act of Noah leaving the ark was to offer sacrifice; he offered it for himself and for all his children. With him, as offering in a public act the homage of his race, the great covenant of which we have been speaking was made. Besides the divine things bound together in the institution of sacrifice—the accord of four acts, adoration, thanksgiving, prayer, and expiation, which express man's knowledge of his condition of God's sovereignty, and of his own last end, as well as the dedication of his will to God—great temporal promises, such as the dominion over all other creatures, and the filling the earth with his race, promises which belong to man as one family and one race, were made to Noah in this solemn covenant ratified in sacrifice. The common hopes of the whole community for the present life and the future also were jointly represented in it. It is, in fact, the alliance of the civil government with religion, of which we see here the solemn ratification. Noah the Father, the King, and the Priest, sacrifices for all, where all have a common hope, a common belief, a common knowledge, a life not only as individual men, but as a family, as a race, as a society.

Thus in marriage, in sacrifice, in the vicarial exercise of divine power by civil government, and in the alliance of that government with the worship of God, we have the four central pillars on which the glorious dome of a sacred civilisation in the human family, when it should be conterminous with the whole earth, was intended to rest. These four things date from the beginning of the race; they precede heathenism, and they last through it. Greatly as man in the exercise of his free-will may rage against them, grievously as he may impair their harmony, and even distort by his sin the vast good which that harmony ensures and guards into partial evil, yet he will not avail to destroy the fabric of human society resting upon them before the Restorer comes.

Noah having lived 600 years before the flood, and having been the preacher of justice for 120 years to a world which would not listen to him, has his life prolonged for 350 years after the flood. During this time he is to be viewed as the great Teacher of his family, like Adam when he came out of Paradise. What the Fall was in the mouth of Adam the Deluge was in the mouth of Noah, a great example of punishment inflicted on man for the disregard of God as his end. It is hard to see how God could have more completely guarded those two beginnings of human society from the corruption of error and the taint of unfaithfulness than by the mode in which He caused them to arise, in that He formed them both through the teaching of a family by the mouth of a Parent, and the government of a race by the headship of its Author. For the larger society sprung actually out of brethren as the brethren themselves out of one parent. "They have," to use Bossuet's striking recapitulation, "one God, one object, one end, a common origin, the same blood, a common interest, a mutual need of each other, as well for the business of life as for its enjoyments." And one common language, it may be added, serves as the outward expression, the witness, and the bond of a society so admirably compacted, based, as it would seem, on so immovable a foundation.

Let us sum up in three words the history so far as it has yet been recorded. The foundation of all is man coming forth by creation out of the hand of God. He comes forth as one family in Adam. Falling from his high estate by his Father's sin, he receives a religion guarded and expressed by a specific rite of worship, which records his fall, and prophesies his restoration. After this the family springs from parents united in a holy bond, which, as it carries on the natural race, is likewise the image of a future exaltation. As he increases and multiplies the divine authority is vicariously exercised in the government of the race as a society. That government is strictly allied with his religion. It is most remarkable that the last end of man dominates the whole history; that is, all the temporal goods of man from the beginning depend on his fidelity to God. Disregard of this works the Fall; the same disregard works the Deluge. It remains to show how that compact and complete society instituted under Noah depended, as to the maintenance in unimpaired co-operation of the great goods we have just enumerated, upon the free-will of man to preserve his fidelity to God; that is, to show how in the constant order of human things there is an inherent subordination of the temporal to the spiritual good, as for the individual so for the race.

2.—*The Divine and Human Society in the Dispersion.*

The divine narrative of the beginning of human society ends with an event of which the consequences remain to the present day, and from which all the actual nations of the earth take their rise. The blessing and command given to Noah and his family were, " Increase and multiply and fill the earth." It would seem that the family of man continued in that highly privileged and guarded state which has just been described during five generations, comprehending perhaps the life of Noah and Shem. Of all this time it is said, " The earth was of one tongue and the same speech." The division of the earth among the families of a race by virtue of a natural growth, which was itself the effect of the divine blessing and command, did not carry with it as a condition of that growth the withdrawal of so great a privilege as the unity of language. God had formed the human family out of one; had built it up by marriage; cemented it by a religious rite of highest meaning; crowned it with His own delegated authority of government, and sanctified that government by its alliance with religion. Unity of language is as it were the expression of all these blessings. The possession of language by the first man, the outer vocalised word, corresponding to the inner spiritual word of reason, was a token of the complete intellectual nature inhabiting a corporeal frame—a fact expressed by the doctrine that the soul is the form of the body—which constituted his first endowment. And in a proportionate manner the possession of one language as the exponent of mind and heart by his race, was the most effective outward bond of inward unity which could tie the race together, whatever its numerical and local extension might be. It is to be noted that though the cause of the deluge was that "the earth was corrupted before God, and was filled with iniquity" (Gen. vii. 11), yet God had not withdrawn from man the unity of language, perhaps because the revolt of man had not hitherto reached to a corruption of his thought of the Divine Nature itself. But now ensued an act of human pride and rebellion which led God Himself to undo the bond of society, consisting in unity of language, in order to prevent a greater evil. The sin is darkly recorded, as if some peculiar abomination lay hid underneath the words; the punishment, on the contrary, is made conspicuous. "And the earth was of one tongue and the same speech. And when they removed from the east, they found a plain in the land of Sennaar and dwelt in it. And each one said to his neighbour, Come, let us make brick and bake them with fire. And they had brick instead of stones, and slime instead of mortar. And they said, Come and let us make a city and a tower, the top whereof may reach to heaven : and let us make our name famous before we be scattered abroad into all lands. And the Lord came down to see the city and the tower which the children of Adam were building. And He said, Behold it is one people, and all have one tongue ; and they have begun to do this, neither will they leave off from their designs till they accomplish them indeed. Come ye, therefore, let us go down and there confound their tongue, that they may not understand one another's speech. And so the Lord scattered them from that place into all lands, and they ceased to build the city. And therefore the name thereof was called Babel, confusion, because there the language of the whole earth was confounded; and from thence the Lord scattered them abroad upon the face of all countries."

It may be inferred that the city and the tower thus begun point at a society the bond of which was not to be the worship of the one true God. As a matter of fact, thenceforth and to all time the name of Babel has passed into the languages of men as signifying the City of Confusion, the seat of false worship, the headship of the line of men who are the seed of the serpent, and of that antagonism which the primal prophecy announced as the issue of the fall.

But the severity of the punishment and its nature seem further to indicate that we are here in presence of the beginning of the third great sin of the human race, in which, as in the former, the free-will of man, his inalienable prerogative and the instrument of his trial, runs athwart the purpose of God. The first was the sin of Adam's disobedience resulting in the Fall; the second the universal iniquity of the race punished by the Deluge; the third is the corruption of the idea of God by setting up many gods instead of one, a desertion of God as the source of man's inward unity, which is punished by the loss of unity of language in man, the voice of the inward unity, as it is also the chief stay and bond of his outward unity. The multiplication of the race and its propagation in all lands was part of the original divine intention. When the bond of living together in one place and under one government was withdrawn, there remained unity of worship and unity of language to continue and to support the unity of the race. Man was breaking his fealty to God not only by practical impiety, as in the time before the flood, but by denial of the Divine Nature itself as the One Infinite Creator and Father; God replied by withdrawing from rebellious vassals that unity of language which was the mark and bond of their living together as children of one Parent. With the record of this event Moses closes his history of the human race as one family, which he had up to this point maintained. He had hitherto strongly marked its unity in its creation, in its fall through Adam, in its first growth after the fall, and in the common punishment which descended upon it in the flood, and again in its second growth and expansion from Noah. Language is the instrument of man's thought, and the possession of one common language the most striking token of his unity; and here, after recording the withdrawal of that token by a miraculous act of God in punishment of a great sin, Moses parts from all mention of the race as one. He proceeds at once to give the genealogy of Shem's family as the ancestor of Abraham, and then passes to the call of Abraham as the foundation of the promised people. He never reverts to the nations as a whole, whom he has conducted to the point of their dispersion and there leaves.

Through this great sin the division of the earth by the human family started not in blessing, but in punishment. "The Lord scattered them abroad upon the face of all countries." He who had made the unity of Noah's family, Himself untied it, and we may conceive that He did so because of that greatest of all crimes, the division of the Divine Nature by man in his conception of it, his setting up many gods instead of one.

Let us see how this sin impaired, and more and more broke down, that privileged civilisation brought by Noah from before the flood, and set up by him in his family.

If God be conceived as more than one, He ceases by that very conception to be self-existing from eternity, immense, infinite, and incomprehensible. He ceases also to have power, wisdom, and goodness in an infinite plenitude; and, further, He ceases to be the one Creator, Ruler, and Rewarder of men.

Thus the conception of more gods than one carries with it an infinite degradation of the Godhead itself, as received in the mind and heart of man.

But it likewise unties the society of men with each other, and lays waste the main goods of human life. Thus it was in the case of Noah's family. As it was planted by God after the deluge, it possessed a distinct knowledge and worship of Him, as the one end and object of human life. This knowledge and worship were contained, as we have seen, in the rite of sacrifice and its accompaniments. Proceeding from this, it possessed the love of God, obliging men to mutual love, a precept the more easy because it was given to those who, as members of one family, were brethren. From these it followed that no man was stranger to another man; that every one was charged with the care of his brother; and that a unity of interest itself bound men to each other.[1]

But all these goods are dependent on the first. For if men do not worship one and the same God, as the Creator, the Ruler, and the Rewarder of all, their life ceases at once to have one end and object; their love to each other is deprived of its root, for they suppose themselves to be the creatures of different makers, or not to be made at all, to spring out of the earth, or to come into the world no one knows how, whence, or

[1] Bossuet sums up the state in these six points: Politique, &c. Art. I.

wherefore. Again, the natural brotherhood of man depends on his origin from one family, which must be the creature of one maker. And if the root of this natural affection and brotherhood be withered, men become strange to each other, rivals in their competition for the visible goods of life; they cease to care for others, and cease to be united in one interest.

When the family which had formed a patriarchal state became by natural growth too large to live together, the natural process for it was that it should swarm, and each successive swarm become a patriarchal state. Here was in each the germ of a nation, as they occupied various countries. Naturally, they would have parted in friendship, and if the bond of belief and of language had continued unbroken, they would have become a family of nations; they would each have carried out and propagated the original society from which they sprang without alloy or deterioration.

What actually took place was this. The division of the race into separate stems, and the corruption of the conception of God into separate divinities, pursued a parallel course, until the deities became as national as the communities over which they presided. As there ceased to be in their thought one God of the whole earth, they ceased to believe in one race of man, nor does any good seem to have more utterly perished from the peoples who sprung out of this dispersion than the belief in the universal brotherhood of man; and the conduct which should spring out of that belief, the treatment of each other as brethren.

That their having lost the consciousness of such brotherhood is no proof that it never existed, has been established for us by the new science of comparative grammar in our own day in a very remarkable instance. The careful study of a single family of languages in the great race of Japhet has proved beyond question that those who came after their dispersion to speak the Sanscrit, the Persian, the Greek, the Latin, the Celtic, Slavic, and Teutonic tongues, all once dwelt as brethren beside a common hearth, in the possession of the same language. Yet, in ancient times, it never crossed the mind of the Greek that he was of the same family with the Persian, by whose multitudinous inroad he was threatened; to him the barbarian, that is the man who did not speak his tongue, was his enemy, not a brother. As little did the Saxon, when he displaced the Celt, and gave him, too, the name of barbarian,[1] as not understanding his tongue, conceive that he was of the same family. It was with no little wonder that the first French and English students of Sanscrit found in it uneffaced the proofs of its parentage with Greek and Latin.

The study of the comparative grammar of various languages, when carried out as fully in other directions, may have in reserve other surprises as great as this; but the proof of unity in this case, where yet the divergence has proceeded so far, of unity in a family from which the greatest nations of the earth have sprung, and whose descendants stretch over the world, tends to

[1] Welsh, *i.e.*, foreigner, not speaking a language understood.

make the unity of the original language of man credible on principles of science, independently either of historical tradition or of revelation, while it shows into what complete and universal oblivion a real relationship may fall.

With the belief in one God, then, fell the belief in one human brotherhood as well as the existence of one human society. Each separated stem became detached from the trunk, and lived for itself. It is true that each state, as it began, was patriarchal; but identity of interests was restricted to the single state; beyond its range there was war, and within it, in process of time, war led to conquest, and after conquest the conquering leader became head of the conquered. Thus the patriarchal state, in which the head of the family was its priest, passed into kingdoms compacted by war and its results, in an ever-varying succession of victories and defeats.

But it is our special task to see what portion of the goods, which belonged to the race when undivided, passed on to its several stems in the dispersion with which Moses closes his account of the one human family.

The universal society stops at Babel, and national existence begins; that is, a number of inferior local unities succeed to the one universal. It would be well if we had a Moses for guide through the long period which follows, but he restricts his narrative to Abraham and his family, and to such incidental notice of the nations with whom they come in contact as their history requires. When we reach the beginnings of history in the several peoples who took their rise at the dispersion, a long time has intervened. The bond of one society in a race seems to consist in unity of place, of language, of religion, and of government. Now for man in general the unity of place was taken away by the dispersion itself. As to language, the lapse of a thousand years was more than sufficient to make the inhabitants of various countries strange to each other and barbarians. Men of different lands had long utterly ceased to acknowledge each other as brethren. As to religion, the worship of the one true God had passed into the worship of many false gods in almost every country each one of which had its own gods, generally both male and female, whom it considered as much belonging to itself as its kings or its cities. This diversity of deities in each nation, and the appropriation of them by each to itself, was become a most fertile principle of division and enmity among men. But if man had lost the unity of religion he had created for himself in every land an institution which might be said to be universal: the division of men into bond and free, the institution of slavery. That condition of life whereby man ceased to be a member of a family invested with reciprocal obligations and rights, came in fine to be regarded, not as a person, but as the thing of another man, that is the institution which man had made for himself in the interval between the dispersion of Babel and the commencement of authentic history in each nation. Man, who had divided the unity of the Godhead, had not only ceased to recognise the one ineffaceable dignity of reason as the mark of brotherhood in all his race demanding equality of treatment, and the respect due to a creature who possesses moral freedom, but had come to deprive a vast portion of his kindred of the fruit of their labour, and to confiscate their toil for his own advantage.

There remains the fourth bond of unity, government, whether national, tribal, or municipal, without which social existence is not possible ; and this, as the nations emerge into the light of history, appears everywhere among them standing and in great vigour. In the vast majority of cases that government clothes itself in the form of royalty; the king is undoubtedly the most natural descendant of the patriarchal chief, the father passing by insensible gradation into the sovereign. But whether monarchy or republic, whether the rule of the many or of the few, government, by which I mean the supreme dominion in each portion of the race over itself, of life and death over subjects, is everywhere found. Nowhere is man found as a flock of sheep without a shepherd.

Over these unrecorded years of human life, which want their prophet and their bard, sounds yet the echo of perpetual strife. If mighty forms loom among their obscurity, and come out at length with fixed character and a strong and high civilisation, such as the Assyrian and Egyptian, the Indian and Chinese monarchies, and so many others of more or less extent and renown, we know that states have suffered change after change in a series of wars. The patriarchal ruler has given way to the conquering chief; conquest has humiliated some and exalted others. What remains intact in each country, and after all changes, is government itself. This carried on the human race.

But if we examine more closely this race which is thus scattered through all countries, which speaks innumerable tongues, has lost the sense of its own brotherhood, worships a multitude of local gods, is divided, cut up, formed again, and torn again with innumerable wars, and has degraded a large part of itself into servitude, so as to lose as it would seem all semblance of its original unity, we yet find running through it, existing from the beginning as constituent principles which the hand of the Creator has set in it, four great goods.

1. For what hand but that of the Creator could have impressed ineffaceably upon a race, misusing as we have seen to such a degree the faculty of free-will, such an institution as marriage, in which the family, and all which descends from the family, is contained? The dedication of one man and one woman to each other for the term of their lives, for the nurture and education of the family which is to spring from them, is indeed the basis of human society, but a basis which none but its Maker could lay. It exists in perpetual contradiction to human passion and selfishness, for purposes which wisdom or the pure reason of man entirely approves, but which human frailty is at any time ready to break through and elude. If we could so entirely abstract ourselves from habit as to imagine a company of men and women thrown together, without connection with

each other, without any knowledge, any conception beforehand of such an institution, and left to form their society for themselves, we should not, I think, imagine them one and all choosing to engage themselves in such a union, resigning, respectively, their liberty, and binding themselves to continue, whatever might happen to either party, however strength and vigour might decline on one side, or grace and attractiveness on the other, in this bondage for life. Yet this institution of marriage is found established, not, as was just imagined, in a single company of human beings thrown together, but in a thousand societies of men separated by place, by language, by religion, and by government. The most highly policied among them are the strictest in maintaining its purity; and the higher you are enabled by existing records to ascend in their history, the stronger and clearer appears the conception of the duties of the married state. It is surrounded with all the veneration which laws can give it, and the blessing of religion consecrates it. Take marriage among the Romans as an instance. Their commonwealth seems to be built upon the sanctity of marriage and the power of the father. The like is the case with China, the most ancient of existing polities. There is not one nation which has gained renown or advanced in civilisation but shows, as far back as you can trace its history, this institution honoured and supported. I leave to mathematicians the task of calculating what are the chances of such an institution springing up in so great a multitude of nations according to an identical rule, guarded in all of them with whatever protection religion and law could afford, except by the fiat of a Creator in the manner described by Moses. The signet of God impressed on Adam at his origin could alone create such a mark on his race; the Maker alone lay such a foundation for it.

We find this institution in the course of time and in various countries debased by polygamy, and corrupted by concubinage. These aberrations testify to the force of human passion, and the wantonness of power and wealth ever warring against it, but they only enhance thereby the force of the institution's universal existence from the point of view from which I have regarded it.

2. Take, secondly, the rite of bloody sacrifice. It would be hard to find anything more contrary to reason and feeling than the thought that taking away the life of innocent creatures by pouring out their blood could be not only acceptable to the Maker of those creatures, but could be accepted by Him in expiation of sin committed by man. Yet this is the conception of bloody sacrifice; this was expressed in the rites which accompanied it; and besides this particular notion of expiation, which is the correlative of sin, the most solemn duties of man, that is, Adoration, Thanksgiving, and Petition, the whole expression of his obedience to God, and dependence on God, were bound up with this rite, and formed part of it. And we find this rite of sacrifice existing from the earliest times in these various nations; continued through the whole of their history, solemnised at first by their kings and chief men, and then by an

order of men created for that special purpose, and in every nation themselves holding a high rank in virtue of their performing this function. What, again, are the chances of a rite so peculiar being chosen spontaneously by so many various nations, and chosen precisely to express their homage for their own creation and continuance in being, to make their prayers acceptable, and above all, to cover their sin, to serve as an expiation, and to turn away punishment. This is the testimony which Assyria and Egypt, which Greece and Rome, which India and China bear to their original unity. If God instituted this rite, at the fall itself, as a record and token of the promise then made, its existence through the many changes of the race becomes intelligible; on any other supposition it remains a contradiction both to reason and feeling, which is like nothing else in human history.

The institution of sacrifice comprehends with its accompaniments the whole of religion. It suffered the most grievous corruption in that it was offered to false gods, to deified men, to powers of nature, to those who were not gods but demons. Again, its meaning was obscured, and the priests who offered it were not pure in their lives. But whatever abominations were at any time or in any place connected with it, its peculiarity, its testimony to the unity of the race, to the power which established it, remain without diminution.

3. Thirdly, let us take the great good of civil government. The human race is scattered over all countries, in divisions which range as to amount of population

from the smallest independent tribe to the largest
empire. God suffered them to pursue their own course,
to engage in numberless wars, and to pass through
a succession of the most opposite circumstances, but He
implanted in them from the beginning, and preserved in
them throughout, the instinct of society, which develops
in government. And He established that government
in possession by the patriarchal constitution of life,
which each portion of the race at its first start in independence took with it. By this He maintained order
and peace, as a rule, in the bosom of each community;
the smallest and the greatest alike possessed the commonwealth in the midst of them, which was thus, independent of walls and forts, a citadel of safety. Not even
the most savage tribe in the most desolate northern
wilderness, barren shore, or inland lake, was left in
its self-wrought degradation without this support.
In cultured nations, such as the Egyptians, Assyrians,
Persians, Indians, Chinese, the State attained a high
degree of perfection; while from the practice of the
Hellenic cities Plato and Aristotle could draw principles
of government which are of value for all time; and
Rome, the queen-mother of cities, has been the teacher of
state-wisdom to mankind. But what I wish to note here
is that civil government was everywhere throughout the
dispersion of the nations a dam, constructed by Divine
Providence, sufficiently strong to resist the inunda-
tion of evils brought about by man's abuse of his moral
freedom. It was the moon in heaven which shone as
a stable ordinance of God amid the storms and darkness

of human life in the fall of heathendom. It belonged to man as man and never departed from him; because as conscience was given to the individual, the witness and mark of God, sovereignty was given to the community, a delegation of the divine kingship. "It is entirely by the providence of God that the kingdoms of men are set up," says a great father.[1] "He gave to every one of them, said the Son of Sirach, commandment concerning his neighbour. Their ways are always before him, they are not hidden from his eyes. Over every nation he set a ruler, and Israel was made the manifest portion of God" (Ecclus. xvii. 12–15).

The human race, from its beginning and through all its dispersion, was never in any of its parts without civil government. The headship of Adam, repeated in Noah, itself a vicarious exercise of divine authority, rested, amid its dispersion and partial degradation, upon each portion of the race, so that it might never be kingless and lawless: never a herd, always a society.

This great good had also its corruption, into which it very frequently fell; the corruption of tyranny. Against this the Book of Wisdom (vi. 2–5) warned: "Hear therefore ye kings and understand: learn ye that are judges of the ends of the earth. Give ear, you that rule the people, and that please yourselves in multitudes of nations. For power is given you by the Lord, and strength by the most High, who will examine your works, and search out your thoughts: because being ministers of his kingdom, you have not

---
[1] St. Augustine.

judged rightly, nor kept the law of justice, nor walked according to the will of God." But this corruption of tyranny no more destroys the good of government or its testimony as the mark of the Creator, than the corruption of marriage by concubinage, or the offering of sacrifice to false gods, impairs the testimony of those institutions.

4. The fourth good which I shall note as running through all the nations of the dispersion, is the alliance between government and religion. Distance of place, diversity of language, division of the idea of God into separate divinities, which become the guardians of their several peoples, these causes all co-operate to sever from each other the various peoples and to make them enemies. But observe, at the same time, with this hardening and estrangement of the peoples from each other, the enlacement of all human life, public and private, by the rites and ties of religion in each society. At the head of the new race we have seen Noah offering sacrifice for his family, and a covenant with the whole earth struck in that sacrifice between God and man. That aspect of the public society towards religion was not altered during the whole course of heathendom, and in all its parts. It is a relation of the strictest alliance. No nation, no tribe of man, up to the coming of Christ, conceived any condition of society in which the Two Powers should not co-operate with each other. "If it be asked," says Bossuet,[1] " what should be said of a State in which public authority should be esta-

[1] Politique, &c., lib. vii. art. 2.

blished without any religion, it is plain at once that there is no need to answer chimerical questions. There never were such States. Peoples, where there is no religion, are at the same time without policy, without real subordination, and entirely savage." It is a fact which we see stretching through all the times and all the nations of the dispersion, that however tyrannical the government, and however corrupt the belief, still the separation of government from religion was never for a moment contemplated. A Greek or a Roman, and no less an Egyptian or an Assyrian, an Indian or a Chinese, must have renounced every habit of his life, every principle in which he had been nurtured, to accept such a divorce. For all of them alike, "ancestral laws" and "ancestral gods," went together. He who was traitor to the city's worship was considered to overthrow its foundation. In this point of view heathendom in all its parts continued to be profoundly religious. It risked the life of a favourite of the people when the statues of a god at Athens were mutilated, as it was supposed, with the connivance of Alcibiades; and Marcus Aurelius, stoic philosopher as he was, offered countless sacrifices for the Roman people, as Noah offered sacrifice for his family; and the Chinese Son of Heaven is to this day the father of his family who unites religious and civil power in his sacred person, and calls upon his people for the obedience of children.

The corruption of this relation between civil government and religion, which was an original good of the race, was the forcible maintenance of the polytheistic idolatry with all the moral abominations which it had introduced. But the corruption does not belong to the relation itself; it issues, as in the preceding cases, from the abuse of his free-will by man.

Here then are four goods, marriage, religion, as summed up in sacrifice, civil government, and alliance between civil government and religion, which we find embedded in the whole human society from the beginning, going with it through all its fractions, untouched by its wars, dissensions, and varieties of belief, suffering indeed each one of them by man's corruption, but lasting on. The force of any one of them as testimony to the unity of God who alone could have established it in the race, and so through Him to the unity of the race in which it is found established, and so, further, to the whole account of Moses, would be very great and not easily resisted by a candid mind seeking nothing but the truth. But how great is the cumulative evidence of the four together to the exactness of the account of the race's origin, establishment, and education, which we receive through Moses.

How strangely also are these goods of the race contrasted each one of them and all together with a great evil, universal like them, but man's own invention, the result of his wars and of the destruction of the feeling of brotherhood, in the various portions into which the race divided. The hideous plague-spot of slavery, which yet is one institution running through the race, attests also its unity, attests by its contrast with the four goods, by its practical denial of their beneficent action so far as the slave is concerned, the degradation of the race from that condition of a family having one end in the worship of one God, one brotherhood, a common care and charge of its members, a common interest in which it started.

The sum then of the whole period which begins from the dispersion of mankind at Babel and runs on to the coming of Christ is the progressive moral degradation of a race founded in the unity of a family. That unity itself rested upon the fidelity of the race to the belief and worship of the God who created it. The race voluntarily parted from this belief and worship; its own division followed; mutual enmity supplanted brotherhood, and the end is to create two classes of men, dividing society in each nation into the bond and the free. The nations themselves have lost all remembrance that they were once actually brothers by one hearth. Yet they still contain in themselves indisputable proof of that original unity. There is not only the common nature which language, the token of reason, raises to a dignity utterly incommensurable with the condition of any other animal; but great divine institutions planted at the beginning endure amid the corruption which has dimmed their original beauty, and testify to the providence which has preserved them amid the surging flood of heathenism for future restoration of the race.

3.—*Further Testimony of Law, Government, and Priesthood in the Dispersion.*

The account of the human race in its origin and its

dispersion thus presented allows for the existence of tribes in every part of the world, who, through their isolation, the effect of nomad life, war, and severities of climate, but most of all by that tendency to degrade itself—to fall from known truth to error—which is the characteristic of the race, and through the impairing of social life which thus ensues, have left records of their uncultivated or even savage condition, which an eager search is continually discovering. These records have been taken as aids to a theory which, rejecting the scriptural and traditional account of man's origin, would wish him to start from men of different races, or from universal savagery, or even from the ape as an ancestor. But, while on the one hand the existence of such tribes is no difficulty in the scriptural record of the dispersion, where they may be fully accounted for by the causes above-mentioned, the universal existence of the four great goods in the most ancient nations, where they appear also purest at the most remote time, is quite incompatible with either of the three invented origins of the human race. Neither different races of men, originally distinct and separated, nor universal savagery, and far less fathership of the ape, will develop into simultaneous existence four uniform institutions found through the widest range of divided nations, such as marriage, a religion based on sacrifice, civil government, and the alliance between government and religion. An original language accounts for the proofs of unity embedded in the primary structure of the Aryan tongues, and science professes its full belief in such unity. It is but a parallel to this to say that a creative hand impressing itself on the plastic origin of the race accounts for the existence of these goods in the most-widely severed branches of it. But that scattered savages should emerge from savagery into cultivation of the same ideal, or different races in their dispersion pitch upon the same very marked peculiarities of social life, or the ape teach his offspring the highest requirements of human society, such imaginations are contrary to the collective testimony of reason, experience, and history. Perhaps one must go altogether beyond the bounds of true science to account for their arising, and attribute them to that passionate dislike of a creating God, which is the recoil from the condition of a creature subject to responsibility for his actions.

On the contrary, pure historical inquiry, going back in the dry light of science to the archaic society of nations as they first appear to us at the beginning of written records, shows this remarkable chain of facts. A condition of things is found existing, of which the only explanation is that family was the nidus out of which sprung forth the House, then the Tribe, then the Commonwealth with its patriarchal government. When property is traced to its origin it seems to be first found in the family as joint-ownership; and further, its succession is blended inexplicably with the existence and state of the family. Again, the close union of government with religion finds its root in the family. No testimony can be more unsuspicious than that of the learned author of "Ancient Law," who observes (p. 4), that "the earliest notions connected with the conception of a law or rule of life are those contained in the Homeric words θεμις and Themistes." "The divine agent, suggesting judicial awards to kings or to gods, the greatest of kings, was Themis." She is the assessor of Zeus, the human king on earth, not a law-maker, but a judge. "The Themistes are the judgments, in fact, of a patriarchal sovereign, "whose judgment, when he decided a dispute by a sentence, was assumed to be the result of direct inspiration. And Themis and Themistes were (p. 6) " linked with that persuasion which clung so long and so tenaciously to the human mind of a divine influence underlying and supporting every relation of life, every social institution. In early law, and amid the rudiments of political thought, symptoms of this belief met us on all sides. A supernatural presidency is supposed to consecrate and keep together all the cardinal institutions of those times, the State, the Race, and the Family. Men, grouped together in the different relations which these institutions imply, are bound to celebrate periodically common rites and to offer common sacrifices; and every now and then the same duty is even more significantly recognised in the purifications and expiations which they perform, and which appear intended to deprecate punishment for involuntary or neglectful disrespect. Everybody acquainted with ordinary classical literature will remember the *Sacra Gentilicia* which exercised so important an influence on the early Roman law of adoption and of wills. And to this hour the Hindoo Customary Law, in which some of the most curious features of primitive society are stereotyped, makes almost all the rights of persons and all the rules of succession hinge on the due solemnisation of fixed ceremonies at the dead man's funeral, that is, at every point where a breach occurs in the continuity of the family."

Thus every king, as history begins, appears in a position which recalls the memory of Adam or of Noah, as the divinely appointed judge, whose office springs out of his fatherhood. The original consecration, which rested on the government of the race when it begun, is seen not yet to have parted from its scattered members in their tribal or national insulation.[1]

It is observed of Homeric Greece that "the people in its orderly arrangement of family or clans, or tribal relationships coming down from the patriarchal form of life, derives its unity from its king, whose power as little springs from the people as that of the father from his children. Thus he possesses this power not in virtue of compact or choice, but simply from Zeus.

Οὐ μέν πως πάντες βασιλεύσομεν ἐνθάδ' Ἀχαιοί.
οὐκ ἀγαθὸν πολυκοιρανίη· εἷς κοίρανος ἔστω,
εἷς βασιλεύς, ᾧ δῶκε Κρόνου παῖς ἀγκυλομήτεω
σκῆπτρον τ' ἠδὲ θέμιστας, ἵνα σφίσιν ἐμβασιλεύῃ.
—Iliad, 2. 203.

This conception shows itself not merely on occasion in the poet, as perhaps in the well-known epithets, Jove-born, Jove-nurtured, friend of Jove, or in the genealogies which connect with the gods the princely races by

[1] Nägelsbach, Homerische Theologie, 275.

ties of blood, but he has a distinct theory on the subject variously expressed.

ἐπεὶ οὔποθ' ὁμοίης ἔμμορε πμῆς
σκηπτοῦχος βασιλεὺς, ᾧ τε Ζεὺς κῦδος ἔδωκε.

Agamemnon's sceptre, the symbol of his rule over the Peloponnesus, is referred to the immediate gift of Jupiter.

The effect of this evidence, says the author just before cited, derived from comparative jurisprudence, is to establish that view of the primeval condition of the human race which is known as the "Patriarchal Theory." This is, " that the eldest male parent—the eldest ascendant—is absolutely supreme in his household. His dominion extends to life and death, and is as unqualified over his children and their houses as over his slaves; indeed, the relations of sonship and serfdom appear to differ in little beyond the higher capacity which the child in blood possesses of becoming one day the head of a family himself. The flocks and herds of the children are the flocks and herds of the father; and the possessions of the parent, which he holds in a representative rather than a proprietary character, are equally divided at his death among his descendants in the first degree, the eldest son sometimes receiving a double share under the name of birthright, but more generally endowed with no hereditary advantage beyond an honorary precedence." "The sum of the hints given us by legal antiquities" is that " men are first seen distributed in perfectly insulated groups, held together by obedience to the parent. Law is the parent's word. When we go forward to the state of society in which those early legal conceptions show themselves as formed, we find that they still partake of the mystery and spontaneity which must have seemed to characterise a despotic father's commands, but that at the same time, as they proceed from a sovereign, they presuppose a union of family groups in some wider organisation. The next question is, what is the nature of this union and the degree of intimacy which it involves? It is just here that archaic law renders us one of the greatest of its services, and fills up a gap which otherwise could only have been bridged by conjecture. It is full in all its provinces of the clearest indications that society, in primitive times, was not what it is assumed to be at present, a collection of individuals. In fact, and in the view of the men who composed it, it was an aggregation of families. The contrast may be most forcibly expressed by saying that the *unit* of an ancient society was the Family, of a modern society, the Individual."

"In most of the Greek states, and in Rome, there long remained the vestiges of an ascending series of groups, out of which the State was at first constituted. The Family, House, and Tribe of the Romans may be taken as the type of them; and they are so described to us that we can scarcely help conceiving them as a system of concentric circles which have gradually expanded from the same point. The elementary group is the family, connected by common subjection to the highest male ascendant. The aggregation of Families forms the

Gens or House. The aggregation of Houses makes the Tribe. The aggregation of Tribes constitutes the Commonwealth. Are we at liberty to follow these indications, and to lay down that the commonwealth is a collection of persons united by common descent from the progenitor of an original family? Of this we may at least be certain, that all ancient societies regarded themselves as having proceeded from one original stock, and even laboured under an incapacity for comprehending any reason except this for their holding together in political union. The history of political ideas begins, in fact, with the assumption that kinship in blood is the sole possible ground of community in political functions; nor is there any of those subversions of feelings, which we term emphatically revolutions, so startling and so complete as the change which is accomplished when some other principle—such as that, for instance, of local contiguity—establishes itself for the first time as the basis of common political action. It may be affirmed, then, of early commonwealths that their citizens considered all the groups in which they claimed membership to be founded on common lineage."

"The conclusion, then, which is suggested by the evidence is, not that all early societies were formed by descent from the same ancestor, but that all of them, which had any permanence or solidity, either were so descended, or assumed that they were. An indefinite number of causes may have shattered the primitive groups; but wherever their ingredients recombined, it was on the model or principle of an association of kindred. Whatever was the fact, all thought, language, and law adjusted themselves to the assumption" (p. 131).

"On a few systems of law the family organisation of the earliest society has left a plain and broad mark in the life-long authority of the Father, or other ancestor, over the person and property of his descendants, an authority which we may conveniently call by its later Roman name of Patria Potestas. No feature of the rudimentary associations of mankind is deposed to by a greater amount of evidence than this, and yet none seems to have disappeared so generally and so rapidly from the usages of advancing communities" (p. 135).

"It may be shown, I think, that the Family, as held together by the Patria Potestas, is the nidus out of which the entire Law of Persons has germinated" (p. 152).

"When we speak of the slave as anciently included in the Family, we intend to assert nothing as to the motives of those who brought him into it or kept him there; we merely imply that the tie which bound him to his master was regarded as one of the same general character with that which united every other member of the group to its chieftain. This consequence is, in fact, carried in the general assertion already made, that the primitive ideas of mankind were unequal to comprehending any basis of the connection *inter se* of individuals apart from the relations of Family" (p. 164).

"The point which before all others has to be apprehended in the constitution of primitive societies, is that the individual creates for himself few or no rights and few or no duties. The rules which he obeys are derived first from the station into which he is born, and next from the imperative commands addressed to him by the chief of the household of which he forms part" (p. 311).

Then as to the union of government with religion: —" A stage occurs in the history of all the families of mankind, the stage at which a rule of law is not yet discriminated from a rule of religion. The members of such a society consider that the transgression of a religious ordinance should be punished by civil penalties, and that the violation of a civil duty exposes the delinquent to divine correction" (p. 23). At the time of the Code of the Twelve Tables, "Roman society had barely emerged from that intellectual condition in which civil obligation and religious duty are inevitably confounded" (p. 18).

For, in fact, originally, "Law is the parent's word" (p. 125), and "the civil Laws of States first make their appearance as the Themistes of a patriarchal sovereign" (p. 166); that is, "as separate, isolated judgments, which, consistently with the belief in their emanation from above, cannot be supposed to be connected by any thread of principle" (p. 5). Moreover, as to the origin of Property:—" It is more than likely that joint-ownership, and not separate ownership, is the really archaic institution, and that the forms of property which will afford us instruction will be those which are associated with the rights of families and the groups of kindred" (p. 259), as shown in the Indian village-community, the Russian and Slavonic village. And "we have the strongest reasons for thinking that property once belonged not to individuals, nor even to isolated families, but to larger societies composed on the patriarchal model" (p. 268). Thus the author conjectures "that private property, in the shape in which we know it, was chiefly formed by the gradual disentanglement of the separate rights of individuals from the blended rights of a community" (p. 269).

He remarks "a peculiarity invariably distinguishing the infancy of society. Men are regarded and treated not as individuals, but always as members of a particular group. Everybody is first a citizen, and then, as a citizen, he is a member of his order—of an aristocracy or a democracy, of an order of patricians or plebeians; or in those societies which an unhappy fate has afflicted with a special perversion in their course of development, of a caste; next he is member of a gens, house, or clan; and lastly he is member of his *family*. This last was the narrowest and most personal relation in which he stood; nor, paradoxical as it may seem, was he ever regarded as *himself*, as a distinct individual. His individuality was swallowed up in his family. I repeat the definition of a primitive society given before. It has for its units not individuals, but groups of men united by the reality or the fiction of blood-relationship" (p. 183). "The history of jurisprudence must be followed in its whole course, if we are to understand how gradually and tardily society dissolved itself into the component atoms of which it is now constituted; by what insensible gradations the relation of man to man substituted itself for the relation of the individual to his family, and of families to each other" (p. 185).

Such is the strong—may we not say irrefragable?—testimony which the condition of human society, as it emerges into the light of history, bears to the family as the cradle of man's life. It is in the original soil of the family that the four goods we have noted, marriage, religion, government, and the alliance between religion and government, spring up together. Further, also, they are seen to be not separate, one here and another there, but bound together in the strictest coherence. For if this human race be thrown up and down throughout the world, divided and insulated in its several parts by vast distances and by thousands of years, even the scattered limbs are shaped in the mould stamped upon it at its birth, and in them government, law, property in its origin and its succession, and religion bear witness to the family character. This archaic society, from the Pacific to the Atlantic Oceans, from Scythia in the north to India in the south, is never a crowd of individuals but an organic structure: Adam and Eve prolonged and living in their race. We see that in the beginning the fathership of God created a human plant which should reveal Himself in its development, bearing in its structure and fruit an undying witness to His nature; and serving, in spite of corruption and decline, for the future exhibition of His fathership in a yet higher degree, even to the communication of the divine nature.

Whatever may be the interval of time which runs out between the dispersion of the family at Babel, and the appearance of each separate member on the platform of history—and the longer this time, the greater the marvel we note—the family remains in each as a sort of universal θεσμὸς upon which the commonwealth, the government, property viewed in itself and in its descent, law, and religion itself rest. The "natural state" and the "social compact" when inquired into become unsubstantial fictions; "theories plausible and comprehensive," as the author of ancient law observes, "but absolutely unverified" (p. 3.) Man is seen to be the child of Adam; and all the relations of men to each other to have been originally determined by that origin, and persistently maintained in its mould.

Now let us return to the relation between the Spiritual and the Civil Power, which forms part of this original constitution of the race.

At the head of the human race we have seen, first in Adam and then in Noah, the junction of the two orders, sovereignty and priesthood. There never was a time when the race was without government; there never was a time when the race was without sacrifice. The delegated authority of God rested ever upon the former for the prosperity of man's life upon earth; the worship of the one God, man's Creator and End, was summed up in the latter. All human life consists of the tissue formed by the two; and as in his first abode man's condition was subject to his obedience to the divine command, so throughout his course his worship of God ruled his temporal condition. The lot of the antediluvian world bore witness to that truth. With Noah the experience began afresh. Then once again the covenant with Noah and his seed after him was made in sacrifice, in which the unity of God and the religion of man stand recorded, and man's earthly lot is made dependent on the purity of his worship. Thus the two orders are seen in their origin to be both of divine institution; just as the life of man upon earth was from the beginning subordinate to his ultimate end, so government, which was created for the former, was subordinate to worship, which was created for the latter.

Let us follow rapidly the relation between man's social state and his religion, arising out of such origin, that we may note how the degradation of worship entailed the degradation of society.

In Noah and his sons, so long as the earth continued of one tongue and speech, the priesthood belonged to the head of the family. That was its natural descent. We may suppose that the dispersion began with the same rule, but we are not able to say how long that rule continued in force. There was intended to be one priesthood offering one sacrifice over all the earth to the one God. How prodigious became the degradation when the divine unity was lost! A variety of gods was introduced; a similar variety of priesthoods followed: and the sacrifice, which was the rendering of supreme homage to the one Creator and Lord of life, in which was contained the everliving prophecy of man's future restoration, was prostituted to a number of deities, the offspring of man's sensual imagination, or of perverted tradition, or of worship of natural powers, or of demoniacal trickery.

As soon as the patriarchal State was changed by war into the State founded by conquest, the natural appurtenance of the priesthood to the head of the family must at least have been modified. It was probably often attached to the actual head of the State. But it does not need to trace step by step the debasement of worship and the multiplication of deities which took place in the Gentile world. It is enough to see how the whole mass of nations had by the time of Christ become divided from each other in their civil societies and their religious belief. But we may note that as with the loss of belief in one God the nations originally lost the belief in their own brotherhood, so their national gods became the stronghold of national prejudices and hatreds. Thus a debased religion was turned into a source of cruelty to man, who had no bitterer enemy to his life and welfare than a foreign god; and instead of human life being sacred to man, it was sometimes even an act of worship to immolate him to an idol.

It is not too much to say that the profound enmity of the Gentile nations to each other was grounded in the variety of their gods; and in this instance religion, which in its purity is the bond of human society, had become a main cause of alienation between the members of the race.

The alliance of the State in each nation with its religion was, as we have seen, an original good of the race; and it continued through all the debasement of worship. Had that worship maintained its original purity, the alliance would have been an unmixed good. But as the belief became corrupt, it ended in the public force being ever at the command of error. The final issue of this alliance seems to have been when the State had laid hold of religion to deify, as it were, itself. The Roman emperors were the most complete, but by no means the sole, bearers of this corruption. They were considered to embody in their single persons the united majesty of the gods. Whoever refused obedience to their worship was guilty of the double crime of sacrilege and treason.

If this be a correct summary of the relation between the Two Powers as it issued in the final condition of Gentilism, it is clear that the State had far less declined from the high purpose for which it was instituted, that is, the preservation of human society, than the priesthood from the corresponding purpose which belonged to it, that is, the worship of God and the sanctification of human life. The civil power was still in every respect a lawful power. And obedience was due to it for conscience' sake, as expressly declared by our Lord and His Apostles. But the priesthood had been so utterly debased by its worship of false gods, which tore from it the crown of unity, and by the abominations which its rites in too many instances carried with them, that it had ceased to be a lawful power. It had moreover fallen, at least in the Roman empire, and from the time of the Cæsars, under the dominion of the State.

Yet down to the very coming of our Lord the veneration which had belonged to the original character and institution of the priesthood is made manifest by the clear acknowledgment that the authority of the priest was not derived from the king. The Gentiles in the lowest depths of their moral degradation referred the excellency of the priesthood to its divine origin. The honour due to God, and the thought of the future world, were so imbedded in the original constitution of human society everywhere, that even in a pantheon of false gods, and in a service paid to numberless male and female deities, the priest's office itself was held to be divine.[1]

In the case of the Romans, it is true that when the free state was suppressed by the empire, the priesthood and the imperial power were improperly conjoined in the same person. But this conjunction was at once a novelty and an usurpation. Thus the office of Pontifex Maximus, first seized by Lepidus after the death of Julius Cæsar, and after Lepidus assumed by Augustus, and then kept in succession by the following Cæsars, whether through the adulation of the people or their own pride, seemed to pass as a proper title of their principate, and was numbered among the honours, even of the Christian emperors, down to Gratian, who refused and prohibited it. Nevertheless the functions of these two powers were reckoned as distinct; but in the time of the Kings and the free Commonwealth this distinction was much more marked.

[1] See Bianchi, vol. iii. ch. ii.

Dionysius of Halicarnassus thus describes the Roman Pontifical College :—" They have authority over the most weighty affairs; they are judges of all sacred causes, whether among private persons, or magistrates, or ministers of the gods; they legislate for all sacred things which are not written or prescribed by custom, enacting laws and customs as seems to them good; they examine into all magistracies to which sacrifice and worship of the gods belong, and scrutinise all priests; they keep watch over the ministers which these use in their sacred office, so that the sacred laws be not transgressed; they instruct and interpret for lay persons who do not understand what concerns the worship of gods or genii. If they observe any disobedient to their commands, they punish them according to the due of each. They are themselves exempt from all trial and punishment. They render account neither to senate nor to people. It would be no error to call them priests, or sacred legislators, or custodians, or, as we should prefer, rulers of sacred things. On the death of any one another is elected to his place, not by the people, but by themselves, whoever of the citizens they judge the most meet."[1] From this account of the historian, says Bianchi, we may deduce the following conclusions :—Firstly, how great was the power of the Roman Sacerdotes in judging matters of religion, in which the magistrates were subject to them. Secondly, their authority to punish those who transgressed their

---

[1] Ἱεροδιδάσκαλοι εἴτε ἱερόνομοι, εἴτε ἱεροφύλακες, εἴτε, ὡς ἡμεῖς ἀξιοῦμεν, ἱεροφάνται. Dionys. Halic., l. 2.

laws, independently of kings and magistrates. Thirdly, their immunity from the civil power, even of the Commonwealth itself, to which they were not bound to render an account of what they did. Fourthly, the distinction which existed between the power of the priests and that of the civil magistrates, which results not merely from the points recited, but also from the reflection that the Pontiffs were perpetual, while the magistrates under the free Commonwealth were temporary. The latter were created by the suffrages of the people; in the former vacancies were filled by the College of Pontiffs itself. This custom lasted from Numa's time to the year of Rome 601, when Cneius Domitius, tribune of the people, transferred the right of filling vacancies from the College to the people; this was abolished by Sylla in his dictatorship; but again restored by the Tribune Titus Labienus during Cicero's consulship. But finally the right of electing its members was given back to the College of Pontiffs by Augustus.

The Pontifex Maximus, though created by the suffrage of the people, was always taken from the College of Pontiffs, and his office was perpetual. Augustus would not take it from Lepidus during his life, though he took it after his death. Thus the power of the Supreme Pontiff was by no means confused with that of the magistrate or the prince; and the assumption of this priesthood by the Cæsars makes it evident that they recognised it not to be part of the prince's power to intrude into matters of religion; and that they needed a sacerdotal power in order to superintend sacred things. It was for the sake of this superintendence, Dio observes, that the emperor always assumed the office of Pontifex Maximus, in virtue of which he became master of all religious and sacred things.

The example of Cicero pleading before the College of Pontifices for the restoration of his house, which had been dedicated by Clodius to Concord, a plea involving their power to revoke a tribunicial law passed by Clodius, is a remarkable testimony to the pontifical authority: "If ever," he said, "a great cause rested on the judgment and power of the Priests of the Roman people, it is this; in which all the dignity of the commonwealth, the safety, the life, the liberty, the public and private worship, the household gods, the goods, the fortunes, and the homes of all seem intrusted to your wisdom and integrity."[1]

The fair conclusions from these facts, says Bianchi again, are that the Romans knew religion to be directed to a higher end than temporal felicity, though they did esteem it also necessary for the preservation of the State; that the power of the priesthood was distinct from the civil power of the magistrate; that it had the right to judge in all cases of religion without interference from the magistrate; that immunity and exemption from the civil power belonged to it.

It is needless to go through the various nations of antiquity in order to show the veneration which everywhere belonged to the office of the priest. That is

[1] Bianchi, Sect. VI.

shown likewise in the frequent connection of the royal power with the priesthood; but though thus connected, they were not confused; kings were priests, not in virtue of their kingship, but by a distinct appointment. Plato asserts that in some nations the priesthood was reputed so excellent that it was not considered to be properly placed save in the person of the king; and that among the Egyptians it was not lawful for any king to command the people without being first consecrated to the priesthood. By this fact is seen how the sacerdotal dignity was esteemed by antiquity, even in the darkness of idolatry; and, at the same time, how the power of the priest was considered to be distinct from the power of the sovereign. Plato gives his own judgment when he says that the creation of priests should be left to the care of God; and that they should be elected by lot, in order that the person destined to so high an office may be divinely chosen.[1]

All that it is requisite here to point out seems to be that, however great was the degradation of worship produced by the character of the gods worshipped, as well as by the divisions of the godhead which the multiplying of divine beings brought with itself, yet two things survived in the minds of men: one the intrinsic excellence of worship in itself, as the homage paid by man to a power above himself; and the other, the sense that this worship was a thing of divine institution, coming down from heaven upon earth, quite distinct in character from civil rule, and if exercised by

[1] Bianchi, p. 23.

kings, exercised not because they were kings, but in virtue of a separate consecration. Thus, if the patriarchal origin of property, law, and government is borne witness to by the most ancient institutions, customs, and feelings of men, which witness likewise extends to the unity of the race, so likewise the original independence of the priestly order as to all its sacred functions and the sense of its divine origin, which runs through so many nations, bear joint witness to the unity of the race and to the truth of the Mosaic record. They convey a manifest contradiction to the theory that man sprung originally from a number of different races, and likewise to the theory that he grew up originally in a state of savagery.

The force of the testimony consists in this: first, a priesthood appears everywhere; secondly, it is connected with the rite of sacrifice; thirdly, it usually comprises an order of men devoted to the purpose of divine worship, or at least having special functions which by no means belong to the civil ruler as such, so that if he performs them, it is as priest and not as king; fourthly, this order has a special authority from the Divine Being or Beings whom it represents, not subject to the civil rule; fifthly, injury to the priest's person or contravention to his order in divine things is esteemed as an injury done to the God whom he represents.

The peculiarity of a priesthood must therefore be added to the peculiarity of the rite of sacrifice upon which his office rests, and both together form an order of ideas so marked and distinctive as to establish the unity of the race in the several portions of which they appear; and at the same time it establishes, as the common inheritance of that race, an overwhelming sense of human life being founded, preserved, and exalted by a communion between heaven and earth: it is, in short, a sense of man lying in the hand of God.

We have hitherto followed the dispersion of Babel in its Gentile development down to that ultimate issue in which a long and unbroken civilisation is combined with an extreme moral corruption; now let us revert to the divine plan which was followed to repair this evil.

At a certain point of time, when forgetfulness of the divine unity was becoming general, God chose one man out of whom to form a nation, whose function should be the preservation of a belief in this unity. Abraham, the friend of God and the forefather of Christ, was called out of his own country that he might preserve the religion of Noah, and that "in him all the kindreds of the earth might be blessed" (Gen. xii. 3). In the second generation his family was carried down into Egypt, and became, in the security of that kingdom, a people, but it likewise fell into bondage. From this it was redeemed in a series of wonderful events under the guidance of Moses, was led by him into the desert, and there formed into a nation by the discipline of a religious, which was also a civil code. In the law given on Mount Sinai we see once more the constitution of the society established in Noah. The whole moral order of the world contained in the ten commandments is made to rest upon the sovereignty of God: "I am the Lord;

thou shalt have no strange gods." From this precept, which fills the first table, proceed the precepts which, in the second, maintain the order of society: "Honour thy father and thy mother; thou shalt not kill; thou shalt not steal," and the rest. Such, says Bossuet, is the general order of all legislation. The ten words of God form the core of a complete religious and civil code, in which the two Powers exist in an ideal no less than a practical union. The individual and the national worship is the same, and the society springs out of it, the root being, "I am the Lord;" but the persuasiveness of redemption is added to the power of creation: "I am the Lord thy God, who brought thee out of the land of Egypt, out of the house of bondage." Abraham, the father of the people, had exercised the patriarchal priesthood and the patriarchal sacrifice in his family; but just as God had not chosen Abraham because he was the first-born, so Moses, taking the patriarchal priesthood, with a special sanction, set it not in the first-born of the tribes, but in another tribe, and in a family of this tribe. He took, further, the rite of sacrifice, which had existed from the beginning, only developing its meaning in a series of ordinances, which, as St. Paul tells us, all pointed to Christ: "Almost all things according to the law are cleansed with blood, and without shedding of blood is no remission" (Heb. ix. 22). But while there is here a complete union in faith, in practice, and in worship, for every true Israelite and for the whole people, while there is one source of authority to the three, the bearers of the dignities which represent this triple life of man are separated. Moses instituted, in the person of Aaron, a high priesthood which from that time stands through the whole history of his people at the head of their worship, superior in all that concerns it to the civil authority, which is bound to consult it and obey it, not only in the things of God, but in the chief civil acts which regard the nation. The outcome of this work is the creation of a people whose function is to bear on the worship of the one true God and faith in the Redeemer to come, a royal, prophetic, and priestly nation, the special domain of the promised Messias.

I have no need here to follow this people through the trials, revolts, chastisements, and humiliations of 1500 years. It is sufficient to observe the result at the coming of Christ. The nation at length, as the fruit it would seem of captivity and suffering, has accepted with one mind and heart the doctrine and worship of one God; the Jewish priesthood, uncorrupted in its essence by any of the abominations of polytheism, offers the daily morning and evening sacrifice, which typified the Lamb of God, in the spirit of Adam, Noah, Abraham, and Moses. The power of the State had indeed just passed to a Roman lord, but it left the rites and practices and doctrines of the Jewish faith untouched in the hands of the High Priest and the Great Council, which sat in this respect in the chair of Moses, —a great and manifest distinction, perhaps, from the condition in this respect of the whole Gentile world. In Rome, at least, the worship "of the Immortal Gods," though blended with the whole growth of the

State, and seated triumphantly in the Capitol, was simply subservient to the Civil Power : in Judea, a small and despised province of Rome, the religion was the life of the people, which had been made a people that it might be God's domain, and, with all its divisions, was filled from the highest to the lowest with an universal expectation of the promised Christ, who was to be Prophet, Priest, and King.

In the relation between the two Powers, Gentilism required a total reconstruction, in order that the priesthood, existing in it from the beginning, might be completely purified, derived afresh from God, and receive from Him an independence which it had lost from the moment that it lost its fidelity to the One Creator,—and such a gift would be a token of divine power. Judaism, on the contrary, made, after the programme of God, an image in the nation of what the Christian people was to be in the world, required only to acknowledge in the Christ the purpose for which it was appointed, that the law might go forth from Sion and the word of the Lord from Jerusalem.

CHAPTER II.

RELATION BETWEEN THE CIVIL AND THE SPIRITUAL POWERS AFTER CHRIST.

1.—*The Spiritual Power in its Source and Nature.*

TAKING as our basis the historical outline of the relation between the Civil and Spiritual Powers which has preceded, let us attempt to have present to our minds the state of this relation at the death of Christ.

The great world-empire had then been ruled in most peaceful security for half a generation by Tiberius. Under him lay a vast variety of nations, professing as strange a variety of gods and of worship paid to them, but all, with one exception, accepting a religious supremacy in him as Pontifex Maximus of the Roman religion. The Princeps of the civil power, the Imperator of the civil force, was also Chief Priest of religion, and by that union held in his hands those two Powers, an attack upon either of which constituted, as Tertullian testifies, the double guilt of majesty violated and sacrilege incurred. Within these limits, and with this condition, it was free to the several nations to practise their ancestral rites as well as to believe in their ancestral gods, at least within their ancient territorial bounds.

There can be no doubt that these nations generally clung to their several rites and beliefs, not only from the force of nurture and habit, but also as remnants of their former independence as nations. As little can we doubt that the great Roman power was employed to maintain and protect them as part of the constituted order of things and in prevention of *sedition*. This, so far as the Roman dominion extended, was the outcome of that long succession of wars, and changes of rule ensuing on wars, which forms the history of mankind so soon as it leaves the nest of pristine unity at the epoch of the dispersion. It is clear that through the whole of this Gentile world, while amity had not been broken between the Civil and the Spiritual Powers, the priesthood, which represented the latter, had everywhere become the subject of the former. It is no less clear that this subjection was repaid with support. This condition of things was most clearly expressed as well as most powerfully established in the position of the Roman Emperor, who, as he received the tribunitial power, which in union with the consular was distinctive of the imperial dignity, from the Senate, so received also the supreme authority in matters of religion which belonged to the Pontifex Maximus. This authority had indeed been in its origin and its descent from age to age in the Roman city distinct from secular power, but henceforth became practically united with the civil principate. That undivided supremacy betokened the ultimate constitution of the heathen State, antecedent to the coming of Christ, in what concerns the relation between the two Powers. According to this, the Civil Power prevailed over the Spiritual, and casting off the subjection to religion in which itself had been nurtured, directed all its actions to a temporal end.

Far otherwise was it with that people which Moses, under the divine command, had created according to the pattern which he saw in the Mount. Chosen by God to conduct the race of Abraham out of captivity into the promised land, he alone in the history of the Israelitic race united in himself the three powers bestowed by unction of Priest, of Prophet, and of King. These powers he left to the people he was forming, but did not deposit them all in the same hands. His creation of the priesthood in the tribe of Levi, and of the high priesthood in the person of his brother Aaron and his lineal descendants, stands without a parallel in all the history of the world before the coming of Christ as an act of transcendant authority. For instead of the original priesthood of the first-born, which he found existing as it had been transmitted from the earliest time, he selected a particular tribe, which was not that of the first-born, to bear from that time forth the priesthood among the children of Israel; and further, he selected a particular person in that tribe, his brother Aaron, to erect in him the high priesthood, the most characteristic institution of the Jewish people. In like manner he took the ancient institution of sacrifice, dating, as we have seen, from Paradise itself, and formed it into an elaborate system to be carried out day by day through the whole succeeding history of his people, by priests springing from the person of the first High Priest. At the door of the Tabernacle, in the presence of all the assembled tribes, Moses invested Aaron with the priestly garments, especially the ephod, bearing attached to it the Rational, which contained the twelve stones indicating the twelve tribes of the holy nation, by which the High Priest, consulting God, issued the oracle of doctrine and truth. Moses further set the mitre on his head, bearing on its golden plate the inscription, "Holiness to the Lord;" and pouring on his head the oil of unction, he anointed and consecrated him. Thus the whole Jewish priesthood descended from above, being gathered up in one person, from whom all succeeding priests were drawn, and the sons of the first High Priest were to continue the line for ever according to primogeniture.

The High Priest's office had in it four points peculiar to him beyond the office of the ordinary priest. First, once in the year, on the great day of the atonement, he alone entered into the most holy place, "not without blood, which he offered for his own sins and the sins of the people" (Heb. ix. 7), inasmuch as he sent into the wilderness one he-goat, charged with the sins of all the people, and sacrificed the other, whose blood he carried into the sanctuary, sprinkling it seven times over against the oracle, to expiate the sanctuary from the uncleanness of the children of Israel (Lev. xvi. 15, 16). He thus once every year represented in his person the whole sacred nation in that most remarkable act of confessing its guilt before God, and offering an expiation of it, which pointed even more to a future Redeemer. Secondly, he consecrated the whole body of the priests and Levites for their several work. The oil of unction poured upon his head was the palpable sign of priestly power transmitted from him to the priest, in which, again, he was an image of the future High Priest. Thirdly, whenever the civil rulers of the nation required advice in matters concerning the good of the whole people, it was the office of the High Priest to inquire for them by means of the breastplate of light and truth, which he carried upon the ephod. The relation of the Civil to the Spiritual Power was symbolised in the first bearer of the former after Moses, to whom Moses was commanded by God to communicate "part of his glory." God said to Moses, "Take Joshua the son of Nun, a man in whom is the spirit, and put thy hand upon him, and he shall stand before Eleazar the priest (who had then succeeded his father Aaron in the high priesthood), and all the multitude, and thou shalt give him precepts in the sight of all, and part of thy glory, that all the congregation of the children of Israel may hear him. If anything be to be done, Eleazar the priest shall consult the Lord for him, he, and all the children of Israel with him, and the rest of the multitude, shall go out and go in at his word" (Num. xxvii. 18). Thus David afterwards consulted God by Abiathar, the High Priest in his day. Fourthly, on all questions concerning the decalogue, or commands in the moral law, or the ceremonial law, which embraced the whole field of the divine worship, or the judicial law, which concerned reciprocal rights and duties between man and man, the High Priest possessed a supreme and decisive jurisdiction, from which there was no appeal.

It is necessary to distinguish between the third of these privileges, the judgment by the breastplate of light and truth, which was an extraordinary gift of God, bestowed at particular times, and analogous in this to inspiration, and the fourth, the supreme jurisdiction and judgment of the High Priest, which belonged to him as an ordinary part of his office, and may be likened to a perpetual divine assistance inherent in it.[1]

2. Such was the high priesthood in its institution, and its operation through the whole of Jewish history down to the final destruction of the Temple corresponds to its institution.

The children of Israel were made a nation for a specific purpose, that is, in order that the race of Abraham, by Isaac his chosen son, should maintain upon earth, in the midst of an ever-growing defection, the worship of the one True God, and should likewise embody and represent no less that which was bound up in this worship, the promise of redemption given at the beginning of the world. The reason of its existence, therefore, was to be the bearer of the Messianic idea. To this all its ordinances and sacrifices pointed, and in the execution of all this purpose the High Priest was the chief organ. The Pontificate was the stem of the nation, of which the civil unity was made from the beginning dependent on the spiritual. On Aaron, by God's com-

[1] See Die Harmonie des alten und des neuen Testamentes, von Dr. Konrad Martin, p. 190.

mand, Moses devolved one "part of his glory;" and when Eleazar had succeeded his father in the office of High Priest, and Moses was about to die, he devolved, by the same divine command, another part of his glory upon Joshua, appointing him to lead the children of Israel into their promised inheritance. To invest him with this solemn charge, the civil leadership of the nation, he brought him before Eleazar the priest, that, according to his instruction, Joshua and the whole congregation "should go out and go in." This relative position of Eleazar and Joshua is continued in the respective religious and civil rulers during several hundred years down to the kingship of Saul. When the Israelites chose themselves a king after the pattern of the nations round them, the word of God to Samuel respecting their act is, "They have not rejected thee, but me, that I should not reign over them" (1 Kings viii. 7). Nevertheless God sanctions the erection of a kingdom, leaving unaltered the position of the High Priest. During the time of the kings the high priesthood continues the centre of Jewish worship; and when the civil unity is broken by the revolt of the ten tribes, they revolt likewise against the worship which had its seat in Jerusalem and was gathered up in the High Priest. The long-persistent iniquity of the people is punished by the captivity, and when a portion of the nation comes back to take root afresh in its own land, it is in the high priesthood more than ever that its unity is restored and maintained. Thus, through the three periods of Israelitic history, under the judges, under the kings, and after the return from captivity, the High Priest remains the permanent centre of Jewish life, the organ of spiritual, and therein of civil unity. Our Lord recognises this spiritual ruler as at the head of the Great Council, "sitting in the chair of Moses." At His birth Herod inquires of this authority where Christ should be born, and receives the undoubting answer, "In Bethlehem of Juda." Of Him Caiaphas, being then High Priest, uttered the famous prophecy denoting the great act of His mediatorial sacrifice ; and the same Caiaphas, sitting as supreme judge of the nation, adjures Him by the living God to declare if He be the Christ; and our Lord answers the adjuration by the explicit declaration of His divine Sonship, and His authority to be Judge of the living and the dead.

The judges pass, the kings pass, the nation goes into captivity ; it comes back chastened, and faithful at length to its belief in the divine unity and the promises attached to it ; and through all this, up to the time of accomplishment, the High Priest sits in the chair of Moses, and offers expiation on the day of atonement, and the priests emanate from his person, and prophecy speaks from his mouth. He is the ordinary judge of the whole people, the guardian and interpreter of the divine law, whose decision is final and supreme.

3. That people lost its civil independence, which was merged in the great Roman empire, but its spiritual independence, centred in its High Priest, was preserved to it. At no period of its history was this independence more remarkably maintained. Philo, himself a Jew

settled in Egypt, says, "Innumerable pilgrims from innumerable cities flock together by sea and land, from East and West, from North and South, on every festival to this Temple (of Jerusalem) as to a common harbour and refuge, seeking peace there in the midst of a life of business or trouble."[1] "The Holy City," he says in another place, "is my country, a metropolis not of the single country of Judea, but of many others, on account of the colonies from time to time thence sent forth." But not only was this city such a metropolis to all Jews in every part of the world, and the High Priest the centre of the worship which drew them from all parts of the world, but his spiritual authority extended over them in the several cities which they inhabited as well as when they came up to Jerusalem. This was the power borne witness to by St. Paul, when "yet breathing out threatenings and slaughter against the disciples of the Lord, he went to the High Priest and asked of him letters to Damascus to the synagogues, that if he found any men and women of this way, he might bring them bound to Jerusalem." This was the power which counterworked and persecuted St. Paul himself wherever he went, through which "five times he received of the Jews forty stripes save one, and was thrice beaten with rods" (2 Cor. xi. 24). This was the power which, wherever the Apostles went, preaching the Gospel under the cover of a religion which enjoyed legal sanction, and so disobeyed no

[1] Philo de Monarchia, lib. 2. Legation to Caius, quoted by Vincenzi, p. 21.

Roman law, encountered them, and, after endless particular persecutions, succeeded at last with Nero in getting them put beyond the pale of the protection which their character of Jews might afford them, and placed under the ban of the empire as preachers of a new and unsanctioned religion. They were but summing up a long course of previous persecution in this act, which was the master-stroke of Jewish antagonism, by which they fulfilled to the uttermost the divine prediction: "Therefore, behold I send to you prophets, and wise men, and scribes; and some of them you will put to death and crucify, and some of them you will scourge in your synagogues, and persecute them from city to city" (Matt. xxiii. 40). And it was followed at once by the destruction of the city, the Temple, and the priesthood, as the prophecy ran, "Behold your house shall be left to you desolate." The position of the High Priest in this last period of Israelitic history, the forty years which elapsed from the day of Pentecost to the destruction of the city and Temple, represents him most vividly as the guardian, judge, and mouthpiece of a religion which, though national, had colonies in all parts of the world, and in which not only the central seat of the worship and the country of Judea, but the colonies also, in whatever part of the world they might be situated, acknowledged his spiritual jurisdiction. This privilege was given by Julius Cæsar, as to the Roman empire, and continued by Augustus. It is of much moment to understand the history of the first forty years of the Christian Church.

4. So completely had the high priesthood created by Moses, and the whole system of worship, sacrifices, rites, and ceremonies which it presided over and guarded, fulfilled the purpose for which it was created. It presented in all its parts a type and a prophecy of Christ and His kingdom—a type and a prophecy which through fifteen hundred years of action and suffering had wrought itself out in the heart of a people who, now deprived of their civil, but enjoying a spiritual, independence, lay scattered through the whole world, ready to receive the spiritual kingdom. Through all Gentiledom the sacerdotal authority had become, by its corruption of the high truths of religion, the serf or minion of the Civil Power, but to the Jews the worship of their God was in its own nature supreme, and did not admit of interference even from that power which they acknowledged to rule absolutely in temporal dominion. The same scribes and pharisees and people who cried out before the Roman governor, "We have no king but Cæsar," were ready a few years afterwards to sacrifice their lives rather than admit into Jerusalem a statue of the Emperor Caligula, which seemed to them an impugnment of their religious law. And the Jewish people during the years of our Lord's teaching and ministry were looking for their Messias, and when they should acknowledge Him, were ready to acknowledge Him not only as Priest and Prophet but as King also. So deeply had the words of Moses sunk in their hearts: "That God would raise up to them a prophet of their nation and of their brethren like unto him, whom they

were to hear" (Deut. xviii. 18); that is, a Prophet bearing, as Moses alone had done, the triple unction, and who was to be supreme in teaching, in priesthood, and in rule. The civil subjection of the people brought out more strikingly by its contrast their spiritual independence, and the banishment, which scattered a number of them into all lands, provided everywhere a seed-plot in which the Gospel might be planted—a little gathering not only of Jews, but of Gentile proselytes, "who feared God" in every place, and so could more readily receive the doctrine of God incarnate and crucified upon their belief of God the Creator. Had the Jews remained in their own land, they would not have had the perception of a spiritual jurisdiction founded upon a divine hierarchy alone, and stretching over the whole earth, disregarding all national divisions and restrictions, and binding Parthians and Medes, Elamites and Mesopotamians, Egyptians and Libyans, Cretes and Arabians, Greeks and Romans into one. The mould into which the Gospel was to be cast had been wrought out even through the obstinacy, the sins, and the punishments of the chosen people, and was now complete to receive and bear the tree for the healing of the nations. The high priesthood had come forth from Moses by express inspiration, and bearing its people through centuries of most various fortune, had imaged out exactly the Christian high priesthood and rule to which it was to yield.[1] A prophecy embodied in a

[1] Observe in St. Clement's Epistle how it is assumed as undoubted that bishop, priest, and deacon had succeeded to the three orders of the levitical worship.

fact which unites a people into an indissoluble organisation, and works through centuries moulding generation after generation, and gathering into one prodigious monument of priesthood, sacrifices, ceremonies, and temple, and the hopes and devotion of a race, this is the ground which our Lord selected for the basis of the spiritual kingdom which He would set up. He had provided Moses as a servant to construct the model of the house which hereafter He would build Himself; He had inspired Moses to create Aaron and draw out of him the levitical priesthood, because Himself would commission Peter, the perpetual fountain of the Christian priesthood, and would make Peter for all nations that which Aaron had been for one.

But, as in all the preceding history, God left to man the exercise of his free-will. It was not open to the Jews indeed to frustrate the divine purpose, but it was open to them to receive or not receive the Christ when He came. They were ready to receive a glorious but not a suffering Christ. And the High Priest, sitting at the head of the Great Council of the nation, in the chair of Moses and in the dignity of Aaron, instead of accepting, rejected and slew Him with the Roman death of crucifixion, by the hand of the Roman governor, the bearer to the nation of the Roman imperial power. The High Priest slew Him further on the affected charge that He was plotting against the emperor's power; in reality because He acknowledged Himself to be the Christ, the Son of God.

Let us take, then, what I am about to say as facts

which have been hitherto undisputed. There have been, and there are, unbelievers in plenty of the Christian truth and Church, but no one has, I believe, hitherto been found to deny that Christ was put to death by Pontius Pilate at the instigation of the Chief Priest and the Sanhedrim. Let us take this as a fact, and put ourselves in thought at the great Sabbath during which His Body rested in the tomb. It is the Body of one executed with the greatest ignominy, between two thieves, by a most cruel death, under the authority of the Roman governor, upon the charge that He claimed a kingship which interfered with that of the emperor, at the instigation of those who rejected His claim to be their Messias, the Son of God. His Body, even when dead, ceases not to be under the jurisdiction of the Roman governor, who commits its custody to His chief enemies, those whose instigation has brought about His death. Their seal is set upon His tomb, and their guards watch it. Taking these bare facts, as acknowledged by friend and foe, can any situation of more complete impotence be conceived by human imagination than this? He has come, and taught, and worked miracles, and been rejected by His own. He has been put to death in the name and by the power of the world's lord, who bears the crown of majesty and wields the authority of worship. The guards of His enemies sit beside His tomb.

Such was the fact on the great Sabbath, the high day of the Jewish Pasch.

What can be conceived more improbable at that

moment, and under these circumstances, than the fact which we have now to record as following in its evolution during so many ages? The sovereign in whose name and by whose power that Body had been put to death held undisputed in his hands the supremacy of Spiritual as well as Civil Power through the great world of Gentilism, represented by the Roman empire. From that Body was to spring, beginning with the morrow, the distinction and independence of the Spiritual over against the Civil Power, which was to dissolve this twofold supremacy throughout the whole range of that empire. And this was to be accomplished by a series of actions arising out of the sole proclamation of envoys taken from the people which had rejected Him—a proclamation derived from the commission which He should give in the Body raised again to life. The distinction, indeed, of the two Powers, so far from being new, has been coeval with the human race itself, as we have seen; but it has been broken down by human sin in all nations but one, and that one, created for its maintenance, made, through all its history, prophetical for its fulfilment when the time of that fulfilment came, has rejected its Bearer; and yet out of its bosom, on the morrow, is to go forth that word of power which in the end shall change the condition of human society, and create it after another order.

It will be well thoroughly to grasp the truth that all which followed depended upon a fact, the supernatural character of which cannot be exaggerated. We are considering the Spiritual Power which arose and diffused itself in the world from the Person of Christ. It took its origin from the Body in which He appeared to His Apostles after His resurrection. Without their belief in that resurrection, as evidenced to all their senses, there was no ground for their conduct. Without the reality of that resurrection there was no source for the Power. It would seem that, whatever else the Christian order of things may be, it must be supernatural and miraculous, since, to exist at all, it presupposes a fact which is a lordship over nature and a miracle in the highest degree. Without this primary miracle all Christian faith is vain, and in the power which worked it all subsequent miracles are included. That the fact took place, let the results which followed testify, at the beginning of which our exposition stands. The Jews expected a Messias, who, according to the prophecies long enshrined in their nation about Him, was to be Priest, Prophet, and King. They put to death one who claimed to come before them in this triple character. From one dead, so long as he continues dead, no life can spring. But life and multifold life sprung up here; therefore He who was dead had arisen, and all of which we have to speak is the result of His life. The fundamental truth on which we have to dwell is the going forth of a supernatural power from the Person of Christ.

We have seen Adam in Paradise created in the full maturity of intellect and will, and placed at the head of a double order of things, of civil and of spiritual authority. We have now to consider that greater One whom Adam prefigured, and who, coming forth from the tomb, assumed forthwith that double headship. When the great act of His pontificate had been accomplished in giving up His Body to death for the sins of the world, and its efficacy acknowledged by His resurrection, He declared to His Apostles "that all power had been given to Him in heaven and upon earth." This all-power in heaven and on earth, given to the God-man as the fruit of His incarnation and the reward of His sacrifice, divides itself into two—temporal and spiritual. The first is that by which He disposes of all persons and all events. This power He has not delegated to any one in chief, but keeps it in His own hands. Yet it is a part of this power of which it is said, "By me kings reign, and princes decree justice." The whole civil sovereignty is founded on an apportionment to it of the divine sovereignty for the maintenance of human society. A part of the second or Spiritual Power He delegated to St. Peter in chief, and to the Apostles, with St. Peter at their head. Out of this all-power He set up and sent forth in them a royal priesthood to proclaim and maintain the truth which He had come to declare to the world; that is to say, He took His own priesthood and put it upon them, investing it with a reproductive ordering and maintaining power in His spiritual kingdom. To it He attached the gift of truth, that is, of communicating, unfolding, guarding, the whole body of doctrine which He came upon earth to declare; and in it He placed the jurisdiction which is necessary to the priesthood in order to exert itself in offering the sacrifice and in dispensing the sacraments which He instituted, and in guarding the truth with which they are bound up.

That power, then, which He designated in the keys given to Peter, in the Rock which He set in his person, in the pastoral charge which He laid upon him over His sheep, and in which He sent forth His Apostles to make disciples all nations, to baptize them in the sacred Name, to teach them to observe all which He had commanded, and in the exercise of which He promised to remain with them to the end of the world, is one and indivisible in itself, and triple in its range and direction—a priesthood proclaiming the truth and ruling in the sphere which belongs to its priesthood and its teachings. As Adam is created one and complete, and his race springs from him, so this kingdom of Christ springs complete from Him in its regimen, which is not the result of history, but formed in His Person before its history begins, as He is at once Priest, Teacher, and King. Thus this Power comes from above, not from below; proceeds from emanation; is not gathered gradually by accretion; is an effect of positive institution, derived from the Head; not the effect of a need or the working out of a natural capacity in the body.

The root of that Power is the act for the accomplishment of which our Lord Himself took our flesh upon Him—the act of His high priesthood, by which, having taken our flesh, He took also the sins of the world upon Himself, and offered Himself for them on the cross. It is as Redeemer that He is Priest, the sacrifice of His body being the offering which He made. It is in the perpetual service and offering of that body that the priesthood which He created for others exists and provides the perpetual bread of life, which is the food of sanctification, for His people. In the priesthood, therefore, we have to deal with the whole range of subject which embraces grace on the part of God and worship on the part of man. It is most fitting that all spiritual power should grow upon this stock. All priesthoods in the world from the beginning had been connected, as we have seen, with the sense and acknowledgment of guilt and with the rite of sacrifice. In the Aaronic priesthood this has been specially noted. Thus it bore a perpetual prophetical witness to the act which Christ accomplished. All future priesthood dated from the accomplishment of that act, and took its force from it. Thus it was truly the central act of human history. Had not the Son of God assumed our nature, He could not have been a Priest. His priesthood, therefore, carried in it the two great divine acts—His incarnation and His satisfaction, which make up the economy of human salvation. The first direction, then, of the power which He delegated is that of the Priest.

The second is that of the Teacher. A principal part of His ministry while on earth certainly was to teach. He was the Prophet that was to come into the world, and all that He taught bore reference to the two acts just dwelt upon, that He came forth from God and was going to God. Not a sentence of His teaching but presupposes His Incarnation and His Passion. That whole body of truth, therefore, which He did not write down Himself, but committed to the living ministry of His Apostles, proceeds, as it were, out of His Pontificate, and rests upon it. It is the truth of the Word made flesh, and of God sacrificed for His creatures. The gift of teaching, as the illuminating power in His Church, corresponds to the virtue of faith in the taught, and implies the possession of truth in the teacher. As the priesthood has a perpetual sacrifice stored up within it, and a perpetual gift of grace accompanying it, so the teaching has a perpetual gift of truth. The fountain of truth, therefore, in this Power, can be no more discoloured and polluted than the fountain of grace in the priesthood can be turned into sin. By virtue of it Christ remains for ever the one Teacher and Master whom all His people have to follow. Theology is an outcome of this Power. The issuing of doctrinal decrees is grounded upon it, and the censure of writings and of all false opinions on whatever subject which may impair Christian doctrine.

The third direction of the one Power is that of ruling and ordering, not to be separated from the former two, since it consists, in fact, in the free, legitimate, and ordered use of them, and has, therefore, been termed Jurisdiction, inasmuch as it is government in the whole domain of grace and truth. In every government there is a power which administers, a power which legislates, a power which judges, and all these in the sovereign degree; that is, in a degree not liable to revision and reversal in the respective subject-matter. If we apply these three acts to the full domain of grace and truth, which is the domain of the Incarnate Son (John i. 14), set up in the world, we express that royalty which is the third attribute of the priesthood. It comprehends supreme pastorship in all its range; legislation in the kingdom of truth; and judgment, whether external or internal, in the spiritual tribunal.

This was the Power, one and indivisible in itself, triple in its direction, which Christ took from His own Person as part of the all-power given to Him, and delegated to the Ruler of His Church, that in the exercise of it He might fulfil all prophecy concerning Himself, and be at once Priest, Prophet, and King: and out of this He made and makes His people.

In the transmission of that Power to the persons to whom He gave it He observed two principles: that of unity, and that of hierarchical subordination. To maintain the first, He made the Primacy; to maintain the second, the College of Apostles. For the whole of this triple power, the keys of the kingdom of heaven in the priesthood, the guardianship of faith in the office of teacher, and the supreme pastorship of rule He promised to one and bestowed on one, Peter. Thus He made Peter the Primate, and by the centering this triple authority in his sole person set him as the Rock on which the Church is built. At the same time He associated with Peter the eleven, to exercise this same authority in conjunction with Him. Thus at the very founding of the Church we find the two forces which are to continue throughout, and from the union of which the whole hierarchy with its graduated subordination springs. From the Apostolic College descends the Episcopate, the everliving source of which is in Peter the head, by union with whom it is "one Episcopate, of which a part is held by each without division of the whole." Only on this condition is the Episcopate one, without which, in all places and in all time, it would be a principle of rivalry and division, using the triple power of priesthood, teaching, and rule against itself. With this condition we have exactly realised the image of the Rock on which the Church is founded, and against which the gates of hell shall not prevail, in the establishment of the Episcopate, as one indivisible power, having its fountain and fulness in one person, a part of whose solicitude is shared by a body of bishops spread through the whole world, speaking with one voice the faith of Peter, because they are united with the person of Peter.

All that we have hitherto said as to the emanation of power from the Person of Christ is comprehended by St. Peter when he calls our Lord, "the Shepherd and Bishop of our souls," and by St. Paul when he calls Him "a High Priest over the house of God," "the Apostle and High Priest of our confession," "called of God High Priest after the order of Melchisedek." And by Himself when He bade His disciples to have no other Master, that is, Teacher, "for one is your Master, Christ;" and when, treating on the eve of His passion this very subject, He said to His Apostles, "I dispose to you, as my Father disposed to me, a kingdom;" and after His resurrection, saying to them collectively, "As my Father sent me, even so send I you;" and "Behold

I am with you all days, even to the consummation of the world;" and when He said to Peter on the shore of the Lake of Galilee, after He had drawn in the unbroken net full of great fishes, "Lovest thou me more than these? Feed my sheep."[1] For is He not in priesthood, teaching, and government the prolific Father of the age to come? He remains not solitary in His triple dignity, but is the Adam of His race, and rules in it from His resurrection by those whom He appoints.

It may further be observed that in the supernatural regimen thus established by our Lord, viewed as the one indivisible power which constitutes it, there is an image traced upon His spiritual kingdom of the ever-blessed Trinity, its royalty representing God the Father as the source: its priesthood, wherein lies the whole economy of human redemption, God the Son, who carries it out; its teaching, God the Holy Ghost, the Spirit of Truth, whose ever-abiding presence guides its subjects, as by the hand, into all truth. The regimen is the generative power in His kingdom; and this image, wrought indelibly upon its society in all lands and times, is as distinctly Christ's work upon the Christian commonwealth as the image traced upon individual man in the soul's triple constitution of memory, understanding, and will, when it has been sanctified by His grace, is His work upon the individual.

That in the Episcopate there should be a triple power: of priesthood, comprehending the whole divine worship,

---

[1] 1 Peter ii. 25; Heb. x. 21, iii. 1, v. 10; Matt. xxiii. 8; Luke xxii. 29; John xx. 21; Matt. xxviii. 20; John xxi. 15.

and the imparting of grace through the sacraments; of teaching, which contains the communication of the whole divine truth; and of ruling, that is, over the whole region of action comprised by the priesthood and the teaching, the prototype of which exists in the eternal relations of the Blessed Trinity, while itself is that one undivided power which represents the divine unity, seems to shadow out the very citadel in which the Divine Wisdom set up His kingdom.

Who could have imagined beforehand such a constitution of government? Who, placing himself at the time of Christ and contemplating as a fact the actual relations of the Two Powers then in existence *before him*, could ever have devised such a kingdom? Is not this in very deed the kingdom of grace and truth? Have we not here visible to the eye of faith the Priest, the Prophet, and the King, who has set up Altar, Chair, and Throne together in the midst of the nations?

2.—*The Spiritual Power a Complete Society.*

That man, who was originally made after the image and likeness of God, is sent into this life in order that he may in a future life attain the end of his being, that is, the enjoyment of God, is the primary fundamental truth which is presupposed in that whole work of Christ just described. The supernatural society exists for a supernatural end. The total denial of this end would be the complete and perfect heathenism of which the original heathenism was but a shadow; for that state of man in which the whole of his public and private life was encircled by the ties and consecrated by the rites of religion, even though those rites were prostituted by being offered to false gods, was not a denial of this end. In such a state man acknowledged a power beyond himself—beyond visible nature: his mind, his heart, his imagination were filled with the sense of that power. This is true of the great mass of the heathen before the coming of Christ, and is true in a large degree of those nations remaining still outside the Christian faith in their traditional religion, which descends in however fragmentary, however perverted a form, from the religion of Noah, and the primal and universal covenant for all his family struck with him. It is only the apostasy of a few from the Christian faith itself which has reached that final and absolute impiety —the greatest which the human mind can reach—of entirely denying this end of man.

Now, in considering the relation between the Civil and the Spiritual Power in all its bearings, we assume as a postulate this supernatural end of man. As it is the kernel of our belief, so it is the absolute basis of our argument. It cannot be put in a terser form than that in which our Lord stated it to those about Him when He asked the question, "What shall it profit a man if he gain the whole world and lose his own soul?" Those only who have come to such a negation of reason as to suppose that they have no souls can disregard it. And as it is of absolute necessity, so it is all that is required for a full consideration of the subject.

"There is then a certain good beyond the natural

society of man in this his condition of mortal life, which is that ultimate beatitude which is looked for after death in the enjoyment of God. And so the Christian, who has acquired a right to that beatitude by the blood of Christ, and has received the earnest of the Holy Spirit in order to attain it, requires, beyond the aid which temporal government gives him for the concerns of this life, a spiritual care which is given to the faithful by the ministers of Christ's Church. Now, as to the ultimate end which they are to seek, the same must be said of the whole mass of men as of one man. If, then, the one man's end lay in any good existing in himself, the ultimate end of government for the mass of men would be similarly that it should reach such good and secure its possession. But all the goods of this present life offer no such end, whether it be health, or riches, or knowledge, or even virtue. For the virtuous life, whether of the individual or the mass, is subordinate to a further end, which is the future enjoyment of God. If that end could be obtained by a power of human nature, it would belong to the office of temporal government to direct men to it, since that is supreme in things purely human. But since man does not attain the end of enjoying God by any merely human power but by divine power, according to St. Paul's word, that 'the grace of God is eternal life,' it requires not a human but a divine government to lead men to that end. And so it is that such a government belongs to a King who is not only man but also God, that is, to our Lord Jesus Christ, who has introduced men to the glory of heaven by making them sons of God. This, then, is the kingdom which has been delivered to Him, and which shall not be broken up, on account of which He is named in Scripture, not Priest only, but King. Hence a royal priesthood is derived from Him; and, what is more, all the faithful of Christ, so far forth as they are His members, are called kings and priests. Therefore the ministry of this kingdom, in order that spiritual things might be distinguished from temporal, has been entrusted not to the kings of the earth but to priests, and in the highest degree to the priest who is over all, the successor of St. Peter, the Vicar of Christ, the Roman Pontiff, to whom all kings of the Christian people are to be subject as to our Lord Jesus Christ himself; for this is in accordance with the principle that those to whom belongs the care of antecedent ends should be subject to him who has the care of the final end, and be directed by his rule."[1]

What we have just said amounts to this, that the whole life of man, whether single or in society, while he lives upon earth, is subject to the life which he hopes for in heaven as its supreme purpose and end; and that being so subject, as there is a society to aid him in attaining the goods of his natural life, so much more is there a society to aid him in attaining that supernatural good to which the natural goods are subordinate. We have next to compare the regimens of these two societies with each other in regard to their completeness.

The analogy between the Two Powers is full of instruction; but it is to be remembered that as, since the

[1] S. Thos. de Reg. Prin., lib. l. c. 14, translated.

coming of Christ, the Spiritual Power is one in all countries and in all times, whereas the Temporal Power is one only in each country and at each time, the comparison of the two can only take those points which belong to the Temporal Power alike in all countries and times; and this will be found sufficient for our purpose. We have just seen the conception of spiritual jurisdiction as wielding the priesthood and the teaching: it corresponds in this respect to secular sovereignty, under which is ranged on the one hand authority in every degree, as held by all officials in administration, by all councillors in legislating, by all judges in their several tribunals, by all officers in the public force. Whoever in the public service holds a portion of the public authority may be ranged under the general head of magistrate, and stands herein to the sovereign power in the same relation as the priest to the bearer of supreme spiritual jurisdiction. On the other hand, whoever is engaged in the whole circle of human arts and sciences, which comprehends the vast domain of human knowledge as acquired by learning, answers to the spiritual teacher. This triple division runs through every state, at every time, whatever may be its relative advancement in the scale of government. And the comparison as to both Powers is exhaustive with regard to their range, since in both, man, individual or collective, is a being who acts because he first knows and then wills. Sovereignty, presiding in the various kinds of magistracy over all who command, and over all in the various arts and sciences who teach, because they have first learned, covers that triple domain in the one case, and in the other spiritual royalty, which acts through the priest and the teacher. But the society is knit together in a much stricter bond, by a far more perfect interaction of forces, in the spiritual than in the temporal order; and this arises from the fact that all spiritual power in its triple range actually descends from the spiritual head through every degree, which is far from being the fact in temporal sovereignty. That is the pre-eminence of Christ in His spiritual kingdom; and it is the perfection of the Divine Legislator that He exercises His royalty by the indivisible action of His Jurisdiction, Priesthood, and Teaching, communicated to the whole structure at the head of which He stands.

The completeness of the spiritual society in its regimen is likewise shown by the philosophical basis on which it rests. Our knowledge of our dependence upon the Being, the Truth, and the Goodness of God is the foundation of religion in us, and produces in us the idea of three chief duties binding us to God—Faith, Adoration, and Charity.[1] These answer to man's triple nature, which acts upon the basis of knowing and willing; and they correspond likewise to the office of the Teacher, the Priest, and the Spiritual Ruler. Faith is evidently the virtue in man elicited by the Teacher, and its office is to accept the truth which he communicates. It leads on to Adoration, which ensues when the mind and heart dwell upon the divine attributes and their relation to man, and which includes

[1] Taparelli, Saggio teoretico di dritto naturale.

Hope as a part of itself; and this answers to the special work of the Priest, which is to communicate the whole treasure of grace to the human redeemed family. And, lastly, Charity, which is the ruling principle of all action to the Christian, so far as he acts christianly, is the special virtue of the Ruler, according to the condition imposed by our Lord when He instituted the pastoral rule in its highest degree, saying to Peter, "Lovest thou me more than these?" that is, his brother Apostles and the Apostle of Love himself, and then adding, "Feed my sheep." And these virtues, Faith, Adoration, and Charity, it may be added, have as intimate a connection with each other as the several bearers of power in the regimen to which they belong are linked together. To exercise Faith, Adoration, and Charity make the Christian man, as the Teaching, the Priesthood, and the Rule make the Christian order.

Worship, belief, and conduct embrace the whole man in his relations godward; but much more than this is true in the order of the Christian kingdom, for there these three things are inseparably joined with the Person of Christ. As we have said above, the whole power grows upon the root of His Priesthood, the particular act of which is the offering of His Body, the Body of the Incarnate Son, for the sin of the world. His communicated Priesthood consists in the perpetual presentation of that Sacrifice to God by His ministers in the name and in the presence of the Christian people; and the Sacrifice thus offered becomes further to them the food of eternal life. In this great sacrament, carrying with it the perpetual presence of Christ in and with His Church, all the other sacraments are potentially contained. It is the well-spring of the whole sacramental life, which He caused to open when His own Passion was beginning. Of indescribable grandeur is that order, beginning with the eve of His Passion, and stretching unbroken through all times and climes to the consummation of the world. In that great act, carried on by the High Priest through the voice and hands of countless successors, which daily in every generation gathers into one the prayers of His people, the manifold life is concentered which provides for every need.

But this Priesthood it is which carries on the Faith. That Faith is not a belief in God " as the Architect of the universe," but in the love of God the Father, the Creator of man, who sends His Son to be their Redeemer, and in the love of God the Son, who is so sent; so that the Faith grows on the root of the Priesthood. And out of this Faith is developed that vast fabric of doctrine which in the course of eighteen centuries and a half has made Christian theology, and reared for itself a harmonious system of Christian law. The Eternal Priest carries in His hands eternal truth, which He alone can preserve amid the never-ending conflicts of human opinion, the surging strife of the bottomless sea of human imaginations. The gift of maintaining all the truth which concerns human redemption in every one of its remotest issues cannot be parted from the Priesthood by which that redemption was wrought. Thus it coheres with the sacramental life, and is not a fruit of man's intellect by itself, but is bestowed on that intellect in union with grace. It is as it were an atmosphere of thought which the Christian people breathe.

And, once more, Christian conduct is the action of those who have this worship and this faith. It springs from an intention united at least implicitly to the Author and Finisher of the Faith. It is this intention which gives to the action the quality of merit. For an action done with it differs incalculably from an action done without it, though the external appearance and effect of the two actions may be the same. It is to Christ as King that we are answerable for our actions, and worship and belief culminate in action. The inward life of His subjects therefore answers to the triple outward order established by the Priest, the Prophet, and the King. It is in virtue of this answering in His people that He has fulfilled the prophecies concerning Him as to His triple character. Had He left no government for His kingdom, how would He be a King? Had He left no priesthood to be perpetuated in His Church, how would He be Priest after the order of Melchisedek? Had He left no truth inaccessible to error, how would He be the Prophet that was to come into the world?

It is then in their worship, their belief, and their conduct that the Christian people one and all are derived from Christ, as much as the triple regimen of His kingdom. Every individual man, so far as he is a Christian, is a copy of Christ, while the whole people "is Jesus Christ diffused and communicated, Jesus

Christ complete, Jesus Christ perfect man, Jesus Christ in His fulness."[1]

Nothing can show the universality of this Christian society more than this derivation alike of the individual and of the mass from Christ. When the children of Noah were scattered abroad over the face of the whole earth at the dispersion, the great family was broken up and nations arose; but in the baptism of Christ nations disappear and the great family is restored. There it is the member of the human race, the child of Adam alone, who is assumed to be the brother of Christ. All the conditions of human life which have arisen in the society of the nation, which St. Paul has summed up in the words Greek and Jew, barbarian, Scythian, bond or free, disappear also; there arises from that fontal birth only the man "created anew to knowledge after the image of the Creator" (Col. iii. 10, 11). Yet there is no interference with the natural society, with its rights on the one side and its obligations on the other. It is the human being, with body and soul, making one manhood, of which the soul is the form, which is thus taken; but he is taken in his relations to that last end with the mention of which we begun. As to the other relations of his natural state, they continue as they were, subject only to a superior end, which is superior because it is the last.

Our Lord, when traduced before the Roman tribunal as infringing on the sovereignty of the emperor, was solemnly asked if He was the King of the Jews. He

[1] Bossuet.

replied with a threefold assertion: that He was a King; that His kingdom was not of this world, and yet that it was in this world. How far does the kingdom which we have so far attempted to delineate correspond to these three truths?

1. It is a kingdom because, according to the delineation of it which we have just made, it is a royal priesthood, ruling inasmuch as it deals with the belief, the worship, and the conduct of its people—all the relations of man with God. In all this it does for the divine life in man everything which the temporal kingdom does for his secular life. The analogy between the two is precise and complete.

2. It is not a kingdom of this world, inasmuch as it governs with a view to an end which is outside and beyond this life. This end determines everything within it, as also we have seen above.

3. Again, it is not of this world because the source of its regimen lies in the Incarnation and Passion of the Son of God, acts the virtue of which consists in God's supreme government of the world, in His absolute lordship over it as Creator and Redeemer. All authority in it descends from Christ, "as the Apostle and High Priest" by this divine appointment, from whose Person the apostolate and priesthood are transmitted to those whom He sends, in like manner as He Himself was sent by His Father.

4. Again, it is not of this world because its subjects are produced as so many copies of this divine original; it is the only kingdom in which the people proceeds out

of the King as much as the regimen by which it is ruled. He is strictly the Father whom His children imitate so far as they are His children; in Him Fathership and Kingship are identical.

5. Again, it is not of this world because its sacraments bestow grace, a gift of God coming down upon the world, in it, but not of it; the fountain-head of the gift being that God has taken the flesh of Adam and borne the sin of Adam, and therefore, through seven sacramental streams, dispenses the grace which heals the sin, as it affects the whole life of man as the offspring of Adam.

6. Again, it is not of this world in the perpetual witness which it bears to the truth, in which witness specially our Lord declares that His sovereignty lies. If this witness had closed with His death, that would have been the triumph of falsehood. And those who allege that truth has been corrupted in His kingdom do, in fact, declare with the same breath, though they often do not perceive the consequence, that His witness has ceased and failed. But truth, as the token and inheritance of His kingdom, depends, like grace, upon a divine gift attached to His Person, and transmitted through the order of His kingdom's regimen.[1]

7. Furthermore, it is a kingdom because of the complete analogy with that civil government which makes a temporal kingdom. It has jurisdiction for jurisdiction, and a graduated hierarchy of officers descending more directly from the head than exists in any temporal

[1] See Ephes. iv. 11-16.

monarchy. And what the multifold arts and sciences which embellish natural life are to any of these kingdoms, that the divine inheritance of teaching Christian truth, in its bearings upon the acts and thoughts and philosophy of mankind, is with a much higher degree of perfection in the Christian kingdom.

8. And if man has naturally need to live in society, if to do so is a fulfilment of God's purpose in creating him a race, much more has he this need of the supernatural society; and in so living he fulfils the purpose of God in so much higher a degree as Christ exceeds Adam. All the sacraments fulfil this purpose according to the needs of human life, by incorporating him with a divine order; most of all the divinest of them, in which the King appears for ever in the act of His Priesthood, dispensing bread to His people. And here again this spiritual nourishment, whereby His people live in society, testifies that the kingdom is not of this world.

9. Nor is it to be forgotten that the kingdom thus far described generated for itself a law, not confined, like the law of any earthly kingdom, to a particular time or place, but universal as itself, defining and arranging the various relations by which it subsists, that is, the whole order of the internal Christian life and the external Christian society. The power of the Legislator who is seated in this empire nowhere is shown more manifestly than in the great and uniform fabric of Christian law which He has caused to proceed out of it, and which, made for the rule of a Christian people gathered out of all the tribes of the earth, contains

in it, drawn out and applied, all the principles needed to provide a mirror of justice and equity for the nations of the earth in their intercourse with each other.

10. Most striking is this witness to the truth that it is not of this world in the essential and inherent independence of the civil government which the kingdom possesses as to its end, as to its regimen, as to the production of its people, as to its sacraments, as to its maintenance of the truth committed to it, and as to its Canon Law. With regard to all these it is in the midst of these governments, but it is not of them. No one of these things can their mechanism produce, while the divine kingdom consists in the exercise of them all within the limits of these various kingdoms, with or without their concurrence, but never with any originating power in temporal rule as to any of them.

11. And this leads to two of the most striking differences between the Temporal and the Spiritual Power. Every temporal kingdom is limited in space. The proudest and most imperial which has yet existed, that great Roman empire of which Christ was a subject, and in the bosom of which His greater kingdom arose, how small a portion of the earth's surface did it cover! Not so the Kingdom of Truth. It is in place, but not local; it runs through all the kingdoms of the world, grasping them, not grasped by them. By the token of ubiquity it is in them, but not of them; and if it be retorted that this attribute has but imperfectly been fulfilled in fact, I reply that it has been sufficiently fulfilled to mark to all eyes that it is a token of the

one kingdom, fulfilled more and more, and advancing to greater fulfilment; besides that I am here considering the divine kingdom in its conception, in its idea.

12. And still more than in place is the Temporal Power limited in time. Immortal in the institution itself, so far as the human race is immortal, it is subject to decline and death in numberless individual applications. If man is likened to a flower in duration, many a kingdom lasts not so long as a tree. All change in the character of their government, passing from the one to the few, from the few to the many, or again reabsorbed from the many to one. The succession of human governments is likened to the sea in its changes, whose turbulent waves image forth the fluctuations of empires. Where is the government that has remained one and the same but that concerning which Christ said, "Feed my sheep;" "I will give to thee the keys of the kingdom of heaven;" "Confirm thy brethren;" "Thou art the Rock on which I will build my Church"? By its domination over time and space the kingdom of the truth shows that it is in but not of the world.

13. There is yet one more quality, as distinctive and as peculiar as any which we have yet passed in review. It is the kingdom not only of the truth, but of Charity. Not that within it there have not been innumerable scandals; not that within it sin has not ever been fighting with grace; but that the whole kingdom is compacted and held together by a divine charity, and has in it as a common possession the treasure of the merits of Jesus Christ. "The king is one with the

kingdom, because He bears its sins; the kingdom is one with the King, because it bears His cross."[1] This is an interchange of charity which goes on for ever. It is an effect of this bond that no virtue and no suffering in it is lost. The whole kingdom, from the beginning to the end, makes up "that which is wanting of the sufferings of Christ." There is no such bond of unity, no such fruit of communion, in any temporal kingdom comparable to this. I suppose that patriotism in the natural society corresponds to the charity engendered in the supernatural kingdom; and patriotism is limited to the temporal objects of the particular society; charity extends to the eternal interests of the kingdom without end.

3.—*Relation of the Two Powers to each other.*

In the treatment hitherto pursued we have divided the consideration of the two Powers into the period before Christ and the period which ensues upon His coming.

In the period before Christ we have found that both Powers were originally of divine institution in the beginning of man, and that both belonged to him as a race. Civil government began with the family; worship, and with it priesthood, began also with the family; both were united in the head of the race; both were instituted for the good of man as he lived in society. Their subject was the same—man—the secular Power treating him in his relation to his natural end, its object

[1] Bossuet.

being to provide all things which concerned the temporal prosperity of his life; the Spiritual Power treating him in relation to his supernatural or last end, its object being to provide whatever concerned his eternal state after this life. And their relative importance was determined by their end, with regard to which the temporal life was subject to the future life. No fact was more strikingly illustrated by the whole history than this; for three times the condition of the whole race upon the earth was affected by its conduct in regard to the last end, which belongs to the Spiritual Power. Once, and at a stroke, the whole race fell in its first sire from its state of original justice, and from the happiness which depended on the preservation of that state, by disregard of the end for which it was created. A second time the whole race, with the exception of one family, because disobedience to God became universal, fell in like manner, and was destroyed. A third time the lapse proceeded to the corruption of the idea of God Himself; the unity and brotherhood of the race was broken up in consequence; it divided into nations at enmity with each other, and man, from being a family of brethren, became the bitterest foe of his fellow-man, inventing war, and slavery as its result, and inflicting on himself worse evils than those which came to him from any external cause. By the same lapse the Spiritual Power was specially affected. The unity of the priesthood was destroyed with belief in the unity of the Godhead; the truth which it was intended to attest and carry on, that is, the sense of man's guilt and the promise of his restoration, was overclouded; the sacrifice which it was intended to offer to the one God was offered to a multitude of false gods; the rites which accompanied the sacrifice and the prayers which explained its meaning lost their force. The corruption of religion entailed with it a terrible descent in the moral character of its ministers. In this state it may be said that the Spiritual Power was so far fallen from its original purpose, that it had almost ceased to have relation to the supernatural end of man. In every country it continued to be, it is true, in amity with the civil government, but at the price of absolute subjection at last. The truth which should have guarded it was all but lost, and the honour which belonged to it was seized by the civil ruler as a decoration of his crown.

In the period which ensued upon the coming of Christ we have found a new basis given to the Spiritual Power. As it lay through all Gentilism with its truth corrupted, its power appended to the State, its offices stripped of all moral meaning, it needed to be renewed from its very source. A foul pantheon of male and female deities, differing as to names and functions with every country, could generate no priesthood. Such generation was the work of the Most High God, and for it He sent His Son. The nation which He had built up to form the Altar, the Chair, the Throne of His Son refused, through the worldliness of its rulers, to discharge its office. Yet in its despite He sent forth the law from Sion, where the act of His Son's high priesthood was effected by the very sin of His people; and henceforth we find the Spiritual Power a derivation from the Person of Christ as the Incarnate God in His work of redemption. We have seen it one and indivisible in its essence, triple in its direction or modality; in its Priesthood representing the Son; in its Teaching of the truth, the Holy Spirit; in the Spiritual Royalty, from which Priesthood and Teaching both proceed, and which both exercise, the Father, the source of the Godhead; thus rendering an image, perfect so far as the weakness of created things allows, of the Divine Trinity in Unity, according to the prayer offered for it by our Lord in His Passion: "They are not of the world, as I am not of the world: as Thou hast sent me into the world, I also have sent them into the world; that they all may be one, as Thou, Father, art in me, and I in them, that they also may be one in us."

It is, then, out of the union of the divine and human natures in Christ, in virtue of His Passion, and from His Person when He rose from the dead, that the Spiritual Power is drawn. The Spiritual Power itself makes its subjects; and thus the Father of the future age creates His people from Himself, as of old time and in figure of Himself He made the race out of Adam. Thus, as regards Gentilism, He formed anew the priesthood to replace that original priesthood which had so fallen from its duties, so corrupted its witness, so lost its honour. The act in view to which that original priesthood was set up being accomplished, He resumed its power, for the symbolical sacrifice became useless so soon as the real sacrifice was offered. As regards Judaism, He fulfilled the purpose for which it had been created, offering Himself as the Paschal Lamb in the midst of it; and by His resurrection He caused the prophet-nation to subserve for the generation of an universal kingdom of truth, whose power lay henceforth in Himself.

This is the condition of things established by Christ, and all that we have further to say as to the relation between the Two Powers is a deduction from it.

1. And, first, it is clear that all Christians are subject to the Spiritual Power. This subjection rests upon the same ground as subjection to Christ Himself, for the power represents Him. As regards any individual Christian this will hardly be contested. But it is equally true of all corporate bodies, whether small or great. This obligation touches as strictly the mightiest kingdom, if it be Christian, as the humblest private person. There is nothing in the quality of numbers or of temporal sovereignty which exempts from obedience to the law of Christ those who acknowledge Him for their King; and the King's government is as the King Himself. Of course it is only so far as the spiritual domain extends—that is, over the things which belong to the Priesthood, the Teaching, and that Spiritual Jurisdiction which makes their Royalty—that the obligation of obedience extends.

2. Secondly, all Christians are subject likewise, as all men in general, to the Temporal Power, in the respective country in which they live, so far as the domain of that Temporal Power extends, which even more than the Spiritual has its limits. The Spiritual Power has itself

laid down in absolute terms the obligation of this obedience and the ground on which it rests. "Let every soul be subject to higher powers, for there is no power but from God, and the powers which are have been ordained by God. So that he who resists the power, resists the ordinance of God, and they that resist purchase to themselves condemnation, for the power is God's minister to thee for good." And again, "Be subject to every human creature for God's sake, whether it be to the king as excelling, or to governors as sent by him for the punishment of evil-doers, and for the praise of the good; for so is the will of God." This may be termed the comment of the two chief apostles, Peter and Paul, upon the words of their Lord, "Render to Cæsar the things which are Cæsar's," which is followed by the limitation, "and to God the things which are God's." Temporal government is herein declared to be the vicegerent of God; to have been such from the beginning of the world; to continue to be such to the end of it. The statement that authority, as such, is the minister of God to man for good applies, of course, not to any particular form of temporal government, as emperor, king, or republic, in which the government is administered in the persons of many or few, and in various degrees of delegation, but to temporal government in itself, in the principle of its authority. And being spoken by the highest Christian authority in regard of what was actually a heathen government, it manifestly belongs not only to Christians under Christian governments but to the subjects of civil power in all times and conditions of things. And, further, it is remarkable that our Lord and His apostles, who so strongly recognise civil government as the ordinance of God, "as the minister of God for good," themselves suffered the loss of their lives in obedience to it, by an unrighteous judgment.

We have, then, the two Powers set forth as two Vicegerences of God, in the government of His human world: the temporal Vicegerency belonging to each sovereignty for the country which it rules, so far as the sphere of that sovereignty extends; the Spiritual Vicegerency belonging to His one spiritual kingdom in all times and places in the sphere of its sovereignty.

3. Here we are in presence of two societies, the authority in each of which is a divine Vicegerency, whose subject is the same man, whether individual or collective. The one is the minister of God for good to man in all his natural relations in every country; the other is the very authority of the Incarnate God Himself, unlimited as to time and place, over the same man in all his supernatural relations. Not only do both represent God, but both govern the same man. These two conditions fix what is the divinely intended relation between them. It cannot but be one of amity. As these powers existed in the beginning they were united even as to the person bearing them. The great sin of unfaithfulness to God in the race caused them to be placed in different bearers. Amid all the corruption which ensued, as to worship on the one hand, as to civil government on the other, the two Powers never ceased

to be in amity with each other. For the basis of this amity is, in truth, a condition of human nature which never varies, being, in fact, the subjection of man's natural life to his supernatural end. As long as man is sent into this world for the purpose of trial, to live in another world an endless life, the quality of which shall be determined by his conduct as a free moral agent in this life, so long the power which rules him in reference to the concerns of this life is bound to live in amity with the power which rules him as to the concerns of that future life. This, on the one hand, being the reason for amity in man himself; on the other hand, both Powers proceeding from the same God, must be intended by Him to work in harmony. He has no more made them rivals in the government of His moral world, than He has made the sun and moon rivals in the physical enlightenment of the earth, and the government of its motions.

To illustrate further the necessity of amity between the two Powers for the good of man's life, let us consider three other relations which have been conceived as possible to exist.

4. A separate action of the two Powers in their respective spheres, that is, a complete division between Church and State, has been imagined by some as feasible and desirable. But with regard to this it must be observed that the two Powers rule over one human commonwealth, whether that be viewed as existing within the limit of any particular state, or as spread over the whole world. Again, that they rule conjointly

over both soul and body. For, if we use accurate language, it is not as if the Church ruled over the soul, and the State over the body. It is, indeed, true that, in order to bring home the relative importance of the two ends pursued by the two Powers, this illustration has been constantly used, by the Fathers first, and by other writers afterwards; but it is only an illustration, not an accurate statement of a real relation. They rule, in fact, over both soul and body, but in different relations; the State over soul and body as to their natural end, the Church over soul and body as to their supernatural end. The State's rule is over all those things which are ordered for the tranquillity and stability of human society; the Church's rule is over all those things which concern the salvation of souls, all those things which fall under the domain of her priesthood, her teaching, and her jurisdiction. It is obvious that both these classes of things belong both to soul and body. How, for instance, can rule over the soul be denied to the State if it can demand of its subjects, for the defence of country, the sacrifice of life, in which the condition of the soul as well as that of the body is involved? How can rule over the body be denied to the Church, when the body enters into every act of worship and receives the sacraments?—when the inward belief requires to be testified by word and deed, in order to confess Christ before men?

The Temporal Power, therefore, rules over all temporal matters, that is, those which concern natural right and man's natural end; the Spiritual Power rules over spiritual things, those which concern man's supernatural end. Can the former perform rightly the duties which belong to it without considering the rights appertaining to the latter?

To answer this question, let us take the case of the individual man. Is it possible for a man rightly to perform his duties to the State without consideration of his duties to God? As we have before seen, all the duties of man in life are subject to his supernatural end. Every particle of natural right rests upon the authority of God the Creator; and if God has created man for a supernatural end, to discharge the civil duties of life without regard to that end is simple impiety. It is plain that, according to the intention of God, every part of man's natural life has been ordered with a view to the end of his supernatural life.

But in this the case of the individual in no respect differs from the case of the collective mass. The State has been created with a view to the ultimate end of man as much as the individual. In fact, the cause of its creation was to establish an order in human things which should help man continually to attain that end. It was not created for itself. The society of man in this life is not the ultimate fact. Once more : the Fall, the Deluge, and the Dispersion have uttered three voices upon that truth which can never be silenced, which have echoed through the whole world and touch all human nature. The State, then, as much as the individual, must perform all which it is intended to perform in the government of man, in obedience to the principle that man's present life is ordered with a view to his future life.

To apply this more particularly, it means that the State, in its administration of all temporal things, is bound incessantly to have regard to the free exercise by the Spiritual Power of its authority over spiritual things. It must allow that power to administer the whole work of the priesthood, and the whole work of the teaching, with that liberty of internal government which constitutes its jurisdiction, the seat of its royalty. It is not the place here to enumerate in detail how much that involves. It is enough to say that the ordinary action of the State and the ordinary action of the Church run daily into each other, as being concerned with the same man and the same society of men; and accordingly, that the allowing such a liberty to the Church by the State carries with it great consideration and regard for the Church by the State. But such a consideration and regard are quite incompatible with separate action of the two Powers in their respective spheres. An instance in point would be the State compelling a subject, who is a minister of the Church, to become a soldier. It is a purely natural right of the State to require the service of the subject for such a purpose. It is a purely spiritual right of the Church to have the use of her ministers for her own work. The use of the former right without consideration of the latter would constitute a separate action of the State in its sphere. But it would be at the same time an act of the utmost hostility on the part of the State to the Church. And other instances of the same kind present themselves through the whole domain of things which, in themselves, are purely temporal or purely spiritual. Besides these there is the class of mixed things, and, as one of them, let us take education.

Education, so far as it embraces instruction in the several arts and sciences which subserve man's natural life, belongs to the domain of the State; so far as it embraces the formation of the spiritual character in man, which includes instruction in religion, and that not only as it concerns dogma, but also philosophy and science, belongs to the domain of the Church. If the State exercises its natural right over education with regard to the former, without allowing the supernatural right of the Church over the latter, which in itself would be no more than a separate action in its own sphere, it would constitute, at the same time, a complete infringement of the Church's rights in her spiritual power of teaching and jurisdiction.

This is enough to show that the separate action of the two Powers in their respective spheres leads to the disjunction of man's natural life from his supernatural end. This was not the intention of God in creating the two Powers, and placing man's life under their joint government.

5. Another relation between the two Powers which may be conceived, is that of hostility upon the part of the State to the Church. This cannot be reciprocal. The Church can indeed and must resist, with her own weapons, unlawful aggression against the exercise of

her rights in administering the "things of God," but she cannot war against the State as such, because it is in her sight "the minister of God." The hostility of the State which invades the Church's exercise of her Priesthood, Teaching, and Jurisdiction constitutes persecution. There are many degrees of this. A heathen State may aim at the complete destruction of the Christian Church within its borders, as at times the Roman emperors did. A Christian State may also vex and hamper with every form of impediment the exercise of the Church's powers. A State which has been Christian, becoming heretical or apostate, may assault the Church with a hatred, combined with deceit, which shall surpass the malignity of the Roman State of old or the heathen State at any time. In the course of centuries every degree of persecution has been exercised by the State, heathen, Christian, heretical, or apostate, against the Church, by the permission of the divine Providence; but no one will pretend to say that such a relation as hostility on the part of the State, and of suffering on the part of the Church, is the normal relation intended by God in the establishment of the two Powers. On the contrary, the States which persecute the Church, while they fulfil the divine purpose for its trial and purification, incur punishment in many ways for their crime against God in assaulting His kingdom, and, if they persevere, have been and are to be rooted up and destroyed.

6. In contrast to such relation between the two Powers, let us look for a moment at the divine Idea as it is thrown out in strong projection upon the background

of ages. We have human government founded indeed
by God at and with the commencement of the race,
and continued by the strong sanction of His power
ever since, through the dispersion, through the various
races of men, one rising and another falling; human
government possessed in common by a vast number
of sovereignties, great and small, particular in place,
with changing constitutions, everything about them,
the people who bear them, the boundaries within which
they flourish, the laws by which they are administered,
shifting and transitory: no one of these sovereignties
having a claim to say that it was founded by God,
inasmuch as they all spring out of a long series of
conquests and changes which succeed after the original
patriarchal rule. These are distinctively the kingdoms
of men, and in them is fulfilled, with a little longer
range, what the poet says of each human generation—

"Like leaves on trees the race of man is found;"

the only thing about them which is not shifting and
not transitory is the one thing which is of divine
appointment, government itself. And in the midst of
these nations, borne upon them, and shaken indeed,
but imperturbable amid their fluctuations, behold the
one government founded immediately by Christ in St.
Peter, as no other sovereignty has been founded; in
St. Peter, made by express language His Viceregent.
Here is one sovereignty, universal in time and place,
with no changing constitution, after the fashion of its
human shadows, which are a royalty one day, a demo-

cracy another day, an empire a third, but one and the same for ever. Here is the kingdom of Christ.

But that which rules the relation of the one kingdom and the many kingdoms to each other, is the *end* for which they are constructed: human government, the one abiding because divine element in the many kingdoms, exists for the peace, the order, and the prosperity of man's life on earth. But this, its highest end, is subject, like all the natural goods of man, to a higher end, the eternal beatitude of man. In the last resort temporal government itself was originally founded and actually exists only for this purpose. But the one kingdom of Christ is directed immediately to this very purpose. Because there is an inseparable relation of all earthly things to that highest end, therefore each of these temporal kingdoms and the one spiritual kingdom have a bond between them which cannot be broken. If it were not for this, their range is so apart from each other, their powers so independent of each other, that they would speedily part company. The strong hand of God has joined them to draw together the chariot of human government by the yoke of the last end.

How entirely independent in themselves are their constituent parts! On the one hand, earthly might, grounded indeed in right but ruling by force, cemented by riches, carrying the sword of life and death in its hands, exulting in all the vast accumulation of human arts and sciences, the work of civilised man through long ages; on the other hand, a royal priesthood, with a divine truth, carried through the ages by an order of men generated spiritually in virtue of the consecration once given by the hands of Christ to Peter and his brethren. The temporal government marked by wealth and force; the spiritual by poverty and weakness. Yet both reign over the soul and body of man individual and collective. These powers are both ordained by God; can they be also ordained with co-ordination?

The following passage of St. Thomas[1] leads, I think, to a full answer to this question:—

"As the life by which men live well here on earth is as means to the end of that blessed life which we hope for in heaven, so whatever particular goods are obtained by man's agency, as, for instance, riches, profits of trade, health, eloquence, or learning, have for their end the good of the mass. If then, as we have before shown, the person charged with the care of the last end ought to be the superior of those who are charged with means to an end, and to direct them by his authority, it is evident from what we have said that, just as the king ought to be subject to that domain and regimen which is administered by the office of the priesthood, so he ought to preside over all human offices and regulate them by his supreme authority. Now whoever has the duty of doing anything which stands to another thing as means to an end, is bound to see that his work is suitable to that end; so the armourer furbishes his sword for fighting, and the builder arranges his house to be lived in. Since, then, the beatitude of heaven is

[1] De Regimine Principis, lib. l. c. xv.

the end of that life by which we live at present virtuously, the king's office requires him to promote such a life in his people as is suitable for the attainment of blessedness in heaven, by ordaining what tends thither, and by forbidding, so far as is possible, the contrary."

The king will here stand for whoever has sovereign authority. That sovereign authority therefore is itself subject to the law of God through all its exercise. The bearer of that law of God is the Spiritual Power which stands over against all sovereigns, in all countries, with the commission placed expressly in its hands by Christ. So far, therefore, as the law of God is concerned, which is precisely the same for the individual and the multitude, the sovereign is in every country subject to it, and the more stringently because, in the words of St. Thomas, he presides over all *human* offices. These by their nature are subject to the *superhuman* office.

This is the indirect Power over temporal things possessed by the Royal Priesthood which has been instituted by Christ. The indirect Power rests simply on the supernatural end of man, and cannot be denied without the denial of that supernatural end. And on account of this end the relation between the two Powers cannot be one of co-ordination, and must be one of subordination.

Nothing can be further removed from the confusion of the two Powers, or from the absorption of the one by the other, than this Idea of their relation. For it is a purely spiritual power which belongs to the priesthood: any power which it exerts over temporal things is indirect, based simply upon the subjection of those temporal things to the bearer of the divine law; and therefore this indirect Power extends over *all* temporal things without exception, but over all only so far as they concern the last end of human life.

The sum is this. God is the one Creator, Designer, and Ruler of the order of Nature and the order of Grace, and in both has one end in view, the glorification of Himself by His creatures; which glorification in beings possessed of reason can only consist in the knowledge and love of His infinite perfections.

There is no power on earth of man over man but that which is derived from God, either mediately or immediately; and therefore every power is, strictly speaking, vicarious, a portion of His lordship over the human race, committed to man, and subject to the end of His glorification by His creature; in which is comprehended the ultimate happiness of that creature; since that happiness is itself the exercise of his mind and his will in knowing and loving his Creator, so that God's honour is the creature's bliss.

But, further, the order of nature was in its origin united with the order of grace, and subordinated to it. The intervention of the Fall did not dissolve this subordination. The long ages of the Revolt only led up to the Restoration, which was prophesied at the moment of the Revolt, and intended even before it. Thus the Power divinely instituted to carry on the human race— the Power of civil government—the power which represents God in the order of nature, is yet subordinated by

Him to the power which He Himself has instituted in the order of Grace.

This second Power at the time of the Restoration springs directly from the Person of the Son; who as He was sent by the Father, so sent His apostles; but He conveyed that power especially to Peter and his heirs in the fulness of a royal priesthood which teaches His faith for ever; so that no power on earth exists so directly instituted by God, and so manifestly vicarious of God's own power, as that of Peter, viewed in himself and in his heirs; and given with the express promise that all the power of the enemy shall not prevail against it.

In all this God, who cannot be at variance with Himself, made the two Powers to help each other, conferring upon each distinct offices, which concern respectively the natural and the supernatural life of man, but likewise subordinating the natural to the supernatural end in the person and race of the Second Adam, as He had subordinated it in the person of the First Adam.

One of the greatest saints and rulers, who shines in the firmament of the Church with almost unparalleled lustre, has expressed this union under the image of a human body, seeing the natural light by two eyes, but directed by one mind, the mind of Christ. He is the one Head of the two Powers, ruling in temporal sovereignty by the hand of kings, in spiritual by the Priesthood which He has inaugurated. If we imagine the one mind of the God-man thus ruling the Christendom which He has made out of Himself by the two eyes of the kingdom and the priesthood, we reach the divine ideal of the relation between the two Powers. Thus St. Gregory VII. observes in his letter to Rodolph, Duke of Suabia, A.D. 1073:[1] "The sovereign reigns most gloriously, and the Church's vigour is strengthened, when priesthood and empire are joined in the unity of concord. There should be no fiction, no dross, in that concord. Let us then confer together, for as the human body is directed in the natural light by two eyes, so when these two dignities are united in the harmony of pure religion, the body of the Church is shown to be ruled and enlightened with spiritual light. Let us give our best attention to these matters, so that when you have well entered into what is our wish, if you approve of our reasons as just, you may agree with us. But if you would add or subtract anything from the line of conduct which we have marked out, we shall be ready, if God permit, to consent to your counsels." The words "if God permit" indicate very gently that subordination, grounded upon the pre-eminence of the divine law, and the divine Ruler who upbears it, which, in case of difference, the natural must yield to the supernatural authority. There is the fullest recognition that to temporal sovereignty all things belong which concern natural right. In these few words I think that St. Gregory VII. has summed up the settled view, policy, and practice of all his predecessors and of all his successors upon the relation between the two Powers, and the importance of their agreement for the good of

[1] Mansi, Collectio Conciliorum, xx. p. 75.

human society. Never has any one of them denied to human sovereignty the exercise of all those rights which belong to natural law. Never has any one of them failed to maintain that all things which belong to natural law are subordinate to those things which touch the salvation of man, and accordingly that when the two orders of things come into conflict, the natural must yield to the supernatural. It is obvious to add how many mixed things there must be, which enter into both domains, and the treatment of which will affect the harmony between the two Powers.

From all the above it results that the denial of the supernatural end in man, individual or collective, constitutes that which is the complete heathenism. In proportion as the bearers of the Temporal Power have more or less approached this heathenism has their opposition to the Spiritual Power been more or less intense; in proportion as they have acknowledged and acted with a due regard to the supernatural end, they have also acknowledged the Spiritual Power and acted in harmony with it.

The perfect ideal relation between the two Powers has been expressed by the term of marriage, in which Christ, the celestial Bridegroom in the Spiritual Power, espouses the temporal order. This image is in remarkable accordance with the origin of the race, and with the prefiguration of Christ in Adam. It is as if the divine order at the Fall fell into the background, and in its slumber the human was taken out of it. But when the human race awoke in the new Adam, the divine order greeted the human as bone of its bone and flesh of its flesh, and wooed it to rule the world with it in the stable union of wedlock. This image at least may serve to indicate the various relations which have hitherto existed between the two Powers. It is itself the ideal relation intended by God. Then, as a matter of fact, during the first three centuries the Church, with her divine claims, turns to the Temporal Power inviting it to an alliance. This is the Church's relation to the heathen State, as it were the time of wooing. Next the Temporal Power accepted this invitation and united itself with the Church, so that each preserving its own domain, they ruled the world together. That was the relation of the Church to the truly Catholic State, a marriage disturbed by no division and separation, when unity of faith preserved the marriage vow unbroken. Each then, indeed, might have misunderstandings, because the bearers of the two Powers, like husband and wife, are human beings; but since there was the stable will in both to preserve the marriage vow undefiled in Christ, such misunderstandings were easily overcome. Perhaps this expresses the whole mediæval condition of things in this respect as accurately as can be done. Thirdly, the Temporal Power divorced itself from the Church's faith, and from obedience to her in divine things; that is the state of broken wedlock. It has various degrees. First, the housewife divorces her husband and breaks the marital band: that in itself constitutes the apostate State. Secondly, she dissolves the marriage by entering into connection with another, to whom she

I

gives power over the household, and with his aid oppresses the lawful husband: that is the position of the heretical State. Thirdly, the housewife will no longer tolerate the single rule of him who has alienated her from her husband; she is willing to have more than one temporary connection, and amongst the many perhaps the husband, if he will accept such terms: that is the position of the indifferent State. Thus we get from this image of marriage[1] an adequate measure of all the relations which have hitherto subsisted between Church and State.

But the purpose of the foregoing chapter has been to set forth the ideal relation between the two Powers intended by God in the Incarnation and the Passion of His Son, and springing out of the junction of these two mysteries of His love.

[1] I am indebted to Phillipps' "Kirchenrecht" for this illustration of marriage. It is a work to which I am under many obligations.

CHAPTER III.

THE ACTUAL RELATION BETWEEN CHURCH AND STATE FROM THE DAY OF PENTECOST TO CONSTANTINE.

Transmission of Spiritual Authority from the Person of Our Lord to Peter and the Apostles, as set forth in the New Testament.

THE Spiritual Power rests for its origin, so far as all Christians are concerned, upon the transmission of spiritual authority from the Person of our Lord to Peter and the Apostles.

That transmission runs up as a fact by a living unbroken line of men to our Lord Himself. It subsists as a kingdom subsists. As the governments of England, or France, or Russia, or China, occupy a portion of the earth, and by that fact are recognised quite independently of any records which attest their rise and growth, so the far greater and more widely spread government of the Church exists, and is in full daily action, independently of any records which attest its origin. Day by day in the sacrament of Baptism it admits children into the Christian covenant; day by day upon myriads of altars, from the rising to the setting sun, it offers the unbloody sacrifice of the Body and Blood of Christ; day by day in unnumbered confessionals it exercises in binding and loosing the sacrament of Penance; day by day its priests teach, support, console, uphold, in ways which it would exhaust the power of language to describe, a multitude of its people. This is its vital force as a kingdom, which it has gone on exerting for eighteen hundred and fifty years without a moment's suspension. This vital force does not proceed from any record which attests it: it is not stored up in any book, but in a divine presence resting on a living succession of men, which perpetuates itself—which, as a fact, goes on increasing in volume and in the effects which it produces from age to age.

Nevertheless, it is desirable to draw out as accurately as we can the account of the first transmission of that spiritual authority by which this kingdom exists, as we have it recorded for us in the writings of the New Testament. For this purpose I shall quote the terms which express it as given in each of the four Gospels and in the Acts of the Apostles and the Epistles of St. Paul and in the Apocalypse.

First of all is the institution of that Priesthood which supports the whole spiritual superstructure, and from which, as the stem, all its branches spring. And this is seen to take place at a moment when our Lord's Passion may be said to have begun—to be, as it were, the first act of it. The fullest record we have is that given by St. Paul in the First Epistle to the Corinthians, which runs thus: (1 Cor. xi. 23) " For I have received of the Lord that which also I delivered unto you: the Lord Jesus, the same night in which He was betrayed, took bread, and giving thanks, broke, and said, Take ye, and eat: this is My Body which shall be delivered for you: this do for the commemoration of Me. In like manner also the chalice, after He had supped, saying, This chalice is the new testament in My Blood: this do ye, as often as ye shall drink, for the commemoration of Me." The Apostle adds in His own words that this was an everlasting memorial of the Lord's death, to continue until His second coming, and that it so contained the Lord's Body and Blood that he who ate or drank unworthily was guilty of the Body and Blood of the Lord. "For as often as you shall eat this bread, and drink this chalice, you shall show the death of the Lord until He come. Therefore, whosoever shall eat this bread or drink the chalice of the Lord unworthily, shall be guilty of the Body and Blood of the Lord."

St. Luke in the Gospel mentions the institution in terms similar to those of St. Paul, especially in that he uses in respect of the Body the sacrificial words, "Do or offer this in commemoration of Me," which St. Paul uses of the chalice also, while St. Luke omits them. St. Matthew and St. Mark record it more briefly still, not giving the sacrificial words in either case; and St. John passes over the institution itself of the Blessed Sacrament, while he adds very largely to the record of what was said by our Lord on the eve of his Passion, and gives three whole chapters which might almost be considered as a comment upon that act of divine love. Indeed, the opening words, "I am the true Vine," seem to point to the rite as having just been accomplished, and to give a divine interpretation of the graces stored up in it. On the whole, it must be said of these four accounts, even including that of St. Paul, that they are rather an allusion to a thing otherwise well known to those for whom it was written than a description of it. When St. Paul wrote, the Priesthood and the Sacrifice had been in daily operation for twenty-five or thirty years, and every Christian knew by the evidence of his senses the full detail, both as to Priesthood and to Sacrament, of that to which reference was made. This is a consideration which it is requisite to bear in mind. Nothing could be further removed from the truth than to suppose that we were intended to obtain our knowledge of what the Priesthood, the Divine Sacrifice, and the Blessed Sacrament were, merely or mainly from the record of them in the Gospel narrative. When this was first published in writing, they were institutions upon which the Church had been already founded; every detail of them was imprinted upon the heart of every Christian, associated with his daily life, and enshrined in his practice. To a heathen reading the Gospel, the words, "Do this in commemoration of Me," might be an enigma; while to a Christian they carried the power of which his whole spiritual being was the growth.

The institution of the Blessed Sacrament and of the Priesthood which is to offer the Sacrifice is enacted by our Lord on the eve of His Passion before the Apostles collected together, as He is about to make the offering in commemorating which for ever, until His final coming, the Priesthood consists. Thus the moment of the institution is so chosen as to connect it most intimately not only with His Person, but with that act of our Lord wherein He is our High Priest, and in reference to which His own words of institution carry so deep a significance. That which was given by our Lord to His Apostles, that which they were to receive themselves and give to others to the end of the world, was precisely that which was to be offered on the same day for the sin of the world, which is very exactly intimated in the tense used in the original; not a future but a present tense: "Take, eat: this is My Body which is being broken for you;" as if the action of His immolation had begun.

As the whole divine mission of our Lord is collected up in his Priesthood, and no less the whole power which He left to His Church, every circumstance of time, place, and occasion which belongs to its institution has to be noted, and this in particular, that it is bestowed before His death, and that it is the only power which is recorded to have been actually bestowed before it. Perhaps it would be more correct to say that His death is the crowning act of the eucharistic institution, and accompanies the institution, understanding in this sense the words of St. John, "Jesus knowing that His hour was come that He should pass out of this world to the Father, He loved them unto the end," words by which he introduces the account of that last evening of our Lord's life.

The basis of the whole structure being thus laid in the act which began our Lord's Passion and commemorates it for ever, we proceed to the testimony of the several Gospels as to the investiture of the Church's rulers which followed the Passion.

1. The words in which St. Matthew records the transmission of spiritual power from the Person of our Lord after His resurrection are the following:—" The eleven disciples went into Galilee, unto the mountain where Jesus had appointed them. . . . And Jesus came and spoke to them, saying, All power is given to Me in heaven and in earth. Go forth, therefore, and make disciples all nations, baptizing them in the name of the Father, and of the Son, and of the Holy Ghost, teaching them to observe all things whatsoever I have commanded you: and behold I am with you all days, even to the consummation of the world."

The power thus given, as recorded by St. Matthew, comes direct from Christ, as an outflowing of His all-power in heaven and on earth: it is an universal power, co-extensive with all the purposes for which the Church has been created, and enduring so long as the Church endures, through the accompanying presence of the Lord; and it is given to the Apostles collectively as to one body.

But St. Matthew, in a former part of his Gospel, had recorded a most remarkable and singular promise made to Peter, or rather a group of four promises forming one mass: the first, that he should be the Rock on which Christ would build His Church; the second, that against this the gates of hell should not prevail; the third, that Christ would give to him the keys of the kingdom of heaven; the fourth, that whatsoever he should bind on earth should be bound in heaven, and whatsoever he should loose on earth should be loosed in heaven. Matthew (xviii. 17, 18) had also recorded, a little later, a promise made to the Apostles collectively, in which our Lord, after referring to the Church as an authoritative tribunal for all His people, had added, "Amen, I say to you, whatsoever you shall bind upon earth shall be bound also in heaven, and whatsoever you shall loose upon earth shall be loosed also in heaven." This promise then contained a part of the fourfold promise already made to Peter, with the limitation, however, not only that it was made to the Apostles conjointly, whereas it had been made to Peter singly, but also that it was detached from the other part of the promise so given to Peter. With respect to the first point, a power vested in a Body, with the condition that it be exercised by common consent, differs greatly from the same power vested in the Head of that Body, to be exercised by him singly. It differs, as far as the conception of aristocracy differs from the conception of monarchy. And the second point above noted, that the promise thus given to the Apostles is detached from the other parts of the promise which had been given to Peter, corroborates this distinction. The powers which indicate monarchy lie in those parts of the promise which were not given to the Apostles conjointly.

The whole testimony of Matthew, therefore, consists in the promise of powers which he records to have been made before the Resurrection, and in the giving of powers which he records to have been made after it.

2. The testimony of Mark is contained in the last six verses of his Gospel: "And He said to them (the eleven), Go ye into the whole world and preach the gospel to every creature. He that believeth and is baptized shall be saved, but he that believeth not shall be condemned. And these signs shall follow them that believe: in My name shall they cast out devils; they shall speak with new tongues; they shall take up serpents; and if they shall drink any deadly thing, it shall not hurt them; they shall lay their hands upon the sick, and they shall recover. And the Lord Jesus, after He had spoken to them, was taken up into heaven, and sitteth on the right hand of God. But they went forth and preached everywhere, the Lord working withal, and confirming the word with signs that followed."

Here also the power comes direct from Christ; it is universal in its range and permanent in duration; it is given to the Apostolic Body, and St. Mark attaches to it the perpetual accompaniment of miraculous effects, which he connects with the session of our Lord at the right hand of God, as witnessing to the truth of the Apostolic mission; and not only so, but as further implying that so long as the session at the right hand of

God continues, the divine effects which proceed from it shall continue also.

It is remarkable that St. Mark's Gospel, which is the Gospel of Peter, set forth by his disciple at his instance, is the only one of the four which does not record either the promise or the conveyance of the special power bestowed upon Peter.

3. St. Luke's record is this : Our Lord coming to the Apostles on the evening of His Resurrection bestows upon them His peace ; convinces them that He has risen again ; eats with them ; illuminates their mind to understand the Scriptures and the need of His Passion. "And He said to them, Thus it is written, and thus it behoved Christ to suffer, and to rise again from the dead the third day ; and that penance and remission of sins should be preached in His name to all nations, beginning at Jerusalem. And you are witnesses of these things. And behold I send the promise of my Father upon you ; but stay you in the city until you be indued with power from on high. And He led them out as far as Bethania, and lifting up His hands, He blessed them. And it came to pass while He blessed them He departed from them and was carried up into heaven."

Luke completes his account in the Acts, where he says our Lord " showed Himself alive, after His Passion, to the Apostles whom He had chosen by many proofs, for forty days appearing to them and speaking of the kingdom of God. And eating together with them He commanded them that they should not depart from Jerusalem, but should wait for the promise of the Father, which you have heard, saith He, by My mouth. For John indeed baptized with water, but you shall be baptized with the Holy Ghost not many days hence. They, therefore, who were come together asked Him, saying, Lord, wilt Thou at this time restore again the kingdom to Israel? But He said to them, It is not for you to know the times or moments which the Father hath put in His own power; but you shall receive the power of the Holy Ghost coming upon you, and you shall be witnesses unto Me in Jerusalem, and in all Judea, and Samaria, and even to the uttermost part of the earth. And when He had said these things, while they looked on, He was raised up, and a cloud received Him out of their sight."

The power thus promised as about to be bestowed in terms so concise and yet so simple, as "the promise of the Father sent down by the Son," "the power from on high," "the power of the Holy Ghost coming upon you," is afterwards described in the events which took place on the Day of Pentecost, which therefore supplement or give their full meaning to St. Luke's account of the transmission of spiritual authority. It is a power coming down on the Apostles in a Body direct from Christ—the power, in fact, which makes the Church to be what she is; it is a visible descent of that perpetual presence of the Holy Ghost within her which is her life, by which she is the kingdom of God on earth—a power universal and permanent.

It is given to the Apostolic College collectively, and

there is no mention here of a special power given to Peter. But St. Luke in his account of the Last Supper introduces in a manner peculiar to himself a special prerogative promised by our Lord to Peter. To gather its whole force, it is necessary carefully to study the context in which it is found.

Immediately after his reference to the institution of the Lord's Supper and the announcement that there was one among them who should betray his Lord, St. Luke writes: "And there was also a strife among them which of them should seem to be greater. And He said to them, The kings of the Gentiles lord it over them; and they that have power over them are called beneficent. But you not so; but he that is the greater among you, let him become as the younger, and he that is the leader, as he that serveth. For which is greater, he that sitteth at table or he that serveth? Is not he that sitteth at table? but I am in the midst of you as he that serveth. And you are they who have continued with Me in My temptations; and I dispose to you, as My Father has disposed to Me, a kingdom; that you may eat and drink at My table in My kingdom, and may sit upon thrones judging the twelve tribes of Israel. And the Lord said, Simon, Simon, behold Satan has desired to have you, that he may sift you as wheat. But I have prayed for thee, that thy faith fail not; and thou being once converted, confirm thy brethren. Who said to Him, Lord, I am ready to go with Thee both into prison and to death. And He said, I say to thee, Peter, the cock shall not crow this day till thou thrice deniest that thou knowest Me. And He said to them, When I sent you without purse and scrip and shoes, did you want anything? But they said, Nothing. Then said He unto them, But now, he that hath a purse let him take it, and likewise a scrip, and he that hath not, let him sell his coat and buy a sword. For I say unto you that this which is written must yet be fulfilled in Me, 'And with the wicked was He reckoned.' For the things concerning Me have an end. But they said, Lord, behold here are two swords. And He said to them, It is enough."

We may judge of the importance of this conversation by the fact that the space given to it by St. Luke makes much more than half of his whole record, so far as the events are concerned which took place in the upper chamber, while it exceeds the whole record of those events given either by St. Matthew or St. Mark. In fact, it constitutes the main addition which St. Luke has made to the record of the first two Evangelists, and, viewed as that addition, it specially draws our notice to his reason for inserting it. The incident thus dwelt upon by St. Luke with so much detail is omitted not only by St. Matthew and St. Mark, but by St. John also. If we view the narrative of the Passion as a whole, given by the four Evangelists, it is as special a contribution to it by St. Luke as the conversation given by St. John.

And here, first, it may be again remarked, that our knowledge of the institution either of the Priesthood or of the Blessed Sacrament did not depend upon its record in the Gospels, because both were institutions of the divine kingdom carried into effect before the Gospels were published, and exhibited in the daily action of the Church. But our knowledge of a contest having arisen among the Apostles at the very time our Lord was speaking of one out of the Apostolic College itself who was to betray Him—a contest the subject of which regarded the person who should be the greater in that College—does depend upon the written record of it; and the selection of it to occupy so large a part in so short a narrative, as well as to form almost the whole addition which St. Luke was to contribute to the previous record of St. Matthew and St. Mark, shows that something was contained in it which was to be kept in perpetual remembrance among Christians.

First, then, our Lord does not put aside this contest, but proceeds to determine it. He draws the strongest contrast between heathen domination, such as it both was then and had been in past time, and Christian government, which as yet was not, but was to be. "The kings of the earth lord it over them, and they that have power over them are called beneficent. But you not so; but he that is the greater among you, let him become as the younger, and he that is the leader as he that serveth." Thus "a greater" and "a leader" in the Apostolic College is pointed out as to be. But it is also pointed out that the type and example of this superior is our Lord Himself. It is the character of one who represents Him. "For which is greater, he that sitteth at table or he that serveth? Is not he that sitteth at table? But I am in the midst of you as he that serveth." If the character of our Lord's example is here pointed at on the one hand, on the other the greatness of the rule to be exercised is indicated. In both, in the character of the rule as being a service to those who are ruled, and as representing our Lord Himself, the application makes itself felt. The superior was to exercise not a domination which had become the mark of Gentile kings, but a service for the good of the governed such as Christ in all His ministry had shown. The words recorded by St. Luke bring back those recorded by St. John, which our Lord had uttered just before: "Know you what I have done to you? You call me Master and Lord, and you say well, for so I am. If then I, being your Lord and Master, have washed your feet, you also ought to wash one another's feet. For I have given you an example, that as I have done to you, so you do also." If this had been all which St. Luke had recorded, the existence of a Superior in the Church after the pattern of Christ Himself might have been inferred as to come.

But our Lord then proceeds to speak positively of a kingdom which He was setting up, and of the place in it which the Apostles should hold: "And you are they who have continued with me in my temptations; and I dispose to you, as my Father hath disposed to me, a kingdom; that you may eat and drink at my table, in my kingdom, and may sit upon thrones, judging the twelve tribes of Israel." From these words we gather that in the kingdom thus announced there should be not only one Superior after the pattern of Christ—"the greater and the leader"—but the College of the twelve, sitting on thrones, and judging the whole people of God. The kingdom and its rulers are correlative and co-enduring. And is not the whole of the order of the Episcopate symbolised in these words, as well as the distinctive rank of the twelve Apostles? For do not they in their heirs carry on through the whole duration of the kingdom on earth the mysteries of that wonderful priesthood instituted at this moment, eating and drinking at His table in His kingdom, and judging His people in the tribunal which has reference to it?

This interpretation seems intimated in the words which follow, in which an attack is spoken of as to be made upon all the rulers of this kingdom; and not, as it would seem, a passing, but a continuing attack. "And the Lord said, Simon, Simon, behold Satan hath desired to have you, that he may sift you as wheat. But I have prayed for thee, that thy faith fail not; and thou, being once converted, confirm thy brethren." He singles out one Apostle, and speaking of the whole Body in the plural as the object of the attack, declares that He has prayed for that one, that he may be able, at a future time, when he has been converted, to confirm his brethren. Peter, supposing that our Lord spoke of the actual moment, said to Him, "Lord, I am ready to go with Thee both into prison and to death. And He said, I say to thee, Peter, the cock shall not crow this day, till thou thrice deniest that thou knowest Me."

Thus pointedly did our Lord exclude the time then present from that at which Peter should confirm his brethren; and the event showed that, so far from confirming them during the night of the Passion and the subsequent Crucifixion, his faith and his conduct conspicuously failed: while all deserted Him and fled, he denied Him.

But of what time, then, did our Lord speak? of what attack? of what confirmation to be rendered by Peter?

The words which follow seem to give an answer to these questions. "And He said to them, When I sent you without purse, and scrip, and shoes, did you want anything? But they said, Nothing. Then said He unto them, But now he that hath a purse, let him take it, and likewise a scrip, and he that hath not, let him sell his coat, and buy a sword. For I say to you, that this that is written must yet be fulfilled in Me, ' And with the wicked was He reckoned.' For the things concerning Me have an end. And they said, Lord, behold here are two swords. And He said to them, It is enough."

What is this but that our Lord contrasts all the time of His ministry, when He was with them, their visible Master, Lord, and Comforter, when He sent them forth with instructions, after fulfilling which they were to return to Him, with another period—that in which the things concerning Him had an end: when He was to be taken from them: when they were to go forth in His power, but without the resource of His visible Headship and the comfort of His visible presence. That period is the whole time during which the apostolic ministry —the eating and drinking at His table, and the sitting on thrones judging the twelve tribes of Israel—continues. During all this time the attack of which our Lord spoke is going on: there is one who desires to have them that he may sift them as wheat: there is one also whose faith, in virtue of our Lord's prayer, fails not, and who is appointed to "confirm his brethren." Peter and the eleven, as individual men, passed away and went to their reward; but the kingdom of which our Lord was speaking, and which He disposed to them, did not pass, nor by consequence its rulers, neither those who were to be sifted as wheat, nor he who was to confirm his brethren. Thus during all that time which was to begin after His passion, death, and resurrection, when the kingdom was disposed to the Apostles, when the apostolic ministry was being carried on, and when the undying enmity of the great enemy was to be shown in the persistence of his attack, the chaff is burnt, the wheat is sifted, and the Confirmer, after having been converted, is in the midst of his brethren and performs his work.

Thus completely does our Lord answer the question of the strife which had arisen among the Apostles, and so great is the pertinence of the narrative thus introduced by St. Luke, so important its bearing upon all future history. If, then, these fifteen verses be considered in their whole context, not forgetting that they constitute the insertion of a totally new incident, in which consists mainly the addition made by St. Luke to the two points which are common to his own record and that of the first and second Evangelist, that is, the declaration of our Lord as to the disciple who should betray Him, and the institution of the Blessed Eucharist, it will appear that St. Luke distinguishes Peter from the other Apostles, and the power promised to him of confirming his brethren from the powers given to him in common with them, no less markedly than St. Matthew and St. John, though in quite other language. And it must be added that, as his narrative in the Acts of what took place on the Day of Pentecost completes his statement in his Gospel concerning that "promise of the Father," and "power of the Holy Ghost" coming down, with which the Apostles were to be endued; so his narrative, from the Day of Pentecost through eleven chapters of the Acts, to the end of the time during which he speaks of the whole College of the Apostles, their preaching and miracles, illustrates what is meant in his Gospel by the special office here promised to Peter of "confirming his brethren." For Peter throughout appears at the head of the Apostles: his Primacy is exhibited in action from the first mention on the Day of Pentecost itself, as in the words, "Peter, standing up with the eleven, lifted up his voice and spoke to them;" while his supervision of the whole work, which comprises the first period of the Church's history, while the Apostles acted in one country together and until they separated, is stated in the words, "Peter, as he went through, visiting all," which indeed may be said to be a compendium of the whole narrative. And of him alone is it recorded that, when he was in prison, "prayer was made without ceasing by the Church unto God for him."

This, then, is the testimony of St. Luke considered as a whole, contained partly in the Gospel, partly in the Acts, as to the transmission of spiritual power, and such is the very remarkable addition which he contributes to the narrative given by his predecessors, St. Matthew and St. Mark.

4. The testimony of St. John as to the transmission of spiritual power may be divided, as in the cases of St. Matthew and St. Luke, into the promises which he records as made before our Lord's Passion and the fulfilment which he records as made after His resurrection.

The promises are contained in that same wondrous discourse of our Lord to His Apostles, of which St. Luke has preserved for us another portion in the passage just transcribed. They are given to the apostolic Body collectively, and, so far as they refer to this particular point, the transmission of spiritual power, are contained in the following verses:—

"Whatsoever you shall ask the Father in My name, that will I do: that the Father may be glorified in the Son. If you shall ask Me anything in My name, that will I do.—And I will ask the Father, and He shall give you another Paraclete, that He may abide with you for ever: the Spirit of truth, whom the world cannot receive, because it seeth Him not, nor knoweth Him: but you shall know Him, because He shall abide with you, and shall be in you. I will not leave you orphans:

I will come to you.—These things have I spoken to you, abiding with you. But the Paraclete, the Holy Ghost, whom the Father will send in My name, He will teach you all things, and bring all things to your mind, whatsoever I shall have said to you. Peace I leave with you, My peace I give unto you: not as the world giveth, do I give unto you.—If you abide in Me, and My words abide in you, you shall ask whatsoever you will, and it shall be done unto you.—You have not chosen Me: but I have chosen you; and have appointed you, that you should go, and should bring forth fruit; and your fruit should remain: that whatsoever you shall ask of the Father in My name, He may give it you.—I tell you the truth: it is expedient to you that I go: for if I go not, the Paraclete will not come to you: but if I go, I will send Him to you.—But when He, the Spirit of truth, is come, He will teach you all truth. For He shall not speak of Himself: but what things soever He shall hear, He shall speak, and the things that are to come He shall show you. He shall glorify Me: because He shall receive of Mine, and show it to you.—And in that day you shall not ask Me anything. Amen, amen, I say to you: if you ask the Father anything in My name, He will give it you.—Sanctify them in truth. Thy word is truth. As thou hast sent Me into the world, I also have sent them into the world."

In these words our Lord foretells and promises the coming of the Paraclete to His Apostles, whom He would send to them from His Father, and the perpetual possession of truth which the Paraclete, by His presence, would confer upon them, and our Lord also says how He would bestow on them His own mission, received from the Father. There was the promise of a vast and manifold spiritual power involved in these things, which we do not attempt to draw out; but we pass to the record of St. John as to the bestowal of spiritual power made by our Lord on the eve of His resurrection to the assembled Apostles. A clear and striking connection and correspondence between the bestowal and the promise are here to be seen. An interval of three days only in time had taken place, but in it the passion and resurrection of our Lord had been accomplished.

"Now when it was late that same day, the first day of the week, and the doors were shut, where the disciples were gathered together for fear of the Jews, Jesus came and stood in the midst, and said to them: Peace be to you. And when He had said this, He shewed them His hands and His side. The disciples therefore were glad when they saw the Lord. He said therefore to them again: Peace be to you. As the Father hath sent Me, I also send you. When He had said this, He breathed on them; and He said to them: Receive ye the Holy Ghost. Whose sins you shall forgive, they are forgiven them: and whose sins you shall retain, they are retained."

In these few words, addressed to the Apostles together, our Lord would seem to have conveyed a power as universal and as direct from Himself as that contained in the corresponding passages of the three preceding Evangelists. Nothing could be wanting to that mission of which it is said, "As the Father hath sent Me, I also send you;" nothing to the fulness of the grace communicated by the Lord breathing on them, and saying, "Receive ye the Holy Ghost;" while the concluding words coincide exactly with the promise made to the Apostles in St. Matthew, that they should receive the power to forgive or to retain sins. In this interview with His Apostles on the evening of the day of His resurrection, He conveys to them the full apostolate in terms the simplicity of which is only equalled by their majesty.

Had the testimony of St. John stopped here, it would have seemed to give to the Apostles every attribute of power needed for their work. And it is to be noted that St. Peter was present with his brethren, St. Thomas alone being absent, and so, notwithstanding his recent fall, was included in that grant to the Apostolic College.

But St. John, in the last chapter of his Gospel, has added to it a record of that famous scene wherein our Lord bestowed on Peter singly a power as universal as that contained in the fourfold promise recorded by St. Matthew, a power also completely including the power given collectively to the Apostles in the four Evangelists. Indeed, we seem to hear the same voice sounding which said, "The kings of the Gentiles lord it over them, and they that have power over them are called beneficent. But you not so; but he that is the greater among you, let him become as the younger, and he that is the leader as he that serveth:" when the Lord said to Peter,

"Simon, son of John, lovest thou Me more than these? Feed My lambs: be shepherd over My sheep; feed My sheep." How else was it possible for Eternal Love to give so stupendous a charge and power in language so tender?

But considering that our Lord had already bestowed a mission on the Apostles collectively, which He likened to the mission received by Himself from the Father, what could these words mean save the universal pastorship of the flock of Christ? What *more* could Peter receive than the others, in answer to his greater love for his Master, except this?

The passages which we have now cited contain the whole account which we possess, as written in the Gospels, of the spiritual authority first promised, and then communicated by Christ to the Apostles and to Peter.

They comprehend two classes of passages, those which regard the Apostolic .College collectively, and those which regard Peter singly. And this division is made the more remarkable by the fact that no power is either promised or conveyed to any Apostle distinctly from the rest except to Peter.

In estimating their relative force, on the one hand, the full meaning must be given to each of these classes; on the other, no interpretation can be admitted which puts one class into conflict with the other. That interpretation alone can be sound which binds them in one harmonious whole.

If we take the passages which we have above cited,

and which are addressed to the Apostles collectively, that is, Matt. xxviii. 18 20, Mark xvi. 15-20, Luke xxiv. 46-49, with Acts i. 3-9, and the passages from our Lord's last discourse in St. John together with John xx. 21-23, we find them to contain an universal supernatural power which is conveyed to a Body consisting of the Apostles, and which is coextensive with the needs of that Body, and which lasts so long as the Body is to last. Moreover, the language used by each Evangelist is sufficient by itself, without reference to the others, to express the conveyance of this power, but at the same time the language of each several Evangelist corresponds to the meaning of the others.

If we take the passages addressed to Peter singly, that is, Matt. xvi. 17-19, Luke xxii. 31, 32, John xxi. 15-17, we find a power of Headship superadded to the former power which had been conveyed to the Apostles as a College. This Headship is conveyed in various expressions, such as the Rock on which the divine House is built, while to it the promise of perpetual stability is attached; the Keys, which indicate the supreme power in the divine Kingdom; the power to bind and to loose everything in heaven and earth, as given not to a collective Body, but to one singly, which distinction in the terms of the grant greatly enlarges the authority of the recipient by removing all restraint arising from common action; the Confirming the brethren in the divine Family; the Pastorship of the divine Flock. Each of these five things indicates sovereignty; together they express it with cumulative evidence: but each of these five things also indicates not collective sovereignty given to a college of men, but the sovereignty proper to a single person.

These passages in three several Evangelists addressed to Peter singly correspond to each other even more closely than the former class of passages corresponds to each other, and the power conveyed in them is a power more definitely marked than the power conveyed in the other.

Again, the two classes of passages, as given in the several Evangelists, may be separately compared in the case of each; as Matt. xxviii. 18-20, given to the College, with Matt. xvi. 17-19, promised to the individual; as Luke xxiv. 46-49 and Acts i. 3-9, as said to all, with Luke xxii. 31, 32, prophesied of Peter singly; and, lastly, the various words addressed to the Apostles collectively in the discourse after the Last Supper, and the gift of the Holy Ghost breathed on them together in John xx. 21-23, with the charge to Peter alone recorded in John xxi. 15-17. The result of the most careful and accurate comparison will be to see that the full power given to the Apostolic College in the concluding words of St. Matthew's Gospel is not interfered with by the Headship promised to Peter in chap. xvi. 17-19: that in Luke, the power from on high, and again the power of the Holy Ghost coming down upon the Apostolic College, do not exclude the confirming power promised to one of them: that in John, the universal Apostolic mission and the imparting of the Holy Ghost, bestowed by Christ upon the Apostles in common, so far from being opposed to the universal Pastorship conferred upon Peter by our Lord on the shore of the lake, receive as it were their completion and crown in the privileges of the Head.

It may be noted that in St. Mark alone, the Evangelist who wrote from St. Peter's side and at his direction, there is an absence of this distinction of passages, some of which relate to the Apostles collectively, others to Peter singly. He gives only one class of passages, that which expresses the powers given to the Apostles in common. But Matthew and Luke, while they record only the first class of passages relating to powers given after the Resurrection, record also singular promises made to Peter by our Lord before His Passion. St. John alone, writing last, and in that purpose of supplementing the preceding Gospels which so remarkably belongs to him, gives both words addressed and powers assigned after the Resurrection to the Apostles collectively, and words addressed and powers assigned to Peter singly. His record of the creation of the universal Pastorship following upon his record of the apostolic mission, following also the promise of the Holy Ghost to dwell perpetually with the Apostles, and the gift of the Holy Ghost breathed upon them from His mouth, seems to bind together in one harmony the whole narrative in the four Gospels of the power given by our Lord for the establishment of His Church. "As My Father sent Me, I also send you," addressed to a company of men, and the gift of the Holy Ghost accompanied with the power to remit or retain the sins of men, seem to embrace all the powers of the Apostolate.

So, too, the words in the promise, "When He, the Spirit of truth, be come, He shall lead you by the hand into all truth," seem to embrace the whole gift of maintaining revealed truth in the world; while the solemn charge, thrice given, and in the presence of his brethren, to feed the sheep of Christ, addressed to one singly, contains all the powers of the Primacy.

St. Luke says of our Lord, that "He showed Himself alive after His Passion, by many proofs, for forty days appearing to the Apostles, and speaking of the kingdom of God." We have cited all that we possess in the written record of that intercourse, so far, that is, as concerns the government of the kingdom which He was establishing. It would be a great error to suppose that what we possess in the written record is all that took place. There is a double warning of St. John given to prevent precisely such an error. Immediately after his account of our Lord's first and second appearance to the Apostles together, he adds, "Many other signs also did Jesus in the sight of His disciples, which are not written in this book. But these are written that you may believe that Jesus is the Christ, the Son of God, and that, believing, you may have life in His name." And immediately after his record of the Pastorship conferred on Peter, he closes his Gospel with the words, "But there are also many other things which Jesus did, which, if they were written every one, the world itself, I think, would not be able to contain the books that should be written."

The inference from these passages would be the same

which meditation on the whole subject would suggest, that in the great forty days between His Resurrection and Ascension our Lord instructed His Apostles perfectly in all which they needed to know concerning the kingdom of God for the execution of their office as God's ministers for its propagation. Under this head would fall the number and nature of the sacraments, their ritual—in short, the government of the Church as a spiritual society. Of the details which regarded these subjects, nothing was made known in the writings, of which even the first in time, the Gospel of St. Matthew, began to be published many years after the Church had been carried on in its appointed order. The simple statement of such a fact is enough to show that for the Christians themselves such details were not needed to be expressed in a writing which might fall into other than Christian hands; while to lay them open to the heathen empire, in the midst of which the Church was rising, would have constituted a gratuitous danger, and would have contradicted what we know to have been the discipline of discretion long practised during the era of persecution. It was precisely the polity of the Church at which the Roman State would take umbrage. Thus the powers which are requisite for establishing and perpetuating this polity were recorded as having been conveyed to the Apostles under general heads. The language used for this purpose has a terseness, a concentration, a sublimity which betokens the voice of a Sovereign, the fiat of a Legislator. It befits the Person of the Word in the construction of His divine work. It harmonises admirably with those eight words upon the Mount which sustain and reveal a whole fabric of divine philosophy and Christian life.

Thus the central mystery of divine love, carrying in it the perpetual presence of the Incarnate God in His Church and the institution of the Priesthood, is referred to in the briefest terms, as given to the Apostles by our Lord on the eve of His Passion: "This do in commemoration of Me." The authority which He bestowed on them after His Resurrection is, as St. Matthew states it, a power to confer sacraments and to teach all nations, carrying with it an obligation upon those who are taught of obedience to all which the Apostles should enjoin as commanded by Christ, and a promise of His perpetual presence with them in the fulfilment of the office. As St. Mark states it, a power to teach all nations, to dispense sacraments, and to work miracles, accompanied by the co-operation of Christ sitting at the right hand of God. As St. Luke states it, the promise of the Father sent upon them by Christ; power from on high; power of the Holy Ghost coming upon them; baptism with the Holy Ghost: all which is, in this case, elucidated by what took place on the Day of Pentecost. As St. John states it, such a mission of the Apostles by Christ as Christ received from the Father, and the gift of the Holy Ghost proceeding from the mouth of Christ, together with the power of remitting and retaining sins.

All this was power bestowed upon the Apostles collectively, which Peter, as one of them, shared.

The privileges recorded to have been bestowed on

Peter, if we treat, as we must, the promise and the fulfilment as of equal force, are six—

The first, to be the Rock on which Christ would build His Church.

The second, that to the Church thus founded on the Rock, or to the Rock itself, perpetual continuance and victory are guaranteed.

The third, that the keys of the kingdom of heaven, that is, supreme power in the Lord's house, guardianship of the Lord's city, are committed to him alone.

The fourth, that the power of binding and loosing whatsoever shall be bound or loosed in earth and in heaven is committed to him singly.

The fifth, the power to confirm his brethren, in which name the Apostles are specially indicated, because his own faith shall never fail.

The sixth, the supreme Pastorship of the whole flock of Christ.

Comparing carefully together what is said to the Apostles as a body with what is said to Peter singly, we cannot but be struck with the fact that while they received nothing without him, he received a power including and crowning theirs. The terms of conveyance in the two cases are indeed of similar majesty and simplicity, being the language of God in the sovereign disposition of His gifts; but in the case of Peter there is greater definiteness, and to him our Lord employs constantly the parabolic form of expression, calling him the Rock, giving him the Keys, committing to him singly the binding and loosing, and the confirmation of the brethren, which is the image of a tower or structure held together in one mass, charging him finally with the Pastorship of the flock of Christ. This imagery is capable of wider application than any other form of speaking, and as we know by the instance of the parables, contains in it an amount of instruction which direct language can only convey at a much greater length. None of it is given to any Apostle by himself, except Peter; what the rest receive of it together, as in the case of the power of binding and loosing, first promised and then given to them collectively, is greatly exceeded by what he receives alone. And besides, their commission and his throw light upon each other. The Papacy and the Episcopate are their joint result. Give its full force to the Apostolic commission, and Christ is with the one universal Episcopate all days to the consummation of the world. Give the same full force to the words bestowed upon Peter, and he feeds the flock of Christ until the second coming of the Great Shepherd. Perpetuity enters equally into both.

There is thus accordance in the four Gospels and the Acts of the Apostles as to the persons to whom transmission of spiritual power in the Church was made. The Gospels and the Acts record in the form of narrative the institution of the divine kingdom from its beginning and before it was carried into effect. But there is another inspired writer who speaks of it incidentally in his Epistles after it had been in operation between twenty and forty years. The eminence of St. Paul as the Preacher of the Gentiles is so great that we may endeavour to put together his testimony concerning the constitution of that Church which he loved so well, and for which he gave his life.

And, first, it is from him we derive that name of the Church which, more perhaps than any other, expresses her nature, and identifies her with our Lord. The Church to St. Paul is "the Body of Christ." "As the human body," he says, "is one and has many members, and all the members of the body, whereas they are many, yet are one body, so also is Christ. For in one Spirit were we all baptized into one body, whether Jews or Gentiles, whether bond or free; and in one Spirit we have all been made to drink." "There are," he says, "diversities of graces, but the same Spirit; and there are diversities of ministries, but the same Lord; and diversities of operations, but the same God who worketh all in all;" and saying this to the Corinthian disciples he well-nigh repeats it to the Roman. To him, therefore, the whole structure of the Church's government is divine, as drawn from Christ's Person, as animated by His Spirit, as the work of the Eternal Father in and through the Son whom He has sent, and by the Spirit whom He has also sent. And again, as he thus wrote in the middle of his course to his Corinthian converts, so nearly at the end of it he expressed to the beloved Church of Ephesus, the fruit of so many toils, the same doctrine. This passage is sufficient of itself to give the complete Pauline conception of the Church as it was present to his mind in the whole range of time, stretching from the first to the second coming of our Lord. "I therefore, a prisoner in the Lord, beseech you that you walk worthy of the vocation in which you are called, with all humility and mildness, with patience, supporting one another in charity, careful to keep the unity of the Spirit in the bond of peace. One Body and one Spirit: as you are called in one hope of your calling. One Lord, one faith, one baptism. One God and Father of all, who is above all, and through all, and in us all. But to every one of us is given grace according to the measure of the giving of Christ. Wherefore He saith: Ascending on high He led captivity captive; He gave gifts to men. Now that He ascended, what is it, but that He also descended first into the lower parts of the earth. He that descended is the same also that ascended above all the heavens, that He might fill all things. And He gave some apostles, and some prophets, and other some evangelists, and other some pastors and doctors for the perfecting of the saints unto the work of the ministry, unto the edifying of the Body of Christ: until we all meet into the unity of faith, and of the knowledge of the Son of God, unto a perfect man, unto the measure of the age of the fulness of Christ: that henceforth we be no more children tossed to and fro, and carried about with every wind of doctrine by the wickedness of men, by cunning craftiness by which they lie in wait to deceive: but doing the truth in charity, we may in all things grow up in Him who is the Head, even Christ: from whom the whole Body, being compacted and fitly joined together, by what every joint supplieth, according to the operation in the measure of every part, maketh increase of the body unto the edifying of itself in charity."

Are not these words a divine comment from the Apostle himself upon what he means by the Body of Christ? It is no figure of speech, but the grandest reality in the universe. The words contain the beginning, middle, and end of his belief concerning the instrument of our salvation. It is an inspired summary of the record in the Gospels which we have been so long considering. Its compass reaches from the ascension above the heavens to the completion "of the perfect man" in the fulness of the mystical Body, when all the labours and sufferings of earth are at an end. It places the security against error of doctrine, as well as the growth of charity in the working together of one ministry through the whole Church, and through all time, not only drawn from the institution of Christ, but enclosed in the sacred structure of His Body; nor can we conceive of any preaching of the Gospel without a divine mission derived from Christ through this ministry, as he elsewhere wrote to the Roman Church: "How shall they call on Him in whom they have not believed? or how shall they believe Him of whom they have not heard? or how shall they hear without a preacher? and how shall they preach except they be sent?" There is, in his conception, one mission only in the Body of Christ. The splitting of this Body of Christ into two or three parts would be simply the destruction of St. Paul's conception, not an atom of it would remain. There is, in his conception, but one ministry, in unity and harmony with itself, the guardian and the propagator of the truth—Bishops existing outside this one divine ministry and exercising authority are a complete denial of the whole idea.

It is in exact accordance with these passages that St. Paul, in his pastoral letter to his disciple St. Timotheus, reminds him of the grace of God derived to him by the imposition of the Apostle's hands, and the hands of the Presbytery. He speaks manifestly of a divine gift descending through the hands of men from Christ, "who, ascending up on high, gave some apostles, some prophets," and the rest.

Again, it is after a strict and precise charge to St. Timotheus respecting the quality of the persons whom he should choose for the office of the episcopate that St. Paul winds up with the words: "These things I write to thee, hoping that I shall come to thee shortly, but if I tarry long that thou mayest know how thou oughtest to behave thyself in the house of God, which is the Church of the living God, the pillar and ground of the truth." Here then, also, as in the letter to the Ephesians, he describes the divinely appointed ministry as bearing and upholding the truth which it is charged to impart; so that St. Augustine was putting St. Paul's doctrine forth when he wrote, "I should not believe the Gospel unless the authority of the Catholic Church moved me thereto."[1] According to St. Paul's mind, it is the living ministry which carries to the world the knowledge "of the living God," a knowledge which

[1] Contr. Epist. Manichæi, cap. 5, tom. 8, 154.

dwells in "the house of God" alone. Outside the house the truth is corrupted, and the ministry loses its gift.

From the union of these passages, to which many more of like import might be added, we learn that the unity of the Church, in St. Paul's idea and expression, rests upon the very deepest foundation, the unity of Christ's Person as receiving a mission from the Father, which He accomplishes in His own Body, and by the working of His Spirit. If the promise to St. Peter and its fulfilment were for a moment put out of sight, yet this divine unity testified in St. Paul's letters would still remain in all its force, and could not be disregarded without giving up St. Paul's mind altogether. How can it be accomplished except by means of the promises given and the charge imposed on St. Peter? Thus St. Paul, in testifying directly to the unity, a witness the depth, precision, force, and tenderness of which no one can deny, testifies indirectly to the means by which it is obtained. If there be one ministry discharging in the Body of Christ the functions which St. Paul assigns to it, there must be the organ also by which that ministry remains one. Nor does it follow less that, as the ministry is visible and permanent, so likewise must the organ of its unity be visible and permanent. And if St. John records, in the most emphatic manner, the universal pastorship bestowed on Peter by his Lord, St. Paul sets forth as a reality the unity thus created in a symbol more striking, if possible, than the flock of the One Shepherd, for it is the Body of the One Lord. If the Apostle who lay on our Lord's breast and heard Him declare Himself to be the good Shepherd who gives His life for His sheep, recorded the transmission of that charge to St. Peter under that same figure of the Shepherd in the injunction to feed the lambs and the sheep of Christ, St. Paul, who was carried up to heaven and heard unspeakable words, saw from his prison in Rome, through the whole vast period from our Lord's first to His second coming, the growth of that sacred Body which was to fill all in all, compacted together of the apostles, doctors, and pastors, whom at the beginning Christ gave, whom He would continue to the end to give; for does it not run, " until we all meet into the unity of the faith and of the knowledge of the Son of God, unto a perfect man, unto the measure of the age of the fulness of Christ." In all this St. Paul declares that, so long as the Church is militant, her ministry is the organ of truth, and this because the Church is the Body of Christ.

Thus it is a great and striking harmony with the witness of the Gospels and of the Acts to the transmission of Spiritual Power in the Church which the vessel of election, the Preacher of the Gentiles, contributes. Thus the figure of St. Peter stands in the New Testament between St. Matthew and St. John, supporting him on one side, and St. Paul and St. Luke on the other.

Nothing can be clearer than the mind of St. Paul in these passages. To him the fabric of government is inseparably united with the fabric of doctrine. It is one and the same institution which is indivisible in its organic structure and infallible in the truth which it upbears and expounds. He sets forth a Creed at the same moment that he describes a Body. The Creed and the Body make one thing. St. Paul's doctrine of unity is part of his conception of truth. The Church, the Body of Christ, is as completely possessed by all the truth which came by Jesus Christ as it is dowered with the grace which also came by Him. And the Christian ministry, viewed as a whole, as the mantle dropped by Him who, ascending up on high, led captivity captive, and gave gifts to men, is that wherein the double gift of truth and grace resides indefeasibly.

I pass to another point in St. Paul's teaching. Do the recipients of the government which in general and in particular he thus describes receive it from above or below? Does the magistracy draw its authority from a charge which the community bestows, or from a power which creates the community itself? Which is first both in principle and in time, the magistracy or the community?

There are six names by which, in various parts of his epistles, St. Paul describes the commission in virtue of which he spent his life and finally poured forth his blood in preaching the Gospel. These six names are apostle, minister, doctor, steward, ambassador, and herald. Sometimes they are mentioned singly, sometimes they are blended with each other in a way which sheds light upon them reciprocally. He terms himself an ambassador, when he says, "for Christ, therefore, we are ambassadors, God as it were exhorting by us." And he beseeches his converts to pray for him "that speech may be given me that I may open my mouth with confidence, to make known the mystery of the Gospel, for which I am an ambassador in a chain."[1] He refers all his power back to God when he says, " Our sufficiency is from God, who also has made us fit ministers of the New Testament," for this word, the original of deacons, signifies here a ministry to God, not a service of men. The sufficiency was that God had accredited certain men to bear to their fellow-men a certain document, a new covenant. They stood in the relation of ministers to Him who appointed them; to those to whom they came they were the commissioned agents of a sovereign. He calls himself also a steward,[2] where he says, " Let a man so account of us as the servants of Christ, and the dispensers of the mysteries of God. Here now it is required in dispensers that a man be found faithful; but to me it is a very small thing to be judged by you, or by man's day,—but He that judgeth me is the Lord." And in another place he very remarkably joins together three terms which he applies to himself, while he specially connects them with the source and head of all power in that work of the dispensation which He became man to accomplish. St. Paul breaks into a sort of creed, which is like a summary of his whole message, in these most solemn words which he addresses to the archbishop whom he had himself set in the great see of Ephesus: "There is one God and one Mediator of God and men, the man Christ Jesus, who

---

[1] 2 Cor. v. 20; Ephes. vi. 19, 20; 2 Cor. iii. 6.
[2] 1 Cor. iv. 1: ὑπηρέτας χριστόυ καὶ οἰκονόμους μυστηρίων Θεοῦ.

gave Himself a redemption for all, a testimony in due times. Whereunto I am appointed a herald and an apostle (I say the truth, I lie not), a doctor of the Gentiles, in faith and truth." And he joins the same three names together in another letter to the same Bishop, "The Gospel whereunto I am appointed a herald and an apostle and a doctor of the Gentiles.[1] The original word herald was rendered by preacher; and the term Apostle has become so fixed as the name of those to whom our Lord committed His Church in chief, that the lesson as to the source of the authority which it bears in its meaning of "the sent," has been impaired to many minds. A multitude of men preach in these days without any notion that a preacher is a man who bears a divine commission from a Sovereign to announce pardon to His people, and that a man who chooses himself for such a function is an impostor. Now what I wish to remark of these six terms, by which St. Paul expresses his own authority and that of the brethren who held the like rank with himself, is that they all concur in deriving the power and the commission which they represent from the person giving it, that is Jesus Christ, in the name of His Father, and not from the people for whose good it is bestowed. The whole publication of the Gospel is, in fact, called "The Proclamation," which the word preacher and preaching no longer conveys. It is the message of a King to His subjects declared by His heralds. They convey it to those who hear it by a commission from above. Their

[1] Tim. ii. 7; 2 Tim. i. 11.

whole authority comes from above, not from below. It is not the election of brethren which is the principle of their mission, but the charge of the Sender, Christ. And as the Apostles were sent, they sent their successors. Election, in subsequent times, however conducted, indicated the person upon whom power fell; but the power was from God.

A further light is thrown upon this most grand and beautiful doctrine of St. Paul as to the Church being the Body of Christ, and her ministry the appointed organ for maintaining divine truth through the whole course of time upon earth, by the magnificent vision bestowed upon the beloved Apostle when he was by command of Domitian a prisoner in the island of Patmos, "for the Word of God and the testimony of Jesus." As he "was in the Spirit on the Lord's day, he heard behind him a great voice as of a trumpet, saying: What thou seest write in a book, and send to the seven Churches which are in Asia, to Ephesus, and to Smyrna, and to Pergamus, and to Thyatira, and to Sardis, and to Philadelphia, and to Laodicia. And I turned to see the voice that spoke with me. And being turned, I saw seven golden candlesticks; and in the midst of the seven golden candlesticks one like to the Son of Man, clothed with a garment down to the feet, and girt about the paps with a golden girdle. And His head and His hairs were white, as white wool and as snow, and His eyes were as a flame of fire, and His feet like unto fine brass, as in a burning furnace. And His voice as the sound of many waters. And He had in His right hand seven stars. And from His mouth came out a sharp two-edged sword: and His face was as the sun shineth in His power. And when I had seen Him, I fell at His feet as dead. And He laid His right hand upon me, saying, Fear not, I am the First and the Last, and He that liveth, and I became dead, and behold I am living for ever and ever, and have the keys of death and of hell. Write, therefore, the things which thou hast seen, and which are, and which must be done hereafter: the mystery of the seven stars which thou sawest in My right hand, and the seven golden candlesticks. The seven stars are the angels of the seven Churches: and the seven candlesticks are seven Churches."

This vision occupies a quite singular position. It is, as it were, the opening scene of that revelation which was made by our Lord to the Apostle of the things that should happen in His Church from His first to His second coming; and which terminates only in the conclusion of the great conflict between the city of God and the city of the devil, when the seer beholds the Holy City "coming down out of heaven from God, prepared as a bride adorned for her husband." It took place rather more than sixty years after the day of Pentecost, when two persecutions of the Church, the first under Nero, and the second under Domitian, had already tried the patience of the saints. Thus it dates a full generation after the time of St. Paul. In accordance with the position which it occupies at the head of a revelation given by the Lord Himself to him,

> "Che vide tutti i tempi gravi,
> Pria che moriose, della bella sposa,
> Che s'acquistò con la lancia e co' chiavi,"

it is a vision of extraordinary power and majesty, repeating, and if possible excelling, the grandeur of similar visions in the old prophets, Isaiah, Ezekiel, and Daniel.[1] Our Lord appears with the incommunicable name of God, as the First and the Last: as the Redeemer, that Living One who became dead and is alive for ever and ever; as the Ruler who orders all things as to the race of man, having the keys of death and of hell; as the world's Teacher, with the sharp sword of the Word, the instrument of His dominion, proceeding out of His mouth; in the glory of the Resurrection, for His face is as the sun shining in his strength. The disciple who lay upon His breast at the Supper, now, when he saw Him, fell as one dead at His feet; but He, deigning to lay His right hand on him, raised him up, and communicated the meaning of the vision: and we learn from our Lord's own words that it showed Him present in the government of His Church. Write, He commanded the seer, the mystery of the seven stars which thou sawest in My right hand, and the seven golden candlesticks. The seven stars are the angels of the seven Churches, and the seven candlesticks which thou sawest are seven Churches. The mystery, He said—and the number seven is mystical. The seven stars represent the whole Episcopate held in the right hand of the Lord:[2] the seven candlesticks the whole number of

---

[1] Isaias vi. 1; Ezech. iv. 32; Dan. vii. 9.

[2] Compare the strikingly similar and almost contemporary passage in the letter of St. Ignatius to the Ephesians: "For Jesus Christ, our inseparable life, is the mind of the Father, as also the bishops, appointed throughout the earth, are in the mind of Christ."

Churches throughout the world: and that He, the Son of Man, is in the midst of them, His perpetual government in and through those whom He has appointed:[1] and the seven letters directed to the seven Churches, may by parity betoken seven ages or conditions of the one Church.[2] For the vision, taken as a whole, exhibits the perpetual action of Christ, not in one place, but in the midst of His people from the beginning to the end. It is thus equivalent to the scope of the entire Apocalypse, at the head of which it stands. It also conveys to us, with the witness of St. John, a complete agreement with the conception of St. Paul as to the unity of the divine mission centred in the Church, and exerted by her Episcopate; as to the relation of that Episcopate to Christ, which in every age is held in His right hand, as in every age He is in the midst of the seven golden candlesticks; as to the relation also of that Episcopate to the people over which it is set: for our Lord commands what He would say to the Churches to be written to their several angels, to express the truth that they summed up in

[1] Baur, Kirchengeschichte der drei ersten Jahrhunderte, p. 272, remarks, "Nicht ohne Grund hat man daher schon in den Engeln, an welche die den sieben Gemeinden der Apocalypse bestimmten Schreiben gerichtet sind, einen Ausdruck der Episcopatsidee gesehen—da die den sieben Engeln entsprechenden Sterne alle zusammen in der Hand Christi sind, in ihm also ihre Einheit haben, so kann durch den Engel, welchen jede Gemeinde hat, nichts anders ausgedrückt sein, als die Beziehung, die sie mit Christus als dem einen Haupte aller Gemeinden und der ganzen Kirche verknüpft."

[2] "Ideo septem scribi ecclesias ut una Catholica septiformi gratiæ spiritu plena designetur."—*Cornel. a L. in loco.* "Wherefore in the Apocalypse the whole Church is represented by the sevenfold number of the Churches."—*St. Greg.*, l. B. 23, *Morals. on Job.* "Propter quod et Johannes Apostolus ad septem scribit ecclesias, eo modo se ostendens ad unius plenitudinem scribere."—*St. Aug. de Civ. Dei*, xvii. 4.

their person the flock committed to them. The stars are in His hand, while He is in the midst of the candlesticks. They are His angels, and their authority lies in the message which they bear from Him, not in any charge deputed to them by those whom they govern. Each letter gathers up the character of the people, in the single person of the angel: "I know thy works, thy labour, and thy patience:" thus expressing the doctrine of St. Cyprian, "the Church is in the Bishop."

Thus St. Paul's truth of the Body of Christ is delineated in the vision of Him who is the First and the Last, who became dead, and who lives for ever and ever, and from whom not only does all spiritual power originally descend, but is perpetually carried in His right hand; which does not leave Him because it is used by human instruments under Him. And if the vision seen by St. John is in perfect agreement with the conception of St. Paul, no less does it agree with, and convey in visible action, that whole account of the origin and transmission of spiritual power which we have been contemplating in the harmony of the Gospels and the Acts. Only it is to be noted that what the Gospels declare is *to be*, the vision exhibits *as being*.

If we take the whole mass of the Scripture testimony respecting the transmission of spiritual power for the government of the Church and the constitution of her polity, four qualities will appear salient: its coming from above; its completeness; its unity; its independence of civil authority.

1. First, the power thus instituted comes down from

Christ upon Peter and the Apostles, and from them upon their successors. It does not spring from election out of the body, but by an exactly reverse process; the body itself springs from it. On the eve of the Passion, just after the institution of the Priesthood, our Lord said: "You have not chosen Me, but I have chosen you, and have appointed you that you should go and should bring forth fruit, and that your fruit should remain."[1] This is the whole order of the divine appointment, from beginning and throughout. The Apostles develop out of themselves ministry and people. This growth Peter's preaching on the day of Pentecost inaugurated, as the power from on high came down upon him and his brethren. The whole history of the Church through the first three centuries is a faithful continuation of this beginning. But here we have to note how every particle of the Scripture record testifies to the spiritual power coming down from above, not rising up from below. The figure of this in the old law was Aaron invested by Moses with the Priesthood in the face of the whole congregation of the children of Israel; the counterpart in the new is Christ ascending to heaven, blessing His brethren as He ascended, and sending down upon them the promise of the Father. Thus the divine polity unfolds itself in a spiritual descent.

2. The second quality is the completeness of this power. The absence of details in the records, far from being an impeachment of this completeness, subserves to its expression, because the power given is summed

[1] John xv. 16.

up in a general head, which embraces all particulars under it. Of this summing up we have in the same Gospel of St. John an instance both in what is said to the Apostles and in what is said to Peter. As to the Apostles, the Incarnation, often called by the Fathers the Dispensation, embraces the whole work of our Lord; not only His coming in our flesh, but His satisfaction for the sins of the world in the flesh assumed. All this was a mission from the Father. Now, in investing His Apostles with power on the evening of the Resurrection, He used this very expression: "As My Father hath sent Me, I also send you." Whatever there was to be done and ordered in the Church from the beginning to the end was, by the force of the similitude with Himself thus used, included in these words. They are truly imperial words, constituting a spiritual empire. So, again, as to St. Peter, our Lord was "the great Pastor of the sheep in the blood of the everlasting testament." As such He had been marked out by prophecy: it was His name of predilection: "I am the Good Shepherd: the Good Shepherd giveth His life for the sheep." Now, this and none other was the term He used when He would convey to Peter, in the concluding words of the last Gospel, supreme authority: "Lovest thou Me more than these? Be shepherd over My sheep." What could be added to this one word? That which we render "Be shepherd" comprehends all offices which government in the divine polity requires. It is the word chosen of old in psalm and prophecy for the sovereignty of the Messiah. First the Psalmist sung, as he

M

recorded the splendid promise of the future King, "Ask of Me, and I will give Thee the Gentiles for Thine inheritance, and the utmost parts of the earth for Thy possession: Thou shalt *rule* them with a rod of iron."

Again, when Herod, assembling all the high priests and scribes of the people, inquired of them when the Christ should be born, they replied to him out of the prophet Micheas, describing by this word the reign of Messiah: "Out of thee shall come forth the Captain that shall *rule* My people Israel."

Again, when the last prophet saw in the Apocalyptic vision the glory of the Word of God going forth as a Conqueror, he described His power in the same expression: "The armies of heaven followed Him on white horses, clothed in linen white and clean. And out of His mouth goes forth a sharp sword, that in it He may strike the nations: and He shall *rule* them with a rod of iron." Our Lord of set purpose selected the one word[1] which conveyed His regal dominion, and bestowed it upon Peter. Nor did He give it with a restricted but with a universal application: "Be shepherd over My sheep." Who can refuse St. Bernard's comment: "What sheep? the people of this or that city, or country, or kingdom? *My* sheep, He said. To whom is it not plain that He did not designate some, but assign all? Nothing is excepted where nothing is distinguished."[2] On the two sides, therefore, the power is

[1] Heb. xiii. 20; John x. 11, xxi. 16; Ps. ii. 9: Sept. Matt ii. 6, in translating Mic. v. 2, where its equivalent is ἄρχοντα τοῦ Ἰσραήλ ; Apoc. xix. 15; the same word, ποιμαίνειν, is used in all these passages.
[2] De Consideratione ad Eugenium Papam, 2, 8.

complete; in its nature, as that specially belonging to Christ; in its subjects, as universal. This one word includes in itself all inferior derivations, whether of episcopal or other subordinate power, and in virtue of it St. Peter becomes the source of the whole episcopate as well as the type or figure of every local Bishop.

If the special conversations between our Lord and the Apostles which passed in the forty days are not recorded for us in their details, as being privileged communications made only to the chiefs of His kingdom, for their guidance, and as instructions to be carried out by them in practice, yet the institution of an everlasting polity by Him is marked out in the two instances of Mission and Rule just cited, as well as in the other passages before collected. In fact, it is in the institution of such a polity that the perfection of our Lord as Lawgiver and Governor consists. Nothing in His kingdom was left to chance, or to sudden expedients arising in unforeseen dangers. All was from the beginning foreseen and provided for. When He said to Peter, "Follow thou Me," which was His interpretation of the commission He had just before given to Peter, and a crucifixion which ensued upon a crowning in the case of the disciple as of the Master, the whole sequence of His Church through the centuries was in His mind and expressed in His voice.

3. But further, the very basis of the Spiritual Power, as delineated in the testimony of Scripture, is so laid in unity, that if unity be broken the idea itself is utterly destroyed.

"The Captain who should rule My people Israel"

presents a very definite idea. "To feed the flock of Christ" is equally definite. The one is the portrait of Christ in prophecy; the other represents His kingdom in history. It is one people and one flock, as it has one King and one Shepherd. So the Rock on which the Church is built is one structure; the confirmation of the brethren is the holding together one family in that one structure. When St. Paul convoked the ancients of the Church at Ephesus, he expressed the duty of Bishops through all time and place: "Take heed to yourselves and to the whole flock, wherein the Holy Ghost hath placed you Bishops, to rule the Church of God, which He has purchased with His own blood." This work of the Holy Ghost was not limited either as to time or as to place, and belongs to the Bishops of the whole world as much as to those who met at Ephesus to receive the farewell of St. Paul. In precisely similar terms St. Peter charged the Bishops whom he had planted in the provinces of Pontus, Galatia, Cappadocia, Asia, and Bithynia, "to feed the flock of God which is among you;" indicating at once the unity of the flock and the unity of the episcopate held by many shepherds. For it is one flock which they rule everywhere; not each a separate fold. A confederation of Bishops, each ruling a fold of his own, would frustrate the divine idea; also it would be difficult to imagine a government more futile, or a spectacle less persuasive to the world. If we take the account of the Church's ministry quoted just above from St. Paul, its unity runs through the whole as much as its descent from above. The Body of Christ expresses both equally. If either part is taken away, the essence is gone. A ministry such as is there described, existing in a dozen different countries of the earth, even if it possessed the same succession and order would present no such idea as the Apostle contemplates, and offer no such guarantee of divine truth as he dwells upon, unless it were organically one. Its witness in one country might otherwise be diverse from its witness in another country; and as each would have the same claim to be heard, the one would neutralise the other. In fact, the Body of Christ would cease to be. So ineffaceably is the Sacrament of Unity impressed on the whole Gospel account of spiritual government. There is not a single promise made nor a single power given except to the whole Church and to the one Church.

4. The three qualities we have described, the coming from above, completeness, unity, are intrinsic to the essence of spiritual government. They form together an external relation of entire independence with regard to civil government. Nothing can be plainer than the fact that Christ came from God, and that He gave to His Apostles, and not to kings or rulers of the world, the Spiritual Power which He meant to transmit. Equally plain is it that the power so given, being complete, could derive nothing intrinsic to its essence from the Civil Authority; and its unity demonstrates in no less a degree its independence of that authority, for it is the same one power everywhere, whereas civil government is both complete and different in each separate State. Thus the independence of the Spiritual Power is

essential to it, as flowing out of the qualities which make it.

When we view the Spiritual Power as possessing inalienably these four qualities, as coming from above, as complete in itself, as one in all lands, and as independent of the Civil Power, the notion of perpetuity will be found to be inherent in the thing so conceived. Again, the promises made to it last as long as the subject to which they belong. As the kingdom of Christ and the flock of Christ are perpetual from His first to His second coming, so therefore is the Bearer of the keys and the Shepherd of the flock. And yet more, the Body of Christ moves through the ages, ever growing to His full stature and measure, so that this living structure can as little fail as Christ Himself. The Head and the Body live on together. Again, the secular power also, over against which and in the midst of which in all lands and times the Spiritual Power stands, is perpetual. The promise made to the College of Apostles, "Behold I am with you all days to the consummation of the world," is an express grant of perpetuity. The promise to Peter that the gates of hell shall not prevail against the Rock, or the Church which is founded on the Rock, is a grant of perpetuity equally express. The same is implied in St. Mark's closing words, that our Lord sat down on the right hand of God, after giving His commission to the Apostles to preach the gospel through the whole world to every creature; and that as they went forth He worked with them, confirming the word by signs following—a work and a confirmation on

His part which should last equally to the end, so long as He was seated at the right hand of God. So equally the promise of the Father, the Paraclete, sent down from above by the Son, is a permanent power by which the Church was originally made and perpetually subsists. All these divine promises cohere and shed light upon each other. Thus the commission to Peter, "Feed My sheep," is universal, not only as to its subject, which is the whole flock of Christ, but as to its duration, which is so long as there is a flock to feed. It was a charge, not only to a person, but to an office. If the thing itself to which it related was to endure, it is obvious that the longer it lasted, and the more it grew, the greater also the need of the office which should upbear it. The duration of the living organism moved by the Head, which St. Paul so strongly attests, and carries on into the unseen world, attests the reciprocal duration of the Head.

As those divine words which convey the promise or confer the gift of the Spiritual Power cohere and shed light on each other, so the impairing them in any particular destroys their idea, which is to say that they express a real and concrete existence, wherein the idea has passed into an adequate act. This is Jesus Christ in His Kingship, the same yesterday, to-day, and for ever.

CHAPTER IV.

THE ACTUAL RELATION BETWEEN CHURCH AND STATE FROM THE DAY OF PENTECOST TO CONSTANTINE.

The Transmission of Spiritual Authority as witnessed in the History of the Church from A.D. 29 *to* A.D. 325.

It was requisite to draw out the full statement of the transmission of Spiritual Power, as recorded in the Scriptures of the Church, before passing to its historical fulfilment. How exactly the fulfilment corresponded to the promise is attested for us by an unexceptionable authority, almost at the end of the first century. This witness was given just before the closing of the Canon of the New Testament itself. It is to be deplored that almost all the early letters of the Sovereign Pontiffs have been lost, but one of the first is extant in the letter of St. Clement of Rome to the Corinthian Church. It belongs to the year 95 or 96, and was written during or immediately after Domitian's persecution, when St. John the Evangelist was the sole survivor of the Apostolic College. Its occasion was an attempt to depose the Bishop of Corinth by a party in that Church. The matter was referred to the Roman Church, and the Pope gives his judgment in words which we will quote later.

St. Irenæus,[1] about eighty years after this letter was written, referred to it in these terms: "The blessed Apostles (Peter and Paul), having founded and built up the (Roman) Church, delivered up the administration of it to Linus; this is the Linus of whom Paul has made mention in his letter to Timothy. His successor was Anacletus, and in the third degree from the Apostles Clement received the bishopric, who had both seen the blessed Apostles and lived with them, having their preaching yet sounding in his ears, and their tradition before his eyes; not alone in this, for there were still many left at that time who had been taught by the Apostles. In the time then of this Clement, no slight dissension having arisen among the brethren at Corinth, the Church in Rome sent a most authoritative letter to the Corinthians, drawing them together into peace, and renewing their faith, and recording the tradition recently derived by it from the Apostles."

The nature of the dissension which he sought to appease was a violation of the due succession in the episcopate. This fact led St. Clement to give an account of its origin. This account, be it observed, dates sixty-six years, or just two generations after the Day of Pentecost. It is an historical narration of what had intervened, exhibiting the manner in which the Apostles and their immediate successors had understood the commission given them by our Lord, the terms of which we have just been considering. There can be nothing more authentic or more valuable than such a statement com-

[1] Contra Hæreses, 3, 3.

ing from such a source. It is a summary at the end of the first century,[1] giving the order according to which the Church was propagated, and it has the peculiarity of being issued by the authority which stood at the head of all.

St. Clement[2] there enjoins obedience within the Christian body, referring to the discipline of the Roman army, in these terms: "Let us take service, therefore, brethren, with all earnestness in His faultless ordinances. Let us mark the soldiers that take service under our rulers, how exactly, how readily, how submissively, they execute the orders given them. All are not prefects, nor rulers of thousands, nor rulers of hundreds, nor rulers of fifties, and so forth; but each man in his own rank executeth the order given by the emperor and his commanders. The great without the small cannot exist, neither the small without the great. There is a certain mixture in all things, and therein is utility. Let us take our body as an example. The head without the feet is nothing, so likewise the feet without the head are nothing; even the smallest limbs of our body are necessary and useful for the whole body; but all the members conspire and unite in subjection, that the whole body may be saved. So, in our case, let the whole body be saved in Christ Jesus, and let each man

---

[1] For the date of the epistle, as at the end of the century, see the arguments in the Prolegomena, pp. 22, 23, of Funk's "Opera Patrum Apostolicorum."

[2] St. Clement to the Corinthians, 37 and following sections, in which I follow generally Dr. Lightfoot's translation, with a few changes.

be subject unto his neighbour, according as also he was appointed with his special grace.

"Forasmuch, then, as these things are manifest beforehand, and we have searched into the depths of the divine knowledge, we ought to do all things in order, as many as the Master[1] has commanded us to perform at their appointed seasons. Now the offerings and liturgic[2] acts He commanded to be performed with care, and not to be done rashly or in disorder, but at fixed times and seasons. And where and by whom He would have them performed He himself fixed by His supreme will, that all things being done with piety, according to His good pleasure, might be acceptable to His will. They, therefore, that make their offerings at the appointed seasons are acceptable and blessed; for while they follow the institutions of the Master they cannot go wrong. For unto the high priest his proper liturgic acts are assigned, and to the priests their proper office is appointed, and upon the levites their proper ministrations are laid. The layman is bound by the layman's ordinances.

"Let each of you, brethren, in his own rank give thanks to God, maintaining a good conscience, and not transgressing the appointed rule of his service, but acting with all seemliness. Not in every place, brethren, are the continual daily sacrifices offered, or the free-will offerings, or the sin-offerings and the trespass-offerings,

---

[1] 'Ο Δεσπότης.

[2] προσφοράς καὶ λειτουργίας, sacrificial terms, belonging to the Holy Eucharist.

but in Jerusalem alone. And even there the offering is not made in every place, but before the sanctuary in the court of the altar, and this too through the high priest and the aforesaid officiants, after that the victim to be offered has been inspected for blemishes. They then who do anything contrary to the seemly ordinance of His will receive death as the penalty. You see, brethren, in proportion as greater knowledge has been vouchsafed to us, so much the more are we exposed to danger.

"The Apostles evangelised us from the Lord Jesus Christ: Jesus Christ from God. So then Christ was sent forth by God, and the Apostles by Christ. Both therefore came of the will of God in the appointed order. Having therefore received a charge, and having been fully assured through the Resurrection of our Lord Jesus Christ, and confirmed in the Word of God with full assurance of the Holy Ghost, they went forth with the good tidings that the kingdom of God was about to come. So preaching everywhere from country to country and from town to town, they went on appointing their first-fruits, when they had proved them by the Spirit, to be bishops and deacons for those that were to believe. And this they did in no new fashion; for indeed it had been written concerning bishops and deacons in very ancient times: for thus saith the Scripture in a certain place, I will appoint their bishops in justice and their deacons in faith.

"And what marvel if they who were entrusted in Christ with such a work by God appointed the aforesaid persons, seeing that even the blessed Moses, who was a faithful servant in all his house, recorded for a sign in the sacred books all things that were enjoined upon him. And him also the rest of the prophets followed, bearing joint witness with him unto the laws that were ordained by him. For he, when jealousy arose concerning the priesthood, and there was dissension among the tribes which of them was adorned with the glorious name, commanded the twelve chiefs of the tribes to bring to him rods inscribed with the name of each tribe. And he took them and tied them, and sealed them with the signet-rings of the chiefs of the tribes, and put them away in the tabernacle of the testimony on the table of God. And having shut the tabernacle, he sealed the keys, and likewise also the rods. And he said unto them, Brethren, the tribe whose rod shall bud, this hath God chosen to be priests and officiants unto Him. Now when morning came, he called together all Israel, even the six hundred thousand men, and showed the seals to the chiefs of the tribes, and opened the tabernacle of the testimony, and drew forth the rods. And the rod of Aaron was found not only with buds, but also bearing fruit. What think ye, beloved? Did not Moses know beforehand that this would come to pass? Assuredly he knew it. But that disorder might not arise in Israel, he did thus, to the end that the Name of the true and only God might be glorified: to whom be glory for ever and ever. Amen.

"And our Apostles knew through our Lord Jesus Christ that there would be strife over the dignity of the episcopate. For this cause, therefore, having received complete foreknowledge, they appointed the aforesaid persons, and they established a succession, that if these should fall asleep, other approved men should succeed to their liturgic function.[1] Those, therefore, that were appointed by them, or afterward by other men of repute, with the consent of the whole Church, and who performed their office blamelessly to the flock of Christ, with lowliness, gentleness, and a generous spirit, and for a long time have borne a good report with all, these we judge it not consonant with justice to deprive of their office. For it will be no light sin in us to deprive of the episcopate those who offer the gifts blamelessly and holily. Blessed are those presbyters who have gone before, seeing that their departure was fruitful and ripe, for they have no fear lest any one should remove them from their appointed place. For we see that you are displacing certain persons who were living honourably from the office which they had blamelessly performed."

St. Clement, in the above passages, states in few but precise words how the whole Christian ministry was appointed by Christ with the most exact order. "The Master commanded the offerings and liturgic acts to be performed with care, and not to be done rashly or in disorder, but at fixed times and seasons. And where and by whom He would have them performed He himself fixed by His supreme will, that all things being done with piety, according to His good pleasure, might

[1] τὴν λειτουργίαν αὐτῶν.

be acceptable to His will." We have seen that only the appointment of the supreme authority—that of St. Peter and the Apostolic College—is recorded in the Gospels and Acts. All details are omitted. But this does not mean that such details were either unimportant or left to be developed casually. Here it is expressly said that our Lord appointed them all, and left strict injunctions both as to the persons who should execute them and the things to be done. And then St. Clement assumes rather than states—so entirely uncontested and acknowledged seems it to be in his mind—that the Christian order succeeds the Mosaic in the triple division of high priest, priest, and levite. "They therefore that make their offerings at the appointed seasons are acceptable and blessed; for while they follow the institutions of the Master they cannot go wrong." He speaks of a present, not a past time; of an actual, not a typical order, continuing thus: "For unto the high priest his proper liturgic acts are assigned, and to the priests their proper office is appointed, and upon the levites their proper ministrations are laid. The layman is bound by the layman's ordinances. Let each of you, brethren, in his own rank, give thanks to God, maintaining a good conscience, and not transgressing the appointed rule of His service, but acting with all seemliness."[1] It cannot be denied that these are injunctions

[1] On this passage Bianchi, "Della Potestà e della Politia della Chiesa," vol. iii. p. 158, remarks: "In oltre era noto a San Girolamo il senso della Chiesa intorno all' ecclesiastica gerarchia d' ordine, che ella ne' tre gradi de' Vescovi, de' Preti, e de' Ministri, ovvero de' Diaconi, sotto il cui nome altri Ministri inferiori si comprendono, discendeva dal Vecchio Testa-

issued to those to whom he was speaking. And the tacit appropriation of the Jewish names and offices to the Christian order, with the injunction of present obedience, all based upon the direct institution of "the Master," is every way to be noted. But he proceeds to say that, if the Mosaic services are accurately performed according to a divine rule, much more should the Christian be. "Not in every place, brethren, are the continual daily sacrifices offered, or the free-will offerings, or the sin-offerings, and the trespass-offerings, but in Jerusalem alone. And even there the offering is not made in every place, but before the sanctuary in the court of the altar, and this too through the high priest and the aforesaid officiants, after that the victim to be offered has been inspected for blemishes. They then who do anything contrary to the seemly ordinance of His will receive death as the penalty. You see, brethren, in proportion as greater knowledge has been vouchsafed to us, so much the more are we exposed to danger."

How, it may be asked, comes it that he mentions the worship at Jerusalem as going on when the city and temple had been destroyed twenty-five years before?

I would suggest that St. Clement is considering the whole order of the Aaronic priesthood and worship as a

mento, e da origine divina, cioè dall' ordine stabilito da Dio nel sommo Sacerdote, ne' Sacerdoti inferiori, e ne' Leviti : i quali gradi diversi nella potestà componevano la gerarchia della vecchia Chiesa." St. Jerome himself says, Ep. 101 ad Evangelum : "Et ut sciamus traditiones Apostolicas sumptas de V. Testamento, quod Aaron et filii ejus atque Levitæ in templo fuerunt, hoc sibi Episcopi et Presbyteri, et Diaconi vindicent in Ecclesia."

divine appointment. In this point of view, it is apart from time, that is, he mentions it ideally as a divine institution. Moreover, he clearly considers it as carried on in the Christian ministry, as having found in that ministry its complete fulfilment. In this aspect it was of no importance that the worship at Jerusalem, to which he referred, had ceased by a divine judgment to be any longer in existence. It had fulfilled its work; the blood of bulls and goats, which typified the most Precious Blood, was offered no more; but instead the sacrifice to which it had pointed. He quotes it for what had not passed, the divine institution of a certain order in it. If, for the violation of this order, death was inflicted, how much more should those who transgressed the Christian institution, as having been vouchsafed greater knowledge, be exposed to danger. Moreover, was not the fact of Jesus being the Christ a basis in St. Clement's mind for the belief that the Mosaic worship was carried on, with the requisite change, in the Christian? How deeply lay in his mind the feeling that the Christian Church was a continuation of the Jewish—the child coming forth from the embryo of the Jewish womb—is apparent through the whole letter.

The third point, then, which we note is, that the ordinances of Christ, in all that concerns the priesthood and the rites of His Church, were to be observed according to the rule which "the Master" Himself had given even more accurately than the Mosaic ritual, though that also was of divine institution, had been observed.

In the next section St. Clement states very concisely,

but with the greatest energy, that quality in the transmission of spiritual power on which we have dwelt in drawing out the scriptural record, that it came altogether from above, not from below : "The Apostles evangelised us from the Lord Jesus Christ; Jesus Christ from God. So then Christ was sent forth by God, and the Apostles by Christ. Both, therefore, came of the will of God in the appointed order. Having then received a charge, and having been fully assured through the resurrection of our Lord Jesus Christ, and confirmed in the word of God with full assurance of the Holy Ghost, they went forth with the good tidings that the kingdom of God was about to come." As the whole appointment proceeded originally from Christ to the Apostles, so in the appointments of the Apostles it proceeded from them to those whom they chose. Authority, therefore, in the kingdom of Christ, pursued throughout one descent: it came by the mandate of superiors, not by the election of inferiors. Thus St. Clement restates the Apostolic mission as recorded by St. John : "As My Father hath sent Me, I also send you." But he adds a fact to a principle—a fact which, recording as it does the whole order of the propagation of the faith in the first two generations from the day of Pentecost, is of the utmost value. "So preaching everywhere from country to country, and from city to city, they went on appointing their first-fruits, when they had proved them by the Spirit, to be bishops and deacons for those that were to believe." That is, the Apostles when they came into a town, preaching as St. Paul and St. Barnabas are described as doing at Iconium, at Lystra, and at Derbe, were guided by a special inspiration of the Holy Spirit in the choosing of future rulers among those who heard them and listened to them. These "first-fruits" of their labour they invested with the episcopal consecration and office, and themselves passing on to other places, left the bishop and his deacons to form the future people. In the bishop they planted the root of the complete tree; from his person radiated the priests and deacons; from his mouth came the tradition of the divine doctrine, and thenceforth in that place all Christian ordinances began to exist and to be exercised. The bishop is the ecclesiastical unit, the father and generator after the pattern of Christ, whom he represents. The process is entirely different from another which has often in thought been substituted for it, according to which an existing number of believers might elect their superiors, and the ecclesiastical rule be exercised in virtue of a sort of imagined social compact. But the words of St. Clement are precise in excluding any such origin of Christian mission: he says that the Apostles appointed their first-fruits to be bishops and deacons of those who were to believe, not of those who believed already; they created the ministry, that the ministry might form the people as yet future.[1] All this, he adds, was in accordance with ancient prophecy.

He then proceeds to draw attention to the most remarkable origin of the Jewish hierarchy, in that Moses deter-

---

[1] καθίστανον τὰς ἀπαρχὰς αὐτῶν, δοκιμάσαντες τῷ πνεύματι, εἰς ἐπισκόπους καὶ διακόνους τῶν μελλόντων πιστεύειν.

mined the devolution of the high priesthood to Aaron by appealing to a miraculous judgment of God in causing his rod to bear fruit among the rods of the chiefs of the tribes. In truth, there is no act recorded more strikingly typical of the divine economy in the mission of our Lord than the creation of the whole Jewish priesthood in the person of Aaron. In that one act the entire Jewish ritual, with the doctrine which it upheld and propagated, proceeded by a divine interference attested in a miracle from above, exactly as in the Person of our Lord and from His sacrificial act as Redeemer the whole Christian hierarchy and the doctrine which it upbears came forth from the God and Father of all. Under this example, and as an instance of power coming from above, St. Clement places the conduct of the Apostles in determining the appointment and the succession of rulers in the Church. "And our Apostles knew, through our Lord Jesus Christ, that there would be strife over the dignity of the episcopate. For this cause, therefore, having received complete foreknowledge, they appointed the aforesaid persons, and they established a succession that, if these should fall asleep, other approved men should succeed to their liturgic function."

Thus before the end of the first century we have a historical statement of the universal and regular appointment of bishops throughout the world by the Apostles in consequence of "complete foreknowledge received" from our Lord Himself. The principle on which they proceeded is clearly defined; the generation of the Christian people from a hierarchy existing before itself is marked out. This is said to be in accordance with ancient prophecy, and follows the great example of God, who created by the hand of Moses the order of the Aaronic priesthood, the precursor and preparer of the Christian, in which it was merged, when the High Priest at length appeared and consummated the act which the whole Jewish ritual was formed to symbolise.

In all this statement St. Clement not merely confirms the scriptural record, but he supplies those details which it enveloped in general heads. Titus and Timotheus are instances of episcopal appointment in the writings of St. Paul, and the bishops or angels of the seven Churches in the Apocalypse; but here the appointment is recorded as general, as everywhere carried out by the Apostles in each city according to the special instruction of our Lord.

Scarcely less remarkable is the manner in which this Pope, the third from St. Peter, exercises in the lifetime of St. John the supreme pastoral office, the creation of which that Apostle has recorded. The question to be decided is the deposition or the maintenance of the Bishop at Corinth, and there follows immediately upon the text above cited the act of authority. "Those, therefore, that were appointed by them or afterward by other men of repute, with the consent of the whole Church, and who performed their office blamelessly to the flock of Christ, with lowliness, gentleness, and a generous spirit, and for a long time have borne a good report with all, *these we judge it not consonant with justice to deprive of their office.* For it will be no light sin in us to deprive of the episcopate[1] those who offer the gifts blamelessly and holily." He who speaks in this language intimates thereby that he has power to deprive of the liturgic office, that is, of the episcopate, and acknowledges that he will have to answer for the exercise of that power.

But further, the sentence thus given he declares to be the sentence of God Himself. " Receive our counsel, and you shall have no occasion of regret. For as God liveth, and the Lord Jesus Christ liveth, and the Holy Spirit, who are the faith and the hope of the elect, so surely shall he who, with lowliness of mind and instant in gentleness, hath without regretfulness performed the ordinances and commandments that are given by God, be enrolled and have a name among the number of them that are saved through Jesus Christ, through whom is the glory to Him for ever and ever. Amen. But if certain persons should be disobedient unto the words spoken by Him through us, let them understand that they will entangle themselves in no slight transgression and danger; but we shall be guiltless of this sin."[2] Further on in the letter he continues :—

" Therefore it is right for us to give heed to so great and so many examples, and to submit the neck, and, occupying the place of obedience, to take our side with them that are the leaders of our souls, that, ceasing from this foolish dissension, we may attain to the goal which lies before us in truthfulness, keeping aloof from

[1] τῆς λειτουργίας—τῆς ἐπισκοπῆς ἀποβαλεῖν.   [2] Sections 58, 59.

every fault. For you will give us great joy and gladness if you render obedience to the things written by us through the Holy Spirit, and root out the unrighteous anger of your jealousy, according to the entreaty which we have made for peace and concord in this letter."[1]

Let us sum up the force of the words just cited.

St. Clement, after invoking the Three Persons of the Blessed Trinity as witnesses of the judgment he was about to promulgate, declares that "he who performs without regretfulness the ordinances and commandments that are given by God" shall "be enrolled and have a name among the number of them that are saved through Jesus Christ." On the other hand, that those who are "disobedient unto the words spoken by Him through us" "will entangle themselves in no slight transgression and danger." He adds, moreover, "You will give us great joy and gladness if you render obedience to the things written by us through the Holy Spirit."[1]

From all which we learn that a decision of the Church of Rome, issued by its Bishop, as to whether the Bishop of Corinth was rightly or wrongly deposed, is declared, after attestation of the Three Divine Persons to be among the commandments and ordinances given by God; to be "words spoken by God through us," that is, the Pope and the Church of Rome; to be "things written by us through the Holy Spirit," to which absolute obedience was due, and which could not be neglected "without no slight transgression and

[1] Section 63.

danger." The Pope, moreover, takes upon himself the power to deprive of the episcopate by issuing a judgment that an actual possessor of it is in his right, while he says at the same time that it would be "no light sin in us to deprive him of it unjustly."

It is in every way remarkable that the first pastoral letter of a Pope which has been preserved to posterity should contain so undeniable an exercise of his supreme authority. Again, it is another noteworthy matter that this supreme authority should have been exercised in the lifetime of the last surviving Apostle, the Beloved Disciple. Further, would it be possible to apply in a stronger way than St. Clement, issuing an authoritative judgment, here applies them, those words of our Lord: "He that heareth you, heareth Me; and he that despiseth you, despiseth Me; and he that despiseth Me, despiseth Him that sent Me."[1] And again, "Whatsoever thou shalt bind on earth shall be bound in heaven." Lastly, it is to be noted that the authority thus exercised concerns not a point of dogma, but the office of a Bishop; yet disobedience to it is considered as disobedience to "words spoken by God through us."

The part of St. Clement's letter, which contains the whole judgment thus commented on, has only been recovered within the last few years.

But that whole view of the constitution of the Church during the first century which is presented to us in the Epistle of St. Clement is remarkably corroborated by the letters of his contemporary, St. Ignatius

[1] Luke x. 16.

of Antioch. That fervent confessor of God, passing in chains to martyrdom, pours forth, as is well known, the deepest fulness of his heart to the Churches which he visits in his long way of the cross from Antioch to Rome. The letters are short, the style abrupt, the expressions only incidental; he had no thought of writing a treatise on the constitution of the Church. Thus any short quotation is quite inadequate to render the full witness of the saint. It would be necessary to read through the whole series in order to feel how incessantly he dwells upon union with God wrought through obedience to the hierarchy of bishops, priests, and deacons, which is the test in his mind of love to Christ. Thus, at the beginning of his letter to the Church of Smyrna, he speaks of the most blessed Passion of Christ, "a fruit of which are we that He might set up a token for all ages through His Resurrection to His holy and faithful ones, whether they be among Jews or Gentiles, in the one body of His Church."

In his letter to the Church of Ephesus there is a remarkable passage, in which he joins together the thought of the unity of a particular diocese with the unity of the bishops throughout the world. "It is fitting that you should by all means glorify Jesus Christ, who has glorified you, that by a uniform obedience you may be perfectly joined together and subject to the bishop, and the presbytery may be in all things sanctified. I do not command you, as if I were anybody; for though I am bound in the name of Christ, I am not yet perfected in Him. For now I begin to learn, and speak to you as my fellow-disciples. For I ought to be confirmed by you in faith, in admonition, in patience, in long-suffering. But since charity permits me not to be silent in regard to you, I have therefore taken upon me to exhort you that you may run together with the mind of God. For Jesus Christ, our inseparable life, is the mind of the Father, as also the bishops, appointed throughout the earth, are in the mind of Christ. Whence, also, it becomes you to agree with the mind of the bishop, as indeed you do. For your illustrious presbytery, worthy of God, is fitted as exactly to the bishop as the strings are to a harp. Hence it is that, in your concord and harmonious love, Jesus Christ is sung; and one and all you make up the chorus, that, being harmonious in concord, taking up the song of God in unity, you may sing with one voice to the Father through Jesus Christ, that He may both hear you and recognise by your good deeds that you are members of His Son. It is well for you, then, to be in blameless unity, that you may in all things partake of God."

The vivid love and sense of the Church, as the great instrument of unity wrought by the Passion of Christ in the world, and compacted by the ministry which He has set up, distinguishes the letter of St. Ignatius as it does that of St. Paul to the same Ephesian Church, so specially beloved by the Apostle, and the scene of so many of his labours. But St. Irenæus[1] tells us that it

---

[1] Irenæus, iii. 1.—ἔπειτα Ἰωάννης, ὁ μαθητὴς τοῦ Κυρίου, ὁ καὶ ἐπὶ τὸ στῆθος αὐτοῦ ἀναπεσὼν καὶ αὐτὸς ἐξέδωκε τὸ εὐαγγέλιον, ἐν Ἐφέσῳ τῆς Ἀσίας διατρίβων.

was also from the bosom of this Church of Ephesus that the Apostle of love issued the Gospel in which he recorded for the world the great commission to feed the whole flock of Christ given to St. Peter on the shore of the lake of Galilee.

Let us add one more passage from the letter to the Trallians. "For when you are subject to your bishop as to Jesus Christ you seem to me to live not after the manner of men, but according to Jesus Christ, who died for us, in order that, believing in His death, you may escape death. It is therefore necessary that you do nothing without your bishop, but that you be subject to the presbytery also, as to the Apostles of Jesus Christ, our hope, in whom if we walk we shall be found. The deacons also, as being the ministers of the mysteries of Jesus Christ, must be acceptable to all. For they are not the ministers of meat and drink, but servants of the Church of God. Wherefore they must avoid all offences as they would fire. Let all in like manner reverence the deacons as Jesus Christ, and the bishop as the type of the Father, and the presbyters as God's senate and the College of Apostles. Without these there is no Church."

These words expressly state the organic unity of a local Church to be the bishop with his priests and deacons; but he had likewise noted that the bishops established throughout the earth were together "in the mind of Christ."

The words of St. Clement the Pope, and St. Ignatius, the bishop of one of the three original patriarchal Sees, thus complete and corroborate each other. If we put the passages just cited from the latter with the statement of the former, that "the Apostles, preaching from country to country and from city to city, established their first-fruits, after proving them by the Spirit, to be bishops and deacons of a people that were to believe," we have a perfect chain let down from above, and binding the earth in its embrace : God, who sends forth Christ; Christ, who sends forth the Apostles; the Apostles, who appoint local bishops, who are the bond to their clergy and people. In the whole of this the expression of St. Ignatius is verified : "hence in your concord and harmonious love Jesus Christ is sung." If the bishops throughout the world were not united with each other in as complete a harmony as the presbytery with the bishop in a particular diocese, these words would not be true. But, on the contrary, they are together "in the mind of Christ," as He is "the mind of the Father," and they feed not each a separate flock, but together " the flock of Christ."

But who is the bond of their union? It pleased the Divine Providence that, even before St. Ignatius wrote, and even in the lifetime of the Apostle who recorded the commission to feed the whole flock of Christ, the harmony and obedience of which St. Ignatius spoke should be broken in a particular diocese, and that St. Peter's third successor should execute his office and assert the Divine commission by fulfilling it. His conduct in this marks, by a solemn act, the line between the Apostolate and the Primacy. That he speaks in the name of the whole Roman Church, as the voice of a

Body, illustrates further the words of St. Ignatius, "Your presbytery is fitted as exactly to the bishop as the strings are to a harp."[1]

In the testimony of these Apostolic Fathers, each completing the other, we have not only the local bishop planted as the unit of the Church's organism in any particular city, but the bishop who sits in the See of Peter, the tie and bond of his brethren. The harp sounds its notes to Christ throughout the world.

Another point in which their testimony exactly agrees is, that while St. Clement speaks of the government of the Church as enacted with even greater accuracy and enforced with even stronger penalties than the law of Moses, St. Ignatius takes the strict observance of unity and obedience to external authority as a perfect test of the inward disposition, a perfect assurance that those who exercised these virtues were members of Christ. The temper in which these Fathers write is as far as possible removed from the notion that Church government was either lax or uncertain. To them it comes from above, and requires inward obedience, as the appointment of Christ.

Eusebius, the first historian of the Church, compiling

[1] I note this because Dr. Lightfoot, in his recent edition of St. Clement's complete letter, not knowing how to meet the very strong proof of the Primacy contained in the newly recovered part, suggests that the Primacy belonged not to the Bishop of the Roman Church, but to the Roman Church. This is so total a misstatement of the position held by every bishop in his See as to smack of Presbyterianism. But when he goes on to attribute the Primacy thus located in the Roman Church to a supposed superior sanctity residing in the members of that Church, he would seem to be substituting a pure invention of his own for history.

about the year 324 notices of the times before him, with records at his command which are no longer extant, describes in the following terms the first period, that in which the Apostles themselves preached, which we may speak of as running from the Day of Pentecost to the destruction of Jerusalem :—

"Thus, under a celestial influence and co-operation, the doctrine of the Saviour, like the rays of the sun, quickly irradiated the whole world. Presently, in accordance with divine prophecy, the sound of his inspired Evangelists and Apostles had gone throughout all the earth, and their words to the end of the world. Throughout every city and village, like a replenished barn-floor, numerous and populous churches were firmly established. Those who, in consequence of the delusions that had descended to them from their ancestors, had been fettered by the ancient disease of idolatrous superstition, were now liberated by the power of Christ, through the united force of the teaching and miracles of His messengers; and, as if delivered from dreadful masters, and emancipated from the most cruel bondage, they renounced the crowd of deities introduced by demons, while they confessed the one God, the Creator of all things. This same God they now also honoured with the rites of a true piety, under the influence of that inspired and reasonable worship which had been planted among men by our Saviour."[1]

---

[1] Eusebius, Hist. 2, 3. The words are so specific that it is desirable to give the original : καὶ δῆτα ἀνὰ πάσας πόλεις τε καὶ κώμας πληθυούσης ἅλωνος δίκην μυριάνδροι καὶ παμπληθεῖς ἀθρόως ἐκκλησίαι συνεστήκεσαν. The last word

The next period is distinctly marked by Eusebius as the first succession from the Apostles. St. Paul,[1] he says, preaching to the Gentiles, laid the foundations of Churches from Jerusalem in a circle round to Illyricum; and St. Peter preached to the circumcision in the five provinces recorded by him in his letter. He continues, "It is not easy to say how many imitators of these were by them judged worthy to exercise the pastoral office in the Churches founded by them, except so far as St. Paul's own words record them. For he had numberless fellow-workers, fellow-soldiers, as he himself called them, most of whom he has delivered to immortal memory by mention of them in his letters." Thus Timotheus was first Bishop of Ephesus; Titus was set over Crete, and expressly enjoined to appoint bishops in its several cities, for St. Paul draws out what sort of a character the bishop so appointed should be.[2] "Linus, whom he mentions being with him at Rome, has already," says Eusebius, "been named by us as having been first Bishop of the Roman Church after Peter. But likewise Clement, who was the third appointed Bishop of the Romans, is recorded by St. Paul as his colleague and fellow-labourer."

In a third passage Eusebius,[3] after speaking of Ignatius " as the second who received the episcopal succession of St. Peter at Antioch," Evodius having been the first,

indicates the regular formation of a Church, that hierarchical constitution of the bishop, with his attendant ministry, without which, in the words of St. Ignatius, ἐκκλησία οὐ καλεῖται. I have used Cruse's translation, altering it occasionally.

[1] Lib. iii. 4.   [2] Titus i. 5-9.   [3] Lib. iii. 37.

and after quoting at length his letters, proceeds, "There were many others also noted in the times of these men who held the first rank of the apostolic succession. These, as the holy disciples of such men, built up further in every place the foundations of the Churches which had been laid by the Apostles. They spread the preaching further abroad and scattered the saving seeds of the kingdom of heaven far and wide through the breadth of the world. For the most of the disciples at that time, kindled by a more ardent love of the divine word, had first fulfilled the Saviour's exhortation by distributing their substance to the needy. Afterwards, leaving their country, they performed the work of evangelists, filled with a noble ambition to proclaim Christ to such as had not yet heard the word of faith, and to deliver to them the writing of the sacred Gospels. Thus laying merely the foundations of the faith in new and strange places, and, appointing others to the pastoral office, they left them to cultivate the new plantation, and again went on to other places and nations by God's grace and co-operation. For a great number of marvellous works of power were still done by them through the Holy Spirit; so that at the first hearing multitudes of men in a mass received into their souls readily the worship of the One Creator. As I cannot record by name all those who received the first succession of the Apostles as pastors and evangelists in the Churches throughout the world, I will mention those only where tradition of apostolical doctrine is carried down to us by actual memorials."

The gradations thus marked in the propagation of the gospel are three: first, that of the Apostles in Judea before their dispersion; secondly, that of the Apostles with their personal fellow-workers throughout the world; thirdly, that of the men called Apostolic, because they had lived in the time of the Apostles without having been their first co-operators, or, to use the Pauline expression, fellow-soldiers. This carries us over the ninety years from the Day of Pentecost to the end of Trajan's reign, during which reign, the time, as Eusebius calls it, of St. Clement of Rome and of St. Ignatius of Antioch, he notes that there was a specially abundant outburst of such teachers.

Eusebius bears witness through the whole of his History to the universality of the episcopal regimen. Likewise he carefully gives the descent of the three great Sees of Rome, Alexandria, and Antioch. He notes how they took their rise from the person of Peter, who sat at Antioch himself, who sent his son Mark to Alexandria, and whose coming to Rome the historian describes in the words following:—

"Immediately in the reign of the Emperor Claudius, the most benign and man-loving providence of God conducted to Rome Peter, the great and powerful among the Apostles, who for his virtue was chosen to lead them all against Simon, the plague of mankind.[1] Peter, like a valiant commander of God's army, clothed in heavenly panoply, carried from the East to the West

[1] Eusebius appears to say that the Apostle Peter came to Rome very shortly after he had discomfited Simon Magus in Samaria. See lib. ii. 14.

the precious freight of intellectual light, bearing the proclamation of the heavenly kingdom, to be the sure and saving word of souls." He records the martyrdom of the two Apostles, Peter and Paul, together at Rome under Nero, giving for this fact a fourfold testimony; of historians generally; of their tombs, which were still to be seen at Rome; of the presbyter Caius, who, at the beginning of the third century, appealed to the existence of these tombs, the one at the Vatican, the other on the Ostian Road, as a proof where "the sacred tabernacles of these Apostles had been deposited;" and lastly, to the letter of Dionysius, Bishop of Corinth in the middle of the second century, who spoke of their having both taught the Church of Corinth as well as that of Rome, and of both having suffered martyrdom together. "These particulars I have given," says Eusebius, "that the memory of the fact may be the more confirmed."[1] He gives carefully during two hundred years the descent of the bishops in these three Sees, and the number of years they sat—a tacit witness to the eminent rank of the three great Mother Sees established by Peter in the three chief cities of the Roman Empire; and an honour which he gives besides only to the Church of Jerusalem, since all, he says, have ever borne reverence "to the throne of the Apostle James, the first who received the episcopate of the city of Jerusalem from the Saviour Himself and the Apostles!"

In another place he writes: "Again, when I consider the power of the Word, how the most populous churches

[1] Hist. 2, 25.

were constructed by the rudest and most ignoble disciples of Jesus, not in obscure and unknown places, but founded in the most conspicuous cities, in very imperial Rome itself, in Alexandria and Antioch, for all Egypt and Libya, for Europe, and for Asia,—again I am compelled to search out the reason of this, and to confess that they could not have succeeded in so audacious an attempt except by some divine and superhuman power, and the working together with them of Him who said ' Make disciples all nations in My name.'"[1]

Between St. Clement of Rome and St. Ignatius of Antioch at the end of the first century, and Eusebius at the beginning of the fourth, stands at the end of the second century the witness of Tertullian. In setting forth the legal ground of prescription against the heretics of his day, he gives an account of the original propagation of the divine kingdom, which exactly tallies with all that precedes. "Christ Jesus our Lord . . . had chosen twelve disciples to be attached to His side, whom He destined to be the teachers of the nations. Accordingly, after one of these had been struck off, He commanded the eleven others, on His departure to the Father, to go and teach all nations, who were to be baptized into the Father, and into the Son, and into the Holy Ghost. Immediately, therefore, the Apostles, whom this designation indicates as the Sent, having on the authority of a prophecy, which occurs in a psalm of David, chosen Matthias by lot as the twelfth into the

---

[1] Eusebius, Hist. 7, 19; and Præp. Evan. lib. 3, towards the end, quoted by Bianchi, 3, 137.

place of Judas, obtained the promised power of the Holy Ghost for the gift of miracles and of utterance. And after first bearing witness to the faith in Jesus Christ throughout Judea, and founding Churches, they next went forth into the world, and preached the same doctrine of the same faith to the nations. They then, in like manner, founded Churches in every city" (that is, an episcopal See in each city, without which, as St. Ignatius told us, there is no Church) "from which all the other Churches, one after another, derived the tradition of the faith and the seeds of doctrine, and are every day deriving them that they may become Churches. Indeed it is on this account only that they are able to deem themselves apostolic, as being the offspring of Apostolic Churches. Every sort of thing must necessarily revert to its original for its classification. Therefore the Churches, though they are so many and so great, comprise but the one Primitive Church founded by the Apostles, from which they all spring. In this way all are primitive and all are apostolic, while all together make up a unity; while they have peaceful communion, and title of brotherhood, and bond of hospitality, privileges which no other rule directs than the one tradition of the self-same mystery. From this, then, do we prescribe the rule that, since the Lord Jesus Christ sent the Apostles to preach, no other ought to be received as preachers than those whom Christ appointed; for 'no man knoweth the Father save the Son, and he to whomsoever the Son will reveal Him.' Nor does the Son seem to have revealed Him to any other than the Apostles, whom He sent forth to preach that, of course, which He revealed to them. Now what this was which they preached—in other words, what it was which Christ revealed to them—can, as I must here likewise prescribe, properly be proved in no other way than by those very Churches which the Apostles founded in person, by declaring the gospel to them directly themselves, both by word of mouth, as the phrase is, and subsequently by their Epistles. If, then, these things are so, it is in the same degree manifest that all doctrine which agrees with the Apostolic Churches—those wombs and original sources of the faith—must be reckoned for truth, as undoubtedly containing that which the said Churches received from the Apostles, the Apostles from Christ, and Christ from God; whereas all doctrine must be prejudged as false which savours of contrariety to the truth of the Churches and Apostles of Christ and God."[1]

But the whole work of St. Irenæus against heresies is based exactly upon the fact which we are here setting forth. His object was to show that the true faith was preserved intact in all the Churches of the world by means of the bishops appointed by the Apostles. Thus he commences his third book : "For the Lord of all gave to His Apostles the power of the gospel, through whom we have learnt the truth, that is, the doctrine of the Son of God; to whom the Lord said, 'He who heareth you, heareth Me, and who despiseth you, despiseth Me,

[1] Tertullian, De Præscriptione Hæreticorum, 20, 21, Dr. Holmes' translation, with a word or two altered.

and Him who sent Me.'" . . . " For after our Lord arose from the dead, and they had been clothed with the power of the Holy Spirit coming down upon them from on high, they were completely filled and had perfect knowledge : they went forth into the ends of the world, proclaiming the gospel of good things from God, and announcing peace from heaven to men, all of them and every one of them possessing equally the gospel of God."
. . . "All, therefore, who wish to see the truth may behold in every Church the tradition of the Apostles, which was made known through the whole world; and we can number up those who were appointed by the Apostles bishops in the Churches, and their successors down to our own times, who have neither taught nor known any such delirious imagination as theirs." He is speaking of the heresy of Valentinus. " For had the Apostles known recondite mysteries, which they were in the habit of teaching separately and secretly from the rest to the perfect, they would deliver such especially to those to whom they were intrusting the Churches themselves. For they desired those to be very perfect and blameless in all things whom they were leaving as their successors, handing over to them their own place of teaching. For if these acted faultlessly, the good would be great; whereas if they failed, the calamity would be complete."

Irenæus sums up all this view in another place, where he says : "True knowledge is the doctrine of the Apostles, and the ancient compacted fabric of the Church through the whole world, and the character of the Body of Christ, according to the succession of bishops, to whom they delivered that Church which is everywhere."[1]

In what has preceded we have traced carefully the transmission of spiritual authority, putting together the various intimations respecting it which are given in the four Gospels, the Acts, the Epistles of St. Paul, and the Apocalypse. From these intimations a most clear and unambiguous result has been deduced. Then proceeding to historical proofs, we find the third Pope from St. Peter, at the end of the first century, in an official document, summing up in words of great precision what had been the actual course of things in the two generations which lay between the Day of Pentecost and the time at which he was writing. If we compare the Gospels which record the institution of the power, and the history which records its actual beginning and exercise, as thus given by St. Clement, we find the most exact agreement. Another saint and martyr, contemporary with St. Clement, and holding by second succession from St. Peter what became the great patriarchal See of the East, affords the strongest corroboration to him in the doctrinal statements which are found interwoven in the letters addressed by him to various churches as he is carried a prisoner on his way to martyrdom. The first extant historian, writing in 324, on the eve of the assembling of the first General Council, testifies throughout the ten books of his work the universality of the

[1] Irenæus, 4, 33, 8. The same is set forth with great force in Book 5, 20.

episcopal regimen, and intimates its organic structure by giving each link in the spiritual descent of the three great Sees of Peter and of the Church of Jerusalem. Intermediate between these three authorities, Irenæus, Bishop of Lyons, writing seventy years after St. Clement, and Tertullian, writing thirty years after Irenæus, give very graphic accounts of the Church in their day, which exactly accord both with the Pope and Martyr-bishop preceding and the historian following them. Instead of calling in other witnesses, let us attempt to give a general view of the Episcopate as it is found when emerging from the last great persecution, which terminated the first stadium of its course, and was followed by the peace of the Church, proclaimed by the Emperor Constantine 283 years after the Day of Pentecost. The whole of this period marks a time in which the growth of the Church and the form of her constitution were the result of a power proceeding solely from within, never favoured by the civil power, often actively persecuted, and daily in a thousand ways discouraged.

St. Augustine, writing in the year 398, observes precisely of this time, that is, the year 314, that if the Donatists suspected the judgment of their African colleagues, there were thousands of bishops beyond the sea to whom they might have recourse.[1] In his own

[1] Ep. 43, 11: "Nec in illis solis episcopis Afris erat Ecclesia, ut omne judicium ecclesiasticum vitasse viderentur qui se judicio eorum præsentari noluissent. Millia quippe collegarum transmarina restabant, ubi apparebat eos judicari posse, qui videbantur Afros vel Numidas collegas habere suspectos."

time he counted 476 Catholic bishoprics in the African provinces. Throughout the Roman Empire it would seem that, before the peace of the Church, not only every considerable city, but even small towns, possessed their bishop. St. Hilary says: "Though there be only one Church in the world, yet every city has its own Church;" and St. Cyprian and St. Dionysius of Alexandria assert this of their own time.[1]

The conduct, then, of St. Peter, of St. Paul, and of all the Apostles in the propagation of the Church, was from the beginning one and uniform, and impressed itself on the succeeding generations.[2] They founded a Christian colony on the solid basis of a complete administration, and establishing their most fervent disciples as the chiefs of that hierarchic organisation, they left to them the charge of forming new centres of spiritual life in the cities dependent on those first chosen. Thus St. Peter chose first Antioch, Queen of the East, the head afterwards of fifteen ecclesiastical provinces; then Rome, the head of the whole Empire, of which Pope St. Innocent said, writing in the year 416 to the Bishop of Eugubium, that "it was an acknowledged fact that no one had established Churches" (by which he means a Bishop's See) "in all Italy, the Gauls, the Spains, in Africa, in Sicily, and the intervening islands, except those whom the venerable Apostle Peter or his successors had appointed bishops."[3]

---

[1] St. Hilary on Ps. 14, 3; St. Cyprian, Ep. 52.
[2] See Dom Chamard, L'Etablissement du Christianisme, p. 141.
[3] *Sacerdotes;* as ἐκκλησία means a Bishop's See, so *sacerdotes* meant a bishop; that word in the language of the day signified the bishop who

Thirdly, he chose Alexandria, whose bishops became the head of the three provinces, Egypt, Libya, and Pentopolis. But no less St. Paul planted in Ephesus the Mother Church of the province of Asia (one-twentieth only of the great country called Asia Minor); in Thessalonica, the metropolis of Thrace; in Corinth, that of Achaia; he and Barnabas, in Salamis, that of Cyprus; while he set a disciple to appoint bishops over the whole island of Crete. These are specimens of the power which was thus established in every city over the whole world traversed by the Apostles and their descendants, a power fixed, not transitory; local, not roving. It was an occupation of each city by the spiritual authority exactly similar in divine things to the military colonies which Rome planted in its provinces for the propagation of its temporal sway. It was a corporate body with a most compact unity, at the head of which, informing and directing every act, stood the bishop, a name of power and jurisdiction. Of them St. Paul said, "Obey your prelates, and be subject to them." From such words the power of government is a clear inference. If the faithful are obliged to obey the prelates of the Church, these must have authority to command. Thus St. Gregory of Nazianzum, addressing in the year 373 the governor of his province, used these words: "The law of Christ subjects you to my authority and to my tribunal. For we also have a government, nay, I will add a greater and more perfect government,

presided in each Church, pre-eminently the *Sacerdos*, as offering the Sacrifice of the Altar. See Constant, Rom. Pont. Epist., p. 856.

unless spirit must yield to flesh, and heavenly things to earthly. I know that you will accept my freedom of speech, because you are a sheep of my flock, a sacred sheep of a sacred flock, nurtured by the Great Shepherd."[1] Elsewhere he calls it "the government which is innocent of blood," contrasting it with "the government of the sword and the lash." The Greek Fathers universally, in explaining the dignity of the episcopate, use this word government.[2]

Of the way in which the world was thus evangelised we have an instance recorded by Photius, who says that Caius, a grave and learned priest of the Roman Church, was ordained by Pope Zephyrinus (who sat from 202 to 218), Bishop of the Nations, that is, without designation of any particular diocese, as if anointed and crowned for a kingdom, which by his valour and wisdom he was to obtain for himself. In this way the Roman Pontiffs consecrated a great number of bishops, whom they sent to bring the provinces under the yoke of the faith, as recorded above by St. Innocent.[3] But it is to be noted that those who were thus sent out during two centuries from the first age were not elected by the people of the several churches which they founded. They came to them by authority from without—the authority of the Apostles and the Apostolic See, mediately or immediately. In the cases just mentioned the mission was immediate: in other cases, where it was derived from some Patriarchal See or from a metropolis, it still

---

[1] Orat. 17, 8; Ep. 224, Africano.   [2] ἀρχή. Bianchi, 3, 475.
[3] See Bianchi, 3, 484.

descended from that original mission of the Apostles, and the distribution of authority made by Peter at their head.

For the whole of this mission there is one great type and source; our Lord at the head of His Apostles is the prelude to the bishop in the midst of his presbytery. He repeats Himself in every diocese, the first and everlasting Bishop, whose heirs spread throughout the world. All is from above.

But each bishop's chair thus established is a centre of dogmatic truth and of moral force. The government extending thus over the whole Church is a mean between autonomy and centralisation. "The bishop is contained in the Church, and the Church in the bishop:" it is "a flock united to its pastor." This is its local character: a most living authority, and a most careful representation of those governed. What it is in reference to the like authority planted elsewhere, we shall see presently.

The bishop, with his presbyterate and diaconate, fitted to him as the strings to a harp, in the words of St. Ignatius, this was the instrument by which our Lord chose to take hold of the world. "Many nations of barbarians," St. Irenæus observes, "believing in Christ, follow the order of tradition without pen and paper, having salvation written in their hearts by the Spirit;"[1] but nowhere as to this point of episcopal regimen did this tradition vary. The Church having traversed the three centuries, assaulted from within by sects innu-

[1] Irenæus, 3, 4.

merable, and from without by a hostile Empire, emerges under this government alone. Nowhere was it without this settled order of the Episcopate. A presbyter not subject to a bishop, a single church or any number of churches not ruled by a bishop, these were unknown things. In the sects, indeed, there were all sorts of disorder and continued changes of government, just as there was incessant fluctuation of doctrine; the true and only Church showed itself precisely in this, that it preserved its doctrine and its government alike unchangeable.

Eusebius observes how "the devices of opponents destroyed each other by their own violence. New heresies continually rose and fell, one giving way to the other, and corrupting themselves in a long series of the most diverse and strange conceptions. But the one Church, proceeding on the same lines, and in an even tenor, kept upon its path, ever increasing in brilliancy, and shedding forth upon every race of Greeks and barbarians the dignity, sincerity, and freedom, the tempered wisdom and purity, of the divine polity and philosophy;" where it is observable that by the words polity and philosophy he blends together the form of life and the truth of doctrine as coinherent with each other.[1]

Thus in less than three centuries the Episcopate was flung as a golden network over the greatest of the world-empires, and far beyond its borders. But let us

[1] Hist., 4, 7, speaking of the time of Hadrian and the Gnostic heresies.

well understand what this means. It does not mean simply that there were bishops everywhere; that no church existed save under the rule of a bishop; that there were no presbyterian, still more, no independent churches. It is a much greater fact which we have to note; it is that there was "one Episcopate, of which a part was held by each without division of the whole;" "one Episcopate spread abroad in the concordant multitude of many bishops."[1] The doctrine of St. Cyprian is thus set forth by De Marca: "As there is one body of the Church divided into many members through the whole world, so there is in it one only Episcopate, spread abroad in the harmony of many bishops. If these be considered as a body, they hold the entire Episcopate in common. But a certain portion of the flock has been assigned to each bishop to lead and direct it singly, but in consonance with the charity and communion due to the whole body. For if unity be relinquished, the bishop who departs from the body would dry up as a stream deflecting from its source, and wither as a branch cut off from the trunk and root. This distribution of portions, which have been committed to the various bishops, descended from the apostolic rule. For when the Apostles founded churches, though they conferred on the ordained bishop by the imposition of their hands all the power of order and jurisdiction, yet they assigned to him the place in which he should discharge his office. This has been marked with great clearness in the 20th chapter of the Acts,

[1] St. Cyprian, De Unit. Ecc. 4, and Epis. 52.

where we read that the Holy Spirit appointed bishops to govern the Church of God. But since the Church was to be ruled in unity, it was necessary that some mode of communion between the bishops should be established by the Apostles according to the example given by Christ in establishing the College of Apostles, which represented the whole body of the Church."[1] And what this rule was De Marca proceeds to state in the words of St. Leo the Great, which, as written in the middle of the fifth century by the highest authority, will serve better to convey a lucid view of the one Episcopate than any more modern statement. In the year 446 St. Leo writes: "It is the connection of the whole body which makes one soundness and one beauty; and this connection, as it requires unanimity in the whole body, so especially demands concord among bishops. For though these have a common dignity, yet have they not a general jurisdiction; since even among the most blessed Apostles, as there was a likeness of honour, so was there a certain distinction of power; and the election of all being equal, pre-eminence over the rest was given to one. From which type the distinction also among bishops has arisen, and it was provided by a great disposition that all should not claim to themselves all things, but that in every province there should be one whose sentence should be considered the first among his brethren; and others again, seated in the greater cities, should undertake a larger care, through whom the direction of the universal Church should converge

[1] De Marca, De Concordia Sacerdotii et Imperii, lib. 6, 1.

to the one See of Peter, and nothing anywhere disagree from its head."[1]

It is thus that the Church appeared when it came out of the fire of persecution and the perpetual conflict with heresies into peace and recognition by the Civil Power. It was not merely that by an innate force—which all the Fathers attribute to the gift of the Holy Spirit dwelling in it—a uniform episcopal government had been established wherever it extended, but that it was one Episcopate ruling one flock. Between a bishop viewed as the centre of unity in his own diocese, but unconnected with other bishops, and independent of them, and an Episcopate organically one, ruling one flock through the whole world, there is all the difference which exists between what is human, weak, and perishable and what is divine, strong, and enduring. In the former case the bishop's throne would simply be a seat of rivalry, confusion, and error; in the latter, the union of the body is the test of health, and makes that divine beauty which our Lord in His prayer for His Church at the entrance of His Passion contemplated, which He likened even to the divine unity. This was the vision which lay before St. Cyprian's eyes when he cried out, "The Spouse of Christ cannot be adulterated; she is incorrupt and chaste; she has one single home; she guards the sanctity of one marriage chamber with inviolable modesty. The Lord says, 'I and the Father are one;' and again, of the Father and the Son and the Holy Spirit it is written, 'These three are one.'

[1] St. Leo I., Ep. 14.

Can any one believe that the unity which springs from the divine strength, which is bound together by heavenly sacraments, can be broken in the Church and torn asunder by the collision of opposing wills."[1] But St. Cyprian's safeguard against this was the one Episcopate, which he views as centred in the See of Peter, its origin and matrix, and which, two hundred years after him, the great successor of St. Peter describes in act.

The Fathers regarded the establishment of bishops everywhere as a wonderful fulfilment of the Psalmist's vision: "Instead of thy fathers, sons are born to thee: thou shalt make them princes over all the earth."[2] And, in truth, the uniform planting in every city and town of a divine government such as we have described, the doing this, moreover, without favour or protection from the civil power, nay, in spite of its jealousy, resistance, and persecution, is a wonder of divine power. But this is only half what was done. This is not yet the One Episcopate, but there is to be added to it that "Sacrament of unity" whereby every one of these bishops belonged to an indivisible whole, and fed a portion of the one "flock of Christ." Bishops, holding each in his own person the fulness of the priesthood, its generative and ruling power, whether the number of their people were small or great, whether their presbyters and deacons were many or few, in these respects equal to each other and complete in themselves, were in a fur-

---

[1] De Unitate Ecclesiæ, 4. [2] Ps. xliv. 17.

ther point of view members of one hierarchy, which could no more be multiplied than the Body of Christ or His Flock. The one Saviour could not have two bodies, nor the one Shepherd two flocks. Hence, what St. Leo calls "the provision of that great disposition that all should not claim to themselves all things, but that in every province there should be one whose sentence should be considered the first among his brethren;" in which words he marks the Metropolitan and his suffragans; "and others again seated in the greater cities should undertake a larger care"—as, for instance, the Bishop of Antioch, when he had fifteen Metropolitans subject to his chair—"through whom the direction of the Universal Church should converge to the one See of Peter, and nothing anywhere disagree from its head." What terser and clearer statement of the actual government of the Church could be given now, though more than fourteen hundred years have passed since it was written?

This, then, is the full meaning of the One Episcopate; this is the marvel superadded to the sons of the Church who are made princes over all the earth, that they are not individual governors only of a local republic, but bound together by a manifold subordination, Bishop to Metropolitan, Metropolitan to Patriarch, Patriarch to Pope. There is the twofold beauty of unity and order; the first, "sweet and comely as Jerusalem;" the second, "terrible as an army set in array."

And it may be said that if there be any one feeling which shows itself on all occasions in the writings of the

Fathers, any one conviction which sways all their arguments, it is the feeling that the flock of Christ is one and indivisible; that the Episcopate which rules it throughout the earth is one and indivisible also; and both because the Great Shepherd is one, and the Father who sent Him is one; as we have heard St. Cyprian in unsurpassable words declaring sixteen hundred years ago.

We see, then, the two forces of the Primacy and the Episcopate coexist at the end of this first great stadium of the Church's course, as they coexisted on the Day of Pentecost. It is precisely when setting forth the testimony given to the one Christian faith against all heresy by the churches as established throughout the world, especially those which had Apostles for founders, that Irenæus, a hundred years after St. Peter's death, dwelt upon this bond of the one Episcopate, "that necessity by which, on account of its superior principate, every Church, that is the faithful everywhere, were bound to agree with the Roman Church."

The two great Fathers, one the glory of the East, as the other of the West, Chrysostom and Augustine, born within a few years of each in the middle of the fourth century, and thus placed at a period sufficiently near, and yet not too near to contemplate the whole course of the Church during her conflict with the Roman Empire, both speak in numberless passages and in enthusiastic words of the wonder of the Catholic Church spread in all lands. The wonder was increased by the existence of heresies and schisms, which seemed by force of contrast the better to delineate the form of the one Spouse of Christ. St. Epiphanius and St. Augustine himself had recorded a number of these when that notable sentence of the great Father, "The judgment of the whole world is a safe one," which has passed into a proverb, was pronounced against the Donatists. What was the marvel which especially convinced their minds and touched their hearts? The Roman Empire, as they still saw it and lived in it, was, in fact, a vast confederation of many peoples, lands, and religions: the only unity which it possessed, amid endless varieties and contradictions, was that unity of civil government which Roman discipline, energy, and valour had so long maintained; which, the one of African the other of Hellenic race, equally felt and appreciated. This is the greatness especially of the imperial period. Now, springing up in the midst of this endless variety, this most profuse and party-coloured polytheism, this antagonism and rivalry of countless races, and no less in the light of a proud, refined, and most ancient, if also most corrupt, civilisation, they saw the establishment of one uniform government, bearing in its bosom one uniform religion, carried on through ten generations of men, and accomplished after manifold persecutions. They saw the religion and the government start together from the Person of one who claimed to be the Son of God, while He certainly died, as a malefactor would be condemned to die, upon the cross. They saw the religion and the government carried on in the second degree by twelve men, poor, illiterate, and powerless. And before their own time their fathers had told them how the chief of this mighty empire had bowed his head before the religion and the government springing from One who hung upon the cross, and in His name taught by the Fisherman and the Tentmaker. Was it not the One Episcopate with its one doctrine planted in all these lands, and imposing a uniform rule of life on men and women of every degree, attested by its hosts of martyrs, the purity of its virgins, the patience of its people, which seemed to them a miracle, the force of which they were never tired of proclaiming? That stately fabric in which doctrine and government permeate each other, "that unity coming from the strength of God, and seated in heavenly sacraments," was it not this to which St. Augustine appealed in combating a heresy in the errors of which he had long been himself ensnared?—an appeal couched in words the force of which is vastly greater when they can be applied with equal truth in the nineteenth as in the fourth century. "I am held in the bosom of the Catholic Church by the agreement of peoples and nations; by the authority which took its rise in miracles, was nurtured in hope, reached its growth in charity, is confirmed by antiquity. I am held by the succession of bishops, down to the actual episcopate, from the very See of the Apostle Peter, to whom after His resurrection the Lord intrusted His sheep to be fed. Lastly, I am held by the very name of Catholic, which, not without reason, among so many heresies that Church alone has possessed; so that though all heretics would like to be called Catholics, yet if a stranger ask where the Catholic

Church is, no heretic would venture to show him his own church or house."[1]

These words were written before the end of the fourth century, and exhibit the aspect in which the Church of Christ presented itself to St. Augustine. That which he has summed up in a few sentences was drawn out at somewhat greater length by St. Chrysostom about ten years before, when the worn-out religion of paganism was falling to the ground, and the judgment of Theodosius in levelling heathen temples only expressed the victory of the Christian society. His words[2] portray so graphically the several features of that "divine and invincible power" to which he attributed the growth and expansion of the Church as he beheld it 350 years after the Day of Pentecost, that I will quote them here notwithstanding their length.[3] He begins with saying: "If a heathen says to me, How can I know that Christ is God? for this is the first thing to be established; the rest all follows from it; I will not make my proof from heaven, or such things. For if I say to him, He made the heaven, the earth, and the sea; he will not receive it. If I say, He raised the dead, He healed the blind, He cast out devils; that too he will not accept. If I say, He promised a kingdom and blessings unspeakable; if I talk to him of the resurrection, not only will he not receive it, he will laugh at it. How, then, can we ap-

---

[1] Cont. Epist. Manichæi, 5.
[2] θεία τις καὶ ἄμαχος δύναμις τοῦ ταῦτα προειπόντος καὶ τελέσαντος.—St. Chrysostom, tom. i. p. 579.
[3] Against the Jews and Gentiles to demonstrate that Christ is God, tom. i. p. 558, and pp. 574, 577, 578.

proach him, especially if he be an ordinary man? How but by those things which both of us admit without contradiction, of which there is no doubt. What, then, does he admit Christ to have done which he will not dispute? This, that He founded the race of Christians. He will not deny that Christ Himself established the Churches throughout the world." Afterwards he thus comments on the marvellous fulfilment of our Lord's prophecy on this subject: "Twelve disciples followed Him; of the Church no one had then conceived so much as the name, for the synagogue was still flourishing. When, then, almost the whole world was under the dominion of impiety, what was His prophecy? 'Upon this Rock I will build My Church, and the gates of hell shall not prevail against it.' Weigh as you please this word, and you will see the splendour of its truth. For the wonder is, not that He built it throughout all the world, but made it impregnable, and that though assaulted by such conflicts. For 'the gates of hell shall not prevail against it' are dangers which drag down to hell. Now, compare the distinctness of the prediction with the force of the result; behold words which have their evidence in facts, and an irresistible power producing its effects with ease. They are but few words: 'I will build My Church.' Do not run over them simply, but draw them out in your thoughts. Form a conception how vast a thing it is to fill the whole world with so many Churches in a short time; to change so many nations; to persuade multitudes; to break up hereditary customs; to extirpate rooted habits; to

scatter like dust the tyranny of pleasure, the strength
of vice; to sweep away like smoke *altars of blood*, and
temples and idols and mysteries, and profane festivals,
and the impure odours of victims, and everywhere to
raise *unbloody altars*[1] in the country of Romans, Persians, Scythians, Moors, and Indians, beyond the limits
of our own world. For even the British Islands, lying
in the ocean beyond our own sea, have felt the power
of this word; for there too churches and altars have
been erected. The word then uttered by Him has been
planted in all men's souls, is current in all their mouths.
The world, which was overgrown with thorns, has been
cleared of them, is become pure arable soil, has received
into it the seeds of piety. It would be a proof of exceeding greatness, an evidence of divine power, if nobody
offered resistance, in the midst of peace and in the
absence of opponents, for so vast a portion of the earth
to be changed in a mass from a long inveterate bad
habit, and to assume another habit far more difficult.
It was not merely custom which offered resistance, but
pleasure which held possession, two tyrannous things.
For men were persuaded to reject what they had inherited from a long succession of ancestors, from philosophers, and from orators; and not only so, but what
was most difficult, to receive a new habit of life, in
which the hardest point of all was, that it carried with
it much endurance. For it led away from luxury to

[1] The contrast is marked in the original by totally distinct words, which the rendering both by the same word *altar* would efface: 1. βωμούς, altars of the religion with bloody sacrifices; 2. θυσιαστήρια, which are altars whereon the Unbloody Sacrifice is offered.

fasting, from the love of money to poverty, from impurity to temperance, from anger to meekness, from enviousness to kindliness, from the broad and wide way to the narrow and straight and rugged way; and this too the very men who had been nurtured in the former. For it did not take men of another world and another habit of life, but the very men who, through their utter corruption, were softer than mire in their old habit of life; on these it enjoined to tread the narrow and straight way, in all its roughness and sharpness, and they listened. How many? Not two, or ten, or twenty, or a hundred, but the vast majority of a world-wide population. And by whom did the persuasion come? By eleven men without literature, without station, ineloquent, ignoble, poor, who had no country, nor abundance of resources, nor bodily strength, nor distinguished reputation, nor renown of ancestors, nor strength of words, nor skill in rhetoric, nor eminence of knowledge; fishermen, tentmakers, foreigners. For they had not even the same language as those they persuaded, but that strange and outlandish Hebrew tongue. Through them He built this Church, which stretches from one end of the earth to the other.

"Nor was this the sole wonder, but there was a further one. These few, poor, private men, undistinguished, untaught, and unvalued, foreigners and despised, had the remodelling of the whole world placed in their hands, and were bidden to change it into a far more difficult condition of things. Yet this was not to be done in peace, but amid wars of all kind surrounding them. War was in every nation and every city; nay, they felt its blast in every house. For this doctrine entering in, and severing often the child from the father, the daughter-in-law from the mother-in-law, brother from brother and servant from master, subject from ruler, husband from wife and wife from husband, and the parent from his offspring, since conversions did not take place in a mass, produced daily enmities, perpetual conflicts, a thousand deaths to its bearers, from whom men turned as common enemies. All persecuted them—emperors, rulers, private persons, freemen, slaves, cities and their peoples; nor them alone, but, hardest of all, their neophytes, while they were yet under instruction. War was waged equally upon the taught and the teachers, since the doctrine was opposed to imperial commands, to the common habit, to inherited manners. They were bidden to abstain from idols, to despise the altars of blood, which their fathers and all their ancestors had served, to quit impure beliefs, to ridicule festivals and reject initiations—things to them the most formidable and tremendous, and for which they would rather have given up their life than choose what the others said to them, to believe, that is, on the Son of Mary, on One who stood before the procurator's tribunal, who was spit upon, who suffered unnumbered horrors, who endured an accursed death, who was buried, who rose again. But the strange thing of all was this: the sufferings were manifest to all, the scourging, the blows on the cheek, the spittings on the face, the strokes from the palms of the hand, the cross, the long mockery, the being put to scorn by all, the burial granted by favour. Not so the facts of His Resurrection; for when He rose again He appeared to them alone. And yet when they told these things they persuaded men, and so they built up the Church.

"But how did they do this? By the power of Him who commanded it. He Himself levelled the way for them; He made the difficulties easy. For had not a divine power given success here, there would not even have been a beginning, not even the first step. How otherwise was it? He who said, 'Let there be a firmament,' and produced it in fact; 'Let the dry land appear,' and it came; 'Let the sun shine,' and it shone; He who did all things with a word planted also these Churches, and the saying, 'I will build my Church,' produced all these effects. For such are the words of God, creative words, of creations wonderful and strange. . . .

"Thus, then, they build the universal Church. Yet no workman who was driven about and hindered could with stone and mortar build a single wall; but these men erected so vast a number of churches through the inhabited world while they were being beaten and imprisoned, pursued and put to flight, banned and scourged, slaughtered, burned, and drowned, together with their disciples. They built not with stones, but souls, in the fulness of free choice. How can one compare a mason's work with that of changing by persuasion a soul wherein demons had so long revelled, so that from a state of madness it should reach the height of a sound mind. Yet such was the strength of men who went about all the world naked and discalced, and with a single coat; for they had fighting with them the irresistible power of Him who said, 'Upon this rock I will build My Church, and the gates of hell shall not prevail against it.' Count up the number of tyrants who were ranged in battle against it from that time, what persecutions they raised, in what position the faith stood all that first time when it was newly planted and men's minds were tender. Heathens were the emperors Augustus, Tiberius, Caius, Nero, Vespasian, Titus, and all those who succeeded them down to the time of the blessed Constantine. All these fought against the Church, some with more, some with less violence; all all of them, however, fought. If some of them seemed to be quiet, the very fact that those who reigned were conspicuous for impiety was a cause of warfare against the Church, because those around them flattered and served them therein. Yet all these snares and attacks were scattered like spiders' webs, smoke, or dust. For the effect of their plotting was to produce a great host of martyrs, to unfold the immortal treasures of the Church, to disclose its pillars and towers. They, not only by their life but by their death, were the assurance of a great help to all who came after them.

"Here is the strength of the prediction: the gates of hell shall not prevail against it. From that which has been trust concerning that which is to be, and that no one shall overcome the martyrs."

In reflecting on the history thus sketched out, the thought occurs how completely the ideal of Pope St.

Clement, St. Ignatius, St. Irenæus, Tertullian, St. Cyprian, St. Chrysostom, St. Augustine, St. Epiphanius, and St. Leo, nay, not their ideal only, but that spritual kingdom which they described as they saw before their eyes, would have been overthrown, if there were substituted for it a number of bishops scattered through the world in a variety of temporal kingdoms, some holding one part and some another part of an original revelation, with a multitude of discrepancies, and all deriving their authority to exercise their mandate from the several temporal powers to which they were civilly subject. The wonder which these Fathers one and all testify in gazing upon a divine Church would have passed into disgust and derision for an institution over which "the gates of hell" had prevailed by destroying its spiritual independence together with its doctrinal unity.

Let us proceed to examine how these two were both maintained, penetrating the divine work so far as to reach that intimate union which made one substance of outward regimen and inward belief by the force of an indissoluble life; for if the Episcopate had been a mere government, it would have had neither such unity nor such vitality, nor have been capable of supporting the Church's fabric.

CHAPTER V.

THE ACTUAL RELATION BETWEEN CHURCH AND STATE FROM THE DAY OF PENTECOST TO CONSTANTINE.

The One Episcopate Resting upon the One Sacrifice.

ONE of the points on which Pope St. Clement most strongly dwells is the care with which our Lord communicated to His Apostles definite and accurate instructions as to the kingdom which they were to set up. And from this care he draws the conclusion that, if infringement of the Mosaic law was punished by death, how much more guilty were they who showed insubordination to a precept of Christ in the institution of Christian rule? Thus St. Clement affirms that our Lord, far from leaving the government of His Church to be evolved out of local circumstances or individual temperaments or political affinities, determined it from the beginning. We shall now further show that He enshrined in it the very life of His people; and so that their worship, their government, their belief, and their practice were wrapped up together. Their government contained their doctrine, and set before their eyes in distinct vision Him in whom they trusted, Jesus Christ and Him crucified. It was not a human device but a divine ordinance, and the preaching of Christ through it was His action also. His words were deeds as much in the teaching of His Church as they were in the days of His flesh.

Our Lord created the priesthood of His Church on the eve of His Passion. It is the basis on which all spiritual power and all doctrinal truth rest in His kingdom; and He willed that the episcopate should be the instrument to communicate both power and truth to His people, and that the priesthood should be stored up in the person of each bishop. This plant of life, complete in itself, but only as a sucker of the One Vine,[1] the Apostles deposited in every city and town by the inspiration of the Holy Ghost; as St. Clement says, they passed on themselves and left it to grow by virtue of the same Spirit. The result was that when Constantine gave the acknowledgment of the Civil Power to the great Spiritual Kingdom, its Episcopate had far outgrown the limits of his empire.

In what does the High-priesthood of Christ consist? In two acts, which it is well carefully to distinguish.

The first is that divine act of the Blessed Trinity by which the Second Person, the Eternal Son of the Father, assumed a created nature into the unity of His Person, and that the nature of man. The act whereby He became man is the act constituting His Priesthood.[2] Before His Incarnation He was not a Priest; in the divine

---

[1] "A quibus traducem fidei et semina doctrinæ cæteræ exinde ecclesiæ mutuatæ sunt." *Tradux*, the vine branch carried along above the ground from the parent stem, so that there is but one tree. Tertullian, De Præscrip. Hæret. 20. [2] Franzelin, De Verbo Incarnato, p. 520.

nature in which alone He is from eternity, He does not offer but receive sacrifice. St. Paul describes the act, and the instantaneous acceptance by the Divine Son, as man in His human nature, of the mission to be High Priest for the human race in these words : " When He cometh into the world He saith : Sacrifice and oblation Thou wouldest not : but a body Thou hast fitted to me : Holocausts for sin did not please Thee. Then said I, behold I come : in the head of the book it is written of Me, that I should do Thy will, O God." The whole purpose of His Incarnation and the whole course of His future human life are here summed up, as accepted by Him in the first moment of His human existence, when He says : " A body Thou hast fitted to Me—behold I come—that I should do Thy will, O God." The whole Christian faith rests upon this divine act. It is the simply inconceivable humiliation of the Divine Majesty, the simply unutterable effect of the Divine Love. The angels, who have had it before them from their creation in vision, and for more than eighteen hundred years in effect, have not yet mastered its depths; nor is the Mother of fair Love herself—the nearest to it—equal to the task either of expressing it or of comprehending it. How, then, was it to be impressed on the human race in a manner which should cause its full force to be received by those who learnt it for the first time; and when it had been thus learnt what further provision was to bring about that it should never be forgotten, nor pass into the crowd of things which have once been and then cease to be ?

We have, first, in these words of St. Paul, the Divine Son accepting His mission as the first act of His human nature, and, further, expressing the nature of His mission—to do the will of His Father, that will being that He should take the body which His Father had prepared for Him. In that acceptance is comprised all the labours and sufferings of the thirty-three years foreseen from the beginning, willed by the Father, freely chosen by the Son in His manhood, as the first act of that manhood, which yet is prolonged through His whole life.

After this the Apostle goes on to exhibit the second act of His High-Priesthood, springing out of the first, and its consummation—the abrogation of the ancient sacrifices, although divinely instituted, and the substitution for them of that Body which God had fitted to Him. "In saying before, Sacrifices and oblations and holocausts for sin Thou wouldst not, neither are they pleasing to Thee, which are offered according to the law: then said I, Behold I come to do Thy will, O God: He taketh away the first, that He may establish that which followeth. In the which will we are sanctified by the oblation of the Body of Jesus Christ once." As the first act, the Incarnation, runs on into the second, the Atonement, so the second depends on the first. Without the assumption by God the Son of a created nature, the nature of man, there would be no sacrifice for man and no reconciliation. The source of sanctification is the offering of the Body of the God-man, of no other body; and without the Godhead of Christ His religion would be the shadow of a dream.

How, again, was this second act of His High-Priesthood, the oblation of His Body on the cross once for all for the sins of the whole world, to be impressed upon the world?

Human acts pass away into the abyss of past time, and the ever-flowing tide of successive existence sweeps them into the background. The sufferings and teachings of our Lord Himself, even His death upon the cross, would in themselves as human acts be subject to this lot. How were they to be made ever-living and ever-present, rescued from oblivion, carried in the heart and professed by the lips of men in every succeeding generation until the day of doom?

Truly there was wisdom needed for this effect, and what did our Lord do?

He was at the very point of completing that will of God which He came to do, and for which a Body was fitted to Him. Having celebrated the Pasch of the Law, which had been instituted so many ages before, as the speaking type of what He was to accomplish, He with a word made His disciples priests to offer that Body which He then first gave to them, which on the morrow He was to offer on the cross, and in doing this utter the " Consummatum est." The Priesthood, which was to carry in itself the whole power and virtue of His Church, He created before the sacrifice of the cross, but in immediate view of it, as the first act, as it were, of His Passion.

But the Priesthood which He created, and the offering in which it consisted, sprung from the union of the two acts which formed His own High-Priesthood, the assumption of the manhood for the purpose of redeeming man, and the execution of that purpose by His death on the cross. The Priesthood contained them both in itself, for the Body given was the Body broken on the cross, the Blood given was the Blood shed on the cross; and they were both the Body and Blood of a God-man. "Do this, He said, in commemoration of Me;" and as long as it was done daily, the double truth, the double benefit of God to man, the double marvel of redeeming love, offering itself and offering what is divine for the erring creature, could not fade from remembrance. It is as present now as it was at the hour of the crucifixion, and will be equally present to the end of the world.

But in order better to understand the force and meaning of our Lord's action, it is necessary to consider the institution which, at the time of it, was in existence and full operation all over the world, the institution, that is, of bloody sacrifice.

From the beginning of history, and in all countries, the intercourse between God and man consisted in two things, prayer and sacrifice, and they were carried on together. For this much the Greek may fitly represent all Gentilism. Now Plato represents Euthyphron as saying to Socrates, "If any one knows how to say and to do things acceptable to the gods by praying and by sacrificing, that is piety, and such conduct preserves both private families and the commonwealth; and the contrary to these acceptable things is impiety, which overthrows and destroys everything." To which Socrates replies, "You call, then, piety a certain knowledge of sacrifice and prayer." "I do." "Then sacrifice is giving to the gods, and prayer asking of them."[1]

A most careful student[2] of the Greek mind tells us: "As the need of the gods was felt by man in all the events of his life, in every work and every purpose, sacrificial worship, the burnt-offering, or the briefer libation-offering, ran through the whole of his being, and seemed to be prayer clothed in action." And again, "We have shown that man conceived of the Godhead not only as by its immortality infinitely exalted above himself, but likewise as the Ruler and Administrator of the whole universe and the being of man; and moreover, that man, in spite of all doubt and error as to the nature of his gods, in spite of his allowing impersonal powers to be at their side who threaten their dignity, yet never detaches himself from them, because he always feels himself impelled to seek a living personal Godhead. To this he was riveted by the insoluble bonds of a spiritual and natural need; and the recognition of this dependence, the expression of human subjection, the tribute of homage which man offers in the certainty of needing its grace, that is piety, as it is shown in action and in word, that is to say, in sacrifice and in prayer." And "the whole worship, that is, all sacrifices and divination, are made by Plato to be identical with the communion of gods and men with each other."[3]

[1] Plato, Eutyphron, 14.
[2] Nägelsbach, Homerische Theologie, 207; Id., Nachhomerische Theologie, 193.
[3] The Banquet, p. 188 *e*.

Another writer,[1] most learned in Greek and Roman antiquity, says: "These two constitute the oldest and most general form of honouring God. It might perhaps be said that the first word of the original man was a prayer, and the first act of the fallen man a sacrifice. Moses in Genesis, at any rate, carries the origin of sacrifice up to the first history of man, to Cain and Abel; the Greek legends, to Prometheus and the centaur Chiron, or to the eldest kings, Melisseus, Phoronæus, and Cecrops.

"In Gentilism as in Judaism, actual sacrifices of animals are everywhere the rule; beside them, in particular cases, offerings also of vegetable substances. Indeed, sacrifices were offered not merely for expiation, but wherever man had need of the gods, or reason to thank them, on all important moments of life, at the beginning and end of every weighty action, in order to maintain and make manifest the unbroken connection of man with God.

"Those most ancient domestic precepts recorded by Hesiod enjoin on every one, at declining and at dawning day, to conciliate the gods, with pure and chaste heart, by holy sprinklings and fragrant perfume, that their heart may incline to us with good-will and peace, and as often as thou returnest from a journey, offer fair sacrifices to the immortal gods. In family life sacrifices were made specially at birth, marriage, and death. The Cretans, who considered human marriage as a transcript of the heavenly marriage between Zeus and Hera, made offerings on occasion of it specially to these gods. If a

[1] Lasaulx, Die Sühnopfer (extracts from), pp. 234-270.

man wished to marry at Athens, he first made his prayers and sacrifices to the so-called Tritapatores, the first fathers of life, for the happy generation of children, since no birth takes place without God. At the marriage itself, again, there were sacrifices, when the gall of the victim was thrown behind the altar to signify that no bitterness should infect their union. Moreover, the bride at Athens was introduced by a sacrifice into her husband's race; and again, a victim was offered upon the inscription of children on the tribe list. At Sparta mothers were wont, on the espousal of their daughters, to make offerings to Aphrodité Hera, the goddess of married love; the Bœotians and Locrians to Artemis Euklea; the maidens of Haliartus made a preparatory gift to the fountain Kissoessa, according to ancestral custom. If the marriage was blest by a child, a sacrifice was offered for this on the seventh or tenth day after the birth, and thereupon the child was named. At death, again, sacrifices were offered for the peace of departed souls, as well by individuals as by the commonwealth. According to Plato, it was an orphic doctrine that there were certain deliverances and purifications which availed also for the dead. The gravestones were anointed and crowned with flowers, pyres were erected, and victims slaughtered on them, or cakes were thrown into the fire, holes made in the earth, and libations of wine, milk, and honey poured into them. Only no sacrifices were offered for children, because, as they had departed unstained by intercourse with earthly things, they needed no further reconcilement. Plutarch describes the great public sacrifice for the dead which the Platæans, in late times, continued to offer yearly for those who had fallen in battle against the Persians.

"In agricultural life, also, which is the beginning and foundation of all religious habit, every important moment was sanctified by sacrifice. The Athenians, at the beginning of tillage, before they turned up the land, offered the preparatory sacrifice to Demeter[1] for the prosperity of the future fruits, and are said on one occasion, in the fifth Olympiad, at a time of general dearth, to have made such an offering for all Hellas at the command of the Delphic god. So at the end of the winter, when the fruits of the field began to grow, all the magistrates, from eldest time, offered the previous thanksgiving[2] to Athené, the protectress of the city. So they offered at Rome, at the time of the pear-tree blossom, before ploughing, vows and grain cakes, for the health of the labouring oxen; then before harvest offerings to Ceres of bread and wine, and so again when a wood was cleared, at the digging and blessing of the fields. So both peoples were wont in general to give the first-fruits of everything which the favour of the gods gave to them; fruits of the field as of the herd, of the vintage, and of the trees; the former liquid, and the latter solid. These first-fruits represented the whole mass, for all the productions of nature belong to the Giver thereof. Aristotle holds the offering of such first-fruits of the field to be the oldest kind of offerings in general, and a Roman writer finely says, since the

[1] προηρόσια. [2] προχαριστήρια.

ancients lived in the belief that all nourishment, the fatherland, nay, life itself, is a gift of the gods, they were wont to offer something to these of everything, more to show their gratitude than because they believed that the gods needed it. Hence, before they ate anything of the new fruits, they consecrated a portion to the gods; and since they possessed both fields and cities in fee from the gods, they dedicated to them a portion for temples and chapels, and some were wont to offer to them the hair, as the topmost portion of the body, for the sound state of the rest. Thus the Bhagavadgita[1] says: 'Sacrifice to the gods; they will give you the wished-for food. He who eats what they have given without first offering therefrom is a thief; they who ate what remained of the sacrifice are free from all sins.' The fathers of families made an offering every month to Hecaté for reparation of sins committed in the house. Certain dishes were prepared and carried through the whole house, while the curse which rested on evil deeds committed was put therein, and then they were placed at midnight upon a cross-road. Whoever ate of this, it was believed he took the curse into him with the food. Only curs and currish men did it.

"Sacrifices were connected not less with all important acts of political life. 'Those before us,' says Philo, 'began every good action with perfect victims, deeming this the best means to bring about a good end to them.' In the consciousness that all were stained with sin, but that sinful men could discover no good counsel, swine

[1] 3, 12.

were sacrificed before every assembly of the people at Athens, and their blood sprinkled as a purification over the seats of the meeting. A priest then carried certain parts of the victim round the assembly, and cast their sins into these parts. When this was done, incense was offered, and the same priest went with a vessel of holy water round, blessing the assembled people therewith for the matter which it was to undertake. Then the herald recited the customary prayers, and the consultation at last began. The sacrifices by which the council, the generals, the Prytanes, and all public magistrates entered on office were similar. In like manner sacrifices preceded the sittings of justice and the taking of oaths. In war no important step was taken before the sacrifices were prosperous and announced a good result. Sacrifice was offered at the first start, at the passage of boundaries and rivers, at making an advance, at taking ship, at landing, before assault of besieged cities, before battle, and after victory. The Athenian generals were wont specially to sacrifice to Hermes, the leader. All truces, peace-makings, leagues, and treaties were accompanied with sacrifice. A direction was attached to all sacrifices ordered by law or oracular decrees, that they should be according to the hereditary three customs, that is, take place on months, days, and years, *i.e.*, solar years, lunar months, and days of the month. Plato enjoins, as in Athens was really the fact, that on every day of the year the magistrate should offer sacrifice to a god or genius for the city and its inhabitants, their goods and chattels. Of Julian, the last emperor attached to the

Hellenic worship, it is expressly said that he, not only on new moons, but every day, welcomed the rising sun-god with a bloody victim, and accompanied his setting with another, and served the gods not by other hands, but himself took part in the sacrifice, ran about the altar, took up the mallet and held the knife, and that, in order the better to discharge these duties, he had built a temple to the sun-god in the midst of his palace. The shedding of blood was everywhere the bond of union between man and man, and between man and God; to the commonwealth the guarantee of its security, the firmest pillar of its government."

If we extend this description of the prevalence of sacrifices among the Greeks and Romans to all the nations of antiquity, we shall be able to form a conception which, after all, will be very feeble when compared with the reality, of the degree in which the whole religious life between man and God, the national life in the various nations, the social life in each nation, the domestic life in each family, was alike dominated by the idea and practice of bloody sacrifice.

The ceremonial of sacrifice was as follows: "The sacrificial usages themselves were very solemn. Everything expressed that the sacrifice was made freely and joyously. Those who offered to the heavenly gods wore white robes, and crowns on the head and in the hands. Those who offered to the gods beneath the earth were robed in black. The victim was also crowned and adorned with ribbons, and on solemn occasions its horns were gilt. It was led by a loose cord, to indicate that it followed willingly and of its own accord. If the animal took to flight, that was a bad prognostic. It had to be put to death, but might not be led up again to the altar. Before touching the sacrificial utensils, the hands were washed in order to approach the holy with purity. As with us, a boy poured water over the hands of the sacrificant. Then the sacrificial cake or sacred salt-meal and the knife of sacrifice were brought in a basket and carried round the altar. A branch of laurel or olive, symbol of purification and peace, was dipped in the water-stoup and the bystanders sprinkled therewith. The holy water itself was consecrated with prayers and the dipping into it of a firebrand from the altar. Silence was then enjoined, and when the profane had been dismissed with such words as 'Depart, depart, whoever is a sinner,' the herald cried with a loud voice, 'Who is here?' those present answered, 'Many, and they pious.' Then the proper prayer of sacrifice began for the gracious acceptance of what was offered; and after the victim had been proved sound and faultless, a line was drawn to mark its willingness with the back of the sacrificial knife from the forehead to the tail, and grain was poured over its neck until by nodding it seemed to give its consent to be sacrificed. Then there were fresh prayers; the priest took a cup of red wine, tasted the blood of the vine, allowed also those present to drink of it, and poured the remainder between the animal's horns. Then the hair of its forehead was cut off and cast into the fire as a firstling; incense was kindled, and the remaining grain finally poured upon the altar with music of pipe and flute, that no ill-omened word might be heard during the sacred action. In specially solemn sacrifices there were also choral hymns and dances. The animal was struck with the axe and its throat cut; when the sacrifice was to the gods above, with hands raised towards heaven; when to the gods below, with head bowed to the earth. The blood was then received in a vessel and partly poured out upon the altar, partly sprinkled on those around, that they might be delivered from sin. Especially all who wished to have a portion in the sacrifice had to touch the victim and the sacrificial ashes. According to the oldest usage the whole victim was burnt; later only certain portions—the head and feet (the extremities for the whole), the entrails, especially the heart as the seat of life, the shanks as the place of strength, and the fat as the best portion. Then red wine, unmixed, was poured upon the flames. The sacrificers consumed the rest, as in the Hebrew thank-offerings and among the Egyptians and Indians, in a sacred festive meal; among the Arcadians, masters and slaves altogether. Such meals were usual from the most ancient time after the completion of the sacrifice, and in them originally the gods were considered to sit as guests with men. All sang thereby, as law and custom determined, sacred hymns, that during the meal moral comeliness and respect might not be transgressed, and the harmony of song might consecrate the words and the conduct of the speakers. By this common partaking of the pure sacrificial flesh, the communion of the offered meats, a substantially new life was to be implanted in the partakers; for all who eat of one sacrifice are one body.

"Hence the first Christians obstinately refused to eat of the flesh of heathen victims. 'I had rather die than feed on your sacrifices.' 'If any one eat of that flesh he cannot be a Christian.'[1] At the end of the feast, as it seems, the herald dismissed the people with the words λαοῖς ἄφεσις—Ite, missa est."

Thus we find that sacrifice existed from the beginning of history in all nations, and was associated with prayer; the two together made up worship, and the spiritual acts of the mind, expressed in prayer, were not considered complete without sacrifice, a corporeal act as it were, so that the homage of soul and body together constituted the complete act of fealty on the part of man to his Maker. But we find also more than this. The spiritual acts which are contained in prayer, as the expression of an innocent creature to his Creator, are three: adoration, which recognises the supreme majesty of God; thanksgiving, which specially dwells on the benefits received from Him; and petition, which speaks the perpetual need of Him felt by the creature. And with these in a state of innocence prayer would stop. But if the harmony between the Creator and the creature has been broken, if sin has been committed, and a sense of guilt arising from that sin exists, then prayer expresses a fourth need of the creature, which does not exist in the state of innocence—the need of expiation. Now offerings of the natural fruits of the earth, of what-

[1] Ruinart, Acta Martyrum, pp. 350 and 527.

ever kind, correspond, it is plain, to the three former parts of prayer—to adoration, thanksgiving, and petition for support; but the bloody sacrifice of living creatures, in which occurs the pouring out of their blood in a solemn rite, the presentation of it to God, and the sprinkling of the people with it, can only be accounted for by a consciousness in man of guilt before God. The existence of a rite so peculiar in so many nations, and its association everywhere with the most solemn act of prayer, is not accounted for even by such a consciousness alone; for what power had the shedding of an animal's blood to remove the sense of guilt in man or to propitiate God? There was no doubt the consciousness of guilt on man's part, but what should ever lead him, of himself, to conceive such a mode of expiating his guilt, such a mode of propitiating God? It was much more natural for him to conceive that the act of pouring out the blood of a creature, in which was its life, the most precious gift of the Creator, would be an offence to that Creator, the Lord of life, its Giver and Maintainer. Thus the act of bloody sacrifice can only be accounted for as in its origin a directly divine institution, a positive law of God. As such it is plainly recognised by Moses when he introduces it in the history of Cain and Abel, where, in the first man's children, it appears as already existing. God alone, the absolute Lord of life, could attach together prayer and bloody sacrifice, and enact that the worship which He would receive from His creature, the worship which not only adored Him as Creator, thanked Him as Benefactor, asked His help as Preserver, but likewise acknowledged guilt before Him for sin committed, should be made up of a compound act, that of solemn prayer, and that of shedding and offering blood, and partaking of a victim so offered. The rite of bloody sacrifice is, therefore, the record of the Fall stamped by the hand of God on the forehead of the human race at its first starting in the state of guilt. The death of a vicarious victim was the embodiment of the doctrine that man had forfeited his life by disobedience to God his Creator, and that he should be restored by the effusion of the blood of an innocent victim. The fact of the concentration of these four acts of prayer about the rite of bloody sacrifice, through all Gentilism, as well as in Judaism, has no end of significance.

This conclusion was drawn by St. Augustine,[1] who says : " Were I to speak at length of the true sacrifice, I should prove that it was due to no one but the one true God; and this the one true Priest, the Mediator of God and men, offered to Him. It was requisite that the figures promissive of this sacrifice should be celebrated in animal victims, as a commendation of that flesh and blood which were to be, through which single victim might take place the remission of sins contracted of flesh and blood, which shall not possess the kingdom of God, because that self-same substance of the body shall be changed into a heavenly quality. This was signified by the fire in the sacrifice, which seemed to absorb death into victory. Now such sacrifices were

[1] Contr. Faustum, l. 22, s. 17, tom. viii. 370.

duly celebrated in that people whose kingdom and whose priesthood were both a prophecy of the King and Priest who was to come, that He might rule, and that He might consecrate the faithful in all nations, and introduce them to the kingdom of heaven, the sanctuary of the angels, and eternal life. Now this being the true sacrifice, as the Hebrews celebrated religious predictions of it, so the Pagans celebrated sacrilegious imitations; for in the Apostle's words, what the Gentiles sacrifice they sacrifice to devils and not to God. For an ancient thing is that immolation of blood, carrying an announcement of the future, testifying from the beginning of the human race the Passion of the Mediator that was to be, for Abel is the first in sacred writ recorded to have offered this."

The rite of bloody sacrifice, thus enacted by God, and set by Him upon flesh and blood as a perpetual prophecy, is one of those acts of supreme worship which may be offered to God alone. "Genuflexions," says St. Thomas,[1] "prostrations, and other indications of such-like honour, may be offered also to men, though with a different intent; but no one has judged that sacrifice should be offered to any one unless he esteemed him to be God, or pretended so to esteem him. But the external sacrifice represents the internal true sacrifice, according to which the human mind offers itself to God. Now, our mind offers itself to God as being the Source of its creation, as being the Author of its operation, as being the End of its beatitude; and these three things

[1] S. Tho. contr. Gentilis, 3, 120.

belong to the supreme principle of things alone. Whence man is bound to offer the worship of sacrifice to the one supreme God alone, but not to any spiritual substances."

The Gentile world broke this primary law of worship in offering the rite of bloody sacrifice to numberless false gods. It is, therefore, no wonder that, falling so low in its conception of the Godhead as to divide God into numberless parts, it fell likewise into oblivion of the meaning and prophecy contained in the sacrifice itself; yet though it might forget, it could not efface the idea enshrined in the act, so long as it preserved the material parts of the act, which in so striking a manner exhibited to the very senses of man the great doctrine that without effusion of blood there is no remission of sins. And this was declared not merely in the Hebrew ritual, divinely instituted for that very purpose, and in full operation down to the very time of Christ; but in all those sacrifices of the dispersed and corrupted nations, which, debased in the persons to whom they were offered, and performed with a routine oblivious of their meaning, yet bore witness to the truth which God had originally impressed on the minds of men, and committed to a visible and prophetic memorial.

If we survey the whole world at the coming of Christ, we may say that the institution of bloody sacrifice is the most striking and characteristic fact to be found in it. This conclusion will result in the mind if four things be noted which are therein bound up together. The first of these is its specific character; for surely the ceremonial of sacrifice, as above described, deserves this title, if anything ever did. It is a very marked and peculiar institution, conveying an ineffaceable sense of guilt in those who practise it, and a quite singular manner of detaching from themselves the effects of that guilt. Secondly, it is found everywhere; without sacrifice no religious worship is complete; its general diffusion has with reason been alleged as a proof of its true origin and deep meaning. Were it only found in single or in rude nations, it might have been attributed to rude and barbarous conceptions; but all nations had it, and the most civilised offered it in the greatest profusion. Thirdly, it had the most astonishingly pervading influence; from the top to the bottom of the social scale it ruled all; the king made it the support of his throne; the father of the family applied it to his children; bride and bridegroom were joined together in its name; and warring nations made peace in the blood of the sacrificed victim. Fourthly, the three notes just given are indefinitely heightened in their force when we consider that the institution, far from being of itself in accordance with man's reason, is quite opposed to it. Reason does indeed suggest that the fruits of the earth should be offered in mark of honour, gratitude, and dependence to that Almighty Lord by whose gift alone they are received; but reason of itself, far from suggesting, flies back from the notion that the Giver of life should accept as a propitiatory offering from His creature the blood of animals, in which, according to the general sense of antiquity, their life itself consisted. That this blood should be poured out, and sprinkled on those present as an act of religious faith; that it should be accompanied by words expressing adoration, thanksgiving, and petition; and further, that it should be considered to remove guilt,—the whole of this forms a conception so alien from reason, that he who reflects upon it is driven to the conclusion of a positive enactment, bearing in it a mysterious truth, which it was of the utmost importance for man to know, to bear in mind, to practise, and not to forget. And if we put together these four things, the specific character of the bloody sacrifice, its universality, its pervading influence, and the token of unreason, apart, that is, from the significance of a deep mystery, which rests upon it, we must feel that there is nothing in the constitution of the world before our Saviour's time more worthy of attention than this. There is no solution of it to be found but that of St. Augustine, " that the immolation of blood, carrying an announcement of the future, testified from the beginning of the human race the Passion of the Mediator that was to be."

But there is likewise a series of portentous facts, bearing upon the institution of bloody sacrifice, which runs through all human history. This is the offering of human sacrifices in expiation of guilt, or to ward off calamities. The religious ideas which lie at the bottom of this are, that as life is a gift of God to man on the condition that he fulfils God's commands, every sinner has thereby forfeited his life. The rule of inexorable justice is set forth in strongest language by the Greek tragedians, as when Æschylus says, "It abides, while Jove abides through the series of ages, that he who has done a deed shall suffer for it. It is an ordinance."[1] But as all men stand in a real communion of life to each other, and as members of one living whole are bound in one responsibility to the Godhead, the idea also prevailed that one man's life could be given for another's; that one might offer himself in expiation for another, and the willing sacrifice of the innocent was esteemed to have the more power in proportion as the vicarious will of the offerer was pure, and therefore acceptable to the gods: "For I think that a single soul performing this expiation would suffice for a thousand, if it be there with good-will," says Œdipus in Sophocles. So kings offer themselves for their people; so the royal virgin gains for the host with her blood prosperous winds. But from such acts of self-devotion, freely performed, we proceed to a further step, in which men are sacrificed against their will. At Athens is found the frightful custom that two miserable human beings, one of each sex, were yearly nourished at the public cost, and then solemnly sacrificed at the feast of the Thargelia for expiation of the people. Not only did the Consul Decius, at the head of his army, solemnly devote himself for his country, but so often as a great and general calamity threatened the existence of the Roman State human sacrifices were offered, and a male and female Gaul, a male and female Greek, or those of any other nation whence danger threatened, were buried alive in

[1] Agamemnon, 1520.

the ox-market, with magic forms of prayer uttered by the head of the college of the Quindecemviri. Nay, the human sacrifices yearly offered upon the Alban Mount to Jupiter Latiaris were continued down to the third century of our era.

What thus took place in Greece and Rome is found likewise amongst almost all the Eastern and Western peoples. The most cruel human sacrifices were nowhere more frequent than among the idolatrous races of Shem, whether Canaanites, Phœnicians, or Carthaginians. These specially offered the eldest or the only son. Egyptian, Persian, Arabian, the most ancient Indian history, and that of the Northern peoples, Scythians, Goths, Russians, Germans, Gauls, British, and the Celts in general, give us examples of the same custom.

The conclusion from all this is, how strong and general in the religious conscience of all ancient peoples was the sense of sinful man's need to be purified and reconciled with God, and that the means of such reconcilement were thought to be in the vicarious shedding of human blood.

At any rate, we may draw from this custom a corroboration of the meaning which lay in the rite of bloody sacrifice of animals, that the vicarious offering of an animal's life, which was deemed to be seated in the blood, was made in the stead of a human life as a ransom for it, as is exactly expressed in the lines of Ovid—

"Cor pro corde precor, pro fibris accipe fibras,
Hanc animam vobis pro meliore damus."—*Ovid, Fasti*, 6, 161.

The vicarious character of animal sacrifice is shown in

the Egyptian usage, wherein a seal was put upon oxen found pure and spotless for sacrifice, which represented a man kneeling with hands bound behind his back, and a sword put to his throat, while the bystanders lamented the slaughtered animal and struck themselves on the breast. The same idea that the victim was a ransom for man's life is also found in the Indian sacrificial ritual.[1]

The institution of bloody sacrifice, then, was not merely an instinctive confession by man of guilt before God, though this confession was contained in it in an eminent degree, but sprung from a direct divine appointment. This conclusion is borne in upon the mind by its existence everywhere, and by the astonishing force with which it seemed to hold all parts of human life in its grasp. Such an influence, again, shows the extent to which, in the original constitution of things, all human life was bound up in a dependence upon God. Not mental acts only, acts of adoration, thanksgiving, petition, and expiation were enjoined, but all these were expressed in a visible, corporeal action, and associated with it. It is precisely in this association that I trace the stamp of the divine appointment, as well as a seal of permanence, which is shown in the unbroken maintenance of the rite through so many shiftings of races and revolutions of governments in the lapse of so many centuries.

---

[1] The above account of human sacrifices is drawn from Lasaulx's treatise, pp. 237-255. He gives a profusion of examples, with their references in ancient authors.

Thus on the original human society, the family of the first man, God had impressed the idea that man by sin had forfeited his life before God; that there must be reparation for that forfeiture; that such reparation was one day to be made by the offering of an innocent victim; that in the meantime the vicarious sacrifice of animals should be offered to God as a confession of man's guilt; that their blood poured out before Him and sprinkled on the sacrifices should be accepted by God in token of an expiation.

Now what we have seen of the original institution of sacrifice will help to show how absolutely divine an act it was which our Lord took upon Himself in establishing a sacrifice for His people. But He was not only ordering a new worship; He was likewise at once fulfilling and abolishing by that fulfilment the old, that which had prevailed from the beginning of man's race. Instead of the blood of animals poured out profusely all over the world, He said, "This is the chalice, the new testament in My Blood, which shall be shed for you;" and speaking as the Lamb of God who takes away the sin of the world, using also the special sacrificial term, He said, "This is My Body, which is given for you; do this for a commemoration of Me." The act was doubly a divine act, in appointing a sacrifice for the whole human race, and in making His own Body that sacrifice; the first an act of divine authority, the second not that only, but pointing out the personal union of the Godhead with the Manhood, in virtue of which the communication of His flesh gives life to the world, as He had foretold a year before : "The bread which I will give is My flesh for the life of the world."[1] Thus the Christian sacrifice is the counterpart of the original institution, and throws the light of fulfilment upon that offering of the blood of bulls and goats which seemed in itself so unreasonable; which would have been so, but that it carried in itself the mystery hidden from the foundation of the world. Thus it was that the animal creation placed below man was chosen to bear witness in its flesh and blood to the offering which was to restore man, and the Lord of life made use of the life which He had given to signify in a speaking prophecy that supreme exhibition of His mercy, His justice, and His majesty, which He had purposed from the beginning. If the earth without Calvary might seem to have been a slaughter-house, Calvary made it an altar.

But if this be the relation of the Christian sacrifice to the original institution in general, it has a special relation to that whole order of hierarchy and sacrifice which was established by Moses. The whole body of the Mosaic law, from head to foot and in its minutest part, was constructed to be fulfilled in Christ. It was alike His altar and His throne, prepared for Him fifteen hundred years before His coming. Moses found the patriarchal priesthood and the patriarchal sacrifice, and drew out both so as to be a more detailed picture of the Priesthood and Sacrifice which were to be.

Then as the whole ancient worship, whether Patri-

[1] Luke xxii. 20; John vi. 52.

archal, or Jewish, or Gentile, had been concentrated in sacrifice, the Lord of all, coming to create the world anew, in the night of His Passion, and as the prelude of it, instituted the new Priesthood, and made it the summary of His whole dispensation. The Priest according to the order of Melchisedec came forth to supply what was wanting in the Levitical priesthood. Signs passed into realities, and the Precious Blood took the place of that blood which had been shed all over the earth from the sacrifice of Abel onwards.[1] St. Paul has told us how the King of justice and of peace, fatherless, motherless, and without genealogy in the sacred narrative, having neither beginning of days nor end of life, as then recorded, was the image of the Son of God, who remains a Priest for ever. For though He was to offer Himself once upon the altar of the cross, by death, to God His Father, and to work out eternal redemption, His Priesthood was not to be extinguished by His death. Therefore in the Last Supper, on the very night of His betrayal, He would leave to His beloved bride the Church a visible sacrifice, such as the nature of man required. This should represent the bloody sacrifice once enacted on the cross; this should preserve its memory fresh and living to the end of time; this should apply its saving virtue to the remission of sins daily committed by human frailty. Thus He declared Himself a Priest for ever after the order of Melchisedec. He presented His Body and His Blood under the species of bread and wine to God His Father.

[1] See Council of Trent, sess. 22, cap. i.

Under these symbols He gave them to His Apostles to receive, and so doing He made them priests of the new testament, and charged them, and those who should succeed them in this priesthood, to make this offering, by the words, "This do in commemoration of Me;" thus, as St. Paul adds, "showing the death of the Lord until He come."[1] For when He had celebrated that old Pasch which the multitude of the children of Israel immolated in memory of their coming out of Egypt, He made Himself the new Pasch, that this should be celebrated by the Church through her priests in visible signs, in commemoration of His passage from this world to the Father, when by the shedding forth of His own Blood He redeemed us and delivered us from the power of darkness and translated us into His own kingdom. This is the pure oblation, incapable of being stained by the unworthiness or malice of those who offer it, which God by the mouth of His prophet Malachias prophesied, saying, "From the rising of the sun even to the going down thereof My name is great among the Gentiles, and in every place there is sacrifice, and there is offered to My name a clean oblation." This St. Paul pointed out with equal clearness when he wrote, "The things which the heathens sacrifice, they sacrifice to devils and not to God; and I would not that you should be made partakers with devils. You cannot drink the chalice of the Lord and the chalice of devils: you cannot be partakers of the table of the Lord and of the table of devils." For as in the one case the table indicates the altar on

---

[1] 1 Cor. xi. 26.

which the heathen sacrifice was offered, so on the other it indicates the altar on which the sacrifice of Christ is offered; and the reality asserted in the one case is equally asserted in the other. And this, in fine, is that offering, the figure of which was given by those various similitudes of sacrifices in the time of nature and the time of the law; for, as the consummation and perfection of all these, it embraces every blessing which they signified.

All the force which sacrifice originally had to represent doctrine in a visible form, in accordance with the twofold nature of man, belonged in the most eminent degree to the sacrifice thus instituted. It became at once the centre of the Church's worship, being celebrated by the Apostles daily,[1] as we are told, while the Liturgies of the East and West make any question as to the character of the sacrifice impossible, and show how the great acts of adoration, thanksgiving, petition, and expiation were united in it and with it. It was the voice of the Christian people evermore mounting to the Eternal Father, and representing to Him in an action of infinite solemnity how He "so loved the world as to give His only-begotten Son, that whosoever believeth in Him may not perish but may have life everlasting."[2]

But more particularly let us observe the doctrines which our Lord taught, and as it were clothed with flesh in the daily sacrifice of the Church.

First, the cardinal doctrine of religion from the be-

[1] Acts ii. 46.   [2] John iii. 16.

ginning, as it is equally the certain witness of human reason, the unity of the Godhead; for the sacrifice is offered to the one God alone. It is the guardian of this great primary truth from all corruption, whether the polytheistic corruption of division and limitation, or the pantheistic corruption of vagueness and impersonality. Wherever this sacrifice is offered, the great Christian unity of the one living and holy God, the God who knows, the God who wills, the God who creates, is maintained by those who offer it.

Secondly, the Trinity of the Divine Persons; for the sacrifice consists in the offering of God the Son in His human nature as a sin-offering for man to His Father: "Wherein the same Christ is contained, and immolated without blood, who once on the altar of the cross offered Himself with blood;"[1] which, moreover, is accomplished by the descent of the Holy Ghost upon the gifts. Thus the three Divine Persons enter into the sacrifice, He to whom it is offered, He who offers it, and He by whose operation it is consummated. So distinct yet so interwoven is their action, so divine in each, that the sacrifice guards the doctrine of the most Blessed Trinity as it guards that of the Divine Unity, and those who offer this sacrifice are faithful in the maintenance of the second mystery as in that of the first. But the Divine Unity and Trinity is the very life of God, the very source of beatitude, to the knowledge and the faith of which this sacrifice subserves. It preaches these truths as no mere word could preach them; for action

[1] Council of Trent, sess. 22, cap. ii.

and word enter into each other and complete themselves reciprocally in the sacrifice.

Thirdly, the stupendous mystery of God the Creator assuming a created nature for the sake of the creature enters into the very substance of the sacrifice. This can scarcely be expressed more distinctly than by the very words of St. Justin Martyr in the second century, who says, "We receive not these as common bread or common drink, but as by the word of God Jesus Christ our Saviour, having been made flesh, had both flesh and blood for our salvation, so we have been taught also that the food which has been blessed by the word of prayer made by Him, from which our blood and our flesh are by their change nourished, are the flesh and the blood of that incarnate Jesus. For the Apostles, in their memorials called the Gospels, have handed down that thus Jesus enjoined them: that He took bread, and having blessed it, said, This do in commemoration of Me: this is My Body; and that He took likewise the chalice, and having blessed it, said, This is my Blood."[1] Here the martyr appeals to the reality of the flesh assumed by the Word, as a supposition necessary to understand the reality of His Body and Blood in the Eucharist, as St. Ignatius had done before him, and as St. Irenæus and others did after him.[2] In this connection, Eusebius of Cæsarea, setting forth the typical character of the Jewish Pasch and its fulfilment in the new covenant, says, "The followers of Moses sacrificed

---

[1] Justin. Apol. i. 66.
[2] Franzelin, De SS. Eucharistiæ Sacramento et Sacrificio, p. 81.

the Paschal Lamb only once a year, on the fourteenth day of the first month about evening tide, but we in the new covenant celebrating the Pasch every Sunday, are ever satisfied with the Body of the Lord, and ever take part in the Blood of the Lamb."[1] And here, once more, wherever this sacrifice is truly offered, the offerers show themselves truly penetrated by that belief which comes next in preciousness and dignity to the belief in the Divine Unity and Trinity—the belief of that assumption by the Divine Son of human nature, on which the Christian faith rests.

Fourthly, the sacrifice in St. Paul's words, "Sets forth the Lord's death till He come," that is, the divine act of redemption; for in it our Lord lies upon the altar in the state of a victim, the flesh and the blood separated, as in the state of death, which He took upon Himself voluntarily for the sin of the world, being offered because He willed it Himself. The sacrifice exhibits most directly this act of the divine love, which with that other act just treated of, the assumption of human nature, makes up the double mystery of God's love to man—the double mystery which, boundless and immeasurable as are the power and the wisdom disclosed to man's reason in the structure of the visible universe, disclosed equally in the infinity of smallness as in the infinity of greatness, disclosed in every branch of science and every portion of nature, makes both power and wisdom to pale before the greatness of condescendence and affection; for truly it is greater that the Maker of

---

[1] Eusebius Cæs.: περὶ τῆς τοῦ Πάσχα ἑορτῆς, cap. 7.

all these things should, for the sake of one of them, descend from His greatness, and that the Lord of life and Author of beauty should encounter death and embrace dishonour, than that He should have created the universe in all its magnificence by the word of His power. But here, in this sacrifice, He lies before His people in the state of annihilation, dishonour, and death. The world's ransom is ever in the sight of those whom He has ransomed, in the very act of paying their debt: the Lamb slain from the foundation of the world goes through its unfolding centuries, ever presenting to His Father the price which He has paid for the salvation of His brethren. And it may be noted that those who offer the Divine Sacrifice in the complete faith of the Church preserve at the same time their full assurance in that redemption which separated sects seem to lose as a consequence of their division, it being too great and awful a doctrine for their weak and paralysed condition to bear.

For it is impossible, fifthly, to separate the gift of adoption from the Divine Sacrifice, which contains it and imparts it. Wherefore does the Son of the Eternal Father lie upon the altar in the state of death? He cries out aloud there, "Behold I and my children whom God has given Me." It is precisely out of the act assuming our nature, and out of the act offering that nature to death, that He draws His human family. It is after the detailed account of His sufferings in the 21st Psalm that He concludes with the words which St. Paul has quoted in this connection:[1] " I will declare Thy name

[1] Heb. ii. 12.

to My brethren : in the midst of the Church will I praise Thee." It is in the act of priesthood that He creates His race. " Because the children are partakers of flesh and blood, He also Himself in like manner has been partaker of them, that through death He might destroy him who had the empire of death." Thus, "It behoved Him in all things to be made like unto His brethren, that He might become a merciful and faithful High Priest before God." And the daily act of His Priesthood thus performed, the unbloody immolation for ever presented before God in the eyes of His people, is the bond and pledge to them of the communicated sonship. They who have the Church's daily sacrifice have never fallen from the belief of the divine brotherhood, have never substituted for it the natural kinship of fallen man. They have not sunk away from the bond of redemption giving sonship, to the phantom of brotherhood, dispensing with faith, and vainly calling on men to unite in the midst of national enmity, broken belief, and thirst for material enjoyment. The Divine Sacrifice, as it is the instrument, so also it is the guardian of divine adoption, and perpetuates it upon the earth.

There are three parts, so to say, of adoption which are further distinctly contained in the Divine Sacrifice. The first of these is the derivation of spiritual life from the Person of Christ; for here especially is fulfilled what He said of Himself, "The Bread of God is that which cometh down from heaven and giveth life to the world." In the act of sacrifice He becomes also the food of His brethren : here He was from the beginning daily; here He is to the end. This is the inmost junction of life with belief, so that the faithful people by its presence attesting belief in the Divine Unity and Trinity, in the Incarnation of the Son of God, in His redemption of the race, in the adoption of man by God, at the same time become partakers of the life which these doctrines declare. The perfection of the divine institution consists in this absolute blending of belief, worship, and practice. The unbelieving Jews strove among themselves, saying, "How can this Man give us His flesh to eat?" Our Lord answered by establishing a rite on which His Church lives through all the ages, in which He bestows Himself on each believer individually, being as much his as if He was for him alone. Space and time disappear before the Author of life in the act of communicating Himself, and He is the sole Teacher of His Church, in that He alone feeds it with the Divine Food, which is Himself.

But this food is the source of sanctification: as that by which man fell away from God was sin, so that which unites him to God is holiness. It is from the Incarnate Son in the act of sacrifice that this holiness emanates to His people; and the gift of His flesh, the banquet at the sacrifice, dispenses it. No teaching of words could so identify the Person of our Lord with the source of holiness as the bodily act of receiving His flesh. It is the command, "Be ye holy, for I am holy," expressed in action. This is the perennial fountain of holiness which wells forth in the midst of His Church; and beside it, as subordinate and preparatory, is the perpetual tribunal of penance : one and the other given to meet and efface the perpetual frailties of daily life, first to restore the fallen, and then to join them afresh with the source of holiness.

There is yet another gift consequent upon adoption, which completes as it were the two we have just mentioned. It is that the flesh of our Lord given in the Blessed Sacrament is the pledge and earnest of eternal life. This He has Himself said in the words, "He that eateth My Flesh and drinketh My Blood hath everlasting life, and I will raise him up at the last day." And St. Thomas, in the beautiful conclusion to the grandest of hymns, has summed up numberless comments of the Fathers on these divine words, where he sings—

> "Bone Pastor, panis vere,
> Jesu nostri miserere,
> Tu nos pasce, nos tuere ;
> Tu nos bona fac videre
>   In terra viventium :
> Tu qui cuncta scis et vales,
> Qui nos pascis hic mortales,
> Tuos ibi commensales
> Cohæredes et sodales
>   Fac sanctorum civium."

The Fathers[1] with great zeal insist that the physical Body of Christ in the Eucharist, being one in all the receivers, is a principle of unity of Christ's mystical Body. St. Augustine especially dwells upon this effect in Christ's mystical Body, but the effect presupposes the cause, which is that physical Body of Christ received by each.

[1] Franzelin, De SS. Eucharistiæ Sacramento, p. 111.

Take an instance of the first statement, that is, the presence of Christ's physical Body, in St. Chrysostom. Commenting on the words, "How can this Man give us His flesh to eat?" he says, "Let us learn what is the marvel of the mysteries, what they are, why they were given, and what is their use. We become, He says, one body, members of His flesh and of His blood. Let those who are initiated follow my words. That we may be so, then, not only by charity but in actual fact, let us be fused with that Flesh. For it is done by that Food which He bestowed on us in the desire to show us the longing which He had for us. He mingled Himself with us, and made His Body one mass with us, that we may be one thing, as a body united with its head. This is what Christ did for us, to draw us to closer friendship and to show His own longing for us; He granted those who desired Him, not only to see Him but to touch Him, and to eat Him, and to fix their teeth in His Flesh, to be joined in His embrace, and to satisfy all their longing. Parents often give their children to be nourished by others; I not so, but I nourish you with My own Flesh; I set Myself before you. I wished to become your Brother, I have partaken of flesh and blood for you; again, I give to you that Flesh and Blood whereby I became your kinsman."[1]

Of the effect proceeding from this cause St. Augustine says, "The whole redeemed city, the assembly and society of the saints, is offered as an universal sacrifice to God by the Great Priest, who also offered Himself in

---

[1] S. Chrys. Hom. in Joan, 46, c. 3, tom. viii. 272.

His Passion for us, according to the form of a servant, that we might be the Body of so great a Head. For this form He offered, in this He was offered, because according to this He is Mediator, in this Priest, in this Sacrifice. When, therefore, the Apostle exhorted us to present our bodies a living sacrifice: 'For as in one body we have many members, but all the members have not the same office, so we, being many, are one body in Christ, and every one members one of another:' this is the sacrifice of Christians, many one body in Christ. Which also the Church constantly performs in the sacrifice of the altar, as the faithful know, where it is shown to her that she is offered herself in that which she offers." As he says a little further on, " Of which thing (that is, Christ being, in the form of a servant, both Priest and Victim) He willed the daily sacrifice of the Church to be the Sacrament; for she being the Body, as He the Head, she learns to offer herself by Him. To this supreme and true sacrifice all false sacrifices have given way."[1]

Thus, then, the question has been answered how our Lord impressed for ever on the world the double act of His Priesthood, the assumption of human nature to His Divine Person, and the offering of that assumed nature in sacrifice. For whereas He made the bloody sacrifice once for all upon the altar of the cross, He ordered the daily sacrifice of His Church to represent it for ever in the name of His people to God the Father, wherein He immolates Himself without blood. " What then ? "

[1] St. Aug. De Civitate Dei, lib. 10, c. 6 and 20.

says St. Chrysostom; "do we not offer every day? We do offer, but making a commemoration of His death. And this is one sacrifice, and not many. How is it one and not many? Because that was once offered which entered into the Holy of holies. This is the figure of that. For we offer ever the same; not to-day one lamb and another to-morrow, but always the same. So that the sacrifice is one. Otherwise, according to the objection, 'Since it is offered many times,' are there many Christs? By no means, but there is one Christ everywhere, complete here and complete there, one Body. As then He, being offered in many places, is one Body and not many bodies, so there is one sacrifice. Our High-Priest is He who offered the sacrifice that cleanses us; that same we offer now which was then offered, which is inconsumable. This is done for a commemoration of that which was then done; for, 'Do this,' He says, 'in commemoration of Me.' We offer not another sacrifice as the (Jewish) high-priest, but ever the same; or rather we make a commemoration of the sacrifice."[1]

The one perpetual sacrifice thus instituted in His Church, to be offered from His first to His second coming, carrying in it indissolubly the great truths of His religion, the life and the unity of His people, this is the instrument which He used to impress His High-Priesthood on the world; and He set up the one episcopate as the bearer of the one priesthood. The government of His Church is not an external magistracy, but rests on the mass of

[1] S. Chrys. 16 Hom. on the Hebrews, tom. xii. p. 168.

worship and doctrine intimately blent together, so that the outward regimen and the inward belief form an indissoluble unity in the daily practice.

In this unity we must likewise comprehend the jurisdiction expressed in planting and maintaining belief and worship throughout the world. For our Lord is a King, and came to establish a kingdom; not several kingdoms, nor a confederation of states, but one kingdom, concerning which His people confesses for ever, in the words of the angel who announced His coming, "Of His kingdom there shall be no end." But without jurisdiction, that is, without the power which says to one man, "Go here," and to another, "Go there," the first foundation of a kingdom was as impossible as was its continuance and permanence.

All the records of that ancient Church which fought a victorious battle with the Roman Empire and received a civil enfranchisement from the Emperor Constantine tend to show that the principle of hierarchical order was very strong in it, and was most severely maintained. It could not be well stated in a more absolute form than in the letter of Pope St. Clement above quoted. But the Church which met in representation at the great Nicene Council offers a perfect picture of what that order was, working itself out in absolute independence of the Civil Power through three centuries from the Day of Pentecost.

In the diocese the bishop's jurisdiction was complete. No priest was independent in the exercise of his functions. Thus jurisdiction in the interior forum entered into the daily dispensing of the sacraments. For a long time the Holy Eucharist was dispensed by the bishop from one altar, and sent from him to the sick. He was the imposer of penance, and when, as churches and priests multiplied, the system of parishes and parish priests arose, they executed all their functions in complete subordination to the bishop, whose title in those early times was taken from the rite on which all his power rested, when he is called pre-eminently Sacerdos, *i.e.*, the sacrificing priest. Within the limits of the diocese there can be no sort of doubt that the idea of jurisdiction was perfectly realised in practice.

But did it stop with the diocese? Was the bishop independent in the exercise of his powers? In the first place, he exercised them all within a certain district. He had no power to encroach upon the district of a neighbouring bishop, nor to execute therein functions which were perfectly lawful and usual in his own. It is plain that had he possessed any such power, the whole system established would not have made one kingdom of Christ, but would have been a congeries of similar governments, not tied together but agitated by perpetual rivalries. Nothing could be more unlike the actual system of government as disclosed by the bearing of the Church of Rome to that of Corinth in the letter of St. Clement, or to that orderly division into provinces which is seen in its full development at the Nicene Council. We may conclude that the tie which held the bishops together was at least as strict and as defined as that which formed the unity of the particular diocese.

We now behold that marvellous spiritual fabric of which St. Chrysostom and St. Augustine, at the head of the Fathers of the fourth century, spoke with such affection, acknowledging that its existence was to them an absolute proof of the Godhead of its Founder. It was not its material extension alone, but its inmost nature and character which moved them thus. It was the evolution of the one indivisible power in its threefold direction of Priesthood, Teaching, and Jurisdiction. It was that the one episcopate tied together in a hierarchy of several thousand bishops was but the outward regimen of an inward polity in which the One Sacrifice is offered, and the one Body of Christ communicated by the work of the one Priesthood, which lives upon and dispenses one doctrine, proclaiming it from age to age to the whole earth.

Thus the words of our Lord, spoken immediately after He had instituted the priesthood according to the order of Melchisedec, committing to it the sacrifice of His Body and Blood, were marvellously accomplished. "I am the true Vine, and My Father is the husbandman.—Abide in Me, and I in you. As the branch cannot bear fruit of itself, unless it abide in the vine, so neither can you, unless you abide in Me. I am the Vine, you the branches: he that abideth in Me, and I in him, the same beareth much fruit; for without Me you can do nothing." The human nature which He had taken had sent forth, in virtue of the Person who took it, the triple power bestowed upon it: His priesthood, His teaching, and His rule had occupied the earth. All the nations composing the Roman Empire had brought in their first-fruits to form clusters of the mystical Vine. They had made the triple offering of the Eastern kings from the peoples of Europe, Asia, and Africa to the Royal Infant; to the King they had given their gold, for His sake and after His likeness becoming poor; to the God their frankincense, worshipping Him at the altar of His love; to the Victim their myrrh, presenting to Him their bodies as a sacrifice, in repetition of His martyrdom. It was the very scoff of the heathen philosopher and magistrate that any one could think to reduce to one worship the various rites of the Empire, a conglomeration of European, Asiatic, and African superstitions. Out of that seemingly hopeless diversity, that endless antagonism, He had constructed a divine unity, a table at which the children of Scipio knelt side by side with the vilest slave, at which many an Aspasia became a penitent, and a Boniface sent back as holy relics to his mistress, Aglae, the body in which he had sinned with her. The vine of the synagogue, planted of old with the choicest care, and protected from the inroads of wild beasts in the security of a single nation of brethren, had brought forth but wild grapes, and therefore it had been plucked up; its hedge had been broken down and its tower ruined. Instead of it, the Vine of His Body had grown abundantly, and from its single root, to use Tertullian's application of the parable, suckers had been carried everywhere, and the harvest of its vintage rendered the earth fruitful; the hills and the valleys of many vast regions were covered with its grapes. But this itself was but the beginning of a vaster growth in the future, the first realisation of an ever-expanding kingdom. Only it was a complete specimen of all that should be. This generation of the Christian people from the person of Christ was the one miracle which St. Chrysostom thought no heathen could deny.

The Eucharistic Sacrifice is the centre and instrument of all this work; the other Sacraments lead up to it or attend upon it. That which is most intimate in man, the forming his soul after a divine type, and the sanctifying it with all its affections; that which is most intellectual, the doctrine of God made man, surpassing all knowledge in its development as in its conception; that government which is necessary to the well-being of every kingdom; that worship which is most exalting, the worship of the Infinite One, the source, example, and giver of personality, which is the last and highest gift of the Creator to the rational creature,—all these were here joined together by the simple act of God when He perpetuated in a visible rite the double power of His High-priesthood, the assumption of our nature, and the dying for our sins, and brought out of it the generation of His people, wherein the resurrection of one Man to bodily life became the resurrection of a countless host to spiritual brotherhood, and created the Family of the Incarnate God.

I have been exhibiting the institution of the most blessed Eucharist, and the planting of it throughout the Church in the three centuries which ended with the

Nicene Council. Throughout these it was the life of the Church; all the marvels of faith, endurance, zeal, and charity spring from it; the works of the Saviour were hidden in it. But since then fifteen centuries and a half have elapsed, and the Church which filled the Roman Empire has dilated itself over the whole earth. In all the countries which it has thus occupied, in all the races of which it has converted the first-fruits, the same blessed Eucharist—that divine banquet of the Flesh and Blood of the Word made man—has continued to be the life of the Church. Upon it the race of martyrs, saints, doctors, and virgins have been nurtured, and the power which in each one of them was supernatural has to be also estimated in its aggregate. Among all the proofs of the Godhead of the Son of Man, that Divine Food which He foretold to the multitude satisfied with the miraculous multiplication of the natural food on the shores of the Lake of Galilee, and which He first gave to His Apostles in the upper chamber on the eve of His Passion, is in its results the most transcendent. It is enough by itself to quench all the doubts of unbelief, to kindle all the fires of an endless charity. It is the Church's unparalleled possession, of which no false religion possesses even a shadow; her testimony, which grows not old; her youth, which never fails. Unnumbered myriads of people of all times and countries have been supported by it through the desert of this world, and been led in its strength to the Paradise in which the Son of God in the glory of His humanity communicates Himself face to face to those whom He has redeemed, and imparts to them the vision of God in His Unity and His Trinity.

But if this Church, possessing this Divine Sacrifice and Sacrament, was a wonder to minds such as St. Chrysostom and St. Augustine in their day of the fifth century, what ought it to be to us at the end of the nineteenth? The Roman Empire broke up, and the tribes of the North dashed into fragments its unrivalled organisation, and destroyed that peace under which the fairest regions of the earth, washed by the inland sea, dwelt for centuries, rich in all the arts of commerce, in all the security of civilisation. The Blessed Eucharist survived this convulsion; far more, it restored this ruin. By founding religious houses through the whole extent of the countries occupied by the German tribes, whose indwellers, in virtue of it, lived *the common life* under the safeguard of the three great vows of poverty, chastity, and obedience, it produced a Christian France, Spain, Italy, Germany, England, and Poland out of the torn and bleeding members of the Empire. This was its work in the Western half of the Roman broken statue.

In the Eastern the savage power of the Mahometan Califate arose, denying at once the redemption of Christ, and the sacrifice in which He had enshrined that redemption, and the divine banquet which ensued upon it. Thousands of Christian Sees fell not before its persuasive power, but its ruthless sword of conquest. The Mahometan Califate has for hundreds of years trampled on the fairest regions of the earth, and turned the Roman peace into a desolation. At length it trembles for its existence; the divine Eucharist remains unimpaired in strength, and is ready to enter into the desolated territory and repeat its work of restoration, to turn the foulness of the Mahometan harem into the sanctity of the Christian home.

Again, when iniquity abounded and the love of many had waxed cold, there arose a defection in the West as terrible as that of the East 900 years before, and it was marked by special enmity to the Blessed Eucharist. It cast down and trampled under the feet of those who approached the desecrated churches the very altars at which for a thousand years the generations of a Christian people had worshipped. It denied the great mystery which was the heart of the doctrine; it enrolled the denial in the coronation oath of its sovereigns; it abolished the belief which had soothed all sorrows as it had made all saints. But that defection has broken into innumerable wavelets against the Rock of the Christian Church, upon which rises, as of old, the impregnable citadel of the faith—the faith which dispenses, as in the first ages, to the children of all the races of the earth that sacred Body and Blood, in virtue of which now, as in the upper chamber, the Word of God declares, " I am the Vine ; ye are the branches: he that abideth in Me and I in him, the same beareth much fruit; for without Me you can do nothing."

Can there be any proof of the Godhead of the Word made flesh to compare with that which has been the life of the living and the hope of the dying to sixty generations of men for eighteén centuries and a half? " For this is the chalice in My Blood of the new and everlasting testament, the mystery of faith, which shall be shed for you and for many, for the remission of sins."

CHAPTER VI.

THE ACTUAL RELATION BETWEEN CHURCH AND STATE
FROM THE DAY OF PENTECOST TO CONSTANTINE.

The Independence of the Ante-Nicene Church shown in her Organic Growth.

THE foundation-stone of the Church of God is the Person of our Lord, a truth embodied with marvellous force and terseness of expression in that famous symbol of the Catacombs, the Sacred Fish, denoting by its initial letters the name of our Lord as Man, His office as Messiah, the two natures in the one Divine Person, the salvation which is their result, Jesus, the Christ, Son of God, Saviour.[1] As in that Divine Person the Godhead and Manhood are joined in that special union which constitutes personality, as He who governs and He who teaches, He who offers sacrifice and He who is sacrificed, is one and the same Saviour throughout, so He continues to be in the life of His Body the Church. And this is very manifest during the first stadium of the Church's course, stretching from the Day of Pentecost to the decree of Constantine, which granted to it civil recognition as a lawful religion; for government and doctrine,

[1] Ἰησοῦς Χριστὸς, Θεοῦ Υἱὸς, Σωτήρ = Ἰχθύς.

like warp and woof, form the robe woven from the top throughout in which our Lord as High Priest appears to the world. According to the prophecy, "He builds a temple to the Lord, and bears the glory, and is a Priest upon His throne."[1] His kingdom resides in this unity. It is one flock, and the pastures in which His people feed upon the truth make the domain of the government by which the kingdom is ruled, and to feed the flock is to rule it. It is the one temple in which the sacrifice offered is the Lord Himself, while in the sacrifice the people is fed and grows, and is reciprocally offered to the Lord.

In all this the Church continues the mystery of her Lord's life, the Divine Incarnation, the suffering of the Nature assumed, the resurrection which follows. We have, then, to deal with one particular but complex fact, the outcome of this whole period in the government, teaching, and worship of the Church inseparably blent together, as borne into and upon the world by its hierarchy, as enacted in its liturgy, as contained in its sacramental life, as exhibited in the living Christian people, the invincible race,[2] which grew up in those centuries without interference by the State. It is a period during which the State's legal position of undeviating hostility served as the guardian of the new spiritual kingdom's independence.

That independence resided in a threefold sanctuary, which is one and the same, being the House, the Temple, the Tribunal which the Blessed Trinity, the source and model of the Church, had constructed for Himself in

---

[1] Zach. vi. 13. [2] τὸ ἄμαχον γένος, St. Chrys., above quoted.

the hearts of His people. First there is the sanctuary of worship, in which Christ is Priest, the starting-point of the whole economy; secondly, the sanctuary of teaching, from which as Prophet He dispenses all that doctrine wherewith He is charged; thirdly, there is the sanctuary of government, whereof jurisdiction is a necessary and inalienable part, and in this He rules as King the distribution of all powers belonging to His kingdom.

We have to consider how, in the first three centuries, all this was actually carried out; and we shall best do so by placing ourselves at the remarkable point of history, the convocation of the Nicene Council in the year 325, and by summing up the result of the long conflict which preceded that event, as regards these three particulars.

The Nicene Council was convoked to terminate the question which Arius had raised as to the Godhead of our Lord. It was the remedy of the Emperor Constantine for the malady which had broken out in the Church. He had just become, by the death of Licinius, sole ruler of the Roman world. Though not yet a Christian by the reception of baptism, he had conceived the highest veneration for the Christian Church. There can be no doubt that he trusted, by means of its spiritual unity, to weld together on a firmer basis the shaken fabric of imperial Rome. Thus he looked with much sorrow and no little perplexity upon the rise of a heresy in the important Church of Alexandria; and when its bishop, in spite of his great authority, as the head of the second Church in the world, which by a most powerful organisation governed the three secular provinces of Egypt, Libya, and Pentapolis, was unable to expel the mischief, he urged the convocation of a General Council. He convoked it, so far as a secular prince could do so, by giving all the assistance which the public authority could render in a State politically absolute; for he not only invited the bishops to attend, but ordered that they should travel free of cost at the public expense. Pope Sylvester, on his side, assented; he sent his legates to the Council, where they alone represented the whole West, and so by his assent and by the mission of his legates gave the Council its œcumenical character.

By this act the Emperor, who, it should be borne in mind, was still the Pontifex Maximus of heathen worship, and the official head of the old State religion, recognised the Church of Christ as a spiritual kingdom, possessing a doctrine of which it was the sole judge and bearer; recognised in its bishops the representatives of the various powers placed by Christ, its Founder, therein, as those who bore throughout his empire a priesthood, and exercised a spiritual rule and jurisdiction, and preached a doctrine all bound together in one whole; who, moreover, in virtue of this triple character, which came upon them from above, by the institution of Christ and through the medium of consecration, which is to say, by the force of a divine unction, and not by any human authority, represented a people which likewise was spread everywhere, while it was one likewise in virtue of a divine consecration, baptism in the threefold name of God.

Such a recognition is an enormous fact, which reason and imagination flag in their effort to realise. Two hundred and ninety-six years before, a Man had died upon a cross the death of a Roman slave, and the evening before His death He had ordered His disciples to commemorate that death for ever in a certain rite which should constitute the central worship of His people. This Man died by the edict of a Roman procurator, which had been extorted from him by the threats of the people and their rulers over whom he maintained Rome's supremacy. This Man also died with the record over His head that the cause for which He died was, the assumption of kingship over a people who refused Him for their King, and chose in preference the Roman Emperor. His death was reported to the Emperor of that day; but we know not whether he took any note of the death of one recorded as a pretender to a provincial throne, or of a death enacted at the command of a very subordinate officer of his empire, a mere procurator under the Proconsul of Syria. The twelve disciples of this Man, made up of fishermen, a publican, and afterwards a tent-maker, went forth, carrying with them this rite, which they delivered to other men throughout the empire. Upon this rite grew up a whole fabric of doctrine and worship; rulers who propagated the doctrine and celebrated the rite, and a people which sprung out of both. The Roman emperors, at first superciliously disregarding the seed which had been so silently dropped in their cities, presently turned to persecute this people and their rulers; during ten generations having always persistently discountenanced them, they imprisoned, tormented, or executed a certain portion. They also destroyed the seat and worship of the people who had rejected this Man as their King, and had chosen the Emperor instead. And now, in rather less than three centuries, the Emperor of Rome, the successor of Tiberius, acknowledged this crucified Man for what He declared Himself to be: acknowledged His kingdom; acknowledged as princes in all lands the missionaries whom He had sent forth; acknowledged as one people, bound together in sacraments, those who had believed in His word, or in the word of others derived from Him; acknowledged, moreover, as a living authority, as judges of what was or was not the true doctrine as so derived from Him, men whose sole claim was the consecration received from that Man on the eve of His public execution, and transmitted by the imposition of hands to their successors; acknowledged the rite of sacrifice which He had created by His word in the offering of His Body as the most august, the most tremendous, the most precious thing existing in the world.

Moreover, in the convocation of the Council, the Emperor acknowledged of his own accord the solidarity of the Christian episcopate. St. Cyprian did not express it more plainly in his famous aphorism, "The episcopate is one of which a part is held by each without division of the whole," than the Emperor in supposing that a point of doctrine on the maintenance of which the whole fabric of revelation rested, since it concerned the Person of the Founder, could be resolved by the common consent of its episcopate. For the decision to be come to would bind the whole as one Body; and herein lay another imperial attestation of Christ's kingdom. The Emperor of Rome looked upon the Church and treated it, not as a beehive of separable cells, but as a Body the force and life of which lay in its oneness; and in causing a single heresy to be thus judged, he was condemning the principle of every heresy which should at any time arise.

All this and much more is comprehended in that act of the Emperor Constantine which sanctioned the convocation of the Nicene Council. It was not a Christianity split up into sects, but the solid unity of the Catholic Church in doctrine, discipline, worship, and constitution, which the Emperor looked to for a support to the tottering political fabric of the State, and as a new bond to its maintenance.[1]

But yet again. The Senate of Rome had been in the day of Rome's freedom a great power. At first representing the authority of a free people who had in course of time established a vast rule, it was a name of dignity and glory on the earth. Next, as the official bestower or ratifier of imperial authority, as even yet representing the Roman people, as collecting in its bosom those who had borne high offices, ruled provinces, gained victories, were the instruments by which the Pax Romana kept the earth quiet and obedient, the Senate was still an august body. But now appeared before

[1] See Hagemann, Die römische Kirche, p. 558.

the world another council, consisting of men each of whom represented in his person a spiritual community while he carried a divine power. These men were not imposers of taxes or rulers of armies, not enactors of laws for human contracts, but men whose rule was over souls, whose word was divine, who announced not to a particular race but to all races of the earth one God, one Christ, one faith; a rule the centre of which was an act of transcendent worship, and the scope and object holiness. And this council, while it met in the empire of an absolute sovereign, who raised up and put down whom he pleased, the lives and fortunes of whose subjects were entirely in his hands, alone possessed freedom, the freedom to worship what they believed, to obey the commands of their conscience as Christians, to acknowledge a power stretching over the whole range of their most secret life, and in nowise derived from the Roman Emperor nor dependent on him. This power Constantine acknowledged in causing the Council to be convoked; and by so doing he pointed out the Council of the Christian Church as that from the imitation of which every future parliament should spring to construct civil liberty under Christian sovereigns. Assuredly the Council, as a deliberative body, possessed a dignity far transcending that of the Senate whether of free or of imperial Rome.

This is the meaning of the Nicene Council in the great arbitrament between the Spiritual and the Civil Powers, or, in Catholic language, between the Priesthood and the Empire. And it is a meaning put upon it by the Roman Emperor himself. Viewed on this side, the Council is a summary of the whole preceding history from the Day of Pentecost to its convocation, the records of which are as scant as the facts are precious. What know we as to the number of the martyrs and confessors in that interval? What infinitesimal portion of individual lives and sufferings then undergone has been preserved for our love and imitation? Among the Fathers present at the Council there was one, Paphnutius, who had lost an eye in the preceding persecution. We are told the Emperor would kiss the empty socket in token of his veneration. That act symbolised his whole demeanour to the Church for whose faith Paphnutius had suffered. It likewise expressed the witness which the fact of the Council convoked and acknowledged by the Roman Emperor gave to all those sufferings the innumerable incidents of which went to construct that victory of patience over force whereby the Christian kingdom was established in its first field of combat. This was the conflict of the natural society of man, as it existed in the grandest empire of Gentilism, with the supernatural society founded in Christ.

Thus the convocation of the Nicene Council is the definitive declaration by the Roman Empire through the mouth of its chief that it recognised a kingdom of Christ upon earth.

To illustrate the spiritual government of this kingdom, as it had grown up in the three centuries which intervene between the Day of Pentecost and the convocation of the Council, let us touch upon five points:

the first shall be the ordered gradation of the hierarchy; the second, the holding of provincial councils; the third, the hearing and the judging of causes; the fourth, the election of the Church's ministers; the fifth, the administration of her temporal goods.[1]

1. As to the first, the Sixth Canon of the Council ordered that the ancient custom should continue in force, according to which the great mother Churches of Alexandria and Antioch possessed jurisdiction over the whole civil diocese, the one of Egypt and the other of the East, in like manner as the Church of Rome possessed a similar jurisdiction in the West. The ground upon which the Council rests this canon is much to be observed; it does not institute this jurisdiction, but orders it be continued because it was the ancient custom. Now as there had been no other Council prior to that of Nicæa, in which this power of jurisdiction over the Metropolitans in the civil dioceses of Egypt and of the East had been granted to the Bishops of Alexandria and of Antioch, the origin of this ancient custom must be referred to apostolic institution, according to St. Augustine's rule, "That which is held by the whole Church, which has not been ordered by councils, but always been kept, we are most right in believing to have been handed down by none other than apostolic authority."[2] Pope Innocent I.,[3] writing to Alexander Bishop of Antioch, about eighty years after the

---

[1] Bianchi, vol. iii. pp. 120, 121.
[2] Aug. l. iv. De Bapt. c. Donat. cap. ult. (B. 120 note).
[3] Innocent. Ep. 18, c. l.

Council, recognises his jurisdiction over not only one province, but over the whole assemblage of provinces which made up the civil jurisdiction of the Prefect of the East, not so much on the ground of the city's civil dignity as because it had been the first See of the chief of the Apostles. St. Gregory the Great [1] repeatedly in his letters speaks of the See of the chief of the Apostles as being the See of one in three places, Rome, Alexandria, and Antioch.

That which the Sixth Canon of the Council witnesses, therefore, is the original jurisdiction of the two great mother Sees of Alexandria and Antioch over their daughter churches, which it corroborates by referring to the norm, as it were, supplied by the still greater See of Rome. Though these Sees were not called at the time of the Nicene Council patriarchal, a name which arose in the fifth century; yet the thing itself, and the institution which it denoted, existed from the beginning. The system of mother and daughter churches is shown in the highest degree in these three great Sees, in two of which St. Peter himself sat, while he founded the third by his disciple Mark. It is, in fact, a derivation from St. Peter's Primacy, and the constituent principle of the hierarchy in its intermediate gradation of ranks. As the institution of bishops throughout the world is a derivation of apostolic authority, so likewise is the repartition of jurisdiction among them. One and the same principle—power coming from above—made the whole hierarchy, whether in the bishop over the simple dio-

[1] S. Greg. I., l. 6, Ep. 39; 8, Ep. 35.

cese, or in the metropolitan over a single province, or in the primate over several metropolitans, or in the central See of St. Peter, the Head of all. The three former of these gradations, the Sixth Canon of the Council recognised as of immemorial existence. With regard to the fourth, when the Roman legate at the Council of Chalcedon cited this canon, he cited it with the heading: "The Roman church always had the Primacy." And although the Greek copies of the Council did not bear this heading, the Greek bishops there did not dispute the fact which it stated. And it must be noted that this heading did not assert the Primacy of Rome to be given by the Council, but that it had always existed; nor was any fact more constantly repeated by Pope after Pope when addressing the Church in her bishops, than this, that his authority, whatever it was, was the gift of Christ to St. Peter, and not bestowed by any Council: and so of divine, not apostolical, institution.

It would appear that the Apostles,[1] in carrying out the divine instructions of their Master for the establishment of His kingdom, followed His own example. Inasmuch as He had given them a head, they would appoint inferior heads in the Church who should hold an order among themselves in its administration, and all refer to the Superior. In doing this they had regard to the civil disposition of the empire, using it as a model upon which they formed the exterior polity of the Church. For just as in the civil and temporal government of each province there was a mother city, the prefect of which

[1] Bianchi, 3, 137.

administered the whole province, ruling under the Prince over the subordinate governors, to whom matters of more grave importance were referred, so the Apostles and their disciples after them instituted in the chief cities bishops to whom they gave all the powers of metropolitans before the name came into use, in order that ecclesiastical regulations of the greatest moment might be treated before them in union with the bishops of their respective provinces.[1] Thus St. Paul, finding Ephesus the metropolis of Proconsular Asia, placed Timotheus to be bishop there, giving him at the same time jurisdiction over the bishops of that province, who should be drawn as it were out of the womb of the parent See; and in his first letter we find instructions as to the quality of the bishops whom he should select. In the 19th chapter of the Acts, we are told that St. Paul had drawn a great number of disciples to him, not only at Ephesus, but in nearly every part of Asia, that is, the proconsular province of that name. In the 17th chapter, at a later date, he summoned at Miletus the bishops of Ephesus and its province to meet him, calling them "all you among whom I have passed preaching the kingdom of God," which words denote that he was speaking, not to the priests of one city, but to the bishops of a province, in which "the Holy Ghost had set them as bishops to rule over the church of God." St. Irenæus also notes that they were bishops and elders from Ephesus and the adjoining cities. St. John recognises these bishops in the seven letters which he is ordered to communicate to

[1] Bianchi, 3, 136.

the angels of the churches in the Apocalypse. At the head of these is the Angel of the church of Ephesus as metropolis. So, again, the Apostle Paul set Titus as metropolitan over the whole of Crete, expressly ordering him to establish bishops in every city, and describing what their character should be. His letters to Corinth and to Thessalonica, as well as to Ephesus, are letters to cities each of which was a metropolis. Thus the 34th of the Canons, called apostolical, runs: "It behoves the bishops of each nation to recognise him, who is the first among them, and to esteem him as their head, and to do nothing of importance without his sentence; but let each of them do only what concerns his own diocese and the places belonging to it, and not that without the agreement of all."[1] Here is seen the discipline of the ancient church, beyond a doubt derived from the Apostles, as to the Metropolitan's superintendence over the bishops of every province.

Thus the distribution[2] of episcopal jurisdiction began with the beginning, and was the outflow of one principle as stable as it was simple. The structure of the diocese, that of the province, that of the patriarchate, that of the whole Church, was identical throughout. It was a series of concentric circles, at the centre of which was our Lord Himself. In the simple diocese He was seen as walking and teaching with His Apostles on earth; in the province the metropolitan, with his suffragans, re-

[1] The Council of Antioch, in the year 341, almost repeats this canon, and lays it down as of universal application.
[2] Bianchi, 3, 132.

peated the same image; in the patriarchate, the Primate and his metropolitans; while in the See of Peter, our Lord stood by the lake of Galilee delivering with the thrice enjoined question, "Lovest thou Me more than these?" the divine pastoral power over His whole flock. This was the example of the Master Himself, which the Apostles faithfully followed.

From the beginning as to this exterior polity of His Church nothing was undefined, nothing was casual; it was the Body of Christ in its natural action gradually filling the world, by which the Head was gradually drawing man to Himself. It was the perfection of order, and yet the perfection of a divine liberty, which took hold of earthly things, such as the civil disposition of a temporal empire, to exalt it into the structure of a supernatural kingdom.

The great builders of the Middle Ages, in these stupendous cathedrals which the piety of generations raised in honour of the Mother of God, represented the Body of our Lord in that form of the cross on which He purchased our redemption. Every wall, every buttress, every chapel therein converged towards the centre, and lent its several portion of support to the whole. Therein the Church in her unity and solidarity was visibly portrayed, the Head with His members, the Mother of fair love, bearing the Divine Child, with His saints and confessors around Him. Therein the mystery of our salvation, the mystical altar of sacrifice, was ever set forth, in which the Divine Presence, the greater Schechinah of the new law, abode without ceasing. Such an intellectual and moral structure is presented to us in the hierarchy of the Church, graduated according to the system just described, from the first Apostolic Council at Jerusalem to the first General Council at Nicæa. No bishop stood apart from his fellows; no important matter of doctrine or discipline, of government or worship, was terminated by him without common council of his brethren. Every province was ranged round the central shrine, and made part of the one edifice. It was the Body of Christ sculptured, not on stone, but on human hearts, joined together by the wisdom of His saints, and cemented with the blood of His martyrs.

2. The second point[1] to be considered is the development of synodical institutions which kept even pace with the metropolitical hierarchy. As the council of his priests stood beside the bishop, so the provincial synod, the earliest form of councils, stood beside the metropolitan. From the second half of the second century these came into action for the subjugation of doctrinal errors and divisions, such as the Montanist heresy, and the contest as to the proper day for the celebration of Easter. The unity and solidarity of the churches and their bishops found more and more expression in these synods; here the heretical attack was stayed, and the common action of the bishops met the common assault of opponents. In the third century these episcopal meetings took place generally once, and in some countries twice a year. In them the bishops only had

[1] The following paragraph is a translation from Cardinal Hergenröther's History, vol. i. pp. 196, 197, sec. 228.

a decisive voice; priests and deacons could take part in them, the latter usually standing, while bishops and priests sat; the laity also were not absolutely excluded. The decrees of councils were usually sent by encyclical letters to other bishops. Bishops who could not appear in person had to be represented either by other bishops, as in A.D. 286 at Carthage, or by clerics of their church, as in 314 at Arles. The bishops of higher rank, who presided over the synod, generally metropolitans, were accustomed to subscribe the decrees alone. Accusations against bishops, and wrong acts on their part, were likewise examined at synods, and decided there. We no longer possess acts of the most ancient councils, except those of some African synods under Cyprian, and of that of Antioch in 269; we have 28 disciplinary decrees of the Council of Amyra in 314, and 14 of that of Neocæsarea held at about the same time.

3. Nothing sheds clearer light upon the constitution of the Church, as a perfect society, than her action in the hearing and deciding of causes.[1] The coercive power of the Church descends to her direct from God, and not from man, and was comprised from the beginning in the twofold jurisdiction of the external and the internal forum, the one criminal and the other penitential. The Son of God, who gave this power to the prelates of His Church, appointed them to be judges of men, granting to them full power to absolve and to condemn, and pledging His divine word that their sentences should be confirmed in heaven. The grant is recorded in the

[1] Bianchi, 3, 468; quoting the constitution of Pope John XXII.

sixteenth chapter of St. Matthew, as promised to St. Peter in his quality as head of the Church, and in the eighteenth chapter as promised to the Apostles collectively, and in their persons to the bishops who descend from them. By this divine disposition they are the sole and ordinary judges of the Church who belong essentially to the ecclesiastical polity; and therefore St. Cyprian wrote: that "heresies have arisen and schisms sprung up from no other reason than the not yielding obedience to God's priest; and from not reflecting that there is at a time but one priest in the Church, and one judge at a time in Christ's place: to whom, if according to the divine commands the whole brotherhood yielded obedience, no one would venture to do anything against the College of Priests;"[1] that is the episcopate.

This power of the keys gave a true and proper jurisdiction as well in the criminal as the penitential forum. But the difference between the two is marked. The punishment inflicted by the Church on those who were accused and convicted in judgment was different from that which was laid upon such as of their own accord, either in public or in secret, confessed their sins. The punishment inflicted on delinquents after accusation and proof of their misconduct was called a sentence, a condemnation, a sacerdotal censure, to use St. Cyprian's

[1] Bianchi, 3, 440. The word *Sacerdos* is here used as the proper appellation of the bishop in his diocese by Cyprian, Ep. 57, according to the usage in the third century, as the word *Ecclesia* indicates the diocese; the argument being that if complete obedience were rendered to the bishop in the diocese, there would be complete peace in the whole Church ruled by the Collegium of Bishops.

term; the other, which was laid upon any one who of his own accord confessed his faults, was properly a penitence, and never called a condemnation, but, on the contrary, carried with it a sacerdotal absolution from the soul's stains. The former belonged to the exterior forum, judicial and contentious; the latter to the interior forum, that of conscience. There was, indeed, a great difference between the two; for the censure laid its stroke upon those who resisted and were contumacious, who refused to confess their crime, if they were once judicially convicted; but penitence was only given to those who, by confession, voluntarily disclosed their fault, and they only who were the guilty parties formed the accusers and the witnesses against themselves.[1]

During the whole period of the first three centuries the Church exercised through her bishops this true and proper jurisdiction, both of the exterior and the interior forum. Instances of the former are the punishment of Ananias and Sapphira by St. Peter; of Elymas the sorcerer and the incestuous person at Corinth by St. Paul. But, further, the latter Apostle in his first Epistle to the Corinthians directed that causes of all kinds among Christians should be settled, not before the secular Gentile magistrates, but before the divine magistracy of the Church. And according to this rule the bishops in the first ages took cognisance of all causes and temporal differences, as well of clergy as of laity, and terminated them by their judgment; and this custom lasted even into the fourth century, after the

[1] This paragraph translated from Bianchi, 3, 445.

peace of the Church, so that the most troublesome occupation which the bishops of those ages had was to exercise this judicial power over secular matters, as St. Augustine confesses in his own case, where he says, "They demand of us that we should occupy ourselves with their vicious and troublesome covetousness, and give them up our time; at least they press the weak, and force them to bring their causes to us; and we do not venture to say to them, 'Man, who made me a judge or a divider among you?' For the Apostle instituted ecclesiastical judges in such causes by prohibiting Christians from pleading before secular tribunals."

Jurisdiction is defined to be "cognition of causes belonging to the magistrate by right of his office."[2] Such a cognition was exercised by the bishops over every sort of cause among Christians in the first centuries. Aristotle says, "Those are most properly to be called magistrates whose function it is to deliberate, to judge, and to command, but especially the latter, as being more characteristic of them." And when St. Paul writes, "Obey those that are set over you, and be subject to them; for they watch as those who will give account of your souls," he says the same, since by the force of relative terms there cannot be the duty of obedience on one side without the right to command on the other. This episcopal magistracy was executed in four degrees, corresponding to the hierarchy and the councils as they have been just described. First, in his

---

[1] Bianchi, 3, 457, 458; St. Augustine in Ps. cxviii.
[2] Bianchi, 3, 474, 475.

diocese the bishop was the proper judge, as Origen in his answer to Celsus draws a parallel between the bishop with his presbytery in each particular city and the chief magistrate of that city with the council. Secondly, the metropolitan with his council of bishops, so that the apostolical canons enjoin that if a bishop be accused by persons of the faith, worthy of credit, he should be brought and judged before that tribunal.[1] Thirdly, if a metropolitan were accused, the higher tribunal of the Primate and his Episcopal Council would intervene. Fourthly, if a Primate, or one of those afterwards termed Patriarchs, were in fault, as Paul of Samosata, holding the See of Antioch in the third century, a council of still greater rank would meet to judge him; and in this case even the secular sovereign, the Emperor Aurelius, recognised that the episcopal house ought to belong to the person indicated by the bishops of Italy, that is, the Pope.

4. The fourth point which I will endeavour to sum up is the practice of the Church in the period preceding the Nicene Council as to the election of bishops and the other ministers of inferior rank to the bishop from the priest downwards, together with the principle on which this practice was founded.

It has been shown above how the first bishops were planted by St. Peter, St. Paul, and the other Apostles, who chose by direction of the Holy Spirit, in the cities wherein they preached, those whom they would invest with the plenitude of the priesthood, to be sources of

[1] Bianchi, 3, 444; Apostol. Canon, 66 and 74.

future spiritual rule and centres of Christian life. But when successors to those had in the course of time to be appointed, what rule was followed?

The form of the sacred elections in those first ages was this: when a bishop died, the bishops of the province, together with the metropolitan, assembled in the city of the defunct prelate. They here took information from the clergy and the people respecting the persons who were considered worthy of episcopal rank. The bishops deliberated by themselves on the matter, and then proposed in public the person whom they considered worthy of the bishop's seat. They heard thereupon the opinion and the wish of the clergy and the faithful people. Having heard these, they issued their judgment, in which the sentence of the metropolitan had the larger share; and the new bishop being elected, they at once consecrated him. As to the election of the priests and the other inferior clergy, the same order was pursued in consulting clergy and people, and the whole judgment was ultimately reserved to the bishop.

St. Cyprian has left us in his 68th letter a most lucid testimony to this being the custom in his day, not only in the Churches of Africa, but in all other provinces. "We must," he says, "diligently observe and maintain the custom which has come down to us by divine tradition and apostolical observance, which is kept among ourselves and in almost every province. In order that ordination be rightly celebrated, the nearest bishops of the province must assemble among that people for whom a superior is to be appointed. The bishop must be chosen in the presence of the people, which has the fullest knowledge of the life of every one, and is thoroughly acquainted with his conduct by his acts." He supports the custom by the example of Eleazar, who, though chosen to be high priest by Moses alone, in obedience to a divine command, was yet set before the people, to show that sacerdotal ordinations should be made in the presence of those who by intimate knowledge can testify the merits of those chosen; and, again, by the example of the Apostles, who, in the election as well of St. Matthias as of the seven deacons, called together the people and heard their testimony, "that no unworthy person might find means to be advanced to a higher rank or the sacerdotal dignity."

The outcome of these three centuries is, that the election of the bishop lay in the hands of the metropolitan, assisted by the bishops of his province, and that the election of the metropolitan lay in the synod of his bishops, but confirmed by the bishops of the first Sees, to whom belonged the consecration of metropolitans.[1] This was the discipline in the East, while in the West the Roman Pontiff, through the dignity of his throne as head of the whole Church and of all particular Churches, did not personally intervene in the election of bishops to vacant Sees, but the successor was chosen by the neighbouring bishops according to the desires of the clergy and people, and the decree of the election was transmitted him, leaving to his choice its confirmation,

[1] Bianchi, 3, 500, translated.

or provision for the vacant See in some other manner, as might seem to him most expedient.

The election of all ministers below the bishop belonged to the bishop alone.

It is evident that the great number of bishops who in the course of two centuries were sent out by the Roman Pontiffs [1] to convert the nations to the faith were not elected by the faithful people which they themselves founded; nor could the testimony or the consent of the people be asked. But if the election of ministers had belonged by divine institution to the faithful laity and the Christian people, neither the Apostles, nor their disciples, nor the successors of St. Peter could have altered a divine disposition, nor elected pastors without the consent of the people.

But the principle on which the Church acted from the beginning is as clear as her practice; for the priesthood and the whole order of pastors in the Church having been established by the Son of God, and the perpetuity of this same priesthood in this same Church being also necessary by this divine disposition, it follows that the election of sacred ministers to maintain the succession and the disposition given by Christ to the Church, must belong by divine order to some one. As it cannot belong to laymen, it must belong to the clergy alone. In fact, St. Paul, in the Epistle to the Hebrews, declares that God Himself prescribed the form of this election in the priesthood of Aaron, and that this form was observed by our Lord. "No one," he says,

[1] Bianchi, 3, 485, translated.

"takes this honour to himself but he that is called by God, as was Aaron. So, too, Christ glorified not Himself to be called High Priest, but He that said to Him, 'Thou art My Son, this day have I begotten Thee;' as also in another place He says, 'Thou art a Priest for ever after the order of Melchisedec.'"

Exactly, then, as Aaron was elected solely by Moses at God's command, without waiting for any consent or any council of the people, so in the Church bishops did not need the consent or counsel of the people to be elected to their ministry, but they required the suffrage and the institution of their own order. And our Lord, on the day of His Resurrection, when He met His assembled Apostles, gave the whole rule, order, and descent of election and institution in His Church in the words, "As My Father sent Me, so I also send you." As He elected His apostles and disciples, excluding all consent of the multitude, so He made them electors and institutors of the ministers who should succeed them, independent of popular election. In His Church power is from above, not from below; from within, not from without; nor is any truth attested with a more complete and unbroken witness in the history of three hundred years than this.

5. The fifth point to be considered is the administration of the Church's temporal goods.

Our Lord died upon the cross in utter want and nakedness; in similar want and nakedness of temporal goods the Church, His Body, began her course. She had to draw by the power of His resurrection from the hearts of men what should be sufficient for her clothing and sustenance. The charge of our Lord in sending out His twelve Apostles is, in brief, the history of His Church during these three centuries. They went out without gold or silver in their girdles; they stayed in the houses which received them, eating and drinking of what was set before them. They preached the kingdom of heaven; freely they had received, and freely they gave; and for their heavenly gifts, since the labourer is worthy of his hire, they received temporal support. The 34th Apostolic Canon expresses the obligation to support the clergy and the divine service, which created all the property of the Church. "The law of God has appointed that those who abide at the altar should live by the altar."

The support of their religion was from the beginning both a natural and a divine obligation lying upon all Christians; the natural obligation, expressed in the words "The labourer is worthy of his hire," received from our Lord a supernatural application, when, using these words, He commanded that they who preached the gospel should live of the gospel.[1]

We may note three states of the Church in these early ages as to this matter.[2] In the beginning, during the first fervour of the disciples in Jerusalem, the clergy and laity were united in one heart and spirit, and had all things in common, and those who possessed property sold it, and laid the price at the feet of the Apostles, that they might provide for the common

---
[1] 1 Cor. ix. 14.   [2] Bianchi, 3, 526, 527.

needs. Those who lived in this manner had no obligation of paying tithes or first-fruits. A second state was that when the faith was spread beyond the bounds of Palestine, and that common life could hardly be maintained. Then the faithful retained their property as individuals, but collections were made on certain days for the support of the clergy and the poor, as St. Paul records.[1] When, subsequently, the Christian faith spread through the whole Roman Empire, and assumed a more complete and established form, these stated collections were retained, while Irenæus, and Origen, and Cyprian bear witness to the institution of tithes and first-fruits. Whether the specific amount of contribution was or was not imposed, at least the sustenance of the clergy and of religion was ever considered a debt of justice.

As to the acquisition and usage of temporal goods, the course of things in these first ages may be thus summed up.[2] It is not easy to know precisely at what time churches began to possess immovable goods; it is, however, very probable that this took place soon after the death of the Apostles, and as soon as the faithful gave up the practice of selling their property. Not that every Church made such acquisitions, but that by degrees, now in one city and now in another, some real property was secured; for it is certain that collections continued to be made for a long time, and the faithful continued to give tithes and first-fruits. These collections were not only made for the local Church, but for

---

[1] 1 Cor. xvi. 1.   [2] Bianchi, 3, 536, translated.

churches of distant provinces which were in need, for such a communication of goods was always enjoined by charity and recommended by unity. And it must be further remarked that these oblations of a particular Church were not only sent to another Church when they were more than were needed at home, but often made on purpose to be sent to a distance, as we learn from innumerable examples of ecclesiastical history. The reason of this is plain; for the whole Church being one, as all particular parts are bound to maintain religious union, so are they bound to have communication of those temporal goods which are the endowments necessary to preserve it, and one must help the other when just reason requires it, that all may help reciprocally in maintaining each other.

There was also in these centuries already made a fourfold distribution of the temporal goods acquired; one portion was given to the bishop, a second to the other clergy, a third for the support and relief of the poor and of strangers, a fourth for the building, reparation, and furnishing of churches, for it would seem that there were from the beginning places destined for divine worship. St. Paul[1] speaks of such for the reception of our Lord's Body and Blood. The Martyrology records the festival of the first Christian Church at Rome, which was consecrated by St. Peter. Justin, Tertullian, Cyprian make mention of churches, sometimes the heathen emperors even allowed these, as is specially mentioned of Alexander Severus.

---

[1] 1 Cor. xi. 22.

If, then, we compare the want and nakedness in which the Church began with the state in which she emerged from the period of persecution terminated by Constantine, we find that in spite of spoliations undergone in so many assaults of the heathen empire, she had created funds to support the whole body of her Episcopate, and the clergy subject to them in each diocese, to make ample relief for the poor, for the reception of strangers, for the support of hospitals; to build, maintain, and adorn churches for the celebration of her sacraments and the preaching of her word. In all this she exerted a parallel force with that which shows itself in the construction of her hierarchy, the system of her provincial councils, the constitution of her tribunals, the free election of her bishops and subordinate ministers. In no one of these things did the temporal government give her any aid. That is, indeed, to say much less than the truth. In no one of them did the temporal government do otherwise than thwart her, from the lowest degree of persecution, consisting in a social contempt and disregard, to the highest, of violent confiscation and bloody torture. The extent of favour which she enjoyed was that here and there a politic emperor shut his eyes to her proceedings, or even remarked in the plenitude of his forbearance that a church was better than a cookshop.[1] As the hierarchy proceeded forth by an inward strength derived from our Lord's command, uniting local autonomy with central authority, exercising a rule at once paternal and majes-

[1] An incident mentioned of Alexander Severus.

tical, the rule of Him who joined the commission to feed His whole flock with the condition to love Him more than all others loved Him, so this same hierarchy, passing from house to house and city to city with the word, "the Kingdom of God is at hand," clothed itself as it passed with such a measure of material goods as was necessary for its maintenance by the offerings of the faithful, which they considered at once a natural and a divine obligation, for throughout they saw in the body they were covering the Body of the Lord, who for their sakes, being rich, had become poor.

The five subjects we have just reviewed belong to the Church's external government, in which she manifested from the beginning a complete liberty and independence of all power outside of herself. It is next in order to show the same liberty and independence in the evolution of her teaching.

In this respect the task which fell upon the Apostles, from the time of her Lord's departure, has been very concisely but, at the same time, very exactly defined in the last words of St. Matthew's Gospel, wherein our Lord Himself charged them to "Go forth and make disciples all nations, baptizing them in the name of the Father, and of the Son, and of the Holy Ghost; teaching them to observe all things whatsoever I have commanded you." Herein the construction of the Church is marked in the authority which makes disciples everywhere, for the disciple stands to the teacher in a relation of obedience; in the rite of baptism, which binds them together in one whole, and which, standing at the head, represents the whole system of sacraments; while the teachers are enjoined to require observance of all those things which Christ had commanded them to teach in His name. These injunctions were recorded by St. Matthew in his Gospel many years after they had been exactly fulfilled by those to whom they were addressed. As soon as the Apostles were invested "with power from on high" at the Day of Pentecost, they began the simple work of making disciples, binding them together with sacraments, teaching them obedience to those things in which they had been enjoined by their Lord to instruct them. Again, we possess in the Gospel of St. Luke, dated, as is supposed, at least thirty years after the Day of Pentecost, a continuous record of what they began to do. But the work done, in all its length and breadth, was independent of these records. It is important to realise as well as we can the fact that the whole settlement of the Church as an institution, which embraces the worship of God, the administration of sacraments, the regulation of discipline, her essential polity, including the vocation, ordination, and jurisdiction of her ministers, and no less the instruction of men in that whole doctrine of salvation which consisted in the confession that our Lord was the Christ; all this, which was effected in the forty years which passed between the Day of Pentecost and the destruction of Jerusalem, was effected by oral teaching and living authority. The chief Sees were planted, and the divine polity in each of them, which formed the life of the Christian people, was laid down before the writings of the New

Testament began to be published, long before they were collected, still longer before the Canon of the writings forming them was closed. The first generation of Christians received their religion from the lips of Messengers, Ambassadors, Heralds, who spoke in Christ's name the words which Christ had put in them. Christians so made entered upon the practice of a life the whole course of which was drawn out for them by their teachers. This is the force of the commission, "Make disciples of all nations." Mysteries were dispensed to them of which these teachers were stewards, and which they accepted from the hands of the teachers. And only when this work had been done, during a course of years and in many great cities, did the first written collection of some of the words and acts of Christ begin to be made public; while the last of this fourfold collection was not communicated to the general body of disciples until more than sixty years after the termination of our Lord's earthly life. Before that time the structure of the Church in those points of her external government which we have touched above had been entirely completed; the sound of the Apostles had gone out into all the world; a multitude of teachers had been commissioned by the Apostles; a multitude of people had been taught by them; martyrs had borne witness to the faith thus planted everywhere.

In this first era, which lasted certainly during the lifetime of the Apostles in general, probably to the death of the last Apostle, John, the tradition of the Christian faith was oral. By all this period the kingdom of Christ preceded the book in which we read at the distance of so many centuries the account of its origin. The book did not make the kingdom, but the kingdom made itself, and in making gave us the book, as a part of itself, a permanent though not a complete record of our Lord's words and acts, and a portion of that oral teaching which had been the instrument of its first propagation.

This oral teaching comprehended three classes of facts: first, the things taught by our Lord to His Apostles, whether they were afterwards written or whether they were not written; and as to such a distinction nothing can be more express than St. John's repeated testimony that only a small portion of the things which He did and the signs which He wrought were written—a testimony the more important as it comes from him whose writings close the canon of Scripture. Secondly, it comprehended those things which the Apostles learnt by illumination from the Holy Spirit, according to the promise recorded for us by St. John, "I have yet many things to say to you, but you cannot bear them now; but when He the Spirit of Truth is come, He will guide you by the hand into all truth,"[1] and which under His guidance they taught to the first disciples; and these two classes of things make up together the divine tradition. Thirdly, it comprehended those things which the Apostles in propagating the Church enjoined upon the pastors whom they appointed for the regulation of discipline,

---

[1] John xx. 30, xxi. 25, xvi. 12.

for the administration of sacraments, and for the worship of God, which were not written; and these things make up the apostolic tradition.

It is obvious that out of this treasure-house of the divine and apostolical tradition came the whole planting and propagation of the Church during that first period which elapsed from the Day of Pentecost to the end of the personal teaching of the Apostles. At first, and for many years, the Gospels were not set forth in a written shape, much less were the other books of the New Testament composed. The writings forming the actual canon were not completed until about the year 98. In this interval the acts and the life of Christ were to be impressed on the world; the character of His people was to be formed upon them; the Christian race was born and passed through more than two generations, and the kingdom of heaven upon earth received its definite shape. The divine and apostolic tradition which came from Christ through living men worked these effects. The principle upon which all rested was personal authority. The historical demonstration of the Apostolic Church in this respect is complete and absolute.

It would seem as if this period were of special importance in enabling us to understand distinctly the nature of the Church's teaching office. The work then done comprised the whole evangelical announcement, the preaching, that is, of Christ in His kingdom; the establishment of the worship which He had enjoined, the administering not merely the sacrament of baptism, but the other sacraments in their due order, as they touched the several parts of human life, the discipline which regulated the daily course of life, and also the ordering of penance. In the first community set up at Jerusalem all this would take place; it would be repeated at Antioch, at Rome, at Alexandria, at Ephesus, at Corinth, at every place in which the Apostles established bishops. These things, with the almost interminable series of arrangements and actions which they involve, are all contained in the charge given by our Lord to His Apostles, to which we have just referred. This it is " to make disciples of all nations."

Thus when St. Peter preached on the Day of Pentecost, the immediate effect of his word was the reception of about three thousand hearers into the Church. These had at once to be baptized; therefore the form and ceremonies of baptism were ready prepared for them; but their life is immediately described as a steadfast continuance upon the teaching of the Apostles, in the communion of the breaking of bread, which took place day by day, and in prayers.

From the Day of Pentecost, therefore, the Liturgy of the Church, with all the treasure of doctrine and worship which it contains, was in full operation. I have endeavoured above to give a very short sketch of the vast amount of doctrine contained in the Liturgy, which is at the same time an explicit confession of faith, an act of worship, and an exhibition of spiritual rule. Further, it is an act daily repeated throughout the whole Church, in which she testifies her life, and the dwelling of her Lord in her. The testimony thus given of the threefold power of doctrine, worship, and rule is entirely independent of those allusions to it which are afterwards made in the narrative either of the Gospels or of the Apostolic Epistles. For instance, the term "breaking of bread" points indeed unmistakably to the Eucharistic service, but it gives no description of what that service as celebrated was. We gather this from the ancient Liturgies of the East and West which have come down to us, showing a perfect accord in their parts and meaning and general disposition. Vast is the difference between these Liturgies, viewed in their completeness as acts of worship—that is, not merely in their words, which are so grand and spirit-stirring, but likewise in the function visibly carried out by the bishop, his attendant clergy, and the adoring people—between all this, and the allusion made to it in the few passages of the Gospels, the Acts, and the Epistles. Yet all this existed from the very beginning, and is part of that which St. Peter at the head of the Apostles instituted from the Day of Pentecost. As an act, it is quite independent of any subsequent narrative which records it; but before the end of this first period it was an act which had been carried out daily in a vast number of cities wherein the Church had taken root.

The Eucharistic Liturgy was from the beginning the Church's explicit and solemn exhibition of her faith in her worship. She kept it strictly for her own people, and did not allow it to be divulged. It was an act expressing Christ visibly in the midst of His Church. The altar was His throne. The chiefs ministrant bore His person, and enacted before the eyes of the observant people the work of Christ's Incarnation and Redemption, presenting it to God the Father. The rites and ceremonies which accompanied the words removed, for those beholding and participating the mysteries, that obscurity which may belong in matters of faith to mere words. But, moreover, words of singular simplicity and perspicuity were used in describing the acts by which our Lord became man for us and redeemed us. When the attendant deacon[1] gave warning that all should be in fear and trembling, before the commencement of the sacred action, and before the invocation of the Holy Ghost, did not the words themselves signify the expectation of some signal miracle to be wrought by the Divine Omnipotence? When the people heard the celebrant invoking the descent of the Holy Ghost on the gifts lying before him, that by His presence He might make the bread to be the Body of Christ, and the wine and water the Blood of Christ, transmuting them by His divine power,—when the ministers delivered them to each of the faithful, with the words, "the Body of Christ," "the Blood of Christ," to which he replied, "Amen," what merely verbal announcement could equal in force of teaching that visible setting forth of Christ? On one part, it was Christ giving Himself to His people; on the other, a supreme acknowledgment of joy, gratitude, and prostrate homage by His people for the gift.

[1] Renaudot, Dissertatio de Liturgiarum Orientalium Origine et Auctoritate, p. li.

When the Beloved Disciple, who lay on the Lord's bosom, had a revelation of what was to happen in the time to come, the vision was presented to him under the form of that worship which Peter first, in the company of his brother Apostles, which the bishop of each city afterwards, surrounded by his ancients and in the presence of the faithful people, celebrated. It seems to be the interior of a church in the apostolic age which we have described, and all the meaning of the Eucharistic Sacrifice, as the witness of creative power and redeeming love, set forth. But it is the Lord Himself, who with the voice of a trumpet proclaimed Himself to be the First and the Last, and charged His Apostle with letters to the Seven Churches, who now says with the same voice, "Come up hither, and I will show thee the things which must be done hereafter." "I looked," he says, "and behold a door was opened in heaven, and immediately I was in the spirit; and behold there was a throne set in heaven, and upon the throne One sitting. And He that sat was to the sight like the jasper and the sardine-stone; and there was a rainbow round about the throne in sight like unto an emerald. And round about the throne were four-and-twenty seats; and upon the seats four-and-twenty ancients sitting, clothed in white garments, and on their heads crowns of gold. And from the throne proceeded lightnings and voices and thunders; and there were seven lamps burning before the throne, which are the seven spirits of God." Here, in the likeness of an ancient basilica, with the throne of the bishop in the apse, and the seats of his presbyters in a semicircle round him, we have the court of the Almighty set forth, and the ineffable grandeur of the creating God : when " the four living creatures full of eyes gave glory and honour and benediction to Him that sitteth on the throne, who liveth for ever and ever, the four-and-twenty ancients fell down before Him that sitteth on the throne, and adored Him that liveth for ever and ever, and cast their crowns before the throne, saying, Thou art worthy, O Lord our God, to receive glory and honour and power, because Thou hast created all things, and for Thy will they are (εἰσὶ,) and have been created."

So far the homage paid to God in the great overwhelming mystery of creation. All things have been made by Him and for Him. But another mystery succeeds : the fall and the redemption of man. "And I saw in the right hand of Him that sat on the throne a book written within and without, sealed with seven seals. And I saw a strong angel proclaiming with a loud voice, Who is worthy to open the book and to loose the seals thereof? And no man was able, neither in heaven, nor on earth, nor under the earth, to open the book, nor to look on it. And I wept much because no man was found worthy to open the book nor to see it. And one of the ancients said to me, Weep not; behold the Lion of the tribe of Juda, the root of David, hath prevailed to open the book, and to loose the seven seals thereof. And I saw, and behold in the midst of the throne and of the four living creatures, and in the midst of the ancients, a Lamb standing as it were slain, having seven horns and seven eyes, which are the seven spirits of God sent forth into all the earth. And He came and took the book out of the right hand of Him that sat upon the throne.—And when He had opened the book, the four living creatures and the four-and-twenty ancients fell down before the Lamb, having every one of them harps and golden vials full of odours, which are the prayers of saints; and they sang a new canticle, saying, Thou art worthy, O Lord, to take the book and to open the seals thereof; because Thou wast slain and hast redeemed us to God in Thy blood, out of every tribe and tongue, and people and nation, and hast made us to our God a kingdom and priests, and we shall reign on the earth. And I beheld, and I heard the voice of many angels round about the throne and the living creatures and the ancients; and the number of them was thousands of thousands, saying with a loud voice, The Lamb that was slain is worthy to receive power and divinity, and wisdom and strength and honour and glory and benediction. And every creature which is in heaven and on the earth, and under the earth, and such as are in the sea, and all that are in them, I heard all saying, To Him that sitteth on the throne, and to the Lamb, benediction and honour and glory and power for ever and ever. And the four living creatures said, Amen. And the four-and-twenty ancients fell down on their faces, and adored Him that liveth for ever and ever."

We have now added to the throne of the Almighty, in the midst of the four living creatures and the twenty-four crowned elders, "a Lamb standing as it were slain," who, having received the sealed book from Him that sat upon the throne, becomes Himself the centre of adoration. He takes the place of the altar in the Church, being Himself the altar and the celebrant; He opens the seals of the book which no one in heaven or earth could open but Himself; He rules the evolution of all the events which make up the history of His people; He the victim; He the priest; He the ruler. And under the Eucharist Sacrifice thus exhibited the whole evolution of judgments and victories are drawn out, which ends with "the holy city, the New Jerusalem, coming down out of heaven from God, prepared as a Bride adorned for her Husband."

Only this vision of the Beloved Disciple and the feelings which it exhibits would adequately represent that awe and joy, that gratitude and triumph, with which the faithful took part in what the Fathers call "the tremendous and unbloody sacrifice." And could any Christian of the Apostle's day read the words of this heavenly vision without recognising in it the very order and arrangement of the great worship which formed then, as it forms now, the central act of united Christian life?

No higher act of authority is even conceivable than that establishment of worship. But this was a worship which the Apostles had received in secret from their Lord, which they did not commit to writing, but carefully imprinted upon the memories of their disciples, which they guarded with the utmost care and jealousy from the knowledge of all until they had first instructed them and then baptized them, the participation in which was the crown of all Christian privileges. Thus they understood what Christ had ordered them to do in commemoration of Himself. They began it at Jerusalem; they carried it with them in their dispersion to all Churches. It is found the same in its principal parts and sequence in all places. The same form was received everywhere solely in virtue of an Apostolic tradition, which originally was not written, but conveyed by word of mouth, and at once and incessantly practised.

The commemoration in which they carried out their Lord's command was contained in words, and rites, and vestments illustrating those words, and making up together an act, a permanent act, going through all the life of the Church from end to end. This act in the present day, as in every past age, is not derived from any written authority, though the Gospels and Epistles of the Apostles, and, as we have seen, the Apocalypse, bear witness to it, but from the authority of the Church, immanent in her from the beginning by perpetual descent from the Apostles.

Another instance of the like kind is scarcely inferior in its force. The Apostles, in passing from city to city in the course of their preaching, selected those in whom they would deposit a portion of their power. But this they did by the imposition of their hands, accompanied by a certain rite, which, like the Eucharistic rite in the beginning, was not written, but conveyed by word of mouth. But the life of the Church depended upon this transmission of spiritual power. The conveying of this power was an act of authority similar in character to the institution of worship, with which indeed it was closely allied. Part of the power which they conveyed by their act was the right to celebrate this very worship. The pastoral Epistles of St. Paul speak of the grace and gift bestowed upon Timotheus by the imposition of hands, as well as of the power given both to Timotheus and to Titus to impart these gifts to others, accompanied with advice as to the quality of persons whom they should select. But the Scriptures of the New Testament do not contain the rite itself, than which nothing could be more necessary to the continued existence of the Church.

No acts could possibly exhibit the teaching office of the Church in greater perfection and fulness than the exercise of the rite which admitted men into her fold; of the rite, again, which communicated to them daily the divine life of the Saviour indwelling in her; and thirdly, of the rite which propagated the whole of that hierarchy by the descent of which from our Lord Himself her existence was secured and perpetuated. The immense authority which documents such as these possess is mentioned in a letter of Pope St. Celestine in the year 431 to the Gallic bishops. "Let us have regard," he says, "to the sacred rites used in sacerdotal supplications, which, having been handed down from the Apostles, are celebrated uniformly in the whole world and in every Catholic Church, wherein the law of supplication establishes the law of belief. For when those who preside over the holy people in various places exercise the office of ambassadors committed to them, they plead the cause of the human race before the divine mercy, and offer their requests and their prayers while the whole Church joins with them in urgent entreaty."[1] It is sufficient to mention these several public and official acts without going on to dwell upon the system of penance in its doctrinal aspect, which has been described above in another aspect, that of government. Such a system, it is evident, existed from the beginning, and the act of St. Paul in reference to the incestuous person at Corinth bears witness to it. The society possessing and exercising these rites, and forming a people upon their discipline, had a complete rule of inward life. Such was the Christian society in the first forty years following the day of Pentecost. And this whole life rested upon the personal authority of its teachers, which they exercised in the name of Christ, and by the power of the Holy Spirit continually attending upon their ministry, and attesting His presence as well by the perpetual operation of His grace as by the extraordinary and visible action of spiritual gifts. That authority was complete before the sacred writings of the New Testament were made public, and without their attestation.

The authority divinely instituted[2] to preserve and

[1] St. Cœlestini, Ep. 21, Constant, p. 493. The part quoted is supposed to have been added to St. Cœlestine's letter (which refers to the death of St. Augustine as having just happened) a little later, but was always joined with it afterwards from the beginning of the sixth century.

[2] Franzelin, De Traditione, Thesis vii. p. 49.

propagate the doctrine preached by the Apostles was neither changed in character nor diminished by the writing of the books of the New Testament and by their delivery to the several churches. The proof of this is twofold. First, the nature of the teaching office itself, placed by Christ in the Apostles and their perpetual succession, to which He promised His own ever-abiding assistance, with the gift of the Holy Spirit dwelling in them. For these two things were not accidental or temporary, but the cause for ever of the Christian profession's continuance.

Secondly, the consideration of all the circumstances which surround the writings themselves corroborates this conclusion.

Before these books were written,[1] and much more before they were all collected and read in all churches, these churches themselves had been arranged by the teaching and ordering of the Apostles according to the charge they had received from Christ; bishops had been appointed in them by imposition of the Apostles' hands; the doctrine delivered to them by the Apostles had been committed to them as a deposit to be faithfully guarded through the gift of the Holy Spirit: they had been charged to appoint successors in every place, endowed with the like authority and the same gift. Thus the faithful everywhere depended, with the obedience of faith, upon the authority of the apostolic successors as God's messengers, from whom they were to receive

[1] Translated from Franzelin, Tractatus de Traditione Divina et Scriptura, pp. 50-53, down to "The Teaching Office."

Christian doctrine and discipline. This was not a mere dependence of those who were learning upon the knowledge of those who were teaching, because as yet there were no books from which each individual might learn for himself, but it was a proper office of teaching upon which the obedience of faith depended by Christ's institution, and by which the unity of the churches was maintained. When, therefore, inspired books containing revealed doctrine were gradually delivered by the Apostles to the churches, the ecclesiastical constitution already existing was not destroyed, but documents were added to be used in accordance with that constitution, to be preserved by those same bishops as successors of the Apostles and guardians of the deposit, and to be explained by them should doubt arise as to the meaning.

Further, it is an historical fact, and is evident from the internal arrangement of the books, that each one of them was written on some particular occasion and necessity for some particular end. No one of the sacred writers had the intention to give complete instruction as to the doctrine, discipline, and worship of the Christian religion. Accordingly in no one of them is the whole Christian doctrine found set out in catechetical order and connection; and in each one many most important points are either omitted, or merely alluded to, or can only be deduced from it, if otherwise known. Now such an origin of the books from particular occasions and for a particular scope, and such an internal arrangement, make it evident that it was not the Holy Spirit's design in writing any particular book, or the whole together, nor any purpose of the Apostles, to substitute books so composed for the ministry of those pastors and doctors whom Christ had appointed to teach all nations to the end of the world. It was not meant to abolish the constitution of a teaching office by which, up to the moment when these books appeared, every one had, in virtue of Christ's institution, been taught by the acknowledged messengers of God, in order that he might teach himself from a written book. This would be plain even were it to be granted that the whole revealed doctrine was contained in those books; for the argument holds not so much from deficiency of matter as from the form of teaching, and the manner of proposing and explaining doctrine.

But when we have stated the historical origin of the books, and their internal arrangement which corresponds to their origin, it is a mere gratuitous assertion that all revealed doctrine is contained in them. For as neither the sacred writers, each taken by himself, intended to comprehend the whole Christian doctrine in his own books, nor concerted together to contribute each his portion to make up one whole, but as each wrote on the most diverse occasions what was necessary or opportune for the particular circumstances, the Holy Spirit indeed, who is the chief Author of the Scriptures, might direct everything, so as to form a complete body of doctrine without the knowledge and beyond the intention of the writers, but that He did so can in nowise be shown.

For this the supposition is required that it was the will of God that Scripture should be the sole source, or at least the complete code, from which the entire revelation might be acquired. We have certain evidence from the charge of Christ that the Apostles and their successors should teach to the end of the world all nations to observe whatever He had commanded them, and from the promise of the Spirit of truth teaching all truth and remaining with them for ever, by whom Christ's witnesses are ordered to go to the end of the earth, that the whole revelation was to be preached by an authentic office of teaching in perpetual succession. On the other hand, there is not a vestige of a charge that this revelation should be committed entire to writing, either in the words of Christ or in the sayings of the Apostles, or in the manner of acting and writing of the Apostles or of the other sacred writers, or in the arrangement, scope, and occasion of the books, or in the persuasion of Christians down to the sixteenth century. How, then, is this to be maintained unless you first lay down not to believe the word propagated by preaching which Christ appointed by charges and promises distinct and irrefragable, and enjoined to comprehend the whole revealed truth, but to believe only the word in Scripture, which He did indeed superadd to preaching, but never either enjoined or promised that all revealed truth should be contained in it?

But whatever be the fact as to the material fulness of Scripture, the form of the books, each and all, is such that they evidently are not written for the purpose of teaching the whole Christian religion to each of the faithful independently of the teaching office.

It must be added that these books were addressed to those who were already Christians, and give directions and advice which could not be rightly understood save by those who had been previously instructed, and, moreover, refer the faithful in express words to the preaching which they had heard and received, and in which they are exhorted to abide. They further also refer to guardians of the deposit, and to a line of authentic teachers who shall continue to hand it on from generation to generation.[1]

That which had existed from the beginning by the institution of Christ, and that which was to last unaltered to the end, was an apostolic succession of men, in whom He put His power and presence, to whom He promised the perpetual assistance of His Holy Spirit, and to whom He committed the propagation of His faith. It was impossible that this principle of action, the living personal authority, which, as we have seen, did everything in the first two generations of the Christian people, should ever be changed, because Christ appointed it to bear His Word, the Word of God, whether oral or written, to every succeeding generation.

Among the things which preceded in time the publication of the writings of the New Testament, and which,

[1] As, *e.g.*, Rom. xvi. 17; 1 Cor. vii. 17, xi. 23, xiv. 33, xv. 12; 2 Cor. i. 18; Gal. i. 18; Phil. iv. 9; Colos. ii. 6, 7; 1 Thess. iv. 2; 2 Thess. ii. 14; 2 Tim. ii. 2; Heb. ii. 3, referred to by Franzelin, but especially Ephes. iv. 11-16, which is of itself sufficient to decide the whole question.

therefore, were not derived from them, were these: The hierarchy, including therein the election, ordination, and jurisdiction of bishops throughout the world, and of the ministers inferior to them; the several sacraments, with the rites which conveyed them; the worship, and herein especially the Eucharist, and all which belongs to it; and fourthly, that daily discipline of life which received men into the Christian body, numbered them in it, imposed penance for faults committed, restored the fallen, and, in fact, which was that atmosphere by breathing which the Christian lived. All this the living succession of men, instinct with the power and presence of the Holy Ghost, the Sanctifier and the Comforter, the Spirit of truth, originally conveyed, as the living succession of men perpetuates it from age to age. These things, the writings of the New Testament, as they were gradually, first one and then another, given to particular churches, or intended for classes of believers, and finally collected in one and made the heirloom of the whole body, found in existence and in full operation. With all the instruments of the divine life thus enumerated these writings did not meddle, except that they alluded to them more or less, usually in few words, attesting them, it is true, but in a manner which those only who were in possession of them would understand aright. The action of the Church as a living Body consisted very largely in these things, and this action, at least in all its details, the Apostles were not directed by any charge of their Lord, nor inspired by the Holy Ghost, to commit to a book. These things, from their nature, formed an essential part of the ecclesiastical tradition; in fact, the Church as a society could not exist without them.

Another part of the ecclesiastical tradition was the announcing to men the words and the acts of Christ. The Christian character was to be formed upon the living example of the Shepherd who had gone before His sheep. For this task men were chosen who had been with Him during the whole time of His ministry. So long as they were on earth they would speak with all the authority of those who had seen what they witnessed; but it is not apparent how an accurate account of our Lord's words and acts could be transmitted to succeeding generations except by writing. Thus it pleased the Holy Spirit to inspire some of the Apostles and some of their disciples to commit to writing that record of our Lord's words and actions which we possess in the four Gospels. Inexpressibly dear, indeed, and precious to every Christian, must be the words of the Word; like nothing else upon earth, the sounds which came from the lips of God manifest in the flesh; of untold depth His utterances; of inexhaustible fruitfulness His teaching. And the same may be said of His acts. As a single parable would disclose the nature of His kingdom, so a single act might be rich in endless application to the history of His Church and to the heart of every believer. This most precious part of the ecclesiastical tradition the Evangelists deposited in the bosom of the Church, to be communicated, guarded, interpreted by her for ever to the end of time. It was not the creation of one power to balance another, for a book and a society do not come into competition; it was endowing the society which Christ had created with the breath of His mouth, and investing it with a permanent knowledge of His words and acts—a knowledge to be transmitted under its keeping to all times.

As the Gospels contained words and acts of our Lord, so the Apostolic Epistles contained comments, illustrations, and developments of their personal teaching, bearing witness everywhere to that teaching, and to the society which their own labours had constructed under their Lord's direction, and only by the power of His Spirit working in themselves who preached, and in the hearers who accepted the faith which they preached. These writings the Church collected and placed in her treasury; they became part of that deposit which St. Irenæus[1] celebrates "as being new and fresh in an excellent vessel, and giving perpetual youth to that vessel, which is the divine office intrusted to the Church, as life is given to the body to vivify all the limbs belonging to it."

If we put together that large mass of teaching above described, which consisted in the government everywhere set up by the Apostles, in the sacraments which they carried into effect according to their Lord's instructions, in the worship which they established, in the life of faith, the daily discipline of which they set on foot, with that written mass of documents of which by the end of the first century the Church was in possession, we can form an approximate notion of the written and un-

---

[1] St. Irenæus, iii. 24.

written tradition which it was her abiding office to expound.

That which is primary and essential,[1] the very substance of God's institution, is the perpetual succession of living men from the Apostles. All the rest are means by which that succession acts. These means the providence of God has placed round His own central creation. Such means are the word contained in the Divine Scriptures, the word contained in sacraments, the word contained in worship, the word contained in the most various ecclesiastical monuments, which exhibit the consent and definitive judgment of the successors of the Apostles in past time.

These were the various means which the apostolic succession itself used, under the assistance of the Holy Spirit, to maintain and expound and preserve from error that whole tradition of the truth which Christ in the beginning committed to it. But the subject requires further illustration.

[1] See Franzelin, De Traditione, p. 134.

CHAPTER VII.

THE ACTUAL RELATION BETWEEN CHURCH AND STATE FROM THE DAY OF PENTECOST TO CONSTANTINE.

The Independence of the Ante-Nicene Church shown in her Mode of Positive Teaching and in her Mode of Resisting Error.

THE Church is the Body of Christ as it moves through the centuries from His first to His second coming. We have been tracing the course through the first three of these centuries. Let us recur for a moment to the beginning, when we behold our Lord, at the head of His Apostles, passing through the towns and villages of Galilee, preaching that the kingdom of heaven is at hand, imparting, as in the Sermon on the Mount, the principles of that divine kingdom, healing every infirmity and disease; then sending out His Apostles, and afterwards His disciples, by two and two, as His heralds and messengers. This was the prelude, the type and germ, of what was to come. Then, after His Passion and Resurrection, we see the first stadium in the mission of the Apostles. They speak in His name; they manifest His power; His Person is in the midst of them; His Spirit upon them. The Apostle who once denied Him stands at their head, and speaks with authority, declaring the mission intrusted to him. Forthwith three thousand, who speedily become five thousand, accede to the voice of his preaching. In twelve years Judæa and Palestine and Antioch have had the new doctrine planted among them, and then it is set up in Rome, the sceptred head of heathendom. The forty years of that first mission are crowned by the destruction of the deicide city, after that, by the hands of the Apostles and the fellow-labourers whom they have chosen, the suckers of the Vine have been laid in all the chief places of the Roman world. A kingdom had been preached and a kingdom had been founded; and its basis had been laid in authority—that of a crucified Head, transmitted to His Apostles.

The whole of this forty years' work is a Tradition or Delivery, to translate literally the Greek title. Its bearers gave what they had received. It was intrusted to them, to their truthfulness and their accuracy; and those who received their message did not question it, but accepted it as they gave it. From first to last the Tradition rested on the one principle of authority, which had its fountain-head in the Person of our Lord. He spoke as one having authority in Himself, not as the Scribes and Pharisees, who interpreted an existing law; and they whom He had deputed to follow Him claimed a delegation from that authority, and spoke in virtue of it.

But if this was so in the lifetime of the Apostles, who had seen and touched and handled the Word of Life, it was no less the case in the teachers who immediately followed them. We have seen a most striking instance in St. Clement, who claimed for the decision of the Roman Church in an important matter, and that during the lifetime of the Apostle John, that the words uttered by it were the words of the Holy Ghost, and asserted that those who did not listen to them refused to listen to God Himself. But this language represents the language and the conduct of those who succeeded to the place of the Apostles in the whole three hundred years. There is no break and no change in this respect. The Nicene Council in its decisions has the same tone as the Apostolic Council at Jerusalem; it is no other than "it has seemed good to the Holy Ghost and to us."

For in truth, from first to last, all success in the divine kingdom is the work of the Spirit of Christ. He is the one power who gives life to the whole. In Him lies the secret of its unity, whereby the Body of Christians, or the Christian nation,[1] is one and the same at Rome, Alexandria, Antioch, and a thousand other places; for Jew and Greek, barbarian, Scythian, bond and free, male and female, have all been made to drink into one Spirit.

Thus a living God will have a living Church; and in this first great period—instinct with a character of its own, as the conflict between the new Christian nation and the mightiest offspring of the old civilisation, that heir of Egypt, Assyria, Persia, and Greece, which transcended its ancestors—the great charter lies in the words, "As My Father sent Me, so also send I you." It

---

[1] Corpus Christianorum: τὸ ἔθνος Χριστιανῶν.

is this ever-living mission which perpetuates " the Tradition or Delivery." Thus it is the accordant witness of all that we have hitherto said, from the testimony of the sacred writings to that of the first fathers and teachers, exhibited in all their conduct, that the living apostolic succession is the one thing instituted by God to carry on His revelation and to maintain His kingdom. This succession it is which bears in its hands the various records forming the treasury of the kingdom, whether they be the Scriptures of the Old and New Testaments, or the sacraments which communicate a divine life, or the majestic liturgy which expresses the divine worship, or the daily praxis of the Church, which is, in fact, the embodiment of its unwritten tradition: in all these, and through them in all ages, the apostolic succession works. And the mission through which it works is as living, real, and present, as immediate and efficacious now, as when the words first dropped from the lips of our Lord in the Body in which He rose again, " As My Father sent Me, so also send I you."

We may divide the consideration of the manner in which the Apostles proclaimed the divine kingdom into two heads, the first of which will be the whole work of positive promulgation, and the second the whole defence against error.

As to the first, I will touch on five points—the system of catechesis, the employment of a creed, the dispensing of sacraments, the system of penance, and the Scriptures carried in the Church's hand. And I am considering these especially in one point of view, as illustrating the method of teaching pursued by a body which was intrusted with a divine message.

1. Converts were admitted into the Church after a process of oral instruction of more or less duration; for I am not here concerned with the extent of that duration, but with the fact that such instruction was invariably given by word of mouth, not by placing a book in the hands of those who came to be taught. What the Christian doctrine was it belonged to its teachers to say, and the system by which it was learnt was termed catechesis, *i.e.*, instruction by word of mouth, by question and answer. This is the word applied by St. Luke in the beginning of his Gospel to Theophilus, to whom he addressed it; and the opening verses of the Gospel describe the thing itself with an accuracy which leaves nothing to be desired; for the Evangelist speaks " of the things that have been accomplished among us, according as they have *delivered*[1] them unto us, who from the beginning were eye-witnesses and ministers of the word;"[2] and adds, " It seemed good to me also, having diligently attained to all things from the beginning, to write to thee in order, most excellent Theophilus, that thou mayest know the verity of those things in which thou hast been instructed by word of mouth." By which we see that it was not a book which had been put into the hands of

---

[1] παρέδοσαν, in which is signified that the whole was a παράδοσις, *traditio*, delivery. On the two meanings of the word *tradition*, the one the unwritten word of God, the other the whole doctrine of salvation as handed down by the Fathers, see Kleutgen's Theologie der Vorzeit, tom. i. p. 73, and v. p. 405.

[2] ὑπηρέται τοῦ λόγου.

Theophilus to teach him Christian truth, but a doctrine delivered by personal teachers, and derived from those who were eye-witnesses, and administered to others what they knew. But after Theophilus had become a full Christian, a Gospel might be addressed to him for confirmation of his faith.

The Church of which we know most as to its method of converting Gentiles is the Alexandrine Church, in which, from very early time, there was a famous catechetical school, founded, it is said, by St. Mark himself, the names of whose after teachers, Athenagoras, Pantænus, and still more Clement and Origen, have distinguished it.[1] Its method has been thus described:—

"In the system of the early catechetical schools the *perfect*, or men in Christ, were such as had deliberately taken on them the profession of believers, had made the vows and received the grace of baptism, and were admitted to all the privileges and the revelations of which the Church had been constituted the dispenser. But before reception into this full discipleship, a previous season of preparation, from two to three years, was enjoined, in order to try their obedience and instruct them in the principles of revealed truth. During this introductory discipline they were called *catechumens*, and the teaching itself *catechetical*, from the careful and systematic examination by which their grounding in the faith was effected. The matter of the instruction thus

---

[1] Origen was followed by his pupil Heraclas; then the great Dionysius, afterwards bishop; Pierius, Achillas, Theognostus, Serapion, Peter the Martyr (Reischl in Möhler, i. 377).

communicated to them varied with the time of their discipleship, advancing from the most simple principles of natural religion to the peculiar doctrines of the gospel, from moral truths to the Christian mysteries. On their first admission they were denominated *hearers*, from the leave granted them to attend the reading of the Scriptures and sermons in the church. Afterwards, being allowed to stay during the prayers, and receiving the imposition of hands as the sign of their progress in spiritual knowledge, they were called *worshippers*. Lastly, some short time before their baptism, they were taught the Lord's Prayer (the peculiar privilege of the regenerate), were intrusted with the knowledge of the Creed, and, as destined for incorporation into the body of believers, received the titles of *competent* or *elect*.[1] Even to the last they were granted nothing beyond a formal and general account of the articles of the Christian faith, the exact and fully developed doctrines of the Trinity and the Incarnation, and, still more, the doctrine of the Atonement, as once made upon the cross, and commemorated and appropriated in the Eucharist, being the exclusive possession of the serious and practical Christian. On the other hand, the chief subjects of catechisings, as we learn from Cyril, were the doctrines of repentance and pardon, of the necessity of good works, of the nature and use of baptism, and the immortality of the soul, as the Apostle had determined them."[2]

[1] τέλειοι; ἀκροώμενοι, or *audientes;* γονυκλίνοντες or εὐχόμενοι; *competentes, electi,* or φωτιζόμενοι. Bingham, Antiq., B. x.; Suicer, Thes. in verb. κατηχέω.

[2] Newman's Arians, pp. 45, 46.

It is not needful for our present purpose to go further into the "Discipline of the Secret." It is enough to point out how this whole method, which belonged to the Church everywhere, though carried out no doubt in various degrees of perfectness according to the endowments and zeal of individuals and the energy of pastoral care, testified throughout the magistral character of the Church, and that those who came into her fold must come in the spirit of little children, according to our Lord's saying. Those certainly who so came could not question the doctrines which they received, nor the authority of which they were not judges, but disciples.

2. But the use of a Creed,[1] communicated at a certain advanced period of the instruction given, and as a prelude to the rite which admitted into the Body, was a further token of authority. Nor indeed can any greater act of authority be well imagined than the summing up what is to be believed as the doctrine of salvation in a few sentences. This is not done in the Scriptures themselves, whether of the Old or New Testament, or both together. And how great an act of authority it was in the mind of the Christian people is well expressed in the tradition which not only called the first creed the Creed of the Apostles, but represented them before their separation not again to be reunited, as contributing each one to the twelve propositions forming it. Such a tradition, even if it be not true, is not only a picturesque but a most powerful and emphatic exhibition of the feeling which Christians entertained as to

[1] See upon this use of the Creed, Möhler, Kirchengeschichte, i. 343-347.

the act of authority implied in creating the instrument which conveyed the Christian faith. For if each separate article of the Creed may be attested by the Christian Scriptures, yet the selection of such and such doctrines, their arrangement and force when put together, indicate something quite other than the existence or expression of such doctrines scattered about Scripture, just as the faggot is something much more than the sticks which compose it. And in accordance with this judgment upon the authority of a creed as such, we find that enlargements or explanations of the first Creed have only been made by the highest authority in the Church, and on rare occasions, as a defence against heresies which threatened the very being of the Church, or as the more complete expression of doctrines in which the Church felt her life to be enshrined. But it was a Creed which from the beginning bore the title of the Rule of Faith. The Creed was recited by the baptized, as a token of their acceptance and incorporation into the Church; repeated as a daily prayer of singular power and efficacy; renewed by the dying as a confession of faith and passport to the tribunal of the great Judge. St. Augustine,[1] in a sermon to catechumens, said, even in his time, "You must by no means write down the words of the Creed in order to remember them, but you must learn them by hearing them; nor when you have learnt them must you write them, but hold them ever in your memory and ruminate on them."

Nor, though the doctrines contained in the original

[1] Sermon 212.

Creed may be attested by the Scriptures, was the authority of the Creed and of the power which imposed it derived from the testimony of the Scriptures. It was antecedent in time to such testimony, and it was derived from those who were authors of the Scriptures, and who were at least as infallible in such an act as in the account which they might communicate to the churches of what they had seen and heard.[1]

To the method of catechesis, therefore, as the means of instruction, we add the employment of the Creed, which is the Church's oriflamme, round which her host gathers, and to which it looks in the ever-during struggle of the faith.

3. Next consider the daily life into which the convert was introduced when his course of catechetical instruction was concluded and he was put in possession of the Creed.

The first sacrament, that of baptism, administered with the utmost solemnity at certain times of the year, the one being the eve of the Lord's resurrection, the other the eve of the descent of the Holy Spirit upon the Church, was "an enlightening" which opened to him the wonders of the spiritual world. In virtue of it he became a member of "the household of God," he entered into brotherhood with his Redeemer, he shared in the gift of the Almighty Spirit, the Author and Giver of all grace. At the same time, or shortly after, the chrism of confirmation added to his strength for the perpetual conflict of the Christian life. And here by the imposition of episcopal hands the same sevenfold

[1] On this subject see Newman's Arians, pp. 137–142.

Spirit of grace descended upon him, marking by the rite itself how the Christian society was inhabited by that Spirit, whose power the bishop bestowed upon the newly born Christian. But both baptism and confirmation were sacraments, however enduring in their effects, yet given once and never to be repeated; whereas for the perpetual sustenance of spiritual life a tree was needed which should bear perpetual fruit. And here the Lord Himself was at hand; for the baptized and confirmed Christian was forthwith fed with the Bread of Angels; and that majestic altar was disclosed to his sight on which daily lay the Body of the Lord of Angels, offered for him in mystical sacrifice; and he heard the accents of that divine liturgy which called upon heaven and earth to rejoice together in the great glory of God. It was impossible for any faithful heart to hear the glowing words in which the sacrificant described the mercy of God in bestowing His Son upon men as their Deliverer and their daily food without being kindled into an unspeakable joy, "while the angels praise, the dominations adore, the powers tremble, the heavens, the heavenly virtues, and the blessed Seraphim with common jubilee glorify" that majesty so shown forth in mercy. In the eucharistic service he felt himself at once the citizen of a heavenly kingdom, for the divine polity breathed in all around him. Sight and touch, language and every sense, testified a divine presence, and religion became to all participants a living thing. This was a permanent, not a fleeting gift; the endowment of a life, the super-substantial daily Bread.

But the heavenly blessing encircled every act. It joined the sexes in a consecration which ennobled while it sanctified that lifelong treaty on which rests the whole existence of a home for family and children; it supported the infirmities of the dying with a special strength; it recruited the ministers of the Church in rites which imaged out in most expressive formulas the power from on high, that delegation from the Saviour's Person which was the whole ground of authority.

4. But there is yet another institution, which in as forcible a way as any of the six just mentioned exhibits the Christian Church as a polity; for the one enemy against which a perpetual watchfulness needed to be maintained was the frailty of the human heart itself. Even from the beginning there never was a time in which Christians did not fall, and so from the beginning there was a system of penance to meet that case of their fall, and to provide for restoration. The Apostle Paul found the evil among his converts at Corinth, and used the remedy. But that remedy powerfully illustrates the control of a living society over its members. Those who fell in any way from the Christian profession could only be restored by a double action; the inward repentance of the individual sinning was required on the one hand, but this did not of itself suffice; the outward action of the society itself was needed, and this society imposed such rules as it thought good for the granting of pardon. It is not to my point to go into any details on the subject, because it is the principle itself contained in the system of

penance which I wish to dwell upon alone. Sins of infidelity, impurity, idolatry, as a rule excluded for long periods of years, or even for the whole course of life, from the Church. The bishop dispensed this discipline either in person or through his priests, in a tribunal in which he represented Christ Himself, and exerted His authority, the greatest given to man upon earth, an authority belonging to God alone, the power to remit or retain sins. From the beginning the Church exercised this authority, and in it ruled a kingdom, the kingdom of man's innermost thoughts, the hopes and the fears of an eternal world. They whose lives were not safe a moment from the persecuting powers of heathen magistrates, wielded a much more awful power over their fellow-Christians, subject to them by the bond of a divine hierarchy which had its source, its centre, and its crown in our Lord Himself, which was His gift to the world, which He left behind Him to carry on His kingdom. This power was an essential part of the priesthood borne by the episcopate, in no sense derived from the particular community wherein it was exercised, but descending from above.

5. If we put together the constant action of these divine institutions, which we term sacraments, we gain from the contemplation a picture of the entire Christian life, the daily course of the Christian citizen in his citizenship, subsisting by the force of the Tradition above spoken of. But there is another point to be exhibited. When St. Luke wrote to Theophilus that the intention of his Gospel was to confirm him in the

certainty of those things which he had been taught by word of mouth, he disclosed to us the position which the Scriptures held in this period of the Ante-Nicene Church. They were not the immediate instrument of teaching, and far less were they put in the hands of the neophyte in order that, by an act of his private judgment, he might compare the doctrine which he supposed to be contained in them with the doctrine taught to him by his instructors. The Scriptures, both of the Old and New Testaments, were carried in the Church's hand, and presented to the faithful as documents beyond the reach of their criticism, guaranteed by the authority through which they themselves became Christians. This is a totally different presentment from that of a book which exists without credentials external to itself. The notion of treating the narratives of our Lord's actions and words as common books, subject, like any ordinary history, to the judgments of their readers, would have struck with horror those who had a special name for such weak or unfaithful Christians as in times of danger delivered up their sacred books to the heathens. They called them Traditores, whence we derive the most loathsome appellation which can be applied to a man who disregards the dictates of conscience and the pledges of fidelity. It would have been *treason* indeed to their minds to question the truth of a miracle recorded by St. Matthew or a doctrine set forth by St. John. But why? Because behind the Holy Scriptures lay the whole authority of that living Church in virtue of which they themselves had the privilege of knowing the Scriptures at all. That the Spirit of God dictated these Scriptures they knew only from the Church. The kingdom of which these Scriptures spoke was the Church herself. The Scriptures were *part* of her. They did not produce the hierarchy by which she was governed, nor the sacraments on which her people lived, nor that whole daily discipline in and through which the Christian people existed. Even had they constituted, which they did not, a code of laws, a code is an unexerted power without those who administer it.

But the Church from the beginning literally *dispensed* the Scriptures; she selected portions of the Gospels and Epistles for recitation in her eucharistic liturgy; she referred to them in her daily teaching. They were a treasury out of which she brought perpetually things old and new. The parables of our Lord became in her hands the structure of a living kingdom; she herself was the fulfilment of that great series of prophecies. In her the Sower went forth to sow His seed, and the field in which He sowed was the world, and the time of the sowing the last age—the time between the first and the second coming of the King. She herself was the net which gathered a multitude of fish, "which when it was filled they drew out, and sitting by the shore they chose out the good into vessels, but the bad they cast forth." She herself was "the grain of mustard seed, which a man took and sowed in his field, which is indeed the least of all seeds, but when it is grown up it is greater than all herbs, and becomes a tree, so that the birds of the air come and dwell in the branches thereof." And especially in all this process she was "the leaven which a woman took and hid in three measures of meal until the whole was leavened," whether we regard those three measures as the corporeal, animal, and spiritual nature of the individual man, or as the family, the social, and the political life of the collective man.

And this continued to be the relation between the Church and the Scriptures which were committed to her charge, and which she dispensed to her people, not merely by reading them in her liturgies and the devotions of her clergy and her religious orders, but in the realising and acting them out in her own life during full fifteen centuries. During this vast period of time the Holy Scriptures were received throughout the whole extent of Christendom as the unquestioned Word of God, with an entire faith in their inspiration. The faithful mind was not prone to analyse the basis on which this belief rested, which was the Church's attestation. They had been copied out by the unwearied labours of innumerable hands in religious houses scattered throughout the world, to whose occupants it was the most pious of toils to multiply the sacred books. It was not the paid work of hirelings, indifferent to their contents, which, up to the invention of printing, wrought this multiplication. How many a monk spent his life in adorning a copy of the Gospels not with pen only but with pencil, so that the loving service of years was enshrined in the leaves he wrought! It followed of course, that down to the time in which printing became common, copies of the Sacred Scriptures were costly, and the reading of them never could have been popular. Thus it was physically impossible, if it had not been besides contrary to all Christian practice and principle, that they should be the immediate instrument of teaching. Only when the Church had been for long ages in possession of men's minds, and had built up one harmonious structure of doctrine and practice by the work of a uniform hierarchy in many lands, and when, besides, a new invention had multiplied with a great economy of manual labour copies of the Scriptures, so that they could be produced in thousands and sold as an ordinary book, a notion, until then unheard of, was set up. A man arose who maintained that the Church in her ministers was not the teacher to whom God had committed the propagation of His gospel, but that each Christian was to teach himself by personal study of the written Word. This notion rested upon the assertion that the Holy Spirit coalesces with the written Word in such a manner as to act immediately on the mind of the reader. To those who could embrace such a notion the written Word came to stand to the reader in exactly that relation to divine truth which up to that time the Church herself had occupied. There seems to have been a real confusion in the mind of the man who devised this notion, and in the minds of his followers, between the outward material Word, which they read and construed, and its true sense, or the inward Word. Thus they argued from the possession of the former to that of the latter, and supposed that unity of belief would follow from the individual's study of the same documents. They always refused to see the conclusion which all of the old belief set before them, that they were substituting their own private and subjective interpretation of the Bible for the Church's public and authorised one. They opposed instead what they called the Word of God, that is, the real sense of Holy Scripture, to the word of man, which they called the Church's interpretation of it.

It is true that this notion contained in it something very flattering to the human mind and the natural feelings, for it supposed an immediate relation between Christ and the individual, and an illumination of the reader's mind by the influence of the Holy Spirit, the sole instrument of which was the reading of the Scripture. Thus this notion got rid at one stroke of Church, sacraments, discipline, and all spiritual rule.

The objections to it at once apparent were : First, it was not only without warrant from Scripture itself, but directly opposed to its plainest statement, such as "Go ye into all the world and preach the gospel to every creature," and all those other passages in which the foundation of spiritual authority is set forth. Secondly, it was directly opposed to the historical fact in the way in which the Church was actually instituted. Thirdly, it was no less opposed to the way in which the Church had been carried on in every age and every country through the fifteen centuries. A fourth objection was made to it as soon as it was set up, but only the actual experience of three centuries and a half could adequately express its force. It has been found to produce not unity of belief, but every possible variety and opposition, until at last the final point has been reached, that this variety and opposition are viewed as being a good in themselves, and an assurance of the mind's freedom; and the possession of one faith, which was the glory of all Christians, and viewed by the Fathers as a sensible token of Christ's Godhead, has ceased, by those who received and transmitted Luther's notion, to be deemed practicable or even desirable. In other words, those who deserted the unity of the supernatural kingdom have been broken without hands into a shapeless anarchy.

If, then, we consider as a whole the work of positive promulgation carried on by the Church from the Day of Pentecost to the bestowal of civil liberty upon it by Constantine, we find it to consist in the action of the Spirit of Christ animating that teaching Body which began with the Apostles and was continued in their living succession. We find the method of internal promulgation which that teaching Body pursued was the creation everywhere of a Christian polity. Of this the main parts were the discipline and direction of the whole spiritual being which the sacraments embraced. One of them contained the great central act of daily worship and the supersubstantial bread of daily life. Into this polity men were admitted after careful probation and instruction of each individual by word of mouth, and the chief articles of belief were delivered to him upon his admission by an act of supreme authority. The

Creed was the soldier's oath of fidelity when he entered into the sacred army. The censure and restoration of sinning members were provided for by other acts of supreme authority. Nor did it only impart to the incoming disciple what he should believe summed up in the Creed, but it presented to its members collectively the Sacred Scriptures of the Old and New Testaments. Thus the living society carried both the written and unwritten Word, not as separate and disjointed, but as one treasure-house of truth committed to its perpetual guardianship. For all these means were comprehended in a divine unity which excluded partition. That unity was the mystical Body of Christ, and these means subsisted in and by force of the Body of Christ; for just as the human soul[1] is the life of the human body, without which its members would cease to be an organism and fall back into dust, so the Spirit of God animated this Body of Christ, binding together in one life those manifestations of doctrine, worship, and government the system of which we have been trying to follow.

We proceed to consider the dangers which beset that unity.

What during this period was the defence of the Church against errors of belief?

We may subdivide our answer into two heads: first, the question of the *principle* which actuated the Church in all her conduct of promulgating her faith; and,

---

[1] As St. Irenæus says, 3, 24, and Origen, Contr. Celsus, 6, 48.

secondly, the question of *fact*, or a review of the errors themselves which she had to oppose.

The principle of the Church was, in one word, that which defines her own being—a divine authority establishing a kingdom, Jesus Christ, her Lord and Founder, living and acting in her. The consideration of the faith which she promulgated cannot be severed from that of her government and her worship. If we put together that which we have been observing, we find a hierarchy stretching over the whole earth, developing itself in councils, hearing and deciding causes both in an exterior and an interior forum, having a fourfold gradation, the Bishop in the diocese, the Metropolitan in the province, the Primate in the larger circle of several provinces, the Pope in the whole Church. But, further, the whole of this authoritative government rests upon an identical worship, in which dwells, in a wonderful manner, the very Person of Him who is the Founder and Maintainer of the kingdom, and which exhibits daily to the hearts and minds of His people the sublime truths upon which His presence rests. Again, this worship itself is a part of that daily discipline of life in which the people live, and by which they are subjects of their sovereign in the spiritual world of thought and action. The administration of sacraments, which belongs to practice, embraces a whole world of doctrine. It is also the carrying out and application to daily life of the Scriptures which the Church holds in her hands, and presents to her people under the guarantee of her authority.

Again, in all that we are enumerating, in the whole system of government, worship, and teaching, is comprised *the Word* of God committed to the Church, a word partly written and partly unwritten, but in both its parts equally the word of God, not human thought or inference; and the teaching office is exercised in the living administration of the one and the other part, which cannot in practice be divided.[1]

Again, the knowledge of revealed truth as a whole, and of the system in which it should be enshrined and perpetuated on the earth among men, was a special gift communicated to the Apostolic Body. They could not propagate a religion without this special gift of understanding what they were to propagate. This was part of their endowment as Apostles, a point in which they were superior to all who should come after them, who would have to continue and hand on that which they had established.[2]

Further, from this gift followed the consciousness from the beginning that the revelation made by Christ to His Apostles was complete as to its substance.[3] He was the Teacher whose word was final: they were those whom He *sent* to convey it to men. Their name expressed their office—*the sent*. They transmitted what they had received. Those who followed, even the greatest who sat in Peter's seat, watched over the maintenance of what the Apostles had transmitted. They

---

[1] See Kleutgen's Theologie der Vorzeit, v. 404-409.
[2] Ibid., pp. 395-404.
[3] For which see Franzelin, De Traditione, pp. 228-237.

were *overseers*. The name of predilection which stands at the head of documents declaring the faith, re-establishing discipline, terminating disputes, is, as it may be, Gregory, Leo, Pius, but always *Bishop;* and the whole plenitude of spiritual power is conveyed in the word "Bishop of the Catholic Church."

Since all that we have been so long saying is an illustration of this principle of the Church,—her own divine authority in promulgating her Lord's message,—we need not dwell on it further, but turn at once to a review of those combats which she actually underwent, in order to see how her liberty and spiritual power are manifested during the period of persecution, by the issue of the conflict in which, from the beginning, she was engaged with various enemies.

The first of these conflicts is with unbelieving Judaism, and its period is chiefly from the Day of Pentecost to the destruction of the temple and city of Jerusalem by Roman arms.

When the Apostles went forth to their work, they first addressed themselves to their own brethren, the people of Israel; and for twelve years they addressed themselves to their brethren alone. The great point to which they had to win Jewish consent was that Jesus was the Christ. Those to whom they preached were well convinced that there would be a Christ, and many of them also that the time for His coming was at hand. The work of the Apostles was to show that the life and death of Jesus corresponded to the manifold prophecies concerning the Messiah contained in the books of Moses, 'the Psalms, and the Prophets, and that He had done "the works of the Christ." In this first period of their preaching a considerable number, even of the priests, listened to their call; but a much greater number rejected it. In Jerusalem itself the Sanhedrim began the long list of Christian persecutions, and those who had slain the Lord commanded His disciples not to preach in His name. We cannot doubt that the enmity of those Jews who rejected a suffering Christ was very bitter against their countrymen who proclaimed Him.

But as soon as the Apostles embraced the Gentiles in their teaching this bitterness would greatly increase; for then, besides proclaiming One who had suffered the death of the cross at the hands of His own people to be the appointed Head and Deliverer of that people, the Apostles opened all the benefits of His Headship to the very nations in the midst of which the Jews lived with the proudest sense of their own superior claim to the favour of God. We see, by the example of St. Paul and St. Barnabas, how the Apostles addressed themselves in each city to their brethren in the synagogue, and through them to the Gentile proselytes, male and female, who frequented it; how they received into the communion of the Church such as accepted their message, and these not only when they were Jews, but the Gentiles also; and how, by the decision of the Council at Jerusalem, the Gentiles so entering were not bound to accept the ceremonial law of Moses nor the rite of circumcision. If it was a grievous offence to Jewish pride that a crucified man should be propounded as the son of David and King of Israel, how intense was the anger excited by the fact that the children of the hated and despised nations were allowed to enter into possession of the divine inheritance of Israel's race without receiving circumcision, the pledge of the Jewish covenant, the mark of the children of Abraham !

Such was the double cause of indignation which led the Jews continually to plot against the life of St. Paul, to cut off St. James by the sword of Agrippa, to attempt at the same time the life of St. Peter, and during the whole period of apostolic preaching to set the Roman magistrates against the Christians.

We must add another cause of Jewish enmity, which, coming upon the two great causes already indicated, must have still more inflamed it.

For a considerable time, perhaps down to the persecution of Nero in the year 64,[1] the Christian faith appeared to the Romans to be what Gallio, the proconsul of Achaia, and the brother, be it observed, of Seneca, called it, " a question of a word and names, and of your,' that is, the Jewish, " law ; " so that practically, in this first time, to use the well-known expression of Tertullian, the apostolic preaching " was sheltered under the profession of a most famous, at least a licensed religion."[2] This means that whereas by the laws existing at Rome before the coming of our Lord, the setting up of religions not authorised by the Senate was strictly

---

[1] Baur observes, p. 432 : " Erst die Regierung Nero's führte auf ihrer würdigen Weise die Christen in die Geschichte ein."
[2] Tertullian, Apol. 21.

forbidden; and whereas the profession of their own religion was everywhere allowed to the Jews as subjects of the empire, who were not called upon to renounce their ancestral belief, and whose synagogues were much frequented, as we know from Horace, even in his time; the first teachers of the Christian faith being Jews, and using the synagogue itself as a means of propagating their message, were covered by the protection extended to the Jewish religion. To the unbelieving Jews this protection, thus enjoyed by those whom they considered not only teachers of a false Messiah, but surrenderers of the special privileges and promises of the Jewish race, must have been very galling. Were apostates to be saved by their Jewish character from the very punishment which the Roman law itself imposed on religious innovators? Were they who overturned the very foundation of Jewish distinction to preach their sect under cover of the Jewish name? Accordingly they set themselves to kindle Roman enmity against the Christian faith by every means in their power. In the whole period between the conversion of Cornelius and the destruction of their own temple and city they were sleepless enemies, so that they fulfilled to the utmost the divine prediction, "Therefore, behold I send to you prophets and wise men and scribes: and some of them you will put to death and crucify, and some you will scourge in your synagogues, and persecute from city to city: that upon you may come all the just blood that hath been shed upon the earth, from the blood of Abel the just even unto the blood of Zacharias, the son of

Barachias, whom you killed between the temple and the altar. Amen. I say unto you all these things shall come upon this generation."[1]

Poppæa is said by Josephus to have been a Jewish proselyte, and to have used her influence with Nero in favour of the Jews; and Tacitus[2] records her to have been surrounded with fortune-tellers, which would include Jewish diviners of the future; and the combination of these statements has led to the conclusion by some that Nero was moved by her to those acts which resulted, not only in the sacrifice of that "vast multitude" recorded by Tacitus as suffering in the persecution raised against them for the burning of Rome imputed to them, but in removing for ever from the Christian religion the protection of being "licit," as a part of an allowed religion. If this be so, all the subsequent persecutions were contained as in germ in the decision of Nero. The special cruelties of the punishments inflicted by Nero might cease upon his deposition, but the decision that the Christian faith was not a part of the Jewish, and therefore not "licit," would remain as a principle of imperial legislation,[3] as appears, in fact, in the conduct of Trajan when Pliny appealed to him for guidance. For it should not be forgotten that Pliny had already treated the profession of Christianity as in itself a capital

---

[1] Matt. xxiii. 34-36.
[2] Joseph. Antiq., viii. 8; Tacitus, Hist. i. 22.
[3] Baur remarks, p. 433: "Die neronische Verfolgung war der erste Anfang alles dessen, was das Christenthum von dem römischen Staat, so lange er keine andere Ansicht von ihm hatte, bei jeder Gelegenheit auf's Neue erwarten musste."

crime, inasmuch as he ordered those who were guilty of it to be executed before he applied to Trajan for directions as to how he should treat them in future, on account of the difficulty which arose from their number. This evidence is complete so far as to show that it was not Trajan's answer to Pliny which made the Christian religion illicit, but that it was already of itself a capital crime.

When St. Peter and St. Paul had crowned the Roman Church with their joint martyrdom under the authority of Nero, that Jewish revolt had already begun the issue of which was the accomplishment of the divine prediction that their "house should be left to them desolate." But the stroke of Nero's sword, wielded by his deputies,[1] was but the final act of Jewish enmity to St. Paul; what his life had been at their hands we have vividly described in his own words: "Of the Jews five times did I receive forty stripes save one. Thrice was I beaten with rods, once I was stoned; thrice I suffered shipwreck; a night and a day I was in the depth of the sea."[2] And as to St. Peter, they for whom Herod Agrippa, seeing that the slaughter of St. James pleased the Jews, proceeded to imprison Peter, intending after the Pasch to bring him forth to the people for public execution, would pursue him with their enmity all the rest of his life. And what happened to the chiefs, St. Peter and St. Paul, happened in their measure to the otherfirst teachers of the new faith: they gained their crown of martyrdom through the perpetual enmity of

[1] μαρτυρήσας ἐπὶ τῶν ἡγουμένων.—St. Clem. 5.   [2] 2 Cor. xi. 24.

the unbelieving Jews stirring up the Roman power against them.

The position of bitter enmity to the Christian religion taken up by the unbelieving Jews was far from terminating with the destruction of Jerusalem. As the nation, with its imperishable vitality, survived that blow, and the further severe punishment dealt upon it after the insurrection headed, in the reign of Hadrian, by the false Messiah Barcochba, who inflicted upon the Christians in Judæa fearful torments, so through the whole period of persecution which the Church suffered from the Roman empire, the Jews fanned by every means in their power the heathen hatred of the Christian people. Tertullian, at the end of the second century, represents them as not possessing an inch of land which they could call their own, yet at the same time as propagating every vile report against Christians. He gives this specimen: "Report has introduced a new calumny respecting our God. Not so long ago a most abandoned wretch in that city of yours (Rome), a man who had deserted indeed his own religion—a Jew, in fact, who had only lost his skin, flayed of course by wild beasts, against which he enters the lists for hire day after day with a sound body, and so in a condition to lose his skin—carried about in public a caricature of us with this label, An ass of a priest. This had ass's ears, and was dressed in a toga, with a book, having a hoof on one of his feet. And the crowd believed this infamous Jew. For what other set of men is the seed-plot of all the calumny against us?"[1]

[1] Tertullian, Ad Nationes, 14, translation in Clarke's edition.

Jewish hatred of the Christian faith stopped as little with Constantine's edict of toleration as it had with the destruction of the temple by Titus or the banishment of the people by Hadrian; but here we have only to consider it in the first period of the forty years.

This is one aspect of that first conflict with Judaism, but there is likewise another, of which the issue was the gradual severance of the Christian Church from the synagogue. As the first struggle came from the enmity of those who rejected Jesus as the Christ, so the second came from those who received Him, but at the same time clung to the Jewish law and its observances.

The problem of the first twelve years' teaching was, whether the Jewish nation would, as a nation, receive the faith of Him whom its rulers had crucified. An ardent longing for the salvation of their people as a whole must have lain deep in the heart of those first Jewish converts. But even after it became plain that only a remnant would accept the faith, and after a great number of Gentile converts had been received throughout the empire, on conditions which exempted them from the practice of the law of Moses, when St. Paul, at a late period of his ministry, went up to Jerusalem, he was entreated, because there were many thousands among the Jews that had believed who were all zealots for the law,[1] to perform in his own person publicly in the temple a vow according to the law, with which he complied.

No doubt one of the greatest difficulties experienced in these first forty years was the amalgamation of

[1] Acts xxi. 20.

Jewish and Gentile converts in the one Christian Church; but I would draw attention only to the completeness of the result. Among the questions then settled[1] were the meaning of the Old Testament law in regard to the faith in Christ, the relation of our Lord to the Jewish prophets, His superiority to them, His divine nature, and thus His relation to God the Father. I pass over the consideration of all these to make one remark. The ultimate result is the proof of power, and by the time the Jewish temple and the public worship carried on in it were destroyed by the Roman avenger of the God he did not know, the Christian Church was seen to emerge in its character of a religion for all mankind. The association of St. Paul with St. Peter in the patronage of the Roman Church is the most conclusive refutation of theories as to their enmity and rivalry. The one Christian community, ruled by one Episcopate, derived from the Person of Christ, and containing Jews and Gentiles in the one Body of Christ, is the best proof that the force of that divine unity prevailed over zeal for the law and national privileges on the one hand, as over all the errors and confusions of heathen life on the other. Jewish persecution had its completion in the ruin of the deicide city. Those thousands of believers, zealots for the law, were in a few short years merged in the ever-increasing number of the Gentile converts. That great mother Church of Jerusalem, mindful of her Lord's prophecy dwelling in her thoughts, was warned by the Roman standards encompassing the city to

[1] See Schwane, Dogmengeschichte, i. 68.

migrate to Pella, beyond the Jordan, and thus the centre of Jewish influence in the Church was dissipated beyond recall. The Christian Church took over the inheritance of the synagogue, displaced and destroyed, without being confined to its rites and ceremonies. The high priest, the priest, and the levite of the old covenant, touched with the life-giving flesh of Christ, passed into the ministry of the new; and while the lamb ceased to be offered for the daily sacrifice in the temple, the Lamb of God on every Christian altar became the Sacrifice and the Food of the one Christian people.

Thus the providence of God, offering to His chosen people their Saviour, had, when they rejected Him, worked a double result of their unbelief: one, the destruction of their city and polity; the other, the coming forth in unity and independence of the true Israel, "the nation of Christ."

In all this the Divine Kingdom accomplished its first stage, being founded by Jewish teachers in spite of the enmity of unbelieving Judaism without, and blending the Jew and the Gentile convert within by the force of its potent unity.

The contest with Judaism in both its phases had but a restricted scope, if we compare it with that manifold contest with error which filled the whole history of the Church from the Day of Pentecost to the convocation of the Nicene Council. It is not easy to realise the circumstances under which that contest was waged. First, from the persecution begun under Nero in the year 64, to the edicts of Constantine in 311-313, the Christian Church lay under the ban of the Empire as an illicit religion. It is indeed true that the whole of this long period of two hundred and fifty years is not a time of active persecution. There are intervals throughout, of considerable length, in which the Church carried on her silent course of conversion, without the law being executed against her, with at least anything like a general intention to destroy her. Still, even in these intervals, she was in the condition of a society in opposition at all points to the powers of the world, and, to say the least, discouraged by the spirit of the time. She could not unfold and publish her constitution. The thing of all others which she could least venture to disclose was her *polity*, that episcopate with its centre in Rome which was the bond of her strength as a regimen. In spite of herself, Roman law forced her into the position, in many respects at least, of a secret society; secret, not because her doctrines in themselves required concealment; secret, not because her polity was in itself an infringement of the Empire's civil rights, but because both doctrine and polity involved a change in the religious, social, and civil relations of the world which the Roman Empire was not prepared to concede, and which, had it divined, not Nero alone, or Domitian, "a portion of Nero in his cruelty,"[1] but every Roman emperor, with Trajan at their head, would have stamped out. Again, it is difficult to realise the condition of a religious society which could not carry out its worship under the protection

[1] Tertull. Apol., 5.

which publicity confers. Yet as to this we have no authority to show that there were public Christian churches before the reign of Alexander Severus, two hundred years after the Church began. Her eucharistic liturgy was a secret; her sacred books were kept out of the sight of the heathen; but even so the language and the treatment of subjects in these books, not to speak of the choice of those subjects, betoken that they belonged to a society which needed not only the harmlessness of the dove but the wisdom of the serpent. It had need to keep its head under cover. To take one instance out of many. I do not know a more remarkable example of reticence than that passage in the Acts of the Apostles wherein it is said of Peter, that when delivered by the angel from prison, he sent a message to James and the brethren, and then "went out and departed into another place." Here St. Luke, writing in a time of active persecution, rather more than twenty years after the event which he was recording, and when Nero had broken out against the Church, carefully abstains from saying that the place to which St. Peter went was Rome, and that he went to found the Church there, for such foundation was the thing above all others which Roman law looked upon with most suspicion, in its confusion of temporal with spiritual rule. Now we have to bear in mind, in order to realise the condition of the Church in this whole period, that all her work of promulgation, her daily administration of sacraments, her worship, her defence of the truth which she had received and which she was to guard, were carried on under this state of compression, a perpetual outlawry in the letter of the law, which might be put into exercise at the will of a local magistrate or the rising of a discontented populace, and which on many occasions was actually enforced by the supreme authority of the emperor. And it is not a little to be borne in mind what the political condition of the empire then was. The rights of the citizen, as opposed to the government, were overborne by a tremendous despotism, which only allowed light and air to its subjects so far as the science of government had not reached the complete development of modern times. The Roman emperors were not enabled to wield a secret police, because such an instrument of servitude had not yet been invented, nor had they reached an universal military conscription, because the Roman peace rendered such a sacrifice unnecessary; they had only the supreme power of life and death in their hands without restriction. Into the midst of such a despotism the Christian religion was cast. The seed silently deposited in each city in the episcopal germ grew with its individual life, which was yet the life of one tree; but how little was that secret unity of root apparent to the world, at least in the first half of this time! How truly, indeed, was the prophecy of the Lord fulfilled: "Behold I send you forth as sheep in the midst of wolves;"[1] and how apposite the warning, "Be ye therefore wise as serpents, and harmless as doves!"

But as the Episcopate was a tree growing upon one root, so the faith on which it lived was one sap. Yet

[1] Matt. x. 16.

to what danger of isolation, especially in those first times, were small communities of Christians in so many several cities exposed. The Sees, it is true, were not crystallised units, but associated in provinces under Metropolitans. Yet their bishops did not possess the civil liberty of meeting when they chose. Upon the whole action of the Church there was a perpetual constraint from without. The two forces which held the Church together were the Episcopate viewed as one body, and the directing, controlling, regulating authority of St. Peter's See at its centre. Yet not once in the well-nigh three hundred years could the Episcopate meet in universal councils, and the action of the Roman Church, an action which of all others within the bosom of the Christian society the Roman State would regard with the most jealousy, could only be exercised with a due respect to that jealousy, and in conjunction with that large measure of autonomy which the condition of a compressed and often-persecuted society, sprinkled over a vast number of provinces, imposed.

One of the most effective means for maintaining unity and overcoming error was the regular meeting of Councils. In ante-Nicene times these took place in various provinces of the Church, but did not extend to the whole Church. The first Western General Council was held at Arles in 314, and it needed the permission of the Emperor Constantine to take place. Before the peace of the Church its various provinces stand out in groups, under the presiding influence of the greater Sees. Thus, Alexandria unites all the Churches of

Egypt and Libya, and the great See of Antioch serves as a centre for the numerous Sees of the East. Ephesus collects the churches of Asia Minor, and Carthage those of Africa. A certain local spirit and certain tendencies of thought would grow up. Perhaps a certain school of teaching may be said to characterise each of these groups. Even the natural temperament[1] of the African, the Egyptian, the Asiatic, and the Oriental character, receiving the one seed of Christian doctrine, would show itself in their several developments. The correction of such local tendencies lay in the free and unfettered intercourse and relation with St. Peter's See; but it was this precisely which the above-noted circumstances of the times rendered difficult.

For all these reasons we may look upon the period stretching from the Day of Pentecost to the Nicene Council as one whole, in which the contest between the faith of the Church and the various forms of emergent or antagonistic error was carried on under trials which tested to the utmost her inherent vigour.

We may approach the subject by reflecting that the first condition of Christians was one of simple faith. The Son of God had come upon earth, and being found in fashion as a man, had taught, worked miracles, suffered, died, and risen again. He had thus delivered a divine truth to His Apostles for communication to the world. It was not the result of human inquiry, but the working of a new life derived from the Person of

---

[1] See this learnedly brought out by Hagemann in his introduction to "Die römische Kirche."

the Incarnate God. A new knowledge formed part of this life, and a new speculation was thus begun. But the complete thing was the life, that is, the Church as an institution, with her sacrifice, her sacraments, her daily discipline, her hierarchy; Jesus Christ dwelling in His people, perpetuating in that people the life which He had begun on earth.

This life was received by an act of faith. It was based upon authority, continued by a tradition which carried in its bosom all the things just enumerated. Such a state is borne witness to in the letters of St. Paul, St. Peter, and St. John, and again in the letters of St. Ignatius and in the Epistle to Diognetus. Its force lay in the strength, simplicity, and earnestness of the faith received as a divine revelation. It is vividly expressed by St. John in his opening words: "That which was from the beginning, which we have heard, which we have seen with our eyes, which we have looked upon, and our hands have handled of the Word of life; for the life was manifested; and we have seen and do bear witness, and declare unto you the life eternal which was with the Father, and hath appeared to us: that which we have seen and have heard we declare unto you, that you also may have fellowship with us, and our fellowship may be with the Father, and with His Son Jesus Christ."

The fulness of truth had thus appeared corporally in the Word become flesh, and by this appearance a new epoch had begun to man,[1] and henceforth there were only two attitudes of the human spirit possible towards

[1] See Stöckl, Lehrbuch der Geschichte der Philosophie, p. 244.

the truth thus revealed. On the one hand, it might recognise the revelation as truth given by God, and make it the standard and guiding principle of speculation. On the other hand, it might use its freedom to assume an independent standing-point over against this revelation, which it might subject to its private reason. In the former case revelation would be primary and reason secondary; in the latter case the position would be reversed. Reason would take what it liked and reject what it disliked in revelation. In the former, reason, using the natural powers of the human mind in subordination to revealed truth, and accepting the Christian mysteries as data, would proceed by profound meditation upon them, would connect doctrine with doctrine, and come to the perception of the harmony contained in the structure of the revelation made in Christ; to a system, in fine, of speculative theology. In the latter, following its particular bias, according to the spirit of the time in each period, it would attempt to subject revelation to itself, to alter some parts, to discard others, to improve or reject according to its own inward attraction.

The one is the principle of orthodoxy, the other that of heresy.

As a matter of fact, we find from the institution of the Christian Church—that is, the entrance of Christ's Person into the world—a spiritual war commence, which runs through all the ages, and of which the time from the Day of Pentecost to the convocation of the Nicene Council is only the first period. But in that period the combatants are already well defined, the two standing-points definitely taken up, and the battle waged even upon the most important of all truth, the existence and the character of God Himself. The Christian God is carried through three centuries, and impressed upon the belief of men by the Christian Church; the philosophic god is set up against Him by those who subjected faith to reason; and in the collision between the two the pantheon of false gods is dispersed and shattered, and dissolved in the pure light of the Christian heaven.

That first condition of the Christian Church, during which it lived on pure faith—I mean the simple historical transmission of its worship, its sacraments, its discipline, and its government, as they were instituted—lasted for several generations; it may be said quite to the end of the second century. During this whole time the attacks of human reason acting upon the principle of heresy were incessant, and it was to defend themselves against these attacks that those who stood entirely upon the ground of faith and tradition in the first instance gradually betook themselves to the arms of reason, reflection, and learning superadded to the faith.

But before passing to any intellectual defence of the faith, it is well to remark that the only adequate defence against error in doctrine consisted in the Church's own life diffused amongst its members; that is, the ordinary teaching office, comprehended in worship, sacraments, discipline, and government, including therein the dispensing of the Scriptures, whether of the Old or New Testaments. Wherever error appeared, this was the power which met it first, met it continuously, and in the end met it successfully; and part of this teaching office was the unity of the Episcopate and the uniformity of its teaching, while error was ever various and changing.

Now let us proceed to the assaults of innovators or one-sided thinkers upon this institution of the Church and her faith. No sooner was the Church in action than the attack began. We have a proof of this in the constant warning against false teachers which occurs in the Apostolic writings. It would be hard to say whether St. Peter, St. Paul, or St. John is the stronger in this warning. It shows us that great as the authority of the Apostles was, and built as the Church was upon their living word, transmitting the charge of their Lord intrusted to them, there was full freedom as to the manner in which it would be received. If Hymeneus and Philetus afflicted St. Paul, "and were delivered by him up to Satan, that they might learn not to blaspheme;" if their "speech spread like a cancer;" if St. Peter, using against error words as strong as any used by his successors in the Papal chair, denounced false teachers as "fountains without water and clouds tossed with whirlwinds, to whom the mist of darkness is reserved;" if St. John even wrote his Gospel against Gnostic errors, and in his first chapter attested the Godhead of the Eternal Word, with His relation to the Father and His assumption of human flesh, in the face of their imaginary æons, and their placing the seat of evil in matter—this is but the first page of the never-ending conflict between truth and error ; between "the men of good will" on the one hand, and "the children of malediction" on the other, "who left the right way and went astray."[1]

We possess very few written remnants of the time immediately succeeding the Apostles. The writers are St. Clement of Rome, St. Barnabas, Hermas, St. Ignatius of Antioch, St. Polycarp, Papias, and the writer of the letter to Diognetus. With the exception of the "Pastor," these are all in the form of letters, conveying strong feelings expressed in few words, short and touching exhortations, simple narratives of joys and sorrows. These first Christians were anything but literary; they were only conscious of possessing a divine truth which had incomparable value above all earthly things. Nevertheless it deserves to be remarked, that short as these writings are, we have in them the first outlines of all future learned teaching.[2] In the letter to Diognetus we have a sketch of the course which Christian apology against heathens afterwards took; in the letters of St. Ignatius, the first features of the Church's defence against heretics; in the letter of Barnabas, an approach to speculative theology; in the "Pastor," the first attempt at a Christian science of morals; in the letter of Pope St. Clement, the first development of the government which afterwards produced the Canon Law; and in the Acts of St. Ignatius' martyrdom, the earliest historical production. In these, as it were, infantine movements of His first disciples, the Divine Child was manifesting the future conquests

[1] 2 Peter ii. 14.   [2] Möhler, Patrologie, p. 51.

which He would achieve in leading His people through the whole range of the divine science.

In the second century the Church vastly increased in the number of her faithful and in her influence; at the same time she was exposed to much severer attacks from within and without. Through the whole century the false Gnosis afflicted her. The Greek and the Oriental philosophy had fully detected the presence of a great enemy, and fought against her with all the arms of learning, the brilliance of Eastern imagination, the fire of religious zeal. It is said that in the first fifteen hundred years no sect has pushed the Church more hardly than Gnosticism, which through the brilliant talent of its leaders in Alexandria, Antioch, Edessa, and other great cities gained many adherents. The attacks from the heathen and the defacements which Christian doctrine received through heretics formed thus the strongest challenge to Christians to defend themselves with the arms of learning and science on their own side.

There were great difficulties in the way. The mass of Christians was still drawn from the lower ranks, and was accordingly unlettered. All, too, that were of higher rank had no other than the heathen schools to frequent, and were thus in great danger themselves from the force of heathen culture. A remarkable result ensued: for, one after another, champions of the Christian cause arose from among the heathen themselves who were converted to the Christian faith. Justin, we are told, sought for truth about the being of God and the soul's immortality in the schools of the

Greek philosophy. He tried successively the Stoic, the Peripapetic, the Pythagorean, and the Platonic, and thought that he had found truth in the last; when, in the midst of these dreams, walking out one day in a lonely place by the sea-shore, he met with an old man with whom he entered into conversation. This man, pointing out the futility of his past search, directed him to the Christian teaching. Justin says that he felt a fire in his heart kindled by the old man's words; he followed his advice, and found here what he had in vain sought elsewhere—the only true philosophy. He became a Christian in middle age, dedicated his life to propagate the faith which he had embraced, and died a martyr for it.

His pupil, Tatian, seems to repeat this history. An Assyrian by birth, he was instructed in all branches of Grecian literature, and had tried every shade of the old heathen wisdom. But the corruption of the heathen world inspired him with abhorrence; he was converted by Justin, and found in the Christian doctrine the ideal which he sought. Yet afterwards certain rigorous views led him into error, and he became the head of a Gnostic sect.

Athenagoras of Athens supplies us with another like conversion. He was an adept in the Greek, especially the Platonic philosophy, and was devoted to heathendom. With the intention of writing against Christians he studied the Holy Scriptures, and in doing so was converted. He has left us two brilliant writings, one an apology in defence of Christians, addressed to the

Emperor Marcus Aurelius, and another setting forth the doctrine of the resurrection with admirable skill.

Theophilus of Antioch continues the list of converts. The study of the Holy Scripture led him to become a Christian, and he afterwards rose to the great See of Antioch, and has left learned writings in defence of the faith.

More brilliant than all these, the first as well as the greatest Latin writer in the West of the whole ante-nicene period, Tertullian, born of heathen parents, studied philosophy and literature, was converted about the age of thirty, became a priest, and dedicated himself by word and writing to the defence of the faith. Every subsequent age has admired the force of his reason. It amounted to genius, yet a rigoristic spirit led him to fall off to a sect.

Pantænus, who became head of the catechetical school at Alexandria about 180, had been a Stoic. His conversion repeats that of Justin. A man of the highest renown for his Grecian learning, he became equally distinguished as a Christian. He devoted himself to preaching. He was also noted as the first who not only commented by word of mouth on the Sacred Scriptures, but wrote his commentaries against Gnostic commentators of the day. For it is remarkable that, in their zeal to get the Scriptures on their side, the Gnostics had preceded the Christians in the explanation of Scripture, which they treated with the utmost latitude of private judgment.

Still more distinguished was Clemens, the pupil as

well as the successor of Pantænus. Born about the middle of the second century at Alexandria or Athens, and endowed with great ability, he searched all the systems of Greek philosophy. He was full of learning when grace made him a Christian, and from that time he devoted all his powers to deepen his knowledge of the Christian faith, and to convey that knowledge to others, by drawing out a true Gnosis against the false, a main seat of which was at Alexandria, over the school of which he presided.

I have taken the seven great converts, Justin, Tatian, Athenagoras, Theophilus, Tertullian, Pantænus, Clemens, who all became apologists of the Church after their conversion, as specimens of the power which she exercised in the second century of drawing the higher spirits among the heathen into her fold. That power did not diminish but increase in the third century. It exerted itself with great effect through the establishment in the course of the second century of a system of learned instruction in the great catechetical schools. The chief of these was at Alexandria; for where the munificence of the Ptolemies had planted and richly endowed a seat of Greek learning, science, and philosophy, which had been enlarged by Tiberius, so that youth thronged to it from all parts of the Roman Empire, now the Christian Church, which probably from its beginning had there the usual school for instruction of catechumens, by degrees enlarged the instruction given in that school, and introduced learned lectures upon the Christian faith. Before long a complete learned education, all that we mean by an university, was set up. The object was not only to instruct Christian youths, but likewise to attract cultured heathen, especially the young, to prepare them gradually, and gain them to the Christian faith. Explanation of the Sacred Scriptures formed the chief point, but likewise grammar, rhetoric, geometry, and philosophy were studied. The exact point of time when all this took effect cannot be assigned; it is probable that it took time to perfect the system. Athenagoras is the first named president, who was followed from the year 170 to 312 by Pantænus, Clemens, Origen, Heraclas, Dionysius, Pierius, Theognostus, Serapion, Peter the Martyr. Each of these had fellow-workers under him, who increased in number as time went on. A crowd of learned men, bishops, saints, and martyrs, came out of this school. The envy and hatred of the heathens were so incited by it, that they often surrounded the house with soldiers, seized upon students, and led them away to execution. The renown of the school was so great in the middle of the third century, that Anatolius, a pupil of it, was sought by the heathen themselves to succeed Aristoteles in the headship of the Alexandrian university.

Another school of the like kind was set up by Origen at Cæsarea in Palestine, and became famous. Rome also possessed a learned school, founded by Justin, concerning which, however, we know very little.[1] Edessa and Antioch possessed the like. It is apparent how important such schools must have been for the formation of a

[1] See Möhler, Patrologie, p. 423.

learned clergy. The more the Christian Church increased, and spread to all ranks of society, the more need there became for learning in its defenders.

But great as was the renown won by these schools, and important as were the services rendered by them to the Christian Church in the advance of learning, in building up that progress from faith to knowledge—that growth of knowledge founded upon faith which marks the whole ante-nicene period—nevertheless the development of the sacred science was connected not so much with a regular course of teaching in the schools as with the vehement struggle for life which the Church was then waging on the one hand against Judaism and heathendom, on the other hand against the great heresies which successively attacked all the main truths of religion and the chief mysteries of Christianity.[1] Also, it must ever be remembered that the gift of infallible teaching, derived from the assistance of the Holy Spirit, is lodged, not in science, even not in theological science, but in the magisterium of the Church.[2] The most accomplished defence during all this period of the Church against the attacks of heathenism is, by common consent, allotted to the work of Origen in reply to Celsus. There is also a like consent that the same author's work upon Principles is the first attempt at systematic theology; but with all its ability, learning, and acuteness, it is not free from great errors. The one is a pure success, the other shows that the contact with Platonic philosophy had led the author in certain points astray.

[1] Heinrich, Dogmatische Theologie, i. 71. [2] Ibid., i. 70.

Again, all his genius and all his zeal did not save Tertullian from falling into Montanism, nor from discharging upon the chief ruler of the Church the sarcasm which he had so often employed against its enemies. In inquiring closely into the belief of some of those whose conversion from heathenism I have above instanced, an illustrious writer says: "It must be considered that the authors whom I have above cited whatever be the authority of some of them, cannot be said to speak *ex cathedra*, even if they had the right to do so, and do not speak as a Council may speak. When a certain number of men meet together, one of them corrects another, and what is personal and peculiar in each, what is local or belongs to schools, is eliminated."[1]

But if, as seems to be fully admitted, theology was not treated as an organic body of doctrine up to the Nicene Council, and even much beyond it, and yet, if in this period the Church maintained, as she did maintain, her faith against three great foes, the Jews, the many-sided influence of the Gentile world arrayed with all its powers against her, and the manifold attacks of false doctrines rising from within in the shape of heresies, or in the shape of antichristian systems which simulated Christianity, how was her work accomplished?

I proceed to give as definite an answer as I can to this question.

I have traced above the transmission of spiritual power from the Person of Christ to the College of Apostles presided over by St. Peter, and the planting

[1] Newman, Causes of Success of Arianism, pp. 215, 216.

of bishops throughout the world by the Apostles as a further transmission of that power. The episcopate so appointed formed, instructed, taught, and governed the Christian people, one and identical in itself. This people, with the hierarchy which governed it, the sacraments which contained and dispensed its inward life, most of all the sacrifice wherein was the Lord Himself, made a polity; and the Christian doctrine was, so to say, to that polity what blood is to the body. From the beginning, then, the office of teaching was lodged in those who governed; they conserved, handed down from age to age, all that which constituted the polity, of which doctrine was the life-blood.

Now, I will take as an exponent of this whole belief one who came forth into active life just at the time of the Nicene Council, and whose name has been ever since identified with the defence of that especial doctrine upon which the whole fabric of the Christian faith rested, namely, the Godhead of Christ. St. Athanasius may well stand as the representative of those principles in virtue of which the Church maintained her faith when she could not meet freely in council, when her theology was contained in the form of simple faith rather than drawn out as an organic structure, when her bishops everywhere had to meet the brunt of persecution, when the action of her central and presiding Bishop was hampered by the perpetual jealousy of a hostile government; when, for all these reasons, the unity and impact of the whole body, as one people, were exposed to a severer strain than at any other period.

I take this account of the mind of St. Athanasius from one who has studied his writings with peculiar care, not to say with the affection of a kindred spirit :—

"This renowned Father is in ecclesiastical history the special doctor of the sacred truth which Arius denied, bringing it out into shape and system so fully and luminously, that he may be said to have exhausted his subject, as far as it lies open to the human intellect. But, besides this, writing as a controversialist, not primarily as a priest and teacher, he accompanies his exposition of doctrine with manifestations of character which are of great interest and value.

"The fundamental idea with which he starts in the controversy is a deep sense of the authority of tradition, which he considers to have a definitive jurisdiction even in the interpretation of Scripture, though at the same time he seems to consider that Scripture, thus interpreted, is a document of final appeal in inquiry and in disputation. Hence, in his view of religion, is the magnitude of the evil which he is combating, and which exists prior to that extreme aggravation of it (about which no Catholic can doubt) involved in the characteristic tenet of Arianism itself. According to him, opposition to the witness of the Church, separation from its communion, private judgment overbearing the authorised catechetical teaching, the fact of a denomination, as men now speak,—this is a self-condemnation; and the heretical tenet, whatever it may happen to be, which is its formal life, is a spiritual poison and nothing else, the sowing of the evil one upon the good seed, in whatever age and place it is found; and he applies to all separatists the Apostle's words, 'They went out from us, for they were not of us.' Accordingly, speaking of one Rhetorius, an Egyptian, who, as St. Austin tells us, taught that 'all heresies were in the right path and spoke truth,' he says that the impiety of such doctrine is frightful to mention.

"This is the explanation of the fierceness of his language when speaking of the Arians; they were simply, as Elymas, 'full of all guile and of all deceit, children of the devil, enemies of all justice,' θεομάχοι—by court influence, by violent persecution, by sophistry, seducing, unsettling, perverting the people of God.

"Athanasius considers Scripture sufficient for the proof of such fundamental doctrines as came into controversy during the Arian troubles; but while in consequence he ever appeals to Scripture (and, indeed, has scarcely any other authoritative document to quote), he ever speaks against interpreting it by a private rule instead of adhering to ecclesiastical tradition. Tradition is with him of supreme authority, including therein catechetical instruction, the teaching of the *schola*, ecumenical belief, the φρόνημα of Catholics, the ecclesiastical scope, the analogy of faith, &c.

"In interpreting Scripture, Athanasius always assumes that the Catholic teaching is true, and the Scripture must be explained by it. The great and essential difference between Catholics and non-Catholics was, that Catholics interpreted Scripture by tradition, and non-

Catholics by their own private judgment. That not only Arians, but heretics generally, professed to be guided by Scripture, we know from many witnesses.

"What is strange to ears accustomed to Protestant modes of arguing, St. Athanasius does not simply expound Scripture, rather he vindicates it from the imputation of its teaching any but true doctrine. It is ever ὀρθός, he says, that is, orthodox; I mean, he takes it for granted that a tradition exists as a standard, with which Scripture must, and with which it doubtless does agree, and of which it is the written confirmation and record.

"The recognition of this rule of faith is the basis of St. Athanasius's method of arguing against Arianism. It is not his aim ordinarily to *prove* doctrine by Scripture, nor does he appeal to the private judgment of the individual Christian in order to determine what Scripture means; but he assumes that there is a tradition substantive, independent, and authoritative, such as to supply for us the true sense of Scripture in doctrinal matters—a tradition carried on from generation to generation by the practice of catechising, and by the other ministrations of Holy Church. He does not care to contend that no other meaning of certain passages of Scripture besides this traditional Catholic sense is possible or is plausible, whether true or not, but simply that any sense inconsistent with the Catholic is untrue—untrue because the traditional sense is apostolic and decisive. What he was instructed in at school and in church, the voice of the Christian people, the analogy of faith, the ecclesiastical φρόνημα, the writings of saints,—these are enough for him. He is in no sense an inquirer, nor a mere disputant; he has received and he transmits. Such is his position, though the expressions and turn of sentences which indicate it are so delicate and indirect, and so scattered about his pages, that it is difficult to collect them and to analyse what they imply.

"The two phrases by which Athanasius denotes private judgment on religious matters, and his estimate of it, are 'their own views' and 'what they preferred;' as, for instance, 'laying down their private impiety as some sort of rule, they wrest all the divine oracles into accordance with it,' and 'they make the language of Scripture their pretence, but instead of the true sense, sowing upon it the private poison of their heresy,' and 'he who speaketh of his own speaketh a lie.' This is a common phrase with Athanasius, 'as he chose,' 'what they chose,' 'when they choose,' 'whom they chose;' the proceedings of the heretics being self-willed from first to last.

"Revealed truth, to be what it professes, must have an uninterrupted descent from the Apostles; its teachers must be unanimous, and persistent in their unanimity; and it must bear no human master's name as its designation. On the other hand, first novelty, next discordance, vacillation, change, thirdly, sectarianism, are consequences and tokens of religious error. These tests stand to reason, for what is over and above nature must come from divine revelation; and if so, it must descend from the very date when it was revealed, else it is but matter of opinion, and opinions vary, and have no warrant of permanence, but depend upon the relative ability and success of individual teachers, one with another, from whom they take their names. The Fathers abound in passages which illustrate these three tests.

"From the first the Church had the power, by its divinely appointed representatives, to declare the truth upon such matters in the revealed message or gospel tidings as from time to time came into controversy; for unless it had this power, how could it be 'the pillar and ground of the truth;' and these representatives, of course, were the rulers of the Christian people, who received as a legacy the depositum of doctrine from the Apostles, and by means of it, as need arose, exercised their office of teaching. Each bishop was in his own place the Doctor Ecclesiæ for his people; there was an appeal, of course, from his decision to higher courts, to the bishops of a province, of a nation, of a patriarchate, to the Roman Church, to the Holy See, as the case might be; and thus at length a final determination was arrived at, which in consequence was the formal teaching of the Church, and, as far as it was direct and categorical, was from the reason of the case the word of God. And being such, was certain, irreversible, obligatory on the inward belief and reception of all subjects of the Church, or what is called *de fide*.

"All this could not be otherwise if Christianity was to teach divine truth in contrast to the vague opinions and unstable conjectures of human philosophers and moralists, and if as a plain consequence it must have authoritative organs of teaching, and if true doctrines never can be false, but what is once true is always true. What the Church proclaims as true never can be put aside or altered, and therefore such truths are called *definitions*, as being boundaries or landmarks."

From all the above "it would appear that the two main sources of revelation are Scripture and Tradition, that these constitute one Rule of Faith, and that sometimes as a composite rule, sometimes as a double and co-ordinate, sometimes as an alternative, under the *magisterium*, of course, of the Church, and without an appeal to the private judgment of individuals."[1]

Now I conceive that the picture thus drawn from the writings and the practice of Athanasius gives us, in fact, a palpable embodiment of that spiritual power by which the Church defended and carried on her faith from the Day of Pentecost to the Nicene Council; for the principles and practice of Athanasius were the principles and practice of the whole Church, and nothing short of the continuous action of the Holy Spirit could have created and maintained a polity whose subjects were instinct with such a loyalty of mind, heart, and action. It was not a gift of learning; it was not philosophic power of thought; it was not the scientific labour of theology, as in after medieval times, arranging in a luminous system the results of the Church's doctrine through ages of spiritual warfare and trials of every kind. It is true that in all this period, as well as in the

[1] Newman, Notes on St. Athanasius, pp. 51, 261, 264, 452, 250, 247, 150, 82, 312.

succeeding four hundred years, the armour of theology was wrought out bit by bit through the blows of heresy, and not before St. John of Damascus did any one work the separate pieces into a panoply. The great mind and nobler heart of Origen even failed in the attempt. But from the beginning the Church moved on, filled with a divine consciousness that it was the Body of Christ, carrying the truth in its bosom. Each bishop, each father, each writer, and in a far higher degree the Councils, were conscious of this; but most of all in the Apostolic See, the centre of the whole body, was such a conviction living and active, and exhibited in all the various functions of spiritual rule.

It is not possible from existing documents to form a continuous and detailed history of the ante-nicene Church. Thus, if any will not accept the Church at the Nicene Council as an evidence of what the Church was in preceding times as to its constitution, principles of action, and faith, it is possible, through the mere absence of written proof, to make denials of those very things without which the Nicene Council could never have come together. The spirit of negation luxuriates in that absence of documents which more than anything else the state of persecution caused. On the other hand, to the eyes of faith the grain of mustard seed planted by our Lord on Calvary is become, at the end of three hundred years, a tree which covers the Roman world, and gives its fruits for the healing of the nations.

The writer just quoted says elsewhere, in treating the point how far an accurate presentation of the doctrine respecting the Holy Trinity is found in the apologists of those times, that "it is a great misfortune to us that we have not had preserved to us the dogmatic utterances of the ante-nicene Popes."[1] But I would draw attention to a remarkable proof actually existing of the completeness with which the hierarchic principle had worked itself out in the days of persecution. This testimony is the more valuable because it belongs to the very first year of the Church's freedom, the year 314. In that year, at the instance of the Emperor Constantine, the Council of Arles was convoked as a representative Council of all the West. Up to this time the Council of Antioch, which deposed Paul of Samosata, had been the most important and general. That of Arles was in a much greater degree a Council in which the bishops who sat represented their respective provinces, as, for instance, from the remote Britain the bishops of York and London and another British See were present.

The Council of Arles then addresses in these terms Pope Sylvester:—"We who, by the desire of the most religious Emperor, have been assembled in the city of Arles, bound together by the common bond of charity and the unity of the Church our Mother, salute you, most glorious Pope, with the befitting reverence. We have endured here men grievous and pernicious to our law and tradition, men of unbridled mind. Both the present authority of our God, and the tradition and rule of the

[1] Newman, "Causes of the Rise and Successes of Arianism," p. 252, a treatise which I have found a storehouse of information respecting the Church of the first three centuries.

truth have rejected them, for there was in them no reasonable ground for pleading, no limit or proof for their accusations. Therefore, by the judgment of God and our Mother the Church, who knows and approves her own, they have either been condemned or repudiated; and would, most beloved brother, that you could have been present at so great a spectacle; we believe, indeed, that our sentence would then have been more severe, and had your judgment been united with ours, our assembly would have rejoiced with a greater joy. But you were not able to leave that place in which the Apostles daily sit, and their blood without intermission testifies the glory of God." Then sending to him the subjects of their decrees, they preface them with the words, "It was our pleasure that knowledge of this should be communicated to all by you who hold the greater dioceses. What we have decreed by common counsel we signify to your charity, that all may know what in future they are bound to observe. And, first, as to the observation of the Lord's Pasch, that it may be kept on one day and at one time through the whole world, and that according to custom you direct letters to all to this effect."

But the Emperor, neither a Christian nor a catechumen for many long years to come, writes to the Fathers of the Council: "They (the Donatists) ask for my judgment, who am myself awaiting the judgment of Christ. For I say, as the truth is, the judgment of bishops ought to be considered as if the Lord Himself were present and judging. For these may have no other mind and no other judgment but what they have been taught by the teaching of Christ.¹ What, then, do those malignant men want, instruments, as I truly call them, of the devil? They desert heavenly in their search for earthly things. Oh, the rabid audacity of maniacs! they interpose an appeal, as is customary in secular matters."²

The Council recognised the authority of the Apostles Peter and Paul ruling for ever in the See of Rome, as the Pope at the present day attests in solemn documents that same rule when he uses the words, "By the authority of the Blessed Apostles Peter and Paul," adding to them, "and by our own;" and the Emperor clearly understands the distinction between secular and ecclesiastical judgments. In the former he knows himself to be the judge of ultimate appeal. In the latter he recognises the bishops as holding the magisterium of Christ Himself, and that their judgments are His, as if He were present among them. What stronger attestation of the Church's freedom in her ecclesiastical and dogmatic judgments from the State's control could be given than this spontaneous declaration by the head of the Roman empire? And it is to be noted that he places the ground of that freedom and the force of its authority in the magisterium of Christ transmitted to the rulers of the Church.

How did the successor of Nero, Domitian, Trajan, and Decius come to this knowledge? That is a subject which requires special consideration.

[1] Magisterio.   [2] Mansi, tom. ii. pp. 469–477.

CHAPTER VIII.

THE ACTUAL RELATION BETWEEN CHURCH AND STATE FROM THE DAY OF PENTECOST TO CONSTANTINE.

The Church's Battle for Independence over against the Roman Empire.

IN the period before Christ, the two Powers, as well in every polity over the earth as in the vast conglomerate called the Roman Empire, beginning together, grew up in fast alliance. Such a thing as the Civil Power in any particular polity putting under ban and persecuting the religion of its people was unknown. In the Roman city, as originally constituted, the union with religion, as an everyday work of life, was especially intimate and strong. It subsisted no less when Rome ruled from Newcastle to Babylon; for under the supremacy of the Emperor as Pontifex Maximus all the various nations were allowed the free exercise of their ancestral rites. Such was the state of the relation between the two Powers at the Day of Pentecost; such it had been from the first creation of human society. A foreign conqueror might, it is true, persecute the gods and the priests of a nation which he conquered, as Cambyses, when, with the zeal of a Persian worshipper of the single Sun-god, he burst upon the gods of Egypt; but this state of things usually passed away, when conquest became settled into possession; and in the Roman Peace each country and city was in stable possession of its gods, its rites, its temples, and among the rest the Jew might everywhere have his synagogue for his own people and worship God.

Close and permanent as the alliance between the two powers of civil government and religious worship, founded in the original constitution of human things, had been up to the time of Christ, yet in the minds of the people the two functions of civil government and of worship had ever been distinct. It is true that in matter of practice the ever growing moral corruption of Gentilism had tended to subordinate worship to government, the priest to the ruler. Nevertheless, though the Emperor was Imperator to his army, the possessor of tribunitial and consular power in the State, and likewise Pontifex Maximus in religion, such a concentration of distinct powers in his single person did not efface in the minds of the many peoples subjected to his sway the distinction itself of the powers wielded by him. A vast number of various priesthoods subsisted in the different countries untouched and unmeddled with by him. He was, in fact, by virtue of his religious pontificate, annexed to his civil principate, the conservator of all these rites, religious customs, and priesthoods. The meddling with them was a violation of his pontificate. Anubis in Egypt, Astarte in Syria, Cybele in Phrygia, Minerva at Athens, no less than Jupiter on the capitol, found their defender and guardian on the Palatine Mount, while Augustus did not disdain to have a daily sacrifice offered for him in the temple at Jerusalem, for the Jewish worship was part of the Roman constitution. He was patron as well as suppliant.

Thus at the time the Holy Ghost came down upon the Apostles on the Day of Pentecost there was strict alliance in all the provinces of the world-empire between secular rule and religious worship; an alliance in which worship was, it is true, subordinate to secular rule, but fostered and guarded by it. The eye of a Trajan would, no doubt, discern a common element in all the religions of which he was the official guardian, and it was even for the security of the immortal gods at Rome that Anubis should bark in Egypt, though he would not be allowed with impunity to deceive the matrons of Rome,[1] and that Astarte, under the public authority, should have trains of female priestesses in Syria. The fixed idea of the Roman Emperors might be said to have been to keep these party-coloured provinces, with their ancestral gods and rites, in due and legitimate enjoyment of their own property, without encroaching on that of their neighbours. And Marcus Aurelius was not deterred by his philosophic pantheism from offering multitudes of white oxen for the success of the Roman arms, but he sanctioned the perpetration of the most fearful tortures upon Christian confessors in the arena of Lyons, and imputed their patience of death to a sort of Galilean obstinacy. Why did he, who sacrificed to Jupiter,

[1] See Josephus, Jud. Antiq., l. 18, c. 4.

while he was an outspoken Positivist, persecute belief in Christ?

Let us endeavour to give a distinct and adequate answer to this question.

The subsisting alliance between civil authority and religious worship, which existed in the Roman world, whatever the particular gods worshipped, and rites and customs practised in the various countries composing it might be, was interrupted and snapped asunder by the proclamation of the Gospel as an universal religion. It is true that in the first twelve years, while the Apostles addressed themselves to the Jewish people, wherever they might be, inviting them to accept Jesus as the Christ, the liberty to do this, within the various synagogues, might be covered by the liberty accorded to the Jewish race everywhere on Roman soil to practise their own religion as a thing handed down to them from their ancestors. So long as it was a question of Jewish law—in the words of the Roman pro-prætor, the brother of Seneca, at Corinth—the protection of an undoubtedly sanctioned religion, to use the phrase of Tertullian, would veil from censure the action of the Apostles; but as soon as, and in proportion as the kingdom of Christ came forth to the Gentiles as an universal religion—so soon as Christ was declared to them to be the Son of God, the Saviour of the world—so soon as men were distinguished as Christians, as they were already at Antioch, that is, recognised to be not a Jewish sect, but the adherents of a substantive religion with distinct belief, which was repudiated by the mass of Jews, a

religion of universal import, which was founded on the
Person of a Redeemer, the Godman who had come into
the world, lived as a man, died, and risen again, and
who called upon all men to be His followers, whether
Jews or Gentiles, it became evident that the toleration,
nay more, the support and guarantee for all religions
which were subsisting equally for the various peoples of
the Roman Empire, did not apply to the followers of
the new religion. St. Paul, for instance, as a ringleader
of the Galilean sect, was punishable and was punished
by the Jewish Sanhedrim, as infringing what they considered the orthodox Jewish belief, and this conduct of
the Jewish authority, everywhere pursued towards the
Christians, drew upon them the attention of the Roman
magistrates. The culmination of this conduct and policy
was seen as to its result in the persecution set on foot
by Nero, under Jewish instigation, and the act of Nero
seems to have had the permanent effect of establishing
the illicitness of the Christian faith, in the sight of
Roman law. The destruction of the Temple of Jerusalem, as the seat of Jewish worship, completely established the severance of the Christian people from the
Jews, and gave them religious independence with all its
honour and all its perils.

For what was their position towards that universal
heathendom which surrounded them on all sides?

Take the three great constituents of belief, of worship,
and of government, which we been have considering in
their several departments, in their relations with each
other, and in their co-inherence.

Heathendom, under the sway of Tiberius, lay stretched out over the vast regions of the empire in numberless varieties of costume which covered an identity of substance. The dark mysterious forms of Egyptian gods, the gods of Greece arrayed in human shapes of consummate loveliness, the voluptuous rites of Syrian goddesses, the sober and homely deities of ancient Rome vested somewhat awkwardly in the robes of their Grecian congeners, the local deities, mountain oreads and river naiads, which had their seat in every city and district of civilised or semi-barbarous provinces, the representatives of oriental traditions, philosophies, and religions,—all these had part in a worship offered by some or other subjects of Rome. And now went forth from city to city preachers who proclaimed to all who would hear them that there was one God alone who had made out of nothing, by an act of the purest freewill, the heavens and the earth, and that He made also of one blood the human inhabitants of this earth. And they declared that this one God was not only the Creator of all matter and of all spirit, of all men in all nations, but that in order to redeem them from a terrible slavery into which they had fallen, He had sent His own Son, one in nature with Himself, in human form among them, to die the death of a malefactor upon the cross, which was the legal punishment of the slave in the Roman law for capital crimes; nor only to die, but by rising again in the same body in which He had died, to attest the truth of His mission, and to gather all men together, the freeman and the slave, the

Roman conqueror and the most abject of his serfs, in one religious community. Thus the same one God who was Creator, was proclaimed to be Redeemer. And, further, the name of this God, communicated in the very rite which admitted into membership with the religion, disclosed a third Divine Person, whose work was pre-eminently a work belonging to the one God alone, for it was to sanctify, by His presence in their hearts, all its members.

Thus these preachers proclaimed, as the basis of all they taught to their hearers, belief in a God who was One[1] and who was Three; who was single and alone, but outside the conception of number, and who was at once Creator, Redeemer, and Sanctifier altogether.

And they proclaimed this to peoples who had every conceivable variety of gods, male and female, to whom various functions, down to the lowest employments in the service of mankind, were assigned, according to the caprice or the inherited traditions of their worshippers.

What was the position of these preachers towards the various deities and their worshippers who occupied the Roman empire? It is obvious that it was one of an absolute uncompromising hostility. And it is plain that, on the other side, all who did not closely and impartially examine their doctrine, would count them to be "godless," and treat them accordingly.

This, the barest outline of the primary and fundamental belief as to the all-important being of God, on which all further development of teaching rested, is

[1] See St. Basil, Ep. 141.

sufficient to exhibit the intense opposition between Christianity and that which it was attempting to displace in the matter of belief.

But belief becomes concrete and actual in worship. What was the worship offered by the nations of the Roman empire to their various gods? From end to end this vast region was covered with magnificent temples, rich with the offerings of successive generations, wherein day by day and often many times a day sacrifices of living animals were offered by priests appointed to that end. I only refer here to this rite of sacrifice, because I have dwelt sufficiently upon it in a former place. The varieties of the worship accompanying it were great, but the substance of the rite identical; the number and names and offices of the deities to whom it was offered were bewildering.[1] The customs and traditions which encircled these various temples and the rites offered in them struck their roots into the family, the social, and the political life of the various peoples among which they stood.

What, as over against this " palpable array of sense," was the Christian worship which the new teachers brought with them?

It was withdrawn into the innermost recess of the Christian society itself. For many generations they had not public churches, but were reduced to meet in secret.

---

[1] For instances, see the almost incredible account in De Civitate Dei vi. 9; and, again, Clement of Alexandria, Cohortatio, p. 81 (Potter's ed.); what I have said is in exact accordance with St. Athanasius, de Inc. Verbi, sec. 46.

And those who shared the Christian membership received, in assemblies held in the silence of the early morning, under cover of some private house, a victim which they adored as the very Body and Blood of the God who for their sakes had become incarnate, for their sakes also had suffered His Body to be broken, and His Blood poured out. Instead of the sacrifices of slain animals, whose blood was sprinkled upon the worshippers, the Christian received the Immaculate Lamb of God, offered upon a mystical altar, in commemoration of that one Sacrifice by virtue of which he was a Christian.

If the contrast in belief between the one Christian God and the many gods of heathendom was great, the contrast between heathen sacrifices and the one Christian Sacrifice was at least as great—perhaps the more wonderful in this, that while natural reason fought in every human breast for the doctrine of the Divine Unity, no reason nor thought of man could ever have imagined a Sacrifice at once so tremendous and so gracious as that which the Christian worshipped, wherein the Victim which received his homage contained and imparted his life.

But if the doctrine of the Divine Unity destroyed the heathen gods, and so rendered its adherents liable to be called "godless" by their worshippers, no less did the doctrine of the Christian Sacrifice, which abolished at a stroke the whole worship of heathendom, create the keenest antagonism; they who were without gods were said to be without altars; they who never presented themselves at the heathen sacrifices were accounted as outcasts and sacrilegious men who renounced all piety.

Yet complete and thorough as the antagonism drawn forth in these two great points of belief and worship, perhaps the third constituent element of the Christian society, its government, was even more calculated to awaken the jealousy and excite the resentment, if not of the various peoples which composed the empire, at least of the Roman rulers.

The priests who ministered in the multitudinous temples to the various deities of the Roman world, were as various as the objects of their worship. No common hierarchy held together the priests of Egyptian, Asiatic, Hellenic, Roman gods, and all the intermediate gradations. But far more than this, there was an absence of hierarchy in the particular or national gods of each several country; the priest of Jupiter had nothing to do with the priest of Apollo, the priest of Juno, and the rest. The conception of many gods had introduced unnumbered weaknesses, anomalies, and incongruities into the arrangements of their ministers. When that which was worshipped was divided, the ministers of the several parts became rivals, with this grand result, as it affected the civil power, that it stood in one great mass of solid unity over against different religions, varying in their objects, crossing each other, contradicting each other. Thus it was that the original independence of divine worship had been lost; no one of these various priesthoods could maintain any real opposition to the civil ruler; no one of them presented any body of concordant doctrine which man's mind could approve, or his heart accept. That which ought to be most sacred among men was by internal contradictions become weak and contemptible.

How, on the other hand, stood the case of the Christian society as to government?

And here as for a long time the Christian altar lay concealed from the sight of the heathen, and they knew not Him who was offered on it, so for a long time the Christian ruler was withdrawn from recognition. They did not even surmise that which grew up gradually and silently in the midst of them: the establishment, that is, of a *new* spiritual power, of *one* power for all nations, of a spiritual governor in every city, a member of this one power. It may safely be said that while Trajan did not apprehend the existence of any such power in his empire, Decius had come to the knowledge of it, and he liked it so little that it was said of him by an eye-witness how he would rather hear of a competitor for his throne than of a Bishop being set at Rome in the See of Peter.

But from the beginning the power was there, concealed in the humility of the mustard seed, while it rested upon the authority of Him who had dropped the seed into the soil.

This power of spiritual government was *new*, in that it sprung from the Person of our Lord Himself, and until He communicated the charge contained in it, did not exist. It was pointed out in type and prophecy to Adam, to Noah, and to Moses, but realised in Him at His resurrection. Thus, whereas these priesthoods which it came to displace were the ultimate form of corruption into which the original worship instituted by God when man fell had sunk, the Redeemer, in the work of His dispensation, sent forth this pastorship of spiritual rule afresh from Himself, gave it to Peter and His Apostles, and propagated it through them upon earth.

For this reason, as coming from one who was Lord of all, it was one for all nations. Corresponding to the unity of the Triune God, and the unity of the Christian Sacrifice, it was one in its origin, its duration, its effect. What greater contrast could there possibly be than between the diversity and contradiction of heathen priests ministering in numberless religions, and the unity of the Christian priesthood, a replication in every instance of Christ's person, between worships varying with every country in their bearers and their rites, and the unity of the Christian episcopate, a replication of His charge to feed His sheep, resting on one Sacrifice as unique as its own rule.

And, again, that which was one in origin, duration, and effect, stretched itself forth and dilated itself to embrace every city, placing at its head a spiritual ruler, who was distinct but not separate from his fellows; who preached one doctrine and ministered to one worship, as he also participated in one power.

If we embrace in one view the three constituents on which we have touched—belief, worship, and government—and contemplate the Christian people which is its outcome, how total a contrast does it present in the Christian habit of life to that of the heathen. The Christian worships a single God, who by the greatest of mysteries is at once one and three; who has a triple personality; he partakes of a worship in which that God, offered first as a Victim for him, becomes his Food; he is governed by one who bears the person of that God, whose priesthood is the foundation of his rule, and whose teaching is bound up with both rule and worship. That which the heathen called nature was to the Christian the ever-living operation of a creative hand hiding under shapes which met the senses an illimitable power, wisdom, and goodness; and the majesty of the God whom he thus adored was presented to him in the holiest rite of his worship as the Victim who redeemed him, and the Food which nourished his spiritual life. Greek and Egyptian, Syrian and African, Roman and barbarian, it was difficult to say from which he was most removed in all his thoughts of God and man, and the world around.

But to the whole body of people thus created it was the shifting of the basis on which the heathen State rested, because it was the discovery of the one Lord from whom all rule descended, and in whose name it was administered. The Roman ruled not in virtue of the principle that one God had made all the nations of the earth of one blood, and partitioned the kingdoms of the earth among them, but by virtue of the fact that the children of the wolf-cub had been the strongest in fight and the firmest in discipline, and had reduced a hundred peoples beneath their sway. The Roman himself worshipped and protected in others the worship of ancestral, that is, national gods, and the God of the Christians claimed not to be national, and to dethrone them all. The Roman, and the nations he held in subjection, believed in a multitude of traditionary doctrines respecting the earth and its inhabitants, and the powers presiding over them, some true and some false, mixed up in each case with peculiar and national interests, and all these the Christian swept away in the sublime belief, austere at once and tender, of a single Being who created, sustained, and ruled all, with the love of a Creator for all, while He kept watch over every thought, word, and action of every rational creature; that is, who was Judge and Rewarder, as well as Creator. And, lastly, this new Christian people held as the very bond of its existence that being the Body of Christ, it was to embrace all nations, and be co-extensive with the earth, co-enduring with man's race.

This was the people and the power which, having been more or less concealed during five generations from the watchful eyes of Roman statesmen, may be said to have come forth and shown itself by the multiplication of its numbers and the tenacity of its purpose, and the fixity of its doctrines in the time of Marcus Aurelius, and which five more generations of Romans, until the time of Constantine, either watched with ever-increasing anxiety, or tolerated in the mistaken hope of assimilating, or finally contended with for life or death in fearful persecutions.

And this was the people and power before which the

Emperor Marcus Aurelius, when he saw it in the persons of women and slaves and aged men, who sacrificed their lives for their belief, lost his philosophic indifference, and persecuted it as if he had been a voluptuous profligate like Nero, or a cruel tyrant like Domitian.

That the belief, the worship, and the spiritual government which carried both, had been from their first appearance in the reign of Tiberius independent of the imperial rule, whose officer crucified their Founder, under the title of the King of the Jews, we have seen in all the preceding chapters. But how was this independence actually acquired and maintained? By what talisman did the Christians compel the emperors to acknowledge that there were things of God to be rendered to God, as well as things of Cæsar to be rendered to Cæsar? For when this fight began the Emperor claimed all things, the things of Cæsar as Emperor, and the things of God as Pontifex Maximus.

Melito, Bishop of Sardis, addressing an apology for the Christian faith to Marcus Aurelius, besought him to "protect a philosophy which was nurtured together and began together with Augustus;"[1] and, in fact, it was at the moment when Augustus closed the temple of Janus, and proclaimed that there was peace in the Roman world, that our Lord was born at Bethlehem. Thirty-three years after, He was crucified by the governor of a province who represented the person of the Emperor Tiberius, and on the ground that he had infringed the

[1] A fragment of this apology is preserved for us in Eusebius' History, iv. 26.

rights of that emperor by calling Himself King of the Jews. Forthwith, when "Peter rose up in the midst of the brethren" to propose the appointment of a twelfth apostle, that he might take the place of the traitor who had betrayed his Master to death, we are told the number of the persons together was about a hundred and twenty. This number, then, indicated those disciples of our Lord who had been gained during His ministry, and were then at Jerusalem. We have another indication of numbers, where it is said that our Lord, before His ascension, was seen by "more than five hundred brethren at once,"[1] which would indicate the larger number of His adherents in Galilee.

These two statements give a notion as to the extent to which the teaching of our Lord had been accepted when the event of His public execution took place, which was intended by those who brought it about to effect the destruction of His claim to teach the world, and which was calculated, according to all human judgment, to produce the effect intended.

The empire of Augustus, and "the philosophy nurtured and begun together with it," took their several courses, and at the end of three hundred years the greatest man who had sat upon the throne of Augustus in all that interval came to the conclusion that the Christian Church was become the power of the time. What makes the greatness of Constantine, we have been told, makes him one of those characters in the world's history who are the individual expression of the spirit of their

[1] 1 Cor. xv. 6.

time, is, that he understood his time, that he perceived the weakness and powerlessness of the heathen world, the inward dissolution of the old beliefs; that the Christian faith was alone the substantial power of the time, the Christian faith, as the Corpus Christianorum, in the strong, flexible, and yet compact organisation of the Catholic Church, as seen in its one episcopate. Constantine knew Christianity only in this form; and the majestic unity into which the episcopate of the Church had already grown was for him so imposing that he saw in the Christian Church[1] the power through which the Roman empire, greatly needing a regeneration, could alone be made capable of it. That was the real power which could give a new basis to the State when it was falling into self-dissolution.

To indicate the greatness of the change involved in the action of the Roman emperor, we may here use the words of St. Gregory the Great to the Anglo-Saxon King Ethelbert, when he wrote to him at the end of the sixth century: "Illustrious Son, guard carefully the grace which thou hast received by a divine gift; hasten to extend the Christian faith among the peoples subject to thee, for He will render the name of your glory yet more glorious to your posterity, whose honour you seek and preserve in the world. For so Constantine, most pious emperor of old, calling back the Roman commonwealth from the perverted worship of idols, subjected it with himself to Jesus Christ, our omnipotent Lord God."[2]

---

[1] As Baur, Die drei ersten Jahrhunderte, p. 464, attests.
[2] St. Greg. 1 Epist. xi. 66.

But what had passed in the interval, since the officer of Tiberius crucified the Head, that the successor of Tiberius, Constantine, should recognise the Body as the only power which could hold together his tottering State?

What had happened was such facts as these.

After the Jews had spent their utmost malice in persecuting the Christian messengers, first at Jerusalem, upon St. Stephen's death, and then throughout the empire, wherever the authority of the Sanhedrim could reach them, Nero, the last emperor of the family of Augustus, moved by Jewish instigation, turned upon Christians the accusation of burning Rome, and slew what the Roman historian calls a "huge multitude" of them, with torments so atrocious that pity for them began to arise even among those who hated them.

Secondly, at the distance of another generation, Domitian slew his cousin, even while he held the consulate, and an unknown number of other Christians, on the imputed charge of impiety, that is, of deserting the heathen gods.

Thirdly, twenty years later, in the time of Trajan, we learn, by his correspondence with Pliny, that the mere profession of the Christian faith was a capital crime; and the punishment of Ignatius, in the Roman amphitheatre, made his name famous to all future generations. We know not to how many in the reign of Trajan the profession of the Christian faith was the sacrifice of life. But the Bishop of Antioch, if the most illustrious, was far from the only victim.

Fourthly, an abundance of martyrs in the reign of his successor, Hadrian, testifies the continuance and the exercise of this law proscribing the Christian profession. The noble Roman matron who witnessed the execution of her seven children is an instance how savage a man of letters and curious taste could be, when there was a question of Christian realities crossing his feelings as a heathen.

Fifthly, the reign of Marcus Aurelius, noblest of heathen rulers, is conspicuous for the number of its martyrs, in Asia Minor and in Gaul, as well as at Rome; for the increasing number of the Christians had now brought the religion into general notice. It is of this time that Irenæus, an eye-witness, shortly himself to be one of those he commemorates, writes "that the Church in every place, on account of that love which she bears to God, sends forward a multitude of martyrs in every time to the Father; while all the rest (by which he means the various sects), not only are not able to show this thing among them, but do not even say that such a martyrdom is necessary. . . . For the reproach of those who suffer persecution for the sake of justice, and endure all penalties, and are done to death for their affection towards God and their confession of His Son, these the Church alone continuously maintains, often thereby weakened, and straightway increasing its members, and becoming entire again."[1] Of this time Eusebius writes, that by the attacks made in various cities through the enmity of the populace calling upon the magistrates to

[1] Irenæus, iv. 33, 9.

execute the laws, "martyrs almost numberless were conspicuous through the whole world."[1]

Sixthly, after another generation, in the time of Septimius Severus, Eusebius states that there were martyrdoms in every part of the Church. This is the time of which Tertullian writes that Christians were now everywhere, and from their numbers would have been able to wage a civil war with their persecutors, had their religion permitted them. Of this also an eye-witness, Clement of Alexandria, says, "It was a good remark of Zeno about the Indians, that he would rather see one Indian roasted than hear any number of arguments about the endurance of pain. But we have every day a rich stream displayed before our eyes of martyrs roasted, impaled, and beheaded. All these the fear of the law has been a tutor to lead to Christ, and has wrought them up to show their piety by shedding their blood. 'God hath stood in the congregation of gods, and being in the midst of them He judgeth gods.' Who are these? They who are superior to pleasure; they who conquer sufferings; they who know each thing which they do; possessors of true knowledge, who have mastered the world."[2] This was the time when Origen, a youth of seventeen, tried to share with his father, Leonides, the martyr's crown, while death, as the result of sufferings undergone in confession, was reserved for him fifty years later in the persecution under Decius. Many writings of Tertullian bear witness of the perse-

[1] Eusebius, Hist., v. 1.
[2] Clement, Strom., ii. 20, p. 494, τοὺς γνωστικοὺς, τοὺς τοῦ κόσμου μείζονας.

cution of his own time, respecting which he says : " You crucify and impale Christians; you tear open their sides with hooks; we lay down our necks; we are driven before wild beasts; we are burnt in fires; we are banished into islands." [1]

Again, we pass thirty years, in which, while emperors hold their hands, yet individual Christians suffer under the law which proscribes their religion in general, and then we come to a seventh persecution of great severity under the Emperor Maximinus, which lasts for three years. After another interval of ten years we reach the great persecution of Decius, the eighth in number, which aims with decision at the general destruction of the Christian clergy and people.

The ten years which commence with the reign of Decius contain also two general persecutions under the Emperors Gallus and Valerianus. It is in this period that three Popes, Fabian, Lucius, and Stephen, Cyprian, Bishop of Carthage, and Laurence, Deacon at Rome, are crowned with martyrdom. The extant letters of Cyprian and Dionysius of Alexandria bear witness to the wide extent of suffering inflicted upon all classes.

Upon this succeeds the longest period of rest which occurs during the three centuries, and is terminated by the persecution commenced in the year 303 by Diocletian, which is likewise the longest, and also the most universal, and the most severe of all.

No human record preserves the names or assigns the numbers of all those who sacrificed their lives for the

[1] Apologeticus, cap. 12.

sake of their Master in these ten persecutions, and in the intervals of comparative peace which lay between them; in all of which it needed but the execution of the empire's existing laws to imperil any Christian life. A persecution meant that the sovereign power called upon the several governors of provinces and magistrates in cities to execute the law.

Thus the period from the Crucifixion in the year 29, to the Edict of Toleration in 313, a space of 284 years, bears one character. It is that of opposition by the great world-empire to the free propagation of the religion of Christ. Not only is every human motive which can have force upon the mind of man set against this propagation, but at constantly recurring times men and women and children give up the joys of home, the security of civilised life, wealth, peace, social happiness, in order to maintain and profess their belief in a crucified man as Son of God and Saviour of the world. To this end a great multitude during ten generations sacrifice life itself, and that often not by simple death, but under torments the most severe and prolonged which the ingenuity of savage enemies can invent.

Martyrdom was the ripe fruit of the Christian mind carried to its highest degree of excellence; the imitation of a crucified Lord in finished perfection. The martyr expressed in his own soul and body the truth uttered concerning his Lord, that "though He was a Son, yet learnt He obedience through the things that He suffered." The martyrs were the choice soldiers and champions of the great army of faith which arose upon the earth between Augustus and Constantine. It was by the sufferings of these three hundred years that the Church won, over against the persistent enmity of the Civil Power, the inestimable right of liberty in her faith, her worship, and her government.

But how did the army itself arise of which the martyrs were the champions? When I attempt to collect in one view the history of these first three centuries, what I find most wonderful is, not that they who believed in a crucified Head were ready as His members to suffer in and for Him, but that men and women of the most various nations, characters, and ranks, came to accept a crucified Head. Martyrdom is the outcome of a perfect faith—but the faith itself, whence was it, and how came it? Hear the Apostle who laboured more abundantly than all others describe his own work: "Christ sent me to preach the Gospel, not in wisdom of speech, lest the cross of Christ should be made void. For the word of the cross to them indeed that perish is foolishness, but to them that are saved, that is to us, it is the power of God. For it is written, I will destroy the wisdom of the wise; and the prudence of the prudent I will reject. Where is the wise? Where is the scribe? Where is the disputer of this world? Hath not God made foolish the wisdom of this world? For seeing that in the wisdom of God the world by wisdom knew not God, it pleased God by the foolishness of our preaching to save them that believe. For both the Jews require signs, and the Greeks seek after wisdom; but we preach Christ crucified, unto the Jews indeed a stumblingblock, and unto the Greeks foolishness, but unto them that are called, both Jews and Greeks, Christ the power of God and the wisdom of God. For the foolishness of God is wiser than men, and the weakness of God is stronger than men. For see your vocation, brethren, that there are not many wise according to the flesh, not many mighty, not many noble; but the foolish things of the world hath God chosen, that He may confound the wise, and the weak things of the world hath God chosen that He may confound the strong. And the base things of the world and the things that are contemptible hath God chosen, and things that are not that He might bring to nought things that are: that no flesh should glory in His sight. But of Him are you in Christ Jesus, who of God is made unto us wisdom and justice, and sanctification and redemption, that, as it is written, he that glorieth may glory in the Lord. And I, brethren, when I came to you, came not in loftiness of speech or of wisdom, declaring unto you the testimony of Christ. For I judged not myself to know anything among you, but Jesus Christ and Him crucified. And I was with you in weakness and in fear and in much trembling; and my speech and my preaching was not in the persuasive words of human wisdom, but in showing of the spirit and of power; that your faith might not stand on the wisdom of men, but on the power of God. Howbeit we speak wisdom among the perfect, yet not the wisdom of this world, neither of the princes of this world, that come to nought: but we speak the wisdom of God in a mystery, a wisdom which is hidden, which God ordained before the world, unto our glory: which none of the princes of this world knew, for if they had known it, they would never have crucified the Lord of Glory. But as it is written, That eye hath not seen, nor ear heard, neither hath it entered into the heart of man what things God hath prepared for them that love Him. But to us God hath revealed them by His Spirit."[1]

Thus St. Paul wrote to some of his early converts about the year 50. The records which would have described by a continuous and detailed history the labours of the Apostles and their successors in the two centuries and a half which followed these words, have almost entirely perished. Their result subsists in the conversion of the Roman world, and the recognition of the kingdom of Christ by the kingdom of Cæsar. These words describe the process. We have no more to say than this, and no less. The Church has not to show in all this period great and renowned men among her members; she has not to show men distinguished for their science; she has not to show men who made themselves of mark in public life, who had wealth, or influential connections, or anything which makes power according to the natural constitution of the world.[2] Even her great writers were not yet come; of those whose writings have come down to us, Tertullian and Origen were her sole men of genius. Among those who sat in the chair of Peter, there had as yet arisen no one such as the great Leo, whose word was equal to

---

[1] 1 Cor. i. 17, ii. 9.   [2] See Schwane, Dogmengeschichte, i. 557.

the power which he swayed. Her schools of theology scarcely existed; no golden tongue among her preachers had yet spoken "with lips of flame;" no heathen rhetorician, converted in the middle of life, had become the great doctor for future ages, a fountain at once of philosophy and theology. She knew and she preached nothing but Jesus Christ and Him crucified, and the effect was that no such contrast exists in all history as that supplied by the weakness of that company, the number of whose names was about 120, who met to elect a successor to the traitor apostle, and the grandeur of that body represented by the 318 Fathers at Nicæa, on whom the majesty of the Roman people waited in the person of Constantine. For behind those Fathers was the Christian people, converts of every race, from the haughtiest patrician of Cornelian blood to the humblest slave of Egypt, who had heard and obeyed the call to believe on Jesus Christ and Him crucified. There had been ten generations of youths and maidens who had offered to Him the very flower of human beauty and superhuman purity; mothers who had surrendered their children, husbands who had lost both wives and children, bishops maimed, or one-eyed, for the love of Christ, who had laboured in mines, a host of missionaries who had been treated as "the offscourings of the world," all for the sake of that Crucified One, who was ever before their eyes, and in their hearts; to whom they were joined by suffering with Him, and who promised them, in recompense for those sufferings, that which eye hath not seen, nor ear heard, nor hath it entered into the heart of man to conceive, but God had revealed by His Spirit.

For no greater change can be conceived for man to accept, than to pass from the life which a Pomponia Græcina or a Callista would lead in her Roman or her Grecian home, into the life of a Lucina burying martyred apostles, or the death of a Callista, in a dungeon of the third century; between the prosperous Cæcilius in the midst of the wealth and luxury of Carthage, and the Cyprian who, after ten years of apostolic labour, uttered his *Deo gratias* upon the Proprætor's sentence of death. Nor must we take only as samples those who were conspicuous for their work as Christians, even though it were accompanied by sufferings. We must take rather the staple of the common Christian life in its opposition to the discarded heathendom— the life of charity, of poverty, of chastity pursued by those of humblest position, over against the hatred, the avarice, the impurity out of which they came. The acceptance of such a law as the Christian law, founded upon such a belief as the Christian belief, is in any one case the result of a power quite beyond man, whatever his learning, eloquence, or persuasiveness from any natural gift may be, to bring about in his fellow-men. What, then, was that power shown in instances innumerable—shown when the acceptance of Christ crucified as the exemplar of life involved the risk of losing life, and all which made life naturally sweet or even tolerable, involved a living crucifixion? The state of virginity, confession of any kind, and finally martyrdom, made the highest point of this life; but we must look upon the great mass of the Christian people as that which produced such fruits. The Martyrs, whatever their number, were no doubt relatively few in comparison with those who were not martyred. They were "the first-fruits of the threshing-floor which the world would offer to the Redeemer;" how numerous must have been the grains of wheat out of which they were chosen? They were "the new leaven and the salt of humanity, which by the offering of their bodies and the pouring out their blood would sanctify the whole mass;"[1] but how great was the spiritual power which had descended into that mass? Surely Chrysostom had good reason when he selected the creation of the Christian people as that one miracle of Christ which no heathen gainsayer could deny.

What we find, then, as an ultimate fact in the historical conversion of the heathen world, is this internal action of the Holy Spirit in the preaching of the Apostles and their successors, by which the Christian people was formed in spite of the world around them; in spite of seductions from the pride of life, the desire of the eyes, the terrible empire of sensuous beauty; in spite of terrors which involved every suffering as well as every privation of lawful enjoyments.

All that vast development of doctrine, worship, and government, which we have been endeavouring to trace out, has been from first to last originated, accompanied, and maintained by the action of the Holy Spirit upon

[1] Panegyric of the Martyrs by the Deacon Constantine.

each individual heart. Here at last is the power which we seek in vain to detect as lodged in any natural gift possessed by the preacher. The heart is that sanctuary of liberty which no human power can invade: the heart's free acceptance of the belief offered to it is the result which no human power can win. If the Church's one Episcopate has thrown the net of Christ over the whole empire, and into regions more or less barbarous beyond it; if the Church's one doctrine has grown out into palpable form, scattering the gods of heathendom with the demons who lurked under their masks, and uplifting the strong personality of the divine Triad, in spite of pantheism, to universal adoration; if the Church's one worship has come forth from the catacombs into the light of day, and the celebration over a martyr's body in an obscure vault to a celebration in lordly temple, rich with marble and precious stones; the one adequate cause for all is the manifestation of spirit and of power, the cross set up in the heart of man before it was applied to living members of the body: it is a process inexplicable save upon the supposition of divine power. That world which by wisdom knew not God, which philosophy had failed to convert, was converted in a great proportion of its subjects by the foolishness of God which was wiser than men, and the weakness of God which was stronger than men. A crucified God was the palmary test of this foolishness and weakness; the army of martyrs was its witness; the empire's recognition of the Church's freedom in doctrine, worship, and government, was the victory which it gained.

Those who lived in the midst of this great movement fully recognised its wonderful character. Thus Clement of Alexandria, in his address to the Greeks, exclaimed: "The power of God casting its beams upon the earth with incredible rapidity and most attractive kindness has filled everything with the seed of salvation. For the Lord could not have brought about so great a work in so small a time without a divine goodwill and affection; despicable in appearance, worshipped in deed; purifier, Saviour, propitious, the Divine Word, the most manifest truly God, equal to the Lord of the universe, for He was His Son, 'and the Word was in God.' Nor was He disbelieved when first announced; nor when He took upon Him human form and fashioned Himself after the flesh, and acted the saving drama of the manhood, was He ignored. For He was a lawful combatant and a fellow-combatant with His creature; and when swifter than the sun He dawned upon us at the Father's will, He was communicated most speedily to all men, and with the utmost ease caused God to shine upon us; showing whence He was Himself, and who He was by what He taught and by what He did; bearer to us of the treaty and the reconciliation, our Saviour Word, a fountain of life and of peace, poured over the whole face of the earth; through whom the world has become a very sea of blessings."[1]

No less were eye-witnesses struck with the impotence of

[1] Clement of Alex., Cohortatio, sec. 10, p. 85. It might be fruitful to compare the view of the world taken by the Christian Clement with that taken by the pessimist Schopenhauer.

philosophy in comparison with the doctrine of the cross.
Thus the same Clement in another place says : " The
heaven-taught wisdom is that alone which is with us,
from which spring all the sources of wisdom; such, I
mean, as lead to the truth. For certainly when the Lord
who was to teach us came to men He had innumerable
pointers of His way, to announce, to prepare, to precede
Him, from the very foundation of the world. They pre-
signified Him by action and by word, they prophesied
His coming, the where and the when, and His signs.
From afar off the Law provides for Him, and Prophecy;
then His precursor declares His presence; then the
heralds teaching the power of His appearance signify it.
[But philosophers[1]] pleased their own only, and not all
these, for Socrates pleased Plato, and Plato Xenocrates,
and Aristotle Theophrastus, and Zeno Cleanthes. They
persuaded those only who embraced their own sect.
But the word of our Teacher did not remain in Judea
alone, as philosophy did in Greece. It was poured over
the whole world, persuading from nation to nation,
village to village, city to city, whole houses of Greeks
at once and of barbarians, and each one of the hearers
by himself, and bringing over to the truth not a few of
the philosophers themselves. Now, as for the Greek
philosophy, if any one in authority offers it hindrance,
forthwith it disappears; whereas our doctrine, from its
very first announcement, has been thwarted by kings
and tyrants, and magistrates, and governors, with all
their satellites and men innumerable, who make war

[1] The words inserted seem here to have fallen out of the text.

upon us, and do their utmost to cut us off. For all which it flourishes the more. For it does not die out like a human doctrine, nor fade away like a weak gift, since no gift of God is weak; but it continues unhindered, having the prophecy that it shall be persecuted to the end."[1]

If such was the marvel of conversion, viewed in itself, it is well also to listen to another eye-witness of the consequences which this change of life brought with it. The heathen objected that Christians ought to be thankful for the sufferings which they wanted. Tertullian replied:

"Well, it is quite true that it is our desire to suffer, but it is in the way that the soldier longs for war. No one indeed suffers willingly, since suffering necessarily implies fear and danger. Yet the man who objected to the conflict both fights with all his strength, and, when victorious, he rejoices in the battle, because he reaps from it glory and spoil. It is our battle to be summoned to your tribunals, that there, under fear of execution, we may battle for the truth. But the day is won when the object of the struggle is gained. This victory of ours gives us the glory of pleasing God, and the spoil of life eternal. But we are overcome—yes, when we have obtained our wishes. Therefore we conquer in dying: we go forth victorious at the very time we are subdued. Call us, if you like, Sarmenticii and Semaxii, because, bound to a half-axle stake, we are burnt in a circle heap of faggots. This is the attitude in

[1] Clement of Alex., Strom. vi., at the end.

which we conquer; it is our victory-robe; it is for us a sort of triumphal car. Naturally enough, therefore, we do not please the vanquished; on account of this, indeed, we are counted a desperate, reckless race. But the very desperation and recklessness you object to in us, among yourselves lift high the standard of virtue in the cause of glory and of fame. Mucius, of his own will, left his right hand on the altar: what sublimity of mind! Empedocles gave his whole body at Catana to the fires of Etna: what mental resolution! A certain foundress of Carthage gave herself away in second marriage to the funeral pile: what a noble witness of her chastity! Regulus, not wishing that his one life should count for the lives of many enemies, endured these crosses over all his frame: how brave a man, even in captivity a conqueror! Anaxarchus, when he was being beaten to death by a barley-pounder, cried out, 'Beat on, beat on at the case of Anaxarchus; no stroke falls on Anaxarchus himself.' O magnanimity of the philosopher, who even in such an end had jokes upon his lips! I omit all reference to those who with their own sword, or with any other milder form of death, have bargained for glory. Nay, see how even torture-contests are crowned by you. The Athenian courtezan, having wearied out the executioner, at last bit off her tongue, and spat it in the face of the raging tyrant, that she might at the same time spit away her power of speech, nor be longer able to confess her fellow-conspirators, if, even overcome, that might be her inclination. Zeno, the eleatic, when he was asked by Dionysius what good philosophy did, on answering that it gave contempt of death, was, all unquailing, given over to the tyrant's scourge, and sealed his opinion even to the death. We all know how the Spartan lash, applied with the utmost cruelty, under the very eyes of friends encouraging, confers on those who bear it honour proportionate to the blood which the young man shed. O glory legitimate because it is human, for whose sake it is reckoned neither reckless fool-hardiness nor desperate obstinacy to despise death itself and all sorts of savage treatment, for whose sake you may, for your native place, for the empire, for friendship, endure all you are forbidden to do for God! And you cast statues in honour of persons such as these, and you put inscriptions upon images, and cut out epitaphs on tombs, that their names may never perish. In so far as you can by your monuments, you yourselves afford a sort of resurrection to the dead. Yet he who expects the true resurrection from God is insane if for God he suffers. But go zealously on, good presidents; you will stand higher with the people if you sacrifice the Christians at their wish. Kill us, torture us, condemn us, grind us to dust; your injustice is the proof that we are innocent. Therefore it is of God's permitting (not of your mere will) that we thus suffer. For but very lately, in condemning a Christian woman to infamy rather than to the lion, you made confession that a taint on our purity is considered among us something more terrible than any punishment and any death. Nor does your cruelty, however exquisite, avail you; it is rather a temptation to us. The oftener we are mown down by you, the more in number we grow; the blood of Christians is seed. Many of your writers exhort to the courageous bearing of pain and death, as Cicero in the Tusculans, as Seneca in his Chances, as Diogenes, Pyrrhus, Callinicus. And yet their words do not find so many disciples as Christians do, teachers not by words, but by their deeds. That very obstinacy you rail against is the preceptress; for who that contemplates it is not excited to inquire what is at the bottom of it? Who, after inquiry, does not embrace our doctrines? and when he has embraced them, desires not to suffer that he may become partaker of the fulness of God's grace, that he may obtain from God complete forgiveness by giving in exchange his blood? For that secures the remission of all offences. On this account it is that we return thanks on the very spot for your sentences. As the divine and human are ever opposed to each other, when we are condemned by you we are acquitted by the Highest."[1]

Origen, in replying to the attacks of a very subtle and able Platonic philosopher of the second century, appeals again and again to the divine power shown forth in the conversion of so many, and among them of those who had previously been the slaves of sin. Heathen philosophy could boast of two converts, Phædo and Polemo; on which he says, "We assert that the whole habitable world contains evidence of the works of Jesus, in the existence of those churches of God which have been founded through Him by those who have been

[1] Tertullian, Apology, 50; Edinburgh translation.

converted from the practice of innumerable sins. And the name of Jesus can still remove distractions from the minds of men, and expel demons, and also take away diseases, and produce a marvellous meekness of spirit and complete change of character, and a humanity, and goodness, and gentleness in those individuals who do not feign themselves to be Christians for the sake of subsistence or the supply of any mortal wants, but who have honestly accepted the doctrine concerning God and Christ and the judgment to come."

Celsus, unable to resist the miracles which Jesus is recorded to have performed, had on several occasions spoken of them slanderously as works of sorcery, to which Origen had severally replied. But he also pointed out how far greater a divine power is manifested in healing the maladies of the soul than in raising the daughter of Jairus, or the son of the widow of Nain, or Lazarus four days dead; for indeed these miracles were the symbols of the greater things which our Lord promised to do by His Apostles. "I would say that, agreeably to the promise of Jesus, His disciples performed even greater works than these miracles of Jesus, which were perceptible only to the senses. For the eyes of those who are blind in soul are ever opened, and the ears of those who were deaf to virtuous words listen readily to the doctrine of God and of the blessed life with Him; and many too who were lame in the feet of the 'inner man,' as Scripture calls it, having now been healed by the word, do not simply leap, but leap as the hart, which is an animal hostile to serpents, and stronger than all the poison of vipers. And these lame who have been healed received from Jesus power to trample with those feet in which they were formerly lame upon the serpents and scorpions of wickedness, and generally upon all the power of the enemy; and though they tread upon it, they sustain no injury, for they also have become stronger than the poison of all evil and of demons."

On this point he dwells further. The Jew introduced by Celsus argued that our Lord was a man. Origen replied: "I do not know whether a man who had the courage to spread throughout the entire world His doctrine of religious worship and teaching could accomplish what He wished without the divine assistance, and could rise superior to all who withstood the progress of His doctrine—kings and rulers, and the Roman Senate and governors in all places, and the common people. And how could the nature of a man possessed of no inherent excellence convert so vast a multitude? For it would not be wonderful if it were only the wise who were so converted; but it is the most irrational of men and those devoted to their passions, and who, by reason of their irrationality, change with the greater difficulty so as to adopt a more temperate course of life. And yet it is because Christ was the power of God and the wisdom of the Father that He accomplished and still accomplishes such results, although neither the Jews nor Greeks who disbelieved His word will so admit. And, therefore, we shall not cease to believe in God, according to the precepts of Jesus Christ, and to seek to convert those who are blind on the subject of religion, although it is they who are truly blind themselves that charge us with blindness; and they, whether Jews or Greeks, who lead astray those that follow them, accuse us of seducing men—a good seduction, truly, that they may become temperate instead of dissolute, or at least may make advances to temperance; may become just instead of unjust, or at least may tend to become so; prudent instead of foolish, or be on the way to become such; and instead of cowardice, meanness, and timidity, may exhibit the virtues of fortitude and courage, especially displayed in the struggles undergone for the sake of their religion towards God, the Creator of all things."

The wonder of the formation of the Christian community itself was never absent from the mind of those who were eye-witnesses of the heathendom in the bosom of which it arose. The place now occupied in the minds of men by the sins of professing Christians was then occupied by the sins of heathens in the midst of whom Christians formed so striking a contrast. Origen refers to the moral miracle as supported and in part explained by the material miracle, which, like every writer of those centuries, he presupposed and dwelt upon as a fact which was manifest before the eyes of every one—a fact which might be ascribed to sorcery, but could not be denied.

"I think," he says, "the wonders wrought by Jesus are a proof of the Holy Spirit's having then appeared in the form of a dove; and I shall refer not only to His miracles, but, as is proper, to those also of the Apostles of Jesus. For they could not without the help of miracles and wonders have prevailed on those who heard their new doctrines and new teachings to abandon their national usages and to accept their instructions at the danger to themselves even of death." And elsewhere: "Christians, who have in so wonderful a manner formed themselves into a community, appear at first to have been more induced by miracles than by exhortations to forsake the institutions of their fathers and to adopt others which were quite strange to them. And, indeed, if we were to reason from what is probable as to the first formation of the Christian society, we should say that it is incredible that the Apostles of Jesus Christ, who were unlettered men of humble life, could have been emboldened to preach Christian truth to men by anything else than the power which was conferred upon them, and the grace which accompanied their words and rendered them effective; and those who heard them would not have renounced the old established usages of their fathers, and been induced to adopt notions so different from those in which they had been brought up, unless they had been moved by some extraordinary power and by the force of miraculous events."[1]

This power of miracles, as inherited by the disciples from their Lord, is thus recorded by Irenæus:[2]—

"They who are truly His disciples, having received the grace from Him, effect it in His name for the good of others in proportion as each individual has received the

[1] Cont. Cels., 1, 67; 2, 48; 2, 79; 1, 46; 8, 47; Edinburgh translation.
[2] Irenæus, 2, 32.

gift from Him. Some with true and permanent effect expel demons, so that in many cases the very persons who have been delivered from the evil spirits believe and are in the Church. Some have foreknowledge of future events, visions, and prophetic utterances. Others heal sick people by the imposition of their hands and make them whole. Dead, too, have been raised to life, and have remained with us many years. What shall I say? It is impossible to express the number of the graces which the Church throughout the whole world, having received them from God, effects every day for the good of the nations in the name of Jesus Christ who was crucified under Pontius Pilate. And in this she neither seduces any nor works for filthy lucre; for what she has freely received she freely imparts."

In the time of Irenæus, Clement, Tertullian, and Origen, the proof from the rapid growth of the Church in spite of the world's opposition was by no means complete. Moreover, the greatest and most general persecutions, those of Decius, Gallus, Valerian, and Diocletian, came after this. Probably the struggle between the Church and the Empire was not understood in all its bearings before the time of Decius. But we possess two treatises of Athanasius, composed in his youth, about the year 320. They are extremely beautiful both in style and matter; and in parts of them Athanasius contemplates the whole preceding history of the Church and the effects of her preaching the cross of Christ. I take as a specimen what he says about certain miraculous effects worked by the name and the cross of Christ, for the truth of which he appeals to universal experience.[1]

"When did men begin to desert the worship of idols except from the time that the true God, the Word of God, appeared among men? When did the oracles which were everywhere among the Greeks cease and come to nought, save from the time that the Saviour manifested Himself upon earth? When did the gods and heroes of the poets begin to be condemned as mere mortal men, save from the time that the Lord set up His trophy against death, and preserved incorruptible the body which He had taken by raising it from the dead? And when was the deceit and madness of demons despised, save when the Word, the power of God, the Lord of all, and of these among all, in His condescension for the weakness of men, appeared upon the earth? When did the art and the schools of magic begin to be trodden underfoot, save upon the manifestation of the Word among men? In a word, when did the wisdom of the Greeks become foolish, save when the true Wisdom of God showed Himself on the earth? For of old the whole world and every spot in it was filled with the false worship of idols, and men held that there were no gods but idols. But now through all the world men desert the superstition of idols and fly to Christ, and worship Him as God, through whom they recognise the Father whom they knew not. And observe this wonder. The religions were different and numberless; each place had its own idol, and he that

[1] Athanasius, De Incarnatione Verbi Dei, c. 46-48.

was invoked as god there could not pass to the next spot to persuade his neighbours to worship him, but could only just maintain his own worship; for no one worshipped his neighbour's god, but kept to his own idol, thinking that he was the lord of all; whereas the one and same Christ is worshipped everywhere by all; and what the impotence of idols could not do to persuade its neighbours, this Christ has done, persuading not only those near, but simply the whole world to worship one and the same Lord, and through Him God His Father.

"Of old, also, everything was full of the deceit of oracles, and those in Delphi, and Dodona, and Bœotia, and Libya, and Egypt, and the Kabiri, and the Pythia, were admired in men's imagination; but from the time that Christ is preached everywhere, this their madness also is stopped, and no one any longer acts the prophet. And of old the demons deceived men with spectres, taking possession of fountains and rivers, of wood and stones, and so astonishing the foolish with deceits. All these sights have vanished since the Divine Epiphany of the Word; for a man using only the sign of the cross scatters all their tricks. Of old men deemed those whom the poets called Zeus, and Kronos, and Apollo, and the heroes, to be gods, and were drawn into error by worshipping them; but now that the Saviour has appeared among men, these have been reduced to the nakedness of mortal men, while Christ has been recognised as alone true God, God the Word of God. What shall I say of the magic which had so much vogue among them? Before the Word was spread among us, it prevailed and worked among Egyptians, Chaldeans, and Indians, and astonished the beholders; but it was convicted and utterly brought to nought by the presence of the truth and the appearance of the Word. But as to the Grecian wisdom and the big words of the philosophers, I think it needs no word from us when the strange sight is before the eyes of all, that all the volumes written by the Greek wise men were not able to persuade even a few neighbours of immortality and virtuous life; while Christ, only by a few cheap words in the mouth of men who had no wisdom of the tongue, has persuaded numerous assemblies of men throughout the whole world to despise death and to have immortal longings, to pass by time and see eternity, earth's glory to esteem as dust and ashes, and grasp instead of it a crown in heaven.

"These are not mere words of ours, but appeal to the test of experience for their reality. Let any one who will go and see the proof of virtue in Christian virgins and the youths who cultivate purity, and the assurance of immortality in the vast multitude of martyrs. He that will try the truth of what we have said, let him upon the appearance of demons, the deceit of oracles, and magic wonders, use the sign of the cross which they mock at, with the mere name of Christ, and he will see how the demons fly, the oracles stop, the whole array of magic and trickery disappears. Who, then, and how great is this Christ who has by His mere name and presence cast His shade over and annihilated all these things everywhere, who prevails over all alone, and has filled the whole world with His teaching? Let the Greeks who mock and blush not say. Is He a man? how then has one man been too much for the power of all their gods, and convicted them by His own power of being nothing? Do they call Him a magician? but how can all magic be destroyed by a magician, and not rather be confirmed? For if He prevailed over some magicians, or was superior to one only, He might well be deemed by them to have surpassed the others by greater art; but if His cross carried off the victory over all magic absolutely, and the very name of the thing, it is plain that the Saviour is not a magician, since the demons invoked by other magicians fly from Him as their Lord. If He only drove away some demons, He might be thought to have power over the inferior by the chief of the demons, as the Jews mocking said of Him. But if all the fury of the demons is displaced and scattered by naming Him, it is plain they are wrong, and that our Lord and Saviour Christ is not, as they think, some demoniacal power. If, then, the Saviour is neither simple man, nor magician, nor a demon, but by His own Godhead has annulled and frustrated all the imagination of poets, the display of demons, and the wisdom of Greeks, it must be plain and confessed by all that He is truly the Son of God, the Word, and Wisdom, and Power of the Father. Hence His works are not human, but above man's range, and are recognised to be the works of God in truth by their manifest effects, and by the comparison of them with the works of man."

Athanasius speaks in these words for the whole period preceding him. The apologists of the early Church before him[1] lay the most stress in proving her divine character upon five things—the predictions of the Old Testament, the miracles of Jesus and the Apostles, the miraculous power continuing on in Christians, the rapid propagation of the Church, and the steadfast endurance of confessors under persecution. Our Lord Himself laid the greatest weight upon the proof arising from prophecy, and from the works of power, themselves announced in prophecy, which He did, "the works of the Christ." His answer to the disciples of John the Baptist included both. In fact, He came among a people possessing a divinely appointed priesthood and office of teaching, which He expressly acknowledged when He said, "The Scribes and the Pharisees sit in the chair of Moses; all things, therefore, whatsoever they shall say to you, observe and do." But He did not in any way attach Himself to this authority, much less submit to it in His office of teaching. If we reflect on the fact that He did not submit Himself to the authority which He acknowledged to be divine, yet claimed supreme authority, it is obvious that without miracles He could claim no authority as the Christ. And He said so most plainly Himself when He summed up, as it were, the whole bearing of His ministry towards the Jewish authorities in the words, "If I had not done among them such works as no man ever did, they should not have sin; but now have they both seen and hated both Me and My Father."

[1] Gieseler, i. 208.

Thus, as in His own life, so likewise in the life of His people, miracles and prophecy were of necessity the double external witness to His mission, as martyrdom, including under it every degree of confessorship, was the great internal witness.

And every ancient Christian writer alleges the existence and the exercise of miraculous power in the Church. But there is also another fact; not only all Christians, but Jews and heathens of every class, the bitterest opponents of the Christian faith, agreed in one point, namely, that superhuman[1] power was at work in the world, and in the whole life of man, by which works exceeding man's ability, and often transgressing the laws of nature, were wrought. They were eye-witnesses of these works. About a great number of them, so far at least as the fact was concerned, they could not be deceived, though they might be deceived as to the nature of the cause.

Without martyrdom and also without miracles the conversion which took place between the Day of Pentecost and the Edict of Toleration in 313 was not even conceivable. Let us consider the bond which connects the two together.

The Christian faith itself rests upon two miracles. The first is the assumption of human nature by the Divine Word, the Second Person in the Blessed Trinity, in the womb of the Virgin Mary. This act of the divine condescension is so transcendent in all its bearings as

[1] As admitted by Friedländer, Sittengeschichte Roms., iii. 458, 459, and see the argument of Celsus in Origen, 8, 45.

not merely to surpass the order of nature, but to be, as it were, the parent of miraculous power in all that supernatural order which it creates and maintains. It is the fontal source of grace to man, of his first creation in grace, the first Adam himself being the image of the Second who was to be, and for whose sake the whole creation was made. Take away from the Christian faith that "Gospel of Mary" which St. Luke has recorded in the mission of the Angel Gabriel to her, and that faith is not only altered, but it ceases to be. Everything which the Christian believes and hopes depends, in fact, upon that miracle of miracles, the union of the divine nature with the human in the Person of Jesus Christ. Therefore all His children are born of a miracle, nurtured upon a miracle, live and hope and suffer and die in faith of a miracle, so great, so peculiar, so inconceivable beforehand, that all other miracles are but its progeny.

But, secondly, the very existence of this first miracle was guaranteed and made known by another—the resurrection of Jesus Christ in that very Body bearing the marks of the nails and the wound of the spear in which He was crucified. It was faith in this resurrection which sent forth a College of twelve unlettered men to convert the world, and by that faith they converted it, so far at least that the diadem of its emperors was surmounted by the cross of Christ. They and their successors who went forth in the same faith were misused, calumniated, persecuted, tormented to death in every shape and fashion, until Constantine saw the token in the sky and placed it on his banner.

What, then, we have said as to the Incarnation we may also say as to the Resurrection of Christ; take it away, and the Christian people have no longer a foundation on which to rest. They would simply cease to be.

They are, therefore, doubly the children of miracle.

They were thus from the beginning—and they could not but be—instinct with the sense of miracle.

But these two miracles were no less the ground of martyrdom and of all that life, consisting in the endurance and even choice of suffering, hardship, privation of every kind, of which martyrdom is the seal and crown. The connection between miracle and martyrdom seems to be this: The Incarnation of our Lord is the very reason of miraculous power being exhibited in the world, just as His assumption of human nature is itself the miracle of miracles. The purpose of all miracle is to bring home to the creature a special action of the Creator as Governor of the world, but the head and crown as well as the starting-point of such special action is, in our actual world, the miracle of the Incarnation.

Again, the original need of miraculous action springs from the moral darkness superinduced by the Fall, which the Incarnation repairs. The angelic world, while under probation, or any world of rational creatures unfallen, needs no miracles. And all miracles anterior to Christ are part of a chain of events leading on to Him, just as all martyrs before Christ have their reason of existence in Him alone. The occasion of martyrdom is the enmity between the seed of the serpent and the Seed of the Woman, and miracle is from beginning to end the hand of God showing itself in the contest. "All the just," says St. Augustine,[1] "who have been from the beginning of the world have Christ for their Head. For they believed in the future coming of that One whom we believe to have come, and they were healed by faith in the same One by faith in whom we are healed, that He might be head of the whole city Jerusalem." And the most inspired of Christian poets, when he beheld the great rose of Paradise flowering with the saints of all times, divided them by their preceding or following the coming of Christ:

> "Da questa parte, onde 'l fiore è maturo
> Di tutte le sue foglie, sono assisi
> Quei che credettero in Cristo venturo.
> Dall' altra parte, onde sono intercisi
> Di vôto i semicircoli, si stanno
> Quei ch' a Cristo venuto ebber li visi."
> —*Paradiso*, c. 32, 22.

In like manner the Apostle commences his illustration of the life of faith by the martyrdom of Abel, "who being dead yet speaketh." Thus the one life pleasing to God from the beginning to the end is identical in its substance, and shows the oneness of the divine plan, commencing its execution in the very family of the first man. There the just loses his life for his justice' sake, and Abel becomes the type of Christ and of all who follow the Divine Master. So St. John the Baptist, marking the transition from the old covenant to the new, the precursor of our Lord, with the triple aureole of virginity, doctorship, and martyrdom, gives up his life to maintain the sanctity of marriage.

[1] On Psalm xxxvi. 3.

Further, the Passion of our Lord is the source of martyrdom; and union with Him, especially in the act of His Passion, is the cause of all the effects which martyrdom produces. As He said, in reference to His coming Passion, of Himself, "Except a corn of wheat fall into the ground and die, it remaineth alone, but if it die, it bringeth forth much fruit;" so Tertullian said of His people, "The blood of Christians is seed." In martyrdom lies the perpetuation of faith in Christ. He stands in the midst of the ages, as the Lamb slain from the foundation of the world, working backwards and forwards. The shedding of Abel's blood, the first blood shed, and the blood of the brother shed by the brother, points to the shedding of Christ's blood; and so in the interval between Abel and Christ the blood of all the just ones is shed for the hope of Christ. As all martyrdom preceding Him was for the hope of Him, so all following is in remembrance and participation of Him.

There is a strong parallel between miracle and martyrdom as to their principle, their witness, their power, and their perpetuity.

1. First, as to *principle.* The conception of miracle springs at once from the doctrine of God the Creator, Orderer, and Maintainer of the universe, united with the doctrine of the Fall of man and the ignorance thence superinduced, and requiring to be dissipated by an objective confirmation of the truth. This confirmation is produced when He suspends that order of nature which He has impressed on things. "The divine power can at any time, without prejudice to His providence, do

something beyond the order impressed on natural things by God. This is the very thing which He sometimes does to manifest His power. For in no manner can it be better shown that all nature is subject to the divine will than by this, that sometimes He does something beyond the order of nature; for by this it is made to appear that the order of things proceeded from God, not by a necessity of His nature, but by His free-will." [1]

On the other hand, the conception of miracles is incompatible with the notion of a power evolving itself by a strict necessity in the universe. This involves at the same time the rejection of the notion of sin as a violation of the eternal law. For the evolution itself is the only law admitted, and is incapable of sin, which arises from the misuse of the liberty of the will. A world evolved by eternal necessity denies any liberty to the will. In this the Positivist and Materialist of the present day only take the position which the Stoic took of old. All the three deny miracle, because they deny creation.

And the principle of martyrdom is the intimate union between Christ and Christians, whereby the Head and His members form one Body. The community in suffering rests on this. At the head of persecution is the statement of our Lord Himself (the narrative of which, it may be remarked, is given three times in the Acts), "Saul, Saul, why persecutest thou Me?" Thus a martyr said to martyrs, "He who once conquered death for us is ever conquering death in us. You know that you are

[1] St. Thomas, Cont. Gent., 3, 99.

contending under the eyes of your present Lord; that by the confession of His name you reach His own glory. For He is not as if He was only looking at His servants, but He wrestles Himself, He combats Himself in them; in the contest of our struggle, Himself both crowns and is crowned."[1]

The martyr Felicitas underwent in prison the sufferings of premature childbirth. One of the attendants remarked to her, "You who so much show your suffering now, what will you do when you are thrown before the wild beasts, which you despised when you refused to sacrifice?" And she answered, "It is I who suffer now that which I suffer; but then there will be another in me who will suffer for me, because I also shall be suffering for Him." On which St. Augustine comments: "It was He who caused women to suffer with faith and the courage of men who deigned in His mercy for their sake to be born of a woman. . . . Eve's penalty was not absent, but Mary's grace was present. What she owed as a woman was exacted; what she needed in help was given by the Virgin's Son."[2]

2. As to the *witness* of miracles, in matter of fact the objective proof of our Lord's mission as Messias and Son of God was based, both in His own life and in the propagation of His faith, upon miracles viewed in a double light—first, as they are in themselves, and secondly, as the fulfilment of prophecy. "To confirm doctrines which surpass natural knowledge He showed visibly works which surpass natural power, by the healing of

[1] St. Cyprian, Ep. 8.   [2] Sermon 281.

the sick, the raising of the dead, and, what is more wonderful, the inspiration of human minds, so that untaught and simple men, filled with the gift of the Holy Spirit, obtained in an instant the utmost wisdom and readiness of speech; so that not by the violence of arms, not by the promise of pleasures, but amid the tyranny of persecutors, an innumerable multitude, not merely of simple, but of the wisest men was drawn into the Christian faith. They preached doctrines surpassing man's understanding; they set a restraint on carnal pleasures; they taught contempt for everything that is in the world. It would be the most marvellous of all marvels if the world without miracles had been led to the belief of doctrines so difficult, the working of deeds so arduous, the hoping of rewards so exalted, by simple and ignoble men."[1]

The witness of martyrdom is expressed in its very name, that they who suffered death for the sake of Christ were simply called witnesses. The analogy with miracles is very strong indeed, the one being the witness of God attesting the truth of His messengers by visible signs, which suspend or reverse the order which He has Himself established as a general rule; the other being the witness of men who suffer all those things from which the nature of man recoils in order to attest the truth of God.

3. As to the *power* exercised by miracles over the minds of men, the victory over idolatry and the whole heathen life, which was the reflection of that idolatry,

[1] St. Thomas, Contra Gent., I, 6.

could not have been accomplished—all other powers remaining in the Church—without this one. In fact, a diabolic spiritual power, termed by our Lord "the strong man armed," being, as the result of the Fall, in possession of his captive, could only be cast out by One stronger than he, the Son of God Incarnate. The series of miracles wrought by His disciples were the arms which He used. His name alone when invoked by them is attested in numberless instances to have had a supernatural effect.

As to the power exercised by martyrdom, the whole history is full of that victory over idolatry and the heathen life which was accomplished by the suffering of our Lord's disciples in His name and in community with Him. Over and above the effect which the voluntary endurance of suffering for conscience' sake has upon the minds of men, martyrdom merited the propagation of the faith as if our Lord's Passion required to be repeated in His members for the growth of His Body. Such is the fact expressed by St. Paul in the words, "I rejoice in my sufferings for you, and fill up those things that are wanting of the sufferings of Christ in my flesh for His Body, which is the Church." And, again, "As the sufferings of Christ abound in us, so also by Christ doth our comfort abound." In this martyrdom threw a light upon the divine government of the world; and as the reversibility of guilt had formed the history of fallen man, so the reversibility of merit formed the history of man redeemed. Thus over against the abyss of judgment lies the abyss of grace, the treasure-house of the Church, of which the King of martyrs holds the key. That treasure-house is the communion of saints. The power of martyrdom is one of its great exhibitions. Its source is the Incarnation of the Son. Taking the mass of sufferings undergone by the mystical Body of Christ in the process of its growth, there is nothing in the web of human guilt, how intricate soever it may be, from the beginning to the end of the world, which has not its counterpart in the reversibility of merit, all derived from the Passion of the Incarnate Son.

4. As to the *perpetuity* of the miraculous power, the same reason exists through the whole course of the Church's preaching for the signs in her following them that believe. The promise is most clearly recorded at the conclusion of St. Mark's Gospel, without limit of time or place. The performance in this first age, when she had to meet all the tyranny of rulers and all the rage of unbelievers, is recorded also. The promise clearly extends to the whole time over which the command relating to it extends: "Go ye unto the whole world, and preach the gospel to every creature."

As to the perpetuity of martyrdom, it is clear, to use St. Paul's expression, that what is wanting of the sufferings of Christ will not be made up until His Body is completed "in the measure of the stature of the fulness of Christ."

In all these respects the two great powers of miracle and martyrdom, united in their origin, seem to run into and complete each other. The witness of God and the witness of man concur in the formation of the kingdom of His Son.

It may also be noted that all those who reject God as Creator, Judge, and Remunerator proclaim as a first principle that a miracle is impossible, while they have the same dislike to martyrdom as the great adversary is said to have for holy water.

I have now, then, answered the question which I put above—How came the Roman Emperor to allow to Christians the liberty to render to God the things of God, that is, to believe, to worship, and to be governed according to the law of Christ? It was done by an internal action of the Holy Spirit, forming by a process of individual conversion in the minds of an innumerable multitude a certain type of Christian character, an image in each one of the Founder of the line; and at the same time by an external action of the same Holy Spirit co-operating in this conversion "with signs following." Never before were the divine and the human societies pitted against each other in so absolute a conflict. Perhaps it is even the only period as yet in the 1850 years of Christian life in which the Battle of the Standards, of poverty, affliction, and contempt on the one side, of the lust of the eyes, the lust of the flesh, and the pride of life on the other, has been completely carried out—completely in that the representation on each side embraced the whole society. For if any would not be poor, afflicted, and despised in those times, either they could not become Christians, or becoming so in times of comparative peace, they were speedily scattered by the winnowing flail of persecution. But on the other side, the combative heathenism from Tiberius to Maxentius was pre-eminently corrupt. It should be added, that in the 1850 years, never has there been so astonishing a result as the advance of the Christian Church, from those who met in the upper room on the Day of Pentecost to those who received from Constantine perfect civil freedom to believe that doctrine, to exercise that worship, to be governed by that Episcopate, which formed together the greatest conceivable contradiction to the heathen world of Augustus. It was the result of ten generations, sanctified by suffering and multiplied by martyrdom.

There is another point of view also in which this period should be regarded. What did these champions of conscience do for that very civil order of things to which in their character of Christians they had so often to refuse obedience, and to say simply, in the words of their first leader, "We ought to obey God rather than men"?

They conferred upon all future generations of men an inestimable benefit, for they established the doctrine that the individual man has rights which the collective society of men may not violate. They overthrew the autocracy of the State, which had crushed out the heart of humanity.

During those ages, after the conversion of the original Roman commonwealth into the Cæsarean empire, there was no guarantee of civil liberty. From the city which only refused fire and water to its guiltiest citizens, the Empire had grown into a power wherein a charge of majestas justified the application of every torment to the accused; and the charge of majestas was ever at hand in the case of a Christian. If Augustus, though he slaughtered without mercy when his interests were concerned, studied to give his rule the aspect of moderation, the emperors his successors became more and more uncontrolled. Not only had they legislative power, but the imprisonment and the execution of any obnoxious person was entirely in their hands. In this long period of 284 years, Christians without number suffered loss of goods, confinement in loathsome dungeons, separation from their families, and finally death itself under torment and insult, because they would worship Christ as God, because they would not swear by the genius of the Emperor, because they would not burn a few grains of incense on the altar of an idol, because one who had dedicated herself to God would not marry, because a soldier would not carry out an impious command, for any of the innumerable reasons for which they were offensive to the world, which the world called "their hatred of the human race," that being the phrase of the day for the Kulturkampf.

Thus they suffered and they died, and in so suffering and dying they constructed a new basis of civil liberty. For this it was which the Church's creation of the Spiritual Power betokened. It meant the establishment of the Christian conscience not merely in the individual, but in the great world-wide corporation of the Church, which thus formed an impregnable citadel of defence against civil absolution, by cutting off from it the triple domain of the Church's priesthood, teaching, and jurisdiction. What heathenism had destroyed by corrupting the worship of the one true God into a multitude of false gods, the Church restored by setting up the worship of the Blessed Trinity; and the priesthood, which unutterable degradations had humbled in the dust of human passions and vices, the Church took from the Body of her Lord, dyed red in blood, and invested with the imperishable sanctity of the Priest after the order of Melchisedek; and that kingship which Nero and Domitian, Elagabalus and Galerius, had stained with unspeakable crimes, it renewed in the example of those princes over all the earth who ruled not as the kings of the Gentiles, but as Fathers in God. Christian monarchy is the Church's work, and the Christian State became possible because the Christian people in times of authority which was cruel, and of majesty which was selfish, had shown the example of rulers who governed for their people's sake, governed by the authority of One who created the government of His people when He said by the Lake of Galilee to the disciple who should be the type and mould and origin of the episcopate for ever, "If thou lovest Me, feed My sheep."

This was a purifying and ennobling of civil society wrought by the Church over and above its spiritual end. The kingdom of heaven, whilst it limited, also invigorated the earthly kingdom, showing that Christians alone are freemen, by exercising the highest of all freedoms .in belief, in worship, and in obedience to spiritual government, and in the conduct which is their united result.

Retracing the ground we have traversed, we find that the Church, between the Day of Pentecost and the Edict of Toleration, passed unscathed and victorious through five great trials, which were calculated to test to the utmost the power vested in her. Two of these conflicts—that with Judaism and that with heresy—were internal, and three—the conflict with idolatry, that with Greek and Oriental philosophy, and that with the civil power of the Roman Empire—were external. Moreover, while one of these conflicts—that with the enmity of the unbelieving Jews, and the spirit which urged the obligation of the ceremonial law upon the Christian Church—raged chiefly in the first forty years, and was greatly assuaged in its influence by the destruction of the city and temple of Jerusalem, the remaining four contests lasted continuously, and acted with collective force against the Church during the whole period. For as to heresy, it was rife from the time of the Apostles themselves. Those who became Christians, whether Jews or Gentiles, were all themselves exposed to the danger of intellectual and moral seduction: we find, indeed, that some of the most distinguished converts yielded to it, such as Tatian and Tertullian. Those especially who in middle age had passed over from heathen customs and a youth perhaps spent in the study of Hellenic literature and philosophy into the Christian confession, would naturally remain all their lives liable to the danger of false teaching, if they were not guarded from it by the utmost purity of life, and not only sincerity but humility of mind. Certainly no period of the Church's history shows a greater number of sects than this.

Another enemy which the Church had from the beginning, and which continued in the utmost force through the whole time, was idolatry, and that whole contexture of life of which it was first the prolific source, then the vigilant nurse and the constant support. Every part of Gentile life was flavoured by the spirit of the false worship—the passions of the young, the ambitions of middle life, the avarice of age. Its power was all around the Church, to corrupt morals, to pervert belief, to sensualise worship. As we have seen above, Christian writers dwell upon the fact that vast numbers of those who became Christians had previously been stained with heathen vices: those who had yielded to all manner of sensual passions became chaste: those who had revelled in pride of intellect became humble. But what a force of opposition to the spread of the Christian religion did the moral state of the great cities in which it had its principal seats present! Rome, Alexandria, Antioch, Ephesus, Corinth and Carthage were the very centres of all moral corruption when the Christian seed was dropped upon them. This glamour of the heathen life was an enemy the intensity and ubiquity of whose power lasted without intermission from the beginning to the end of the time.

From the beginning likewise to the end the heathen

philosophy, whether Greek or Oriental, or in that amalgam of both which probably formed the texture of cultured minds in this period, was a most dangerous and influential foe. Against this also the Apostles themselves warn their converts. From a very early time indeed the Gnostic sects put up the pantheistic unity of the philosophic God against the Christian Trinity in Unity. They tried to convert the Divine Logos into an æon. Led by their doctrine that the essential seat of evil was in matter, they attacked Christ in His human nature, denying the verity of His Body. They constructed divine theogonies with all the brilliance of the Eastern imagination and all the cleverness of Greek subtilty; and many who resisted the foulness of heathen idolatry were led away by fantastic schemes of spiritual unity—by pantheism in one of its many shapes. This enemy also lasted through the whole period: the Gnostic systems passed into the Neoplatonic, perhaps the most dangerous enemy which the Church encountered in the three hundred years, and Arianism itself was but a modification of Gnostic error.

But heresy, idolatry, and philosophy were helped throughout by that jealousy of the Civil Power, the most marked perhaps in the best rulers, such as Trajan and Decius, which abhorred above all things the formation of an independent religious community in its bosom. How would an emperor of cultivated tastes and incessant curiosity, such as Hadrian, exult over the divisions of heresies and the varying systems of philosophy, looking down on them all from his superior height! Irenæus observed that heresies had no martyrs—the State did not persecute them. And philosophy did not die for its belief; its essence was free thought—that is, the license to change to-morrow what it asserted to-day. But how would a monarchy which scrupled to authorise a guild of firemen in a provincial city, lest it should form the nucleus of a secret society, abhor the growth of a Church which had its centre in Rome and a governor in every city, bound to the centre at Rome by the accord of a common faith, a common worship, and the undivided rule of a single people, the *corpus Christianorum!* Therefore heresy, idolatry, and philosophy were the friends and allies of the Civil Power throughout this time. It patronised them, and it could use all their influence, their resources, and their intellect against the insurgent Church, while all the time it had at its command every punishment which force can inflict on those who disregard the laws of an empire. To be a Christian was to violate the Roman majestas.

Over against these five enemies the Church received her spiritual authority from the Person of her Lord; she planted it through her episcopate over the earth; she maintained her one doctrine in the teaching of that episcopate, her one worship in the sacrifice which it everywhere offered; she worked out her independence in her organic growth of structure, in the mode of her teaching, in her resistance to error of every sort and kind; and, finally, the empire which had used every arm against her, acknowledged her doctrine, her worship, and her government, and her essential independence in all these as the kingdom of Christ, when Constantine appeared at the Nicene Council, not to control, but to carry into effect its decision, and when he wrote concerning it, "The sentence of the three hundred bishops is nothing else but the decision of God; especially since the Holy Spirit, by His action upon the minds of such men, has brought into full light the divine will."[1]

When the Emperor of Rome, the successor of Tiberius, gave official utterance to such words, he showed that the blood of martyrs shed through ten generations, the endurance of confessors, the labours of priests who refused the joys of domestic life in their imitation of the Virgin's Son, the continence of those who carried out in themselves the vow of the Virgin Mother of that Son, and what is included in all these, the generation of the Christian people, had done their appointed work; and so the kingdom of Cæsar recognised the kingdom of Christ.

[1] Constantine's letter to the Church of Alexandria, recorded by Socrates, Hist. 1, 9.

INDEX.

ADAM, Father and Head of his race, 3; does not lose the Headship by his fall, 11; is likewise Priest and Teacher of his race, 14-16; created in full possession of language, 5; has an infused knowledge of the animal creation, 5; has the Image and Likeness of God both as an Individual and as Head of his race, 6; subserves the mystery of the Incarnation, 8; as does the whole society founded in Adam and his children, 55

Æschylus, his rigid statement of satisfaction due for sin, 260

Alexandria: its catechetical school, 345; becomes a Christian university, 385; its succession of ten distinguished presidents, 386

Altar, the heathen, on which beasts were sacrificed, βωμός, the Christian, on which the Unbloody Sacrifice is offered, θυσιαστήριον, 232

Apostolate, the powers conveyed to it by Christ, 136, 138, 139, 149-151; summary of these powers, 154, 155, 159. (See PRIMACY and EPISCOPATE)

Aquinas, St. Thomas, his doctrine of the subordination of the Temporal to the Spiritual Power, grounded upon the superiority of the end pursued by the latter, 123; Miracles a proof that the order of things proceeds from God, not by necessity of nature, but by His free-will, 450; the conversion of the world without miracles would have been the most marvellous of all marvels, 452; marks that sacrifice must be offered to God alone, 256; his statement of the supernatural government tending to a supernatural end, 94-96; sums up patristic doctrine on the Eucharist in his hymn, Lauda Sion, 274

Athanasius, St., represents the principles on which the ante-nicene Church maintained the faith, 389; how he states the authority of Scripture, 370; the rule of faith, 392; what he thinks of private judgment, 393; his tests of heresy, 393; on ecclesiastical definitions, 394; says Scripture and Tradition are united in the Church's magisterium, 395; how he accounts for the cessation of idolatry, oracles, and magic, 440-443

Athenagoras, his conversion, 383

Augustine, St., his description of the "Connection of Ages" down to Christ, and from him, xxx-xxxii; witnessed the Catholic Church, but did not foresee Christendom, xxxiv; his description of the Two Cities, xxxvii; attests that the shedding of blood in sacrifice from the beginning points to the sacrifice of Christ, 15, 255; that the Christian Sacrifice is the principle of unity to Christ's mystical Body, 276; how he understood the "One Episcopate," 280; mentions thousands of bishops as existing in 314 A.D., 216; why he saw in the Church the Godhead of its Founder, 280; his testimony to the force of the Catholic Church upon his mind, 165, 229; the number, names, and offices of heathen deities, 407; the seven churches in the apocalypse signify the fulness of the one Church, 174; his rule that what has been always kept in the Church, without being ordered by a council, is of apostolical authority, 296; complains of judgments as to secular matters being pressed upon him, 306; forbids the words of the creed to be written down, 348; comments on an answer of St. Felicitas, 451

2 G

BABYLON, type of the kingdom of force, xxvi; identified with heathen Rome by St. Peter and St. John, xxix
Basil, St., places the nature of God outside the conception of number, 406
Baur, Die drei ersten Jahrhunderte, 364, 366; Constantine's view of the Church, 416; sees the episcopal idea in the angels of the seven churches, 174
Bernard, St., his comment on the sheep committed to Peter, 178
Bianchi, Potestà della Chiesa, on the honour given by the Gentiles to their priesthood, 60, 63, 64; how St. Jerome says that bishops, priests, and deacons succeed the high-priest, priests, and Levites of the Mosaic hierarchy, 191; the bishop's office an ἀρχή, 219; selects five points of the Church's organic growth, 296; the Apostles follow their Lord's example in placing power in a head, 298; distribution of episcopal jurisdiction from the beginning, 300; on the Church's hearing and deciding causes, 303; on the criminal and penitential forum, 304; the Apostles prohibited Christians from pleading before secular tribunals, 306; jurisdiction, 307; election of bishops in the first three centuries, 309; bishops sent out from Rome to convert the nations, 219, 310; the Church's administration of temporal goods, 312, 313
Bossuet, his six points of the original human society, 29; what he thinks of a State without a religion, 41; the Christian people's relation to Christ, 101, 108

CATECHETICAL SCHOOLS, at Rome, Alexandria, Antioch, Edessa, 386, 387
Chamard, Dom, L'Etablissement du Christianisme, quoted, 217
Christ, His action as at once and always King, Lawgiver, and Priest, the subject of this volume, xx; kingdom of Christ as prophesied, xxi-xxviii; as fulfilled, xxix-xl; His High-priesthood consists in two acts, 239; His people answer to Him in the triple order established by Him as the Priest, the Prophet, and the King, 101
Chrysostom, St., his epitome of the Church's course preceding his own time, 230; Christ's one undeniable miracle that He founded the race of Christians, 231; contrast of the race with that out of which it was formed, 232; the incessant conflict amid which it was done, 233; dwells on the presence of Christ's physical Body in the Eucharist, 275; the Eucharist one sacrifice, everywhere, and for ever, 277
Cities, the Two, date from the Fall, 14; city of the devil, prevailing, leads to the Deluge, 17; described by St. Augustine, xxxvii
Clement of Alexandria, his conversion, and great ability, 385; attests the persecution in his time, 419; on the power of the κήρυγμα, 429; impotence of philosophy contrasted with it, 430; exposes the heathen deities, 407
Clement, St., of Rome, his letter to the Church of Corinth, the first Papal Pastoral, 184; called most authoritative by Irenæus, 185; likens Christian obedience to Roman military discipline, 186; speaks of minute regulations as to religious ordinances given by Christ, 187; makes all spiritual order to descend from above, 188; argues for the Christian order à fortiori, as compared with the Mosaic, 189; says the Apostles established bishops everywhere, with rule of succession, 190; attests the continuation of the Mosaic hierarchy in the Christian, 191; says Christian ordinances are to be observed more accurately than Mosaic, 193; describes the descent of power from above in the first sixty years, 194-196; confirms in this the Scriptural records, and supplies details, 197; exercises the primacy in the lifetime of St. John, 197-200; St. Clement and St. Ignatius complete and corroborate each other, 203; insists on the care with which our Lord instituted the government of His Church, 238; marks St. Paul to have been martyred by Nero's deputies, 367
Council of Arles, 375; its testimony to the Pope's authority, 397; says the Apostles Peter and Paul sit for ever in the Roman see, 398; Constantine acknowledges its judgment as that of Christ, 398

INDEX. 467

Council of Trent, its description of the Christian sacrifice, 265, 268
Cœlestine, Pope St., how the law of supplication establishes the law of belief, 329
Cyprian, St.—every city has its bishop in his time, 217; meaning of his aphorism on the oneness and solidarity of the Episcopate, 222; which he compares with the divine Unity in the Trinity, 224; his testimony as to the election of bishops in his own time, 308: sees Christ present in the martyrs, 450

Daniel, the prophet, his vision of the kingdom of God set up on earth, xxiii-xxviii
Dante, the great statue, xxix; St. John the Evangelist, 172; the saints before and after Christ form the great rose of Paradise, 448
Dionysius of Halicarnassus, description of the Roman Pontifical College, 61

Episcopate, the One, planted in every city by the Apostles, 194; attested by St. Ignatius, 202; by Eusebius the historian, 207; who gives the succession at Rome, Alexandria, Antioch, and Jerusalem, 210; by Tertullian, 212; by Irenæus, 213; each city and small town had its bishop before the peace of the Church, 216; the bishop said to wield a government, 218; bishops sent out from Rome to convert the nations, 219; episcopal government universal, 220; but the One Episcopate much more than this, 222; a regimen ruling one flock through the whole world, 224-226; the undivided rule of a single people, the Corpus Christianorum, 462; set forth by De Marca, 222; by St. Leo the Great in A.D. 446, 223; co-exists with the Primacy, 227; considered a miracle by St. Chrysostom and St. Augustine, 228; contrasted with national churches, 180, 181, 237; Christian government, worship, belief, and practice wrapt up together herein, 238; organic growth of the One Episcopate in mother and daughter churches, 296; developed in provincial councils, 302; exercised in decisions of coercive power, 303; exhibited in election of bishops, 307; the whole a derivation of the mission of Christ, 311; gradually clothes itself in temporal goods, 312-316; the living personal authority that to which the assistance of the Holy Ghost is promised from beginning to end, 335; our Lord's missionary circuits the germ, 340; the mission carried on by the Apostles, 341-343; personal authority exhibited in the system of catechesis, 344; the use of a creed, 347; the dispensing of sacraments, 349; the inflicting of penance, 351; the dispensing of the Scriptures, 352; all this continued during fifteen hundred years, 355-359; gift of infallibility lodged in the magisterium, 387, 389; which is the Church's divine government and concrete life, as attested by Athanasius, 395
Eusebius, of Cæsarea, notes three periods in the first ninety years, 206, 207; sum of his testimony as to the three great sees and the episcopate, 209; records that Peter came to Rome in the reign of the Emperor Claudius, 209; and the martyrdom of the two Apostles, 210; attests the divine power by which the Church was planted, 211; the Paschal Lamb sacrificed once a year, but Christians are ever satisfied with the Body of the Lord, 270; contrasts the divine polity and philosophy of the Church with the incessant variation of heresies, 221; attests the multitude of martyrs everywhere in the reign of Marcus Aurelius, 418

Fish, the sacred symbol in the catacombs of Christ's person and work, 287
Franzelin, Cardinal, the Church's teaching office, 330-335; that which is essential, the perpetual succession of living men, 339; the revelation made by Christ to the Apostles complete as to its substance, 361; the act of Christ's High Priesthood in the Incarnation, 239; the reality of the Body and Blood of Christ on the altar asserted by St. Ignatius of Antioch, St. Justin, and St. Irenæus, 269; the physical Body of Christ in the Eucharist insisted on by the Fathers, 274
Friedländer admits the universal belief in miracles of Jews and heathens as well as Christians, 445

GIESELER, five things on which the apologists laid stress, 444

Gregory the Great, St., his letter to King Ethelbert, 416; the whole Church represented by the sevenfold number of the churches, 174; repeatedly speaks of the see of the chief of the apostles as the see of one in three places—Rome, Alexandria, and Antioch, 297

Gregory of Nazianzum, calls his office as bishop a government, 218

Gregory VII., St., on the union of Church and State, 127

HAGEMANN, Die römische Kirche, how Constantine looked at the Church, 293; speaks of particular tendencies in local churches, 376

Heinrich, Dogmatische Theologie, 387

Heresy, its principle, as opposed to that of orthodoxy, 378; the apostolic writings full of warnings against it, 380; its incessant attacks through the second century, 382

Hergenröther, on the development of synodical institutions, 302

Hilary, St., attests that every church has its bishop, 217

IGNATIUS of Antioch, St., contemplates the whole Episcopate in the mind of Christ, as the mind of the Father, 173, 202; corroborates St. Clement of Rome, 200, 203; states the organic unity of a local church, 203

Innocent I., Pope, St., grounds the wide jurisdiction of the See of Antioch on its being the first see of the chief of the apostles, 296

Irenæus, St., quoted, 185, 202; describes the propagation of the Church, 213; barbarians believing in Christ follow the order of tradition without pen or paper, 220; the Church's deposit of doctrine like the principle of life in a body, 339; bears witness to the multitude of martyrs everywhere, 418; and of miracles, 438

JOHN, ST., does not record the institution of the Eucharist, but adds what may be considered a comment upon it, 134; records promises made to the Apostles, 149-151; the universal pastorship conferred on Peter, 152; how his expressions sum up both the universal mission of the apostolate, and the supreme pastorship of Peter, 177; his double warning as to the many things concerning Jesus not written, 157; his vision of the heavenly court as the Eucharistic Sacrifice, 324-327; his vision of our Lord in the government of the Church through his bishops, 171-175; identifies heathen Rome with Babylon, xxix

Josephus, 402; states Poppæa to have been a Jewish proselyte, 366

Jurisdiction, how partitioned in the Episcopate, stated by De Marca, 222; by St. Leo the Great, 223; Bianchi, 306; necessary in any kingdom, 278-280

Justin Martyr, St., says the presence of Christ's Body and Blood on the altar is as real as the Incarnation itself, 269; the tale of his conversion, 382

KINGDOM of Christ, thirteen characteristics of, 103-107; foretold by Daniel, xxii-xxviii; subsists from age to age by its own force, 131; disposed to the Apostolic College, 144; jurisdiction necessary to it, 278; as it appeared in A.D. 29 and A.D. 325, 291; recognised by Constantine at the Council of Arles, A.D. 314; and at the Nicene Council, 290, 463; consists in three things, Sacerdotium, Magisterium, Jurisdictio, answering to worship, belief, and government in the people which is its outcome, 411; the intimate cohesion of these three, 87-90; the perfect antagonism which they constituted in Christians to the Pagan empire, 404-411; the five conflicts which the kingdom underwent in the three centuries, 459-463

Kleutgen, on the two meanings of *tradition*, 344; on the word of God, written and unwritten, 361; on the special gift of the Apostolic Body, 361

LASAULX, Die Sühnopfer der Griechen und Römer, und ihr Verhältniss zu dem einem auf Golgotha, extracts from, 245-253; on human sacrifices, 259-262

Leo the Great, St., illustrates the "One Episcopate" of St. Cyprian, 223; his perfect picture of ecclesiastical jurisdiction in his day, 223

Leo XIII. in his encyclical, June 1881, declares civil power to be a vicegerency from God, 20

Lightfoot, Dr., suggests that the Primacy belongs not to the bishop but to the Church of Rome, 205

Luke, St., records the institution of the priesthood, 133; the power given to the Apostles, 139, 159; vast importance of the conversation which he alone records about the disposition of the kingdom, and its ruler, 141-147; distinguishes Peter from the other Apostles, as much as St. Matthew and St. John, 148; his reticence as to the place to which St. Peter went, when delivered from prison, and its reason, 373

MAGISTERIUM, of the Church, shown in her teaching, 316; which at first was oral only, based upon authority, 317; three classes of truths forming the divine and apostolical tradition, 319; the period of exclusively oral teaching specially exhibits the Church's teaching office, 320; seen in the rite of baptism, 321; in the Eucharistic Liturgy, 322; in the rite of ordination, 328; fulness of the magisterium shown in these rites, 329; not changed or diminished by the writings of the New Testament, 330-335; consists in the unchangeable principle of a living personal authority, 335; thus expressed by Irenæus, 213; acts of the magisterium which preceded the New Testament, 336; is the continuation of Christ's personal teaching, 340; and of the apostolic mission, 341; and abides in all ages, 343; is shown in five things, the system of catechesis, the use of a Creed, the dispensing of sacraments, the enjoining of penance, the handling of Scripture, 343-355; unimpeached through fifteen centuries, 355; its principle, a divine authority establishing a kingdom, 360; it transmits the word of God, written or unwritten, 361; which is complete, as to its substance, from the beginning, 361; the defence against error lodged in it, 387; consists in the Church's divine government and concrete life, 389; employs the whole word of God, written or unwritten, as its Rule of Faith, 395

Maine, Sir Henry, author of "Ancient Law," quoted upon original society, 46; the patriarchal theory, 47, 49; family, the unit of ancient society, not the individual, 50-54; universal belief, or assumption, of blood-relationship, 51; the Roman *patria potestas*, a relic of the original rule, 53; union of government with religion, 53; property sprung out of joint-ownership, 53

Marca, De, his statement of jurisdiction in the Episcopate, 222

Mark, St., the only Evangelist who does not record special powers given to Peter, 156; records the institution of the priesthood, 133; the powers given to the Apostolic Body, 138, 154

Martin, Dr., Bishop of Paderborn, on the High-priest's office, 75

Martyrdom, an essential element in the world's conversion, 445; its occasion the enmity between the serpent's seed and the Woman's Seed, 447; before Christ looks to Christ, and after Christ looks back on Him, 448; parallel with miracles in principle, witness, power, and perpetuity, 449-455; martyrs, champions of a great army, 421; endure for God what heroes endure for natural goods, 431-434; fill up what is wanting in the sufferings of Christ, until His mystical Body is completed, 453, 454; hated by all who deny a Creator, Judge, and Remunerator, 455; the Deacon Constantine's panegyric, 427

Matthew, St., records the institution of the priesthood, 133; the transmission of spiritual power, 136; the special promises to Peter, 137; distinguishes the Apostolate and the Primacy, 154-155

Melito, of Sardis, calls the Christian faith a philosophy nurtured together and begun together with Augustus, 414

Miracles, their existence alleged by every ancient Christian writer, 445; by Jews and Heathens of every class, 445; by Origen, who insists on miracles of conversion as greater than bodily miracles, 435; and that miracles only could account for the conversions wrought, 438; attested by Irenæus, of his own time, 439; by Athanasius, of the sign of the cross, and the name of Christ, 442; connection between miracles and martyrdom, as to their principle, witness, power and perpetuity, 449–454; the Christian faith rests upon two miracles, the Incarnation and the Resurrection of Christ, 445–447; the absolute necessity of miracles to substantiate the mission of Christ, 444; the Incarnation, the reason of miraculous power, 447; and the Fall of man its necessity, 447

Möhler, on the use of the Creed, 347; on the first Christian writers, 381; on the Roman catechetical school, 386

NÄGELSBACH, original kingship springs from fathership, 48; sacrifice, an essential of Greek piety, 244; the Greek seeks a living personal God, 244

Newman, Cardinal, describes the system of catechesis, 345; his history of the Arians referred to, 349; notes on St. Athanasius quoted, 390–395; his treatise on the Rise and Successes of Arianism, a storehouse of information, 397; says that particular authors do not speak *ex cathedra*, nor as a Council may speak, 388

Nicene Council, occasion of its convocation, 289; Constantine recognised therein the Church as a divine kingdom, 290; and the solidarity of the Episcopate, 292; compared with the Roman Senate, 293; its force as to the relation between Church and State, 294; its sixth Canon, 297; Constantine, acknowledging its sentence as the decision of God, recognised the kingdom of Christ in the world, 463

Noah, refounds the human race, 18; his first act, an act of sacrifice to which God attaches an universal covenant with his race, 18–21; is Father, King, Priest, and Teacher of his race, 22; among whom he establishes Marriage, Sacrifice, Civil Government, and the alliance of Government with Religion, 22–24

ORIGEN, insists on the divine power shown in converting sinners, 434; on miracles of conversion as greater than bodily miracles, 435; on the spread of the Church and the conversion of sinners viewed together, 436; not possible without miracles, 437; as the soul vivifies and moves the body, so the word arouses and moves the whole body, the Church, 359; sets up a catechetical school at Cæsarea in Palestine, 386

Ovid, his statement of the power of vicarious sacrifice, 261

PANTÆNUS, his conversion, labours, and renown, 384

Paul, St., six names whereby he describes his commission, 168; the Church to him "the Body of Christ," 162-165; says mission is necessary to every herald of the Gospel, 164; attests the grace given by ordination, 165; places in the one Christian Ministry the seat of dogmatic truth, 162; sees an inseparable bond in unity, truth, and government, 167; how he records the institution of the Priesthood, 132; appoints bishops, 165, 217

Peter, St., the six privileges recorded to have been bestowed on him, in which his primacy consists, 160; speaks of Rome under the name of Babylon, xxix

Phillipps' Kirchenrecht, 130

Philo, describes the concourse of Jews to Jerusalem, 78; quoted upon sacrifice, 248

Plato, makes piety to consist in prayer and sacrifice, 243

ποιμαίνειν, force of the word, to be Shepherd, 177–178

Priesthood, begun in Adam, 15; and afresh in Noah, 22; carried on from them through all the race, 56; distinguished from the Civil Power in the Roman Republic, 60; united afterwards to the Principate, but still distinct, 62; the College of Pontifices reverse a tribunicial law, 63; the distinction from civil power in it runs through all ancient nations, 64; witness to the unity of man's race, 65; the Aaronic, 72; special offices of the High-priest, 72; part of the High-priest through the whole history from Moses to Christ,

75; his jurisdiction under the Roman empire, 77; the Jewish priesthood and worship, a prophecy and preparation for Christ, 80; the High-priest's treatment of Christ, 82; the Christian priesthood springs from the Person of Christ, 86; as the human race from Adam, 111; institution of the Christian Priesthood, 132-135; all the mission of Christ collected in his Priesthood, 135; the Christian hierarchy succeeds the Mosaic, 191; Priesthood of the Church springs from the two acts of Christ's High Priesthood, 242; priesthood, teaching, and jurisdiction cohere inwardly, 87, 287-288; acknowledged equally by Constantine, 462

Primacy, the, of the Church, instituted by Christ himself, 137, 143-148, 152-153, 176-179; the words conveying it compared with those which convey the Apostolate, 154; the witness of St. Matthew to the distinction between Apostolate and Primacy, 155; the witness of St. Luke to the same distinction, 155; the witness of St. John to the same distinction, 155, 156; summary of its powers as given in the Gospels, 160; how St. Paul bears witness to it, 166-168; exercised by St. Clement in the lifetime of St. John, 197-200; the two forces of the Primacy and the Hierarchy exist from the beginning, 90; are exactly expressed by St. Leo in the year 446, 223; hold the Church together in the ante-nicene period, 375; are the joint result of our Lord's words, 161

Powers, the Two, appear united in the Headship of Adam, 11-13; and again in Noah, 19; in whom civil government is established by divine authority, 20; it is a common good of all his race, 38-40; the two Powers ever in alliance through all gentilism, 41-42; civil government springs as little from those governed, as fathership from children, 48-52; "Law originally is the parent's word," 53; relation of the two Powers from the beginning, 56, 108; Gentile deification of the State, 58; relation of the two Powers in the Mosaic Law, 67, 72-82; Analogy between them, 95; subjection of the spiritual to the civil power, the final result of gentilism, 70; the spiritual power has a new basis in the Person of Christ, 110; co-operation of the two Powers as stated by St. Gregory VII., 126; Christians subject to both Powers, 111; amity intended by God between them, 114; their separate action not intended, 115; persecution of the spiritual by the temporal not intended, 119; the indirect spiritual power over temporal things, 124; the ideal relation of the two Powers, and the various deflections from it described under the image of marriage, 128; alliance of the two Powers in the Roman empire at the advent of Christ, 400; how and why the civil power acknowledged the triple spiritual liberty of belief, worship, and government, 455, 462

Power, the Spiritual, a derivation from the Person of Christ, out of the union of the divine and human natures in him, 103, 111, 162; creates the supernatural society for a supernatural end, 93; to which the present life is subordinated, 94; and which is beyond the provision of temporal government, 96; a kingdom subsisting by its own force from age to age, 131; divine truth maintained by the perpetual operation of its one hierarchy in the Body of Christ, 162-164; has in Scripture five qualities, 175; the coming from above, 175; completeness, 176-179; unity, 179-181; independence of civil government, 181; perpetuity to the end of time, 182; the transmission of such a power witnessed in the Church's history from A.D. 29 to A.D. 325, 184-237; the resting of this power upon the Sacrifice of His Body instituted by Christ, 238-243, 263-286; its independence as to government shown in its organic growth, 295-316; its independence as to teaching shown in its communication of doctrine, 316-339; in its mode of positive teaching, 340-355; in its mode of resisting error, 359-399; in its conflict with the Roman empire's civil power, 400-463; the creation of such a power by the direct action of God foretold by the Prophet Daniel, 600 years before Christ, xxi-xxviii

RENAUDOT, the Eucharistic Liturgy, 323

SACERDOS, in the language of the third century, signifies the bishop, as offering the sacrifice of the altar, 217, 279; as ἐκκλησία signifies a diocese, 304

Sacrifice, rite of bloody, appears in the family of the first man, and dates from his fall, 15; unintelligible without the notion of sin, 15; its prevalence among the Gentiles, 243-250; specialities of the rite, described by Lasaulx, 250-253; associated with prayer, 253; with the sense of guilt, 254; enacted by God at the Fall as a perpetual prophecy, 256; the most striking characteristic of the world before Christ, 257; human, 259-261; enaction of, a divine act, 263; the Christian Sacrifice counterpart of the original institution, 264; and fulfilment of the whole Mosaic ritual, 264; its prodigious meaning and power, 267-274; presence of Christ's physical Body in it, according to St. Chrysostom, 275; is the principle of unity to Christ's mystical Body, according to St. Augustine, 276; the double act of Christ's High-priesthood thereby impressed on the world, 276; fulfils over the world the parable, I am the true Vine, 280-286; the Eucharistic picture of, by an apostle, 324

Schwane, Dogmengeschichte, 370, 424

Sophocles, his sense of the power of vicarious sacrifice, 260

Stöckl, Lehrbuch der Geschichte der Philosophie, 377

TACITUS, his *compages* of the Roman empire, xxxiv; says that Poppæa was surrounded with fortune-tellers, 366

Taparelli, Saggio teoretico di dritto naturale, philosophical basis on which the spiritual society rests, 98

Tatian, history of his conversion, 383

Tertullian, history of his conversion, 384; marks Domitian as a persecutor of the Church, 372; attests the persecution in his time, 420; sufferings which followed on conversions, 431-434; describes the first propagation of the Church, 211-213; compares the Church to a single vine planted in all lands, 239; the apostles sheltered by their position as Jews, 364; marks the Jews as sources of all calumny against Christians, 368.

Theophilus, bishop of Antioch, his conversion and writings, 384

Tradition, has two meanings, (1) the *unwritten* word of God, (2) the whole doctrine of salvation as handed down, 344; divine and apostolical tradition, 319; announcing the acts and words of Christ, part of, 337; various parts of tradition in its full sense, 338

www.ingramcontent.com/pod-product-compliance
Lightning Source LLC
Chambersburg PA
CBHW051159300426
44116CB00006B/371